Lecture Notes in Computer S

T0238201

Commenced Publication in 1973
Founding and Former Series Editors:
Gerhard Goos, Juris Hartmanis, and Jan van Leeuwen

Oscar Ibarra   Bala Ravikumar (Eds.)

Implementation and Application of Automata

13th International Conference, CIAA 2008
San Francisco, California, USA, July 21-24, 2008
Proceedings

 Springer

Volume Editors

Oscar H. Ibarra
University of California
Department of Computer Science
Santa Barbara, CA 93106, USA
E-mail: ibarra@cs.ucsb.edu

Bala Ravikumar
Sonoma State University
Department of Computer Science
Rohnert Park, CA 94928, USA
E-mail: ravi@cs.sonoma.edu

Library of Congress Control Number: 2008930486

CR Subject Classification (1998): F.1.1-3, F.4.2-3, F.2

LNCS Sublibrary: SL 1 – Theoretical Computer Science and General Issues

ISSN   0302-9743
ISBN-10   3-540-70843-X Springer Berlin Heidelberg New York
ISBN-13   978-3-540-70843-8 Springer Berlin Heidelberg New York

Springer is a part of Springer Science+Business Media

springer.com

© Springer-Verlag Berlin Heidelberg 2008
Printed in Germany

Typesetting: Camera-ready by author, data conversion by Scientific Publishing Services, Chennai, India
Printed on acid-free paper   SPIN: 12442324   06/3180   5 4 3 2 1 0

Preface

The 13th International Conference on Implementation and Application of Automata (CIAA 2008) was held at San Francisco State University, San Francisco, July 21–24, 2008.

This volume of *Lecture Notes in Computer Science* contains the papers that were presented at CIAA 2008, as well as the abstracts of the poster papers that were displayed during the conference. The volume also includes the paper/extended abstract of the four invited talks presented by Markus Holzer, Kai Salomaa, Mihalis Yannakakis, and Hsu-Chun Yen.

The 24 regular papers were selected from 40 submissions covering various topics in the theory, implementation, and applications of automata and related structures. Each submitted paper was reviewed by at least three Program Committee members, with the assistance of external referees. The authors of the papers and posters presented in this volume come from the following countries: Australia, Belgium, Canada, China, Columbia, Czech Republic, France, Germany, Hungary, Italy, Japan, The Netherlands, Poland, Portugal, Romania, Russia, Spain, Sweden, Taiwan, United Arab Emerates, and USA.

We wish to thank all who made this conference possible: the authors for submitting papers, the Program Committee members and external referees (listed in the proceedings) for their excellent work, and the four invited speakers. Finally, we wish to express our sincere appreciation to the sponsors, local organizers, and the editors of the *Lecture Notes in Computer Science* series and Springer, in particular Alfred Hofmann, for their help in publishing this volume in a timely manner.

July 2008

Oscar H. Ibarra
Bala Ravikumar

Organization

Program Committee

John Brzozowski	University of Waterloo, Canada
Cristian Calude	The University of Auckland, New Zealand
Erzsébet Csuhaj-Varjú	Hungarian Academy of Sciences, Hungary
Jean-Marc Champarnaud	Université de Rouen, France
Volker Diekert	Universität Stuttgart, Germany
Omer Egecioglu	University of California, Santa Barbara, USA
Rusins Freivalds	University of Latvia, Latvia
Rudolf Freund	Vienna University of Technology, Austria
Dora Giammarresi	University of Rome, Italy
Jozef Gruska	Masaryk University, Czech Republic
Tero Harju	Academy of Finland, Finland
Jan Holub	Czech Technical University of Prague, Czech Republic
Juraj Hromkovic	RWTH Aachen, Germany
Oscar H. Ibarra (Co-chair)	University of California, Santa Barbara, USA
Lucian Ilie	University of Western Ontario, Canada
Masami Ito	Kyoto Sangyo University, Japan
Kazuo Iwama	Kyoto University, Japan
Juhani Karhumäki	University of Turku, Finland
Nils Klarlund	AT&T Labs-Research, USA
Jarkko Kari	University of Turku, Finland
Martin Kutrib	Universität Giessen, Germany
Sebastian Maneth	University of New South Wales, Australia
Denis Maurel	Université de Tours, France
Giancarlo Mauri	Università degli Studi di Milano - Bicocca, Italy
Mehryar Mohri	Courant Institute of Mathematical Sciences, USA
Andrei Paun	Louisiana Tech University, USA
Giovanni Pighizzini	Universita degli Studi di Milano, Italy
R. Ramanujam	Institute of Mathematical Sciences, India
Bala Ravikumar (Co-chair)	Sonoma State University, USA
Wojciech Rytter	Warsaw University, Poland
Jacques Sakarovitch	Ecole nationale superieure des telecommunications, France
Jeffrey Shallit	University of Waterloo, Canada
Nicholas Tran	Santa Clara University, USA
Bruce Watson	University of Pretoria, Republic of South Africa
Mikhail Volkov	Ural State University, Russia
Sheng Yu	University of Western Ontario, Canada

Additional Reviewers

Cyril Allauzen
Marcella Anselmo
Abdullah Arslan
Marie-Pierre Beal
Daniela Besozzi
Hans-Joachim Boeckenhauer
Pawel Baturo
Mikolaj Bojanczyk
Cezar Campeanu
Maxime Crochemore
Jan Daciuk
Paul Gastin
Zsolt Gazdag
Jens Gloeckler
Csanad Imreh
Christos Kapoutsis
Felix Klaedtke
Andreas Klein
Tomi Krki
Manfred Kufleitner
Ratnesh Kumar
Kamal Lodaya
Gerhard Lischke
Maria Madonia
Francesco Ranzato
Kalle Saari
Kai Salomaa
Nicolae Santean
Helmut Seidl
Ayumi Shinohara
Magnus Steinby
Sara Woodworth
Hsu-Chun Yen

Organizing Committee

Omer Egecioglu   University of California, Santa Barbara, USA
Oscar H. Ibarra   University of California, Santa Barbara, USA
Bala Ravikumar   Sonoma State University (Chair), USA
Nicholas Tran   Santa Clara University, USA

Proceedings Committee

Oscar H. Ibarra   University of California, Santa Barbara, USA
Bala Ravikumar   Sonoma State University, Rohnert Park, USA

Publicity Committee

Andrei Paun   Louisiana Tech University, USA

Steering Committee

Jean-Marc Champarnaud   Université de Rouen, France
Oscar H. Ibarra   University of California, Santa Barbara, USA
Denis Maurel   Université de Tours, France
Derick Wood   Hong Kong Univ. of Science and Technology,
                             Hong Kong
Sheng Yu (Chair)   University of Western Ontario, Canada

Sponsoring Organizations

Citrix Systems Inc., Fort Lauderdale, USA
ELC Technologies, Santa Barbara, USA
Google Inc., Mountain View, USA
Sonoma State University, Rohnert Park, USA
University of California, Santa Barbara, USA

Table of Contents

Nondeterministic Finite Automata—Recent Results on the Descriptional and Computational Complexity

Markus Holzer[1] and Martin Kutrib[2]

[1] Institut für Informatik, Technische Universität München,
Boltzmannstr. 3, 85748 Garching bei München, Germany
`holzer@in.tum.de`
[2] Institut für Informatik, Universität Giessen,
Arndtstr. 2, 35392 Giessen, Germany
`kutrib@informatik.uni-giessen.de`

Abstract. Nondeterministic finite automata (NFAs) were introduced in [67], where their equivalence to deterministic finite automata was shown. Over the last 50 years, a vast literature documenting the importance of finite automata as an enormously valuable concept has been developed. In the present paper, we tour a fragment of this literature. Mostly, we discuss recent developments relevant to NFAs related problems like, for example, (i) simulation of and by several types of finite automata, (ii) minimization and approximation, (iii) size estimation of minimal NFAs, and (iv) state complexity of language operations. We thus come across descriptional and computational complexity issues of nondeterministic finite automata. We do not prove these results but we merely draw attention to the big picture and some of the main ideas involved.

1 Introduction

Nondeterministic finite automata (NFAs) are probably best known for being equivalent to right-linear context-free grammars and, thus, for capturing the lowest level of the Chomsky-hierarchy, the family of regular languages. It is well known that NFAs can offer exponential saving in space compared with deterministic finite automata (DFAs), that is, given some n-state NFA one can always construct a language equivalent DFA with at most 2^n states [67]. This so-called *powerset construction* turned out to be optimal, in general. That is, the bound on the number of states is tight in the sense that for an arbitrary n there is always some n-state NFA which cannot be simulated by any DFA with less than 2^n states [63,64]. These two milestones from the early days of automata theory form part of an extensive list of equally striking problems of NFA related problems, and are the basis of descriptional complexity. Moreover, it initiated the study of the power of resources and features given to finite automata, see, e.g., [21] for a survey on limited resources for finite automata.

O.H. Ibarra and B. Ravikumar (Eds.): CIAA 2008, LNCS 5148, pp. 1–16, 2008.

Our tour on the subjects listed in the abstract of NFAs related problems cover some (recent) results in the field of descriptional and computational complexity. It obviously lacks completeness, as NFAs fall short of exhausting the large selection of finite automata related problems considered in the literature. We give our view of what constitute the most recent interesting links to the considered problem areas. Our nomenclature of finite automata is as follows: A *nondeterministic finite automaton* (NFA) is a quintuple $A = (Q, \Sigma, \delta, q_0, F)$, where Q is the finite set of *states*, Σ is the finite set of *input symbols*, $q_0 \in Q$ is the *initial state*, $F \subseteq Q$ is the set of *accepting states*, and $\delta : Q \times \Sigma \to 2^Q$ is the *transition function*. A finite automaton is *deterministic* (DFA) if and only if $|\delta(q, a)| = 1$, for all states $q \in Q$ and letters $a \in \Sigma$. The *language accepted* by the finite automaton A is defined as $L(A) = \{ w \in \Sigma^* \mid \delta(q_0, w) \cap F \neq \emptyset \}$, where the transition function is recursively extended to $\delta : Q \times \Sigma^* \to 2^Q$. For further details we refer to [36].

2   Determinization and Simulations of NFAs

Since regular languages have many representations in the world of finite automata, it is natural to investigate the succinctness of their representation by different types of automata in order to optimize the space requirements. Here we measure the costs of representations in terms of the states of a minimal automaton accepting a language. More precisely, the simulation problem is defined as follows:

- Given two classes of finite automata C_1 and C_2.
- How many states are sufficient and necessary in the worst case to simulate n-state automata from C_1 by automata from C_2?

Probably the most famous simulation problem in the world of finite automata is the simulation of NFAs by DFAs, which is widely known as *determinization*.

Theorem 1 (NFA Determinization). *Let A be an n-state nondeterministic finite automaton. Then 2^n states are sufficient and necessary in the worst case for a deterministic finite automaton to accept $L(A)$.*

For the particular case of finite and unary regular languages the situation is significantly different. The determinization problem for finite languages over a k-letter alphabet was solved in [70] with a tight bound of $\Theta(k^{\frac{n}{1+\log_2 k}})$. Thus, for finite languages over a two-letter alphabet only $\Theta(2^{\frac{n}{2}})$ states are sufficient and necessary in the worst case for a DFA to accept a language specified by an n-state NFA. The situation is similar when we turn to the second important special case, the unary languages, that is discussed in more detail a bit later. Unary NFAs can be much more concise than DFAs, but yet not as much as for the general case. For languages that are unary *and* finite this is not the case, since in [60] it was proven that nondeterminism does not help in this case. Unary DFAs are up to one additional state are as large as equivalent minimal NFAs.

In the following, we concentrate on simulations between finite automata that may or may not have the features nondeterminism and two-way head motion.

Table 1. State complexities for simulations on general and unary regular languages. Depicted are the bounds for simulating the device of the first column by a device of the second line. A question mark indicates that the precise bounds are not known, in particular it is not known whether the upper bound is exponential.

	General Regular Languages			Unary Regular Languages		
	DFA	NFA	2DFA	DFA	NFA	2DFA
NFA	2^n	—	?	$e^{\Theta(\sqrt{n\cdot\ln n})}$	—	$\Theta(n^2)$
2DFA	$n(n^n - (n-1)^n)$	$\binom{2n}{n+1}$	—	$e^{\Theta(\sqrt{n\cdot\ln n})}$	$e^{\Theta(\sqrt{n\cdot\ln n})}$	—
2NFA	$\sum_{i=0}^{n-1}\sum_{j=0}^{n-1}\binom{n}{i}\binom{n}{j}(2^i-1)^j$	$\binom{2n}{n+1}$	$\Omega(\frac{n^2}{\log n})$	$e^{\Theta(\sqrt{n\cdot\ln n})}$	$e^{\Theta(\sqrt{n\cdot\ln n})}$	?

So, we are concerned with the four devices DFA, NFA, 2DFA, and 2NFA, the latter denoting automata that may move their head to the right as well as to the left. We first sketch the development of results for general regular languages. Then we turn to unary languages, again.

Concerning the simulation of 2DFA by DFA an $\Theta(n^n)$ asymptotically tight bound was shown in [72]. Moreover, the proof implied that any n-state 2NFA can be simulated by an NFA with at most $n2^{n^2}$ states. The well-known proof of the equivalence of two-way and one-way finite automata *via* crossing sequences reveals a bound of $O(2^{2n\log n})$ states [36]. Recently in [53] it was noted that a straightforward elaboration on [72] shows that the cost can be brought down to even $n(n+1)^n$. However, this bound still wastes exponentially many states, as proven in [8] *via* an argument based on length-preserving homomorphisms that $8^n + 2$ states suffice. Recently, the problem was solved in [53] by establishing a tight bound of $\binom{2n}{n+1}$. Furthermore, tight bounds in the exact number of states for the DFA and NFA simulations of 2DFAs and 2NFAs, respectively, which are depicted in Table 1, were presented. The bounds reveal that two-way head motion is a very powerful resource with respect to the number of states. Interestingly, when simulating two-way devices by NFAs, it does not matter whether the two-way device is nondeterministic or not. From this point of view, two-way head motion can compensate for nondeterminism.

Nevertheless, challenging problems are still open. The question of how many states are sufficient or necessary to simulate (two-way) NFAs by 2DFAs is unanswered for decades. The problem was raised by Sakoda and Sipser in [68]. They conjectured that the upper bound is exponential. The best lower bound currently known is $\Omega(n^2/\log n)$. It was proved in [4], where also an interesting connection with the open problem whether L equals NL is given. In particular, if L = NL, then for some polynomial p, all integers m, and all n-state 2NFAs A, there exists a $p(mk)$-state 2DFA accepting a subset of $L(A)$ including all words whose lengths do not exceed m. However, not only are the exact bounds of that problem unknown, but we cannot even confirm the conjecture that they are exponential.

The problem of evaluating the costs of unary automata simulations has been raised in [73]. It turned out that the unary case is essentially different from the general one. For state complexity issues of unary NFAs Landau's function

$F(n) = \max\{\, \text{lcm}(x_1, \ldots, x_k) \mid x_1, \ldots, x_k \geq 1 \text{ and } x_1 + \cdots + x_k = n \,\}$, which gives the maximal order of the cyclic subgroups of the symmetric group on n elements, plays a crucial role. Here, lcm denotes the least common multiple. Since F depends on the irregular distribution of the prime numbers we cannot expect to express $F(n)$ explicitly by n. In [55,56] the asymptotic growth rate $\lim_{n \to \infty} (\ln F(n)/\sqrt{n \cdot \ln n}) = 1$ was determined, which for our purposes implies the (sufficient) rough estimate $F(n) \in e^{\Theta(\sqrt{n \cdot \ln n})}$. An asymptotic tight bound of $\Theta(F(n))$ on the unary NFAs simulation by DFAs was presented in [12,13]. Furthermore, in the same papers it is shown that the costs of the unary two-way to DFA simulation reduces to the same bound $e^{\Theta(\sqrt{n \cdot \ln n})}$. Furthermore, the Sakoda-Sipser problem for NFAs has been solved for the unary case. The tight bound in the order of magnitude is $\Theta(n^2)$. The picture was complemented by the sophisticated studies in [62] which revealed tight bounds in the order of magnitude also for the 2NFA simulations by DFAs and NFAs. Table 1 also summarizes the bounds known for the simulations between unary finite automata. It is also worth mentioning that in [12] also a normal-form for unary NFAs was introduced. Each n-state unary NFA can be replaced by an equivalent $O(n^2)$-state NFA consisting of an initial deterministic tail and some disjoint deterministic loops, where the automaton makes only a single nondeterministic decision after passing through the initial tail, which chooses one of the loops—nowadays the normal-form is referred to as the *Chrobak normal-form* for unary NFAs.

It turned out that nondeterministic as well as two-way automata are hard to simulate for DFAs even if they accept unary languages. Since the bounds are the same, it seems that two-way motion is equally powerful as nondeterminism, but both together cannot increase the descriptional capacity. This observation is confirmed by the bounds for simulations by NFAs, where similarly as in the general case it does not matter whether the two-way device is nondeterministic or not. Nevertheless, from this point of view, two-way head motion can compensate for nondeterminism. Finally, since unary 2DFAs can simulate NFAs increasing the number of states only polynomially, which is not possible the other way around, two-way motion turned out to be more powerful than nondeterminism.

In the remainder of this section we come back to the determinization problem for NFAs. Although a lot is known for the problem, still some important issues were open up to recently. For instance, in [10] the determinization problem was studied for some subregular language families like, for example, combinational languages, definite languages and variants thereof, star-free languages, ordered languages, prefix-, suffix-, and infix-closed languages. Relations between several of these subregular language families are studied in [32]. These subfamilies are well motivated by their representations as finite automata or regular expressions. In all non-trivial cases tight exponential bounds that range from 2^{n-1} to $2^{n-1}+1$ and 2^n were shown.

As already mention above, there are cases, where nondeterminism does not help in succinctly representing a language compared to DFAs. Coming back to the roots of the subset construction, in [42] the question was raised whether there always exists a minimal n-state NFA whose equivalent minimal DFA has α states, for all n and α satisfying $n \leq \alpha \leq 2^n$. A number α not satisfying this condition is called a *magic number*. For NFAs over a two-letter alphabet some non-magic numbers were identified in [42,43]. Recently, in [47] it was shown that there are no magic numbers for languages over a four-letter alphabet. This improved a result from [18] for small growing alphabets to the constant case. Before it was known that for exponential growing alphabets there are no magic numbers at all [48]. Up to our knowledge the case of binary and ternary alphabets is still open. Magic numbers for unary NFAs by revising the Chrobak normal-form for unary NFAs were recently studied in [19], where also a brief historical summary of the magic number problem can be found.

3 Minimization of NFAs

The study of the minimization problem of finite automata dates back to the early beginnings of automata theory. Here we focus mainly on some recent developments related to this fundamental problem—for further reading we refer to [45] and references therein. The minimization problem is also of practical relevance, because regular languages are used in many applications, and one may like to represent the languages succinctly.

It is well known that for a given n-state DFAs one can efficiently compute an equivalent minimal automaton in $O(n \log n)$ time [35]. This is contrary to the nondeterministic case since the NFAs minimization problem is known to be computationally hard. The decision version of the minimization problem, for short the NFA-to-NFA minimization problem, is defined as follows:

- Given a *nondeterministic* finite automaton A and a natural number k in binary, that is, an encoding $\langle A, k \rangle$.
- Is there an equivalent k-state *nondeterministic* finite automaton?

This notation naturally generalizes to other types of finite automata, for example, the DFA-to-NFA minimization problem. The following result on the NFA-to-NFA minimization problem is due to [45].

Theorem 2 (NFA Minimization Problem). *The NFA-to-NFA minimization problem is* PSPACE-*complete, even if the input is given as a deterministic finite automaton.*

In order to better understand the very nature of nondeterminism one may ask for minimization problems for restricted types of finite automata. Already in [45] it was shown that for the restricted class of unambiguous finite automata (UFA) some minimization problems remain intractable. To be more precise, the UFA-to-UFA and the DFA-to-UFA minimization problems are NP-complete. Later in [59] these results were improved in the sense that the minimization of finite automata equipped with a very small amount of nondeterminism is already computationally hard. In particular, the minimization problems for multiple initial state deterministic finite automata with a fixed number of initial states (MDFA) as well as for nondeterministic finite automata with fixed finite branching has been shown to be NP-complete. Prior to this, the MDFA-to-DFA minimization problem in general was proven to be PSPACE-complete in [33]. Recently, the picture was completed in [9] by getting much closer to the tractability frontier for nondeterministic finite automata minimization. There a class of NFAs is identified, the so called δ-nondeterministic finite automata (δNFA), such that the minimization problem for any class of finite automata that contains δNFAs is NP-hard, even if the input is given as a DFA. Here the class of δNFAs contains all NFAs with the following properties: (i) The automaton is unambiguous, (ii) the maximal product of the degrees of nondeterminism over the states in a possible computation is at most 2, and (iii) there is at most on state q and a letter a such that the degree of nondeterminism of q and a is 2. It is worth mentioning that for every n-state δNFA there is an equivalent DFA with at most $O(n^2)$ states.

The situation for the minimization problem in general is, in fact, even worse. Recent work [24] shows that the DFA-to-NFA problem cannot be approximated within $\sqrt{n}/\mathsf{polylog}\,n$ for state minimization and $n/\mathsf{polylog}\,n$ for transition minimization, provided some cryptographic assumption holds. Moreover, the NFA-to-NFA minimization problem was classified to be inapproximable within $o(n)$, unless P = PSPACE, if the input is given as an NFA with n states [24]. That is, no polynomial-time algorithm can determine an approximate solution of size $o(n)$ times the optimum size. Even the DFA-to-NFA minimization problem remains inapproximable within a factor of at least $n^{1/3-\epsilon}$, for all $\epsilon > 0$, unless P = NP [28], for alphabets of size $O(n)$, and not approximable within $n^{1/5-\epsilon}$ for a binary alphabet, for all $\epsilon > 0$. Under the same assumption, it was shown that the transition minimization problem for binary input alphabets is not approximable within $n^{1/5-\epsilon}$, for all $\epsilon > 0$. The results in [28] proved approximation hardness results under weaker (and more familiar) assumptions than [24]. Further results on the approximability of the minimization problem when the input is specified as regular expression or a truth table can be found in [24,28].

For finite languages, NFA-to-NFA minimization can be done by the following algorithm: A nondeterministic Turing machine with an nfa equivalence oracle for finite languages can guess an nfa with at most k states, and ask the oracle whether the guessed automaton is equivalent to the input automaton, and accept if and only if the oracle answer is yes. Since equivalence for finite languages specified by NFA is coNP-complete [74], the minimization problem belongs to Σ_2^P, regardless of whether a deterministic or nondeterministic finite state device is given. Recently, the NFA-to-NFA minimization problem for finite languages was shown to be DP-hard, even if the input is a DFA accepting a finite language. This improved the previously known NP-hardness result, which follows from [3]. The complexity class DP includes both NP and coNP, and is a subset of Σ_2^P. This nicely contrasts with a recent result on the NP-completeness of minimization for finite languages given by truth tables [27]. Hence, the DFA-to-NFA minimization problem for finite languages is more complicated than that with truth tables as input, unless NP = coNP. Whether this lower bound can be substantially raised to, for example Σ_2^P-hardness, is open.

The unary NFA-to-NFA minimization problem is coNP-hard [74], and similarly as in the case of finite languages contained in Σ_2^P. The number of states of a minimal NFA equivalent to a given unary cyclic DFA cannot be computed in polynomial time, unless $NP \subseteq DTIME(n^{O(\log n)})$ [44]. Note that in the latter case the corresponding decision version belongs to NP. Inapproximability results for the problem in question have been found during the last years, if the input is a unary NFA: The problem cannot be approximated within $\frac{\sqrt{n}}{\ln n}$ [22], and if one requires in addition the explicit construction of an equivalent NFA, the inapproximability ratio can be raised to $n^{1-\epsilon}$, for every $\epsilon > 0$, unless $P = NP$ [24]. On the other hand, if a unary *cyclic* DFA with n states is given, the nondeterministic state complexity of the considered language can be approximated within a factor of $O(\log n)$. The picture on the unary NFA-to-NFA minimization problem was completed in [27]. Some of the aforementioned (in)approximability results, which only hold for the *cyclic* case, generalize to unary languages in general. In particular, it was shown that for a given an n-state NFA accepting a unary language, it is impossible to approximate the nondeterministic state complexity within $o(n)$, unless $P = NP$. Observe that this bound is tight. In contrast, it is proven that the NFA-to-NFA minimization problem can be *constructively* approximated within $O(\sqrt{n})$, where n is the number of states of the given DFA. Here by *constructively approximated* we mean that we can build the nondeterministic finite automaton, instead of only approximately determining the number of states needed. This solves an open problem stated in [45] on the complexity of converting a DFA to an approximately optimal NFA in the case of unary languages.

4   Lower Bound Techniques

To estimate the necessary number of states of a minimal NFA accepting a given regular language is stated as an open problem in [2] and [38]. Several authors have introduced communication complexity methods for proving such lower bounds, see, for example, [5,20,37]. The results of [37] have been generalized by the advent of so-called multi-party nondeterministic message complexity [1].

Here we briefly recall a lower bound technique that is widely used, for example, in proofs dealing with the language operation problem on regular languages specified by NFAs, namely the so-called *fooling set* techniques—the fooling set technique [20] and the extended fooling set method [5].

Theorem 3 (Fooling Set Technique). *Let $L \subseteq \Sigma^*$ be a regular language and suppose there exists a set of pairs $S = \{(x_i, y_i) \mid 1 \leq i \leq n\}$ such that (1) $x_i y_i \in L$ for $1 \leq i \leq n$, and (2) $x_i y_j \notin L$, for $1 \leq i, j \leq n$ with $i \neq j$, then any nondeterministic finite automaton accepting L has at least n states. Here S is called a* fooling set *for L.*

The statement of the theorem remains valid if property (2) is changed to (2') $i \neq j$ implies $x_i y_j \notin L$ or $x_j y_i \notin L$, for $1 \leq i, j \leq n$. Properties (1) and (2') form the extended fooling set technique introduced in [5] (here the set S is called an *extended fooling* set). The two techniques are essentially different, although the difference in both theorems looks quite harmless. Obviously, every fooling set is also an extended fooling set, but not the other way around. Moreover, although these techniques are widely used, paradoxically the obtained lower bounds are not always tight, and in fact can be arbitrarily worse compared to the nondeterministic state complexity, see, for example, [26]. This issue was also discussed in [20], where an even unary language was given such that any (extended) fooling set has constant size only, while the nondeterministic state complexity is at least n. An analogous result holds when comparing extended fooling sets *versus* fooling sets.

It was shown recently in [26] that obtaining the best attainable lower bound for the technique under consideration does not require conscious thought and *clever guessing*. In fact, it can be solved algorithmically. To this end, a unified view on these techniques was develop in terms of bipartite graphs—the (extended) fooling set forms a subset of the edges of a bipartite graph G_L, the so called *dependency graph* of a language L, where the left (right) vertices are formed by the equivalence classes of the Myhill-Nerode relation for the language L, (L^R), and the edges are induced by membership in L. Then, a fooling set corresponds to an *induced matching* in G_L, and an extended fooling set to a *cross-free matching* in G_L, and *vice versa*. Based on the graph terminology another lower bound technique, the so called *biclique edge cover* technique, which is a modern formulation of the grid cover approach of [52] used in the minimization algorithm for NFAs, was introduced in [26]. It is worth mentioning that it is also a reformulation of the nondeterministic message complexity method [37] in terms of graphs. Although the fooling set methods cannot provide any guaranteed relative error, the biclique edge cover technique gives an estimate at least as good as the trivial lower bound that is induced by the exponential blow-up from the NFA to DFA conversion. In turn, a result of [39,49] on the gap between nondeterministic message complexity and nondeterministic state complexity was improved in [26].

What concerns the computational complexity of these lower bound techniques, an almost complete answer was given in [26]. It turned out that deciding whether a certain lower bound with respect to one of the investigated techniques can be achieved is in all cases computationally hard, that is, NP-hard or even PSPACE-complete. To be more precise, the fooling set problem

- given a *deterministic* finite automaton A and a natural number k in binary, that is, an encoding $\langle A, k \rangle$,
- is there a fooling set S for the language $L(A)$ of size at least k?,

is classified to be NP-hard and contained in PSPACE, while both, the extended fooling set method and the biclique edge cover method lead to PSPACE-complete problems. That means that this task is already computationally hard as minimizing NFAs [45]. Whether these problems get even harder when the input is given as an NFA instead of a DFA was left open. This would be a surprising phenomenon, since the corresponding minimization problem remains PSPACE-complete.

In the remainder of this section we briefly recall what is known if we draw our attention to the number of transitions as an estimate on the size of a minimal NFA for a regular language. The understanding of transition complexity for NFAs is at its beginning. Lower bound techniques for nondeterministic transition complexity similar to that for nondeterministic state complexity are not known yet. In [29] and independently in [54] it was shown by a counting argument that the nondeterministic transition complexity can be almost quadratic in terms of nondeterministic state complexity, namely in $\Omega(n^2/\log n)$, even for binary alphabets. Recently, explicit languages over a constant size alphabet that need $\Omega(n \cdot \sqrt{n})$ transitions while having nondeterministic state complexity n were constructed in [14]. This somehow improved a result from [40] for growing alphabets to the constant case. The lower bound proof in [14] relies on nontrivial combinatorial properties of finite projective planes. Time will tell whether some of the developed methods can be generalized to a lower bound technique for transitions in the spirit of the above mentioned methods for state complexity.

What else is known for nondeterministic transition complexity? During the last few years, a growing body of research centered around the areas of algorithms for constructing nondeterministic finite automata with a small number of transitions [30,40,41,58,71], computational complexity aspects thereof [23,24,28], and descriptional complexity aspects of nondeterministic transition complexity [14,15,25,29,75]. Finally, let us comment on an interesting phenomenon that state and transition minimization cannot be carried out simultaneously: There are languages for which all n-state NFAs require $\Omega(n^2)$ transitions, but for which allowing a *single* additional state results in a number of $O(n)$ transitions necessary—the result even holds for finite languages. This was first discovered in [25] and is a special case of a more general result shown in [14].

5 Language Operation Problem for NFAs

Let ∘ be fixed operation on languages that preserves regularity. Then the ∘-language operation problem for NFAs is defined as follows:

- Given an n-state and an m-state nondeterministic finite automata.
- How many states are sufficient and necessary in the worst case (in terms of n and m) to accept the language $L(A_1) \circ L(A_2)$ by an nondeterministic finite automaton?

Obviously, this problem generalizes to DFAs as well as to unary language operations like, for example, complementation. These problems are closely related to complexity issues discussed so far. For example, converting a given NFA to an equivalent DFA gives an upper bound for the NFA state complexity of complementation. State complexity results of operations with regard to DFAs are surveyed in [77,78], where also operations on unary regular languages are discussed. Estimations of the average state complexity are shown in [29,65]. A systematic study of language operations in connection with NFAs is [34]. There the following results on Boolean operations were shown:

Theorem 4 (Language Operation Problem). *For any integers* $m, n \geq 1$ *let A be a (unary, respectively) m-state and B be a (unary, respectively) n-state nondeterministic finite automaton.*

1. *Then* $m + n + 1$ *states are sufficient and necessary in the worst case for an nondeterministic finite automaton to accept the language* $L(A) \cup L(B)$ *(if neither m is a multiple of n nor n is a multiple of m, respectively).*
2. *Then* $m \cdot n$ *states are sufficient and necessary in the worst case for an nondeterministic finite automaton to accept the language* $L(A) \cap L(B)$ *(if m and n are relatively prime, respectively).*
3. *Then* 2^n *(*$e^{\Theta(\sqrt{n \cdot \ln n})}$*, respectively) states are sufficient and necessary in the worst case for an nondeterministic finite automaton to accept the complement of* $L(A)$.

We want to comment on some of these results and further operation problems, which are summarized and compared with the deterministic case in Table 2. The tightness of the bounds in the general case are reached even by two-letter alphabets. The upper bound for the union is based on the idea to construct an NFA that starts with a new initial state and guesses which of the given automata is to simulate. For the intersection both given automata have to be simulated in parallel, where in the unary case the lower bound for the intersection additionally requires that m and n are relatively prime. In [66] unary languages are studied whose *deterministic* state complexities are not relatively prime.

In connection with nondeterminism the complementation often plays a crucial role. In fact, compared with DFAs, the complementation of NFAs is an expensive task at any rate. Since the complementation operation on DFAs neither increases nor decreases the number of states (simply exchange accepting and rejecting states), we obtain the upper bounds for the state complexity of the complementation on NFAs by determinization. Unfortunately, these expensive

Table 2. NFA and DFA state complexities for operations on infinite languages. The tight lower bounds for union, intersection, and concatenation of unary DFAs require m and n to be relatively prime.

	Infinite Languages			
	NFA		DFA	
	general	unary	general	unary
$\cup$	$m + n + 1$	$m + n + 1$	mn	mn
$\sim$	2^n	$e^{\Theta(\sqrt{n \cdot \ln n})}$	n	n
$\cap$	mn	mn	mn	mn
R	$n + 1$	n	2^n	n
$\cdot$	$m + n$	$m + n - 1 \leq \cdot \leq m + n$	$(2m - 1)2^{n-1}$	mn
$*$	$n + 1$	$n + 1$	$2^{n-1} + 2^{n-2}$	$(n - 1)^2 + 1$
$+$	n	n		

upper bounds are tight. A sketch of the story about the state complexity of NFA complementation reads as follows: Sakoda and Sipser [68] gave an example of languages over a growing alphabet size reaching the upper bound 2^n. In [6] the result for a three-letter alphabet was claimed. Later in [7] this was corrected to a four-letter alphabet. Moreover, $O(n)$-state binary witness languages were found in [17]. In [34] the lower bound 2^{n-2} is achieved for a two-letter alphabet and finally by a fooling set technique the bound 2^n on the complementation of NFAs was proven to be tight for a two-letter alphabet [50].

More detailed results on the relation between the sizes of NFAs accepting a unary language and its complement are obtained in [61]. In particular, if a unary language L has a succinct NFA, then nondeterminism is useless in order to recognize its complement, namely, the smallest NFA accepting the complement of L has as many states as the minimal DFA accepting it. The same property does not hold in the case of automata and languages defined over larger alphabets.

Now we turn to the concatenation, iteration, and λ-free iteration in more detail. First, for concatenation a tight bound $m + n$ in order to accept the concatenation in the general case was obtained. The lower bound is achieved for a two-letter alphabet. In the unary case, for any integers $m, n > 1$, the lower bound $m+n-1$ of the concatenation misses the upper bound $m+n$ by one state. It is currently an open question how to close the gap by more sophisticated constructions or witness languages. Next, consider iterations. The trivial difference between iteration and λ-free iteration concerns the empty word only. Moreover, the difference does not appear for languages containing the empty word. Nevertheless, in the worst case the difference costs one state. In particular, the tight bounds $n + 1$ and n for the iteration and λ-free iteration for general and unary languages were shown in [34]. So, roughly speaking concatenation operations are efficient for NFAs. Again, this is essentially different when DFAs come to play. For example, in [79] a bound of $(2m - 1) \cdot 2^{n-1}$ states has been shown for the concatenation problem for DFAs, and in [76] a bound of $2^{n-1} + 2^{n-2}$ states for the iteration.

Consider the remaining reversal operation. The bounds for unary NFAs are trivial. For general DFAs one may expect that the state complexity is linear, but it is not! A tight bound of 2^n states for the reversal has been shown in [57]. The efficient bound $n + 1$ for NFAs shows once more that nondeterminism is a powerful concept. The bound is tight even for a two-letter alphabet, and was achieved in [34,50].

Recently, two particular regularity preserving operations were investigated, namely cyclic shift and power of a language. The *cyclic shift* of a language L is defined as $\text{SHIFT}(L) = \{\, vu \mid uv \in L \,\}$. It is an operation known to preserve context-freeness, too. Its nondeterministic state complexity was investigated in [51], where a tight bound of $2n^2 + 1$ states is established. The second operation concerns k-powers of languages. Let A be an n-state NFA and $k \geq 2$ be a constant. Then $n \cdot k$ states are sufficient to accept the language $L(A)^k$ by an NFA. The bound is tight for a two-letter alphabet [16]. For both operations the deterministic state complexity is worse compared to the nondeterministic case.

Table 3. NFA and DFA state complexities for operations on finite languages (k is the size of the input alphabet, t is the number of accepting states of the "left" automaton). The tight lower bounds for union, intersection, and concatenation of unary DFAs require m and n to be relatively prime. More sophisticated bounds on the union and intersection of general finite DFAs are shown in [31].

	Finite Languages			
	NFA		DFA	
	general	unary	general	unary
$\cup$	$m+n-2$	$\max\{m,n\}$	$O(mn)$	$\max\{m,n\}$
$\sim$	$\Theta(k^{\frac{n}{1+\log_2 k}})$	$n+1$	n	n
$\cap$	$O(mn)$	$\min\{m,n\}$	$O(mn)$	$\min\{m,n\}$
R	n	n	$O(k^{\frac{n}{1+\log_2 k}})$	n
$\cdot$	$m+n-1$	$m+n-1$	$O(mn^{t-1}+n^t)$	$m+n-2$
$*$	$n-1$	$n-1$	$2^{n-3}+2^{n-4}$	$n^2-7n+13$
$+$	n	n		

In the remainder of this section we consider the important special case of finite languages. When we are concerned with finite languages we may assume without loss of generality that minimal NFAs not accepting the empty word have only one accepting state. If the finite language contains the empty word, then in addition the initial state is a second accepting one. In Table 3 the bounds on the language operation problem are summarized and compared with the deterministic case. Again, we want to comment on these results.

It turned out, that the state complexity of the union can be reduced by three states compared with the general case. In case of concatenation one state can be saved with respect to general regular languages. Both lower bounds are achieved by languages over a two-letter alphabet. The state complexity for the iterations in the finite language case is as for infinite languages if the iteration is λ-free. If not, the costs are reduced by two states for both unary and arbitrary languages. The tight bounds for union, intersection, and concatenation for finite *unary* languages are found as follows: In [60] it was shown that unary DFAs up to one additional state are as large as equivalent minimal NFAs and that they obey a chain structure. An immediate consequence is that we have only to consider the longest words in the languages in order to obtain the state complexity of operations that preserve finiteness.

The situation for the complementation of finite languages boils down to the NFAs determinization problem, and the tight $\Theta(k^{\frac{n}{1+\log_2 k}})$ bound for languages over a k letter alphabet proven in [70], which was mentioned earlier. Since the complementation applied to finite languages yields infinite languages, for the lower bounds of unary languages we cannot argue with the simple chain structure as before, but obtain a tight bound of $n+1$ [34]. Essentially the exponentially bound for complementation mentioned above is also an upper bound for the reversal operation of finite languages in the deterministic case [11]. From the efficient bounds of n states for NFAs it follows once more that nondeterminism is a powerful concept. Moreover, the fact that NFAs for finite languages do not have any cycles leads again to the possibility of saving one state compared with the infinite case. The bound for the reversal of finite NFA languages is in some sense strong. It is sufficient and reached for all finite languages.

References

1. Adorna, H.N.: 3-party message complexity is better than 2-party ones for proving lower bounds on the size of minimal nondeterministic finite automata. J. Autom. Lang. Comb. 7, 419–432 (2002)
2. Adorna, H.N.: Some descriptional complexity problems in finite automata theory. In: Philippine Computing Science Congress, pp. 27–32. Computing Society of the Philippines (2005)
3. Amilhastre, J., Janssen, P., Vilarem, M.C.: FA minimisation heuristics for a class of finite languages. In: Boldt, O., Jürgensen, H. (eds.) WIA 1999. LNCS, vol. 2214, pp. 1–12. Springer, Heidelberg (2001)
4. Berman, P., Lingas, A.: On the complexity of regular languages in terms of finite automata. Technical Report 304, Polish Academy of Sciences (1977)
5. Birget, J.C.: Intersection and union of regular languages and state complexity. Inform. Process. Lett. 43, 185–190 (1992)
6. Birget, J.C.: Partial orders on words, minimal elements of regular languages and state complexity. Theoret. Comput. Sci. 119, 267–291 (1993)
7. Birget, J.C.: Erratum: Partial orders on words, minimal elements of regular languages and state complexity (2002),
   http://clam.rutgers.edu/~birget/papers.html
8. Birget, J.C.: State-complexity of finite-state devices, state compressibility and incompressibility. Math. Systems Theory 26, 237–269 (1993)
9. Björklund, H., Martens, W.: The tractability frontier for NFA minimization. In: International Colloqium on Automata, Languages and Propgramming (ICALP 2008). LNCS. Springer, Heidelberg (to appear, 2008)
10. Bordihn, H., Holzer, M., Kutrib, M.: State complexity of NFA to DFA conversion for subregular language families (submitted for publication 2008)
11. Câmpeanu, C., Čulik, K., Salomaa, K., Yu, S.: State complexity of basic operations on finite languages. In: Boldt, O., Jürgensen, H. (eds.) WIA 1999. LNCS, vol. 2214, pp. 60–70. Springer, Heidelberg (2001)
12. Chrobak, M.: Finite automata and unary languages. Theoret. Comput. Sci. 47, 149–158 (1986)
13. Chrobak, M.: Errata to finite automata and unary languages. Theoret. Comput. Sci. 302, 497–498 (2003)
14. Domaratzki, M., Salomaa, K.: Lower bounds for the transition complexity of NFAs. In: Královič, R., Urzyczyn, P. (eds.) MFCS 2006. LNCS, vol. 4162, pp. 315–326. Springer, Heidelberg (2006)
15. Domaratzki, M., Salomaa, K.: Transition complexity of language operations. Theoret. Comput. Sci. 387, 147–154 (2007)
16. Domaratzki, M., Okhotin, A.: State complexity of power. TUCS Technical Report 845, Turku Centre for Computer Science (2008)
17. Ellul, K.: Descriptional complexity measures of regular languages. Master's thesis, University of Waterloo (2002)

18. Geffert, V. (Non)determinism and the size of one-way finite automata. In: Descriptional Complexity of Formal Systems (DCFS 2005). Rapporto Tecnico 06-05, Università degli Studi di Milano, pp. 23–37 (2005)
19. Geffert, V.: Magic numbers in the state hierarchy of finite automata. Inform. Comput. 205, 1652–1670 (2007)
20. Glaister, I., Shallit, J.: A lower bound technique for the size of nondeterministic finite automata. Inform. Process. Lett. 59, 75–77 (1996)
21. Goldstine, J., Kappes, M., Kintala, C.M.R., Leung, H., Malcher, A., Wotschke, D.: Descriptional complexity of machines with limited resources. J. UCS 8, 193–234 (2002)
22. Gramlich, G.: Probabilistic and nondeterministic unary automata. In: Rovan, B., Vojtáš, P. (eds.) MFCS 2003. LNCS, vol. 2747, pp. 460–469. Springer, Heidelberg (2003)
23. Gramlich, G.: Über die algorithmische Komplexität regulärer Sprachen. Doctoral Dissertation, Johann Wolfgang-Goethe-Univeristät, Frankfurt am Main (2007)
24. Gramlich, G., Schnitger, G.: Minimizing NFA's and regular expressions. In: Diekert, V., Durand, B. (eds.) STACS 2005. LNCS, vol. 3404, pp. 399–411. Springer, Heidelberg (2005)
25. Gruber, H., Holzer, M.: A note on the number of transitions of nondeterministic finite automata. In: Theorietag "Automaten und Formale Sprachen". Universität Tübingen, pp. 24–25 (2005)
26. Gruber, H., Holzer, M.: Finding lower bounds for nondeterministic state complexity is hard. In: H. Ibarra, O., Dang, Z. (eds.) DLT 2006. LNCS, vol. 4036, pp. 363–374. Springer, Heidelberg (2006)
27. Gruber, H., Holzer, M.: Computational complexity of NFA minimization for finite and unary languages. In: Language and Automata Theory and Applications (LATA), pp. 261–272. Universitat Rovira i Virgili, Tarragona (2007)
28. Gruber, H., Holzer, M.: Inapproximability of nondeterministic state and transition complexity assuming P $\neq$ NP. In: Harju, T., Karhumäki, J., Lepistö, A. (eds.) DLT 2007. LNCS, vol. 4588, pp. 205–216. Springer, Heidelberg (2007)
29. Gruber, H., Holzer, M.: Results on the average state and transition complexity of finite automata accepting finite languages. Theoret. Comput. Sci. 387, 155–166 (2007)
30. Hagenah, C., Muscholl, A.: Computing ε-free NFA from regular expressions in $O(n \log^2 n)$ time. RAIRO Inform. Théor. 34, 257–277 (2000)
31. Han, Y.S., Salomaa, K.: State complexity of union and intersection of finite languages. In: Harju, T., Karhumäki, J., Lepistö, A. (eds.) DLT 2007. LNCS, vol. 4588, pp. 217–228. Springer, Heidelberg (2007)
32. Havel, I.M.: The theory of regular events II. Kybernetica 6, 520–544 (1969)
33. Holzer, M., Salomaa, K., Yu, S.: On the state complexity of k-entry deterministic finite automata. J. Autom., Lang. Comb. 6, 453–466 (2001)
34. Holzer, M., Kutrib, M.: Nondeterministic descriptional complexity of regular languages. Int. J. Found. Comput. Sci. 14, 1087–1102 (2003)
35. Hopcroft, J.E.: An $n \log n$ algorithm for minimizing the state in a finite automaton. In: The Theory of Machines and Computations, pp. 189–196. Academic Press, London (1971)
36. Hopcroft, J.E., Ullman, J.D.: Introduction to Automata Theory, Languages and Computation. Addison-Wesley, Reading (1979)
37. Hromkovič, J.: Communication Complexity and Parallel Computing. Springer, Heidelberg (1997)

38. Hromkovič, J.: Descriptional complexity of finite automata: Concepts and open problems. J. Autom., Lang. Comb. 7, 519–531 (2002)
39. Hromkovič, J., Seibert, S., Karhumäki, J., Klauck, H., Schnitger, G.: Communication Complexity Method for Measuring Nondeterminism in Finite Automata. Inform. Comput. 172, 201–217 (2002)
40. Hromkovič, J., Schnitger, G.: Comparing the size of NFAs with and without ϵ-transitions. Theoret. Comput. Sci. 380, 100–114 (2007)
41. Hromkovič, J., Seibert, S., Wilke, T.: Translating regular expressions in small ϵ-free nondeterministic finite automata. J. Comput. System Sci. 62, 565–588 (2001)
42. Iwama, K., Kambayashi, Y., Takaki, K.: Tight bounds on the number of states of DFAs that are equivalent to n-state NFAs. Theoret. Comput. Sci. 237, 485–494 (2000)
43. Iwama, K., Matsuura, A., Paterson, M.: A family of NFAs which need $2^n - \alpha$ deterministic states. Theoret. Comput. Sci. 301, 451–462 (2003)
44. Jiang, T., McDowell, E., Ravikumar, B.: The structure and complexity of minimal NFAs over a unary alphabet. Int. J. Found. Comput. Sci. 2, 163–182 (1991)
45. Jiang, T., Ravikumar, B.: Minimal NFA problems are hard. SIAM J. Comput. 22, 1117–1141 (1993)
46. Jirásek, J., Jirásková, G., Szabari, A.: State Complexity of Concatenation and Complementation. Int. J. Found. Comput. Sci. 16, 511–529 (2005)
47. Jirásek, J., Jirásková, G., Szabari, A.: Deterministic blow-ups of minimial nondeterministic finite automata over a fixed alphabet. In: Harju, T., Karhumäki, J., Lepistö, A. (eds.) DLT 2007. LNCS, vol. 4588, pp. 254–265. Springer, Heidelberg (2007)
48. Jirásková, G.: Note on minimal finite automata. In: Sgall, J., Pultr, A., Kolman, P. (eds.) MFCS 2001. LNCS, vol. 2136, pp. 421–431. Springer, Heidelberg (2001)
49. Jirásková, G.: Note on minimal automata and uniform communication protocols. In: Grammars and Automata for String Processing, pp. 163–170. Taylor and Francis, Abington (2003)
50. Jirásková, G.: State complexity of some operations on binary regular languages. Theoret. Comput. Sci. 330, 287–298 (2005)
51. Jirásková, G., Okhotin, A.: State complexity of cyclic shift. RAIRO Inform. Théor. 42, 335–360 (2008)
52. Kameda, T., Weiner, P.: On the state minimization of nondeterministic finite automata. IEEE Trans. Comput. C-19, 617–627 (1970)
53. Kapoutsis, C.A.: Removing bidirectionality from nondeterministic finite automata. In: Jedrzejowicz, J., Szepietowski, A. (eds.) MFCS 2005. LNCS, vol. 3618, pp. 544–555. Springer, Heidelberg (2005)
54. Kari, J.: Personal communication (2006)
55. Landau, E.: Über die Maximalordnung der Permutationen gegebenen Grades. Archiv der Math. und Phys. 3, 92–103 (1903)
56. Landau, E.: Handbuch der Lehre von der Verteilung der Primzahlen. Teubner (1909)
57. Leiss, E.: Succinct representation of regular languages by Boolean automata. Theoret. Comput. Sci. 13, 323–330 (1981)
58. Lifshits, Y.: A lower bound on the size of ϵ-free NFA corresponding to a regular expression. Inform. Process. Lett. 85, 293–299 (2003)
59. Malcher, A.: Minimizing finite automata is computationally hard. Theoret. Comput. Sci. 327, 375–390 (2004)

60. Mandl, R.: Precise bounds associated with the subset construction on various classes of nondeterministic finite automata. In: Princeton Conference on Information and System Sciences, pp. 263–267 (1973)
61. Mera, F., Pighizzini, G.: Complementing unary nondeterministic automata. Theoret. Comput. Sci. 330, 349–360 (2005)
62. Mereghetti, C., Pighizzini, G.: Optimal simulations between unary automata. SIAM J. Comput. 30, 1976–1992 (2001)
63. Meyer, A.R., Fischer, M.J.: Economy of description by automata, grammars, and formal systems. In: IEEE Symposium on Switching and Automata Theory (SWAT 1971), pp. 188–191. IEEE Press, Los Alamitos (1971)
64. Moore, F.R.: On the bounds for state-set size in the proofs of equivalence between deterministic, nondeterministic, and two-way finite automata. IEEE Trans. Comput. 20, 1211–1214 (1971)
65. Nicaud, C.: Average state complexity of operations on unary automata. In: Kutyłowski, M., Wierzbicki, T., Pacholski, L. (eds.) MFCS 1999. LNCS, vol. 1672, pp. 231–240. Springer, Heidelberg (1999)
66. Pighizzini, G., Shallit, J.: Unary language operations, state complexity and Jacobsthal's function. Int. J. Found. Comput. Sci. 13, 145–159 (2002)
67. Rabin, M.O., Scott, D.: Finite automata and their decision problems. IBM J. Res. Dev. 3, 114–125 (1959)
68. Sakoda, W.J., Sipser, M.: Nondeterminism and the size of two way finite automata. In: Symposium on Theory of Computing (STOC 1978), pp. 275–286. ACM Press, New York (1978)
69. Salomaa, A., Wood, D., Yu, S.: On the state complexity of reversals of regular languages. Theoret. Comput. Sci. 320, 315–329 (2004)
70. Salomaa, K., Yu, S.: NFA to DFA transformation for finite languages over arbitrary alphabets. J. Autom., Lang. Comb. 2, 177–186 (1997)
71. Schnitger, G.: Regular expressions and NFAs without ϵ-transitions. In: Durand, B., Thomas, W. (eds.) STACS 2006. LNCS, vol. 3884, pp. 432–443. Springer, Heidelberg (2006)
72. Shepherdson, J.C.: The reduction of two-way automata to one-way automata. IBM J. Res. Dev. 3, 198–200 (1959)
73. Sipser, M.: Lower bounds on the size of sweeping automata. J. Comput. System Sci. 21, 195–202 (1980)
74. Stockmeyer, L.J., Meyer, A.R.: Word problems requiring exponential time. In: Symposium on Theory of Computing (STOC 1973), pp. 1–9. ACM Press, New York (1973)
75. Tamm, H.: On transition minimality of bideterministic automata. In: Harju, T., Karhumäki, J., Lepistö, A. (eds.) DLT 2007. LNCS, vol. 4588, pp. 411–421. Springer, Heidelberg (2007)
76. Yu, S.: Regular languages. In: Handbook of Formal Languages, vol. 1, pp. 41–110. Springer, Heidelberg (1997)
77. Yu, S.: State complexity of regular languages. J. Autom., Lang. Comb. 6, 221–234 (2001)
78. Yu, S.: State complexity of finite and infinite regular languages. Bull. EATCS 76, 142–152 (2002)
79. Yu, S., Zhuang, Q., Salomaa, K.: The state complexities of some basic operations on regular languages. Theoret. Comput. Sci. 125, 315–328 (1994)

Language Decompositions, Primality, and Trajectory-Based Operations[*]

Kai Salomaa

School of Computing, Queen's University, Kingston, Ontario K7L 3N6, Canada
ksalomaa@cs.queensu.ca

Abstract. We consider the decomposability of languages and the notion of primality with respect to catenation, as well as, more general operations. We survey recent results and discuss open problems.

1 Introduction

Questions dealing with decompositions of regular languages were studied in depth already by Conway in 1971 [3]: "*How can we express a given regular event E in the form $f(F_1, F_2, \ldots)$, wherein f is a regular function and F_i are regular events? [...] This problem might arise in the construction of large machines from smaller ones – given transducers for the F_i, how can we build a transducer for E?*" On the other hand, the notion of primality, or indecomposability, of languages was introduced and investigated originally by Mateescu, A. Salomaa and Yu [16,21].

Already from the original work of Conway it follows that for a regular language L it is decidable whether or not L is decomposable and in the positive case the factors can be chosen to be regular. (Our terminology follows [11,16], while Conway used "factor" in a slightly different meaning.) Decomposability questions become more difficult when we consider operations other than catenation. Shuffle along trajectories [15] provides a unified formalism to define most of the commonly used language operations.

2 Prime Decompositions

A non-empty language L is said to have a *non-trivial decomposition* if we can write $L = A \cdot B$ where A, B are not the singleton language consisting of the empty word. In the following, by a decomposition of a language we always mean a non-trivial decomposition. A non-empty language $L \neq \{\varepsilon\}$ is said to be *prime* if L has no decompositions. A *prime decomposition* of L is a factorization $L = L_1 \cdots L_m$ where each of the languages L_i, $1 \leq i \leq m$, is prime.

Primality is decidable for regular languages, however, there is no known efficient algorithm to test for primality and also no known hardness result for

---

[*] Supported by the Natural Sciences and Engineering Research Council of Canada Grant OGP0147224.

O.H. Ibarra and B. Ravikumar (Eds.): CIAA 2008, LNCS 5148, pp. 17–22, 2008.

the complexity of this problem. The complexity of deciding primality, at least potentially, depends on whether the language is given by a deterministic or a nondeterministic finite automaton.

Problem 2.1. What is the complexity of deciding primality of a language recognized by a DFA (respectively, by an NFA)?

A finite language always has a prime decomposition but it need not be unique [16,21] even if we disregard the order of factors. It is known that regular languages that satisfy certain types of code properties have unique prime decompositions [4,11]. A regular language has a prime decomposition if and only if it has a prime decomposition where the components are regular [16].

Arbitrary regular languages can have very different (prime) decompositions and, in general, it seems not easy to determine whether a given infinite regular language has a prime decomposition. For example, consider the unary language $L = \varepsilon + a^2 a^*$. The language L is equal to $L \cdot L$ and it has also the prime decomposition

$$L = (\varepsilon + a^2)(\varepsilon + a^3)(\varepsilon + \cup_{i=1}^{\infty}(a^2)^{2i-1}).$$

There exist languages, even unary languages, that provably do not have any prime decomposition [11,19], however, all languages known to have this property are non-regular.

Problem 2.2. Does every regular language have a prime decomposition?

A language L is said to be *strongly prime decomposable,* roughly speaking, if any way of iteratively decomposing L has to end in a finite number of steps. Han et al. [11] give a decidable characterization of strongly prime decomposable regular languages and using this solve the following special case of Problem 2.2.

Theorem 2.1. *Every regular language over a unary alphabet has a prime decomposition.*

Different types of prime factorizations, including infinitary factorizations, have recently been investigated in [20]. Length codes, or numerically decipherable codes [22], provide a useful tool for this work.

Questions of primality become more involved when we consider non-ambiguous (or orthogonal) catenation. We say that L is a *non-ambiguous product* of languages L_1 and L_2, denoted

$$L = L_1 \odot_\perp L_2, \tag{1}$$

if every word $w \in L$ can be written in a unique way as the catenation of $w_1 \in L_1$ and $w_2 \in L_2$. A related, but essentially different, operation of *unique catenation* has been investigated in [18].

We say that L is $\perp$-prime if (1) does not hold for any languages $L_i \neq \{\varepsilon\}$, $i = 1, 2$.

Using power series tools Anselmo and Restivo [1] establish the following strong result concerning one-variable equations.

Theorem 2.2. [1] *For given regular languages L and L_1 it is decidable whether or not the equation $L = L_1 \odot_\perp X$ has a solution for X. A solution, if it exists, is unique and effectively regular.*

Solutions for corresponding one-variable equations with ordinary catenation obviously need not be unique. Deciding whether L is $\perp$-prime involves determining the existence of solutions for a two-variable equation with non-ambiguous catenation for L. We know [5] that $\perp$-primality is undecidable for context-free languages.

Problem 2.3. Is $\perp$-primality decidable for regular languages?

It is noted in [1] that a regular language can be the non-ambiguous catenation of two non-regular languages. For example,

$$a^* = \Pi_{i=0}^\infty (\varepsilon + a^{2^{2i}}) \odot_\perp \Pi_{i=0}^\infty (\varepsilon + a^{2^{2i+1}}).$$

The unary language a^* has different non-ambiguous decompositions into regular components, however, if the components are regular then one of the components has to be finite.

Problem 2.4. Is it possible that, for a regular language L, there exist non-regular $L_1, L_2 \neq \{\varepsilon\}$ such that $L = L_1 \odot_\perp L_2$ but L cannot be expressed as a non-ambiguous catenation of any regular languages distinct from $\{\varepsilon\}$?

In light of the above, we can consider two variants of $\perp$-primality for regular languages depending on whether the factors can be arbitrary languages or the factors are restricted to be regular. Also, the decidability question of Problem 2.3 has, strictly speaking, two variants.

3   Shuffle Along Trajectories

Shuffle along trajectories has been introduced by Mateescu et al. [15] as a model of controlled parallel composition of languages. Extensions of the model have been investigated, for example, in [6,8]. Below we consider decomposability of languages only with respect to the "standard" trajectory-based operations as introduced in [15]. An important tool for finding solutions to language equations involving shuffle along trajectories is an inverse operation called deletion along trajectories [7,14].

A *trajectory* is a word over the binary alphabet $\{0, 1\}$. Consider a trajectory $t = 0^{j_1}1^{k_1} \cdots 0^{j_n}1^{k_n}$, $j_i, k_i \geq 0$, $1 \leq i \leq n$. Consider words $x, y \in \Sigma^*$ where $|x| = |t|_0$, $|y| = |t|_1$. The *shuffle of x and y on t* is defined as

$$x \amalg_t y = \{ \ \Pi_{i=1}^n x_i y_i \ | \ x = \Pi_{i=1}^n x_i, \ y = \Pi_{i=1}^n y_i,$$
$$\text{where } |x_i| = j_i, |y_i| = k_i, \ 1 \leq i \leq n \ \}.$$

If $|x| \neq |t|_0$ or $|y| \neq |t|_1$, $x \sqcup_t y$ is undefined. The operation is extended in the natural way for a set of trajectories T, and if $L_1, L_2 \subseteq \Sigma^*$ are languages we define

$$L_1 \sqcup_T L_2 = \bigcup_{x \in L_1, y \in L_2} x \sqcup_T y.$$

As an example, note that if $T = 0^*1^*$, then $\sqcup_T$ is the language catenation operation and $T = \{0, 1\}^*$ defines the unrestricted shuffle of languages. Many commonly used language operations can be expressed as trajectory based operations [15].

Let T be a set of trajectories. A T-*shuffle decomposition* of a language L is a pair of languages (L_1, L_2) such that $L = L_1 \sqcup_T L_2$. We state the following general open problem.

Problem 3.1. Given a regular set of trajectories T and a regular language L, is it decidable whether or not L has a T-shuffle decomposition?

In the following special case we have a positive decidability result. Recall that a set of trajectories T is said to be *letter-bounded* if $T \subseteq a_1^* \cdots a_n^*$, $a_1, \ldots, a_n \in \{0, 1\}$.

Theorem 3.1. [9] *Let T be a letter-bounded regular set of trajectories. Then given a regular language L, we can decide whether or not L has a T-shuffle decomposition. If a decomposition exists, the components can be chosen to be regular.*

Since catenation is expressed by the set of trajectories 0^*1^*, the result extends the known decidability of primality for regular languages, as well as, covers decomposability with respect to operations such as insertion and bi-catenation. However, the proof of Theorem 3.1 does not extend, for example, to bounded sets of trajectories (that are not letter-bounded).

Several, apparently innocent looking, special cases of Problem 3.1 remain open, in particular, the (unrestricted) shuffle decomposition problem considered by Câmpeanu et al. [2] and Ito [13].

Problem 3.2. Is it decidable whether a given regular language has a non-trivial $\{0, 1\}^*$-shuffle decomposition.

Recall that a language $L \subseteq \Sigma^*$ is k-*thin* [17] if $|L \cap \Sigma^n| \leq k$ for all $n \geq 1$.

Problem 3.3. Given $k \geq 1$, a k-thin regular set of trajectories T and a regular language L, can we decide whether or not L has a T-shuffle decomposition?

Problem 3.3 is known to be decidable when $k = 1$ [10]. To our knowledge it is still open even in the special case $k = 2$.

It is known that there exists a fixed context-free set of trajectories T_0 such that for given regular languages L_1, L_2 and L_3 we cannot effectively decide whether or not $L_1 = L_2 \sqcup_{T_0} L_3$ [10]. This gives an undecidability result for regular languages, in the spirit of the Dassow-Hinz result [12]. The result can be extended to one-variable equations.

Theorem 3.2. [10] *There exists a fixed context-free set of trajectories T_0 such that, for given regular languages L_1 and L_2, it is undecidable whether or not the equation*

$$L_1 = L_2 \sqcup_{T_0} X$$

has a solution for X.

However, a similar result for two-variable equations is not known.

Problem 3.4. Is it possible to construct a fixed context-free set of trajectories T such that for a given regular language L it is undecidable whether or not L has a T-shuffle decomposition?

As was done in Section 2 for decompositions with respect to catenation, we can define primality and consider prime decompositions with respect to shuffle along a set of trajectories. However, so far we seem lack the proper tools to handle the generalized questions, even when the set of trajectories is regular. Since Problem 3.1 remains unsolved, we do not even have a decision algorithm to determine primality of a regular language in this set-up.

References

1. Anselmo, M., Restivo, A.: On languages factorizing the free monoid. Internat. J. Algebra and Computation 6, 413–427 (1996)
2. Câmpeanu, C., Salomaa, K., Vágvölgyi, S.: Shuffle decompositions of regular languages. Internat. J. Foundations of Computer Science 13, 799–816 (2002)
3. Conway, J.H.: Regular Algebra and Finite Machines. Chapman and Hall, Boca Raton (1971)
4. Czyzowicz, J., Fraczak, W., Pelc, A., Rytter, W.: Linear-time prime decomposition of regular prefix codes. Internat. J. Foundations of Computer Science 14, 1019–1031 (2003)
5. Daley, M., Domaratzki, M., Salomaa, K.: On the operational orthogonality of languages. In: Kunc, M., Okhotin, A. (eds.) Proc. of Theory and Applications of Language Equations, Turku, Finland, pp. 43–53 (2007)
6. Domaratzki, M.: Semantic shuffle and deletion along trajectories. In: Calude, C.S., Calude, E., Dinneen, M.J. (eds.) DLT 2004. LNCS, vol. 3340, pp. 163–174. Springer, Heidelberg (2004)
7. Domaratzki, M.: Deletion along trajectories. Theoret. Comput. Sci. 320, 293–313 (2004)
8. Domaratzki, M., Rozenberg, G., Salomaa, K.: Interpreted trajectories. Fundamenta Informaticae 73, 182–193 (2006)
9. Domaratzki, M., Salomaa, K.: Decidability of trajectory-based equations. Theoret. Comput. Sci. 345, 304–330 (2005)
10. Domaratzki, M., Salomaa, K.: Restricted sets of trajectories and decidability of shuffle decompositions. Internat. J. Foundations of Computer Science 16, 897–912 (2005)
11. Han, Y.-S., Salomaa, A., Salomaa, K., Wood, D., Yu, S.: On the existence of prime decompositions. Theoret. Comput. Sci. 376, 60–69 (2007)

12. Hinz, F., Dassow, J.: An undecidability result for regular languages and its application to regulated rewriting. Bulletin of the EATCS 38, 168–174 (1989)
13. Ito, M.: Shuffle decomposition of regular languages. J. Universal Comput. Sci. 8, 257–259 (2002)
14. Kari, L., Sosík, P.: Aspects of shuffle and deletion on trajectories. Theoret. Comput. Sci. 332, 47–61 (2005)
15. Mateescu, A., Rozenberg, G., Salomaa, A.: Shuffle on trajectories: Syntactic constraints. Theoret. Comput. Sci. 197, 1–56 (1998)
16. Mateescu, A., Salomaa, A., Yu, S.: Factorizations of languages and commutativity conditions. Acta Cybernetica 15, 339–351 (2002)
17. Păun, G., Salomaa, A.: Thin and slender languages. Discr. Applied Math. 61, 257–270 (1995)
18. Rampersad, N., Ravikumar, B., Santean, N., Shallit, J.: A study on unique rational operations. Tech. report TR-20071222-1, Dept. of Computer and Information Sciences, Indiana University South Bend (2007)
19. Rampersad, N., Shallit, J.: Private communication (2006)
20. Salomaa, A., Salomaa, K., Yu, S.: Length codes, products of languages and primality. In: Fazekas, S., Martin-Vide, C., Tîrnăucă, C. (eds.) Proc. of the 2nd International Conference on Language and Automata Theory and Applications, LATA 2008, pp. 487–498 (2008)
21. Salomaa, A., Yu, S.: On the decomposition of finite languages. In: Proc. Developments in Language Theory, DLT 1999, pp. 22–31. World Scientific Publ. Co., Singapore (2000)
22. Weber, A., Head, T.: The finest homophonic partition and related code concepts. IEEE Trans. Inform. Theory IT-42, 1569–1575 (1996)

Automata, Probability, and Recursion

Mihalis Yannakakis

Department of Computer Science, Columbia University

Abstract. We discuss work on the modeling and analysis of systems
with probabilistic and recursive features. Recursive Markov chains extend ordinary finite state Markov chains with the ability to invoke other
Markov chains in a potentially recursive manner. The equivalent model of
Probabilistic Pushdown Automata extends ordinary pushdown automata
with probabilistic actions. Both of these are natural abstract models
for probabilistic programs with procedures, and related systems. They
generalize other classical well-studied stochastic models, e.g. Stochastic Context-free Grammars and (Multi-type) Branching Processes, that
arise in a variety of areas. More generally, Recursive Markov Decision
Processes and Recursive Stochastic Games can be used to model recursive systems that have both probabilistic and nonprobabilistic, controllable actions. In recent years there has been substantial work on the
algorithmic analysis of these models, regarding basic questions of termination, reachability, and analysis of the properties of their executions. In
this talk we will present some of the basic theory, algorithmic methods,
results, and challenges.

In recent years there has been a lot of work on the modeling and analysis of
systems that have both probabilistic and recursive features. In the talk we will
present an overview of some of this work. In this paper we will give a brief,
informal introduction to the models, on the type of questions about them that
are investigated, and pointers to the literature.

Markov chains are a useful, standard model for representing the behavior of
probabilistic systems in a broad variety of domains. *Recursive Markov Chains*
extend ordinary finite state Markov chains with a recursive feature [23]. They
can be viewed alternatively also as a probabilistic extension of Recursive State
Machines (RSM) [4]. Informally, a Recursive Markov Chain (RMC for short)
consists of a collection of finite-state component Markov chains that can call
each other in a potentially recursive manner, like procedures. Figure 1 shows an
example RMC $A = (A_1, A_2)$, consisting of two component Markov chains A_1, A_2.
Each component has a set of *entry* nodes and a set of *exit* nodes where execution
starts and terminates respectively; for example A_1 has one entry node *en* and
two exit nodes ex_1, ex_2. In addition, each component has a set of other nodes
and a set of *boxes*, where each box is mapped to some component and represents
a recursive call to that component; for example A_1 has a box b_1 representing a
recursive call to A_2. A box has a set of *call ports* and *return ports* corresponding

O.H. Ibarra and B. Ravikumar (Eds.): CIAA 2008, LNCS 5148, pp. 23–32, 2008.
© Springer-Verlag Berlin Heidelberg 2008

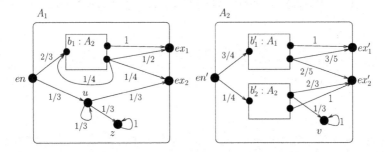

Fig. 1. A sample Recursive Markov Chain

1-1 to the entry and exit nodes of the corresponding component. A transition to a box goes to a specific call port and invokes the corresponding component starting at the corresponding entry node; when (and if) the call terminates at some exit node, then the calling component resumes execution from the corresponding return port of the box. All the transitions are labeled with probabilities as in ordinary Markov chains, summing to 1 for each node, except for call ports and exit nodes that have no transitions; as usual, for computational purposes the probabilities are assumed to be rational numbers.

An RMC A is a succinct finite representation of an underlying (in general) infinite state Markov chain M_A: As an RMC A executes starting from some initial node, at any point in time the process is at a current node of the RMC A and there is a (possibly empty) stack of pending recursive calls (i.e., of boxes); a transition is then selected probabilistically out of the current node, unless the current node is a call port of a box, in which case a new recursive call is initiated, or if the current node is an exit of a component, in which case the component that initiated the last call resumes execution from the appropriate return port of the corresponding box. Note that there is a potentially infinite (countable) number of such 'global' states of the process, because the stack of pending calls may be unbounded, and the stochastic process is a Markov chain M_A on this set of global states.

An RMC in which the calling relation between the components is acyclic is called a *Hierarchical Markov Chain* (HMC), and can be viewed as a probabilistic extension of Hierarchical State Machines [3]. An HMC A represents a finite, but typically exponentially larger, Markov chain M_A. The hierarchical construct is useful to structure and represent compactly large finite Markov chains.

An expressively equivalent model to Recursive Markov Chains is the *Probabilistic Pushdown Automaton* (pPDA) model [19], an extension of pushdown automata with probabilities on the transitions, where the probabilities of all the transitions for each state and top-of-stack symbol sum to 1. The RMC and pPDA models are equivalent in the sense that from a model of one type one can construct efficiently a model of the other type such that the two models represent essentially the same infinite state Markov chain.

Pushdown automata and recursive state machines (without probabilities) were studied for the purpose of analyzing algorithmically the properties (*model checking*) of (abstractions of) programs with procedures [6,17,4]. Similarly, a main motivation for the introduction of RMCs and pPDAs was for the analysis of probabilistic programs with procedures. The procedures correspond to the components of the RMC, the arguments and return values correspond to the entry and exit nodes. The probabilities could arise from randomizing steps or reflect statistical assumptions on the behavior of the program, under which we want to analyze its properties. The properties of interest can range from simple termination and reachability properties, to more complex properties expressed for example by temporal logic or automata specifications. The simplest type of property, and one that plays a central role also for the analysis of more complex properties is termination: Suppose that the RMC starts execution at some node; what is the probability that it will eventually reach a specified exit node (or any exit node), with no pending recursive calls, and terminate? More generally, the nodes and/or edges of a RMC can be labeled from some (finite) alphabet Σ (for example, the letters may correspond to properties satisfied by the states of the program). The executions of the RMC map to words over Σ. A (linear-time) property specification can define the set of desirable (or undesirable) executions by specifying a subset L of finite or infinite words; the question then is, what is the probability that an execution of the RMC starting from some specified initial node (or from some initial distribution) maps to a word in L. Branching-time properties can be similarly specified.

Probability and recursion are fundamental constructs that arise in a variety of contexts, and accordingly several such models have been studied and used in various fields over the years. We discuss next a number of such models.

Branching processes (BP) are an important class of stochastic processes, with applications in various areas such as population genetics, biology and others (see e.g., [34,36,38]). They were introduced first in the single type case by Galton and Watson in the 19th century to study population dynamics, and extended later by Kolmogorov and Sevastyanov to the multi-type case [39]. A branching process models the stochastic evolution of a population of entities of a given (finite) set T of types. For each type $i \in T$, there is a set of probabilistic rules concerning the set of offsprings (their number and types) that an entity of type i produces in the next generation. Starting from an initial population, a branching process evolves from one generation to the next, where in each generation every entity is replaced (independently) by a set of offspring entities chosen probabilistically according to the rules of the type of the entity. There is a well developed mathematical theory of branching processes, see [35] for a comprehensive treatment. Basic quantities of interest in a BP are the *extinction probabilities*: if the process starts with one entity of type i, what is the probability that it will become extinct, i.e. there will be eventually no descendants (these can be used to compute the extinction probability for any initial population). There is a close connection between branching processes and a subclass of RMCs, specifically the class of *1-exit RMCs* where all the components have only 1 exit (denoted *1-RMC*): From a given finite branching process (i.e., with a finite set of types and rules) we can construct efficiently a 1-RMC such that the extinction probabilities of the types in the BP are equal to termination probabilities of nodes in the 1-RMC [23]. There seems to be a distinct difference in expressiveness and complexity between 1-exit RMCs and multiexit RMCs. The one exit restriction means that when a component terminates, it does not return any information about the call beyond the fact that it terminated. Also, as we'll mention later on, some problems can be solved efficiently for 1-exit RMCs, but we do not know how to solve them with multiple exits (and they may well be intractable.) The 1-exit restriction for RMCs corresponds to a 1-state restriction for pPDAs.

Another intimately connected well-studied model is *Stochastic Context-Free Grammars* (SCFG). These have been studied since the 1970's especially in Natural Language Processing (see e.g. [42]), and have been applied also in other areas such as biological sequence analysis [15,49]. A SCFG is a CFG where every production has an associated probability such that the probabilities of the productions for each nonterminal sum to 1. The SCFG models a stochastic process for generating strings, for example, by a leftmost derivation rule, and gives a probability to each string in the language. From a given SCFG G we can construct efficiently an 1-exit RMC A that is 'equivalent' to G in the sense that the two models represent essentially the same infinite state Markov chain. In particular, the probability of the language of G (i.e., the sum of the probabilities of all the strings in the language, which can be less than 1) is equal to the termination probability of a certain 'initial' node in the 1-RMC A, and the 1-RMC (suitably labeled) and the SCFG induce the same probabilities on the strings of the language. Conversely, it is possible to translate efficiently a given 1-exit RMC to an 'equivalent' branching process or to a SCFG, such that the termination probabilities of the nodes of the RMC are equal to extinction probabilities of the types of the BP or to the probabilities of the languages generated by the nonterminals of the SCFG [23].

Another related model, called *Random walk with back button*, was introduced and studied in [31] as a probabilistic model for web-surfing. It is an extension of a Markov chain with a 'back button' (as in a web browser) that enables the process to trace back its steps. This model corresponds to a proper subclass of 1-RMCs and SCFGs [23].

A class of models, called *Quasi-Birth-Death Processes* (QBD), have been studied for performance analysis in the queuing theory and structured Markov chain community [5,41,45]. A (discrete-time) QBD process is a (countably) infinite state Markov chain whose transition matrix has a certain repeating block structure specified by a constant number of finite matrix blocks. Generalizations of QBDs, called *tree-structured* QBDs and *tree-like* QBDs (which are equivalent to each other [53]), have been also studied; they are an extension of QBDs with an additional tree structure on the states. As shown in [22], (discrete) quasi-birth-death processes are expressively equivalent to probabilistic 1-counter automata, i.e., pPDA where the stack alphabet has only one symbol; tree-structured and tree-like QBDs are equivalent to (unrestricted) pPDA and RMCs.

In all the models we discussed above (RMC, pPDA and their subclasses considered in various fields), all the steps are probabilistic. More generally, some steps of a system/program may be probabilistic while others are not probabilistic but rather are controlled by the system or the environment. Markov Decision Processes (MDP) and Stochastic Games (SG) are standard models for systems that have both probabilistic and nonprobabilistic/controllable aspects (see e.g. [47,32,44]); they have been used in various areas, including in particular in verification as models for probabilistic concurrent systems and for open systems that interact with their environment. Extending these models with a recursive feature gives rise to *Recursive Markov Decision Processes* (RMDP) and *Recursive Stochastic Games* (RSG) [25,28]. A RMDP or RSG is like a RMC except that some of the nodes are probabilistic as in an RMC, i.e., have probabilistic transitions, and some nodes are nonprobabilistic, i.e., their transitions are controlled by the player(s). In an RMDP (like in a MDP) there is only one player that controls all the nonprobabilistic nodes, with the goal of maximizing or minimizing some objective, such as the probability of an event, (for example, termination of the process, or more generally, generation of an execution that satisfies a given property); or there can be a reward (payoff or cost) specified for the individual nodes and/or edges of the RMDP, and the player wants to maximize or minimize the reward (cost) accumulated during the execution. In a game there are two opposing players, one trying to maximize the objective, the other to minimize it. In the general form of a stochastic game (sometimes called *concurrent game*) at each (nonprobabilistic) node, each player has a finite set of possible actions that it can choose from; the players select an action simultaneously and the combination of selected actions determines the transition taken out of the current node. In a simpler form, called *simple* or *turn-based* games, only one player can choose an action (has a 'turn') at each node, i.e. the (nonprobabilistic) nodes are partitioned among the players who control the transitions out of them.

We will touch briefly now on some of the issues, methods, and results on the recursive models. The recursive feature introduces several difficulties that are not present in the nonrecursive case. One difficulty is that the probabilities that we want to compute are typically irrational. Recall that we assumed as usual that the given transitions probabilities of the models are rational. In the case of ordinary Markov chains this implies that the probabilities we want to compute of the usual types of events (including probabilities of general properties expressed for example by automata or temporal logic) are also rational, have polynomially bounded size (number of bits), and they can be computed in polynomial time. This is no more true, even for 1-exit RMCs (and SCFGs and branching processes); for example, the probabilities of termination are typically irrational. Thus the probabilities cannot be computed exactly, and can be only bounded or approximated. We distinguish between qualitative and quantitative questions regarding the desired probabilities. In the *qualitative problem* we want to determine whether a certain probability is 0, 1, or strictly between 0 and 1. For example, does a given a SCFG generate a terminal string with probability 1? Does an execution of a given RMC satisfy a given temporal property almost surely? In a *quantitative decision problem* we want to determine how a certain probability compares with a given rational bound r, i.e. is it $<, =$ or $> r$? In a *quantitative approximation problem* we want to approximate a desired probability to a specified precision.

The termination probabilities play a central role in the analysis of RMC and pPDA: For each node u of an RMC and each exit node v of the same component as u, let $q(u, v)$ be the probability that the RMC started at u will eventually reach the exit v (with no pending recursive calls) and terminate (the corresponding quantities for pPDA are the probabilities $q(s, Y, t)$ that the pPDA starting from state s with Y on the stack will eventually pop Y and end in state t). The vector q of termination probabilities satisfies a set of equations $x = P(x)$ (one equation for each termination probability) where P is a vector of polynomials with positive rational coefficients. The system may have many solutions; however the vector P defines a monotone mapping from the nonnegative orthant to itself, and has a least fixed point (LFP), i.e., a componentwise least nonnegative solution. The LFP is precisely the vector q of termination probabilities [19,23]. From the equations $x = F(x)$, we can construct a system of polynomial equations and inequalities and use a procedure for the existential theory of the reals [10,48] to solve the qualitative and quantitative termination problems in PSPACE.

For several important subclasses of RMCs more efficient algorithms can be obtained using different methods. For example, the qualitative termination problem can be solved in polynomial time for 1-RMCs (and SCFGs and BPs), as well as for hierarchical Markov chains, using algebraic and combinatorial methods; for RMCs with linear recursion, the probabilities are rational and can be computed exactly in P-time [23]. For back-button processes the probabilities can be approximated in polynomial time using Semidefinite Programming [31]. It is an open question whether the qualitative and quantitative problems can be solved in polynomial time in general; however, this seems unlikely, and there are results indicating that it would require solving at least some hard longstanding open problems. The quantitative decision problem for 1-RMCs and hierarchical Markov chains subsumes the square root sum problem (a 30-year old simple intriguing problem that arises often in geometric computations [33,52]), and a more general problem (called posSLP) that characterizes P-time computability in a RAM model with unit cost rational arithmetic operations [1]; these problems are in PSPACE but are not even known to be in NP. For RMCs with 2 exits, even the qualitative problem (does the RMC terminate with probability 1?) is at least as hard as these problems, and the same holds for the approximation of the termination probabilities with any nontrivial constant error [29,23].

The procedures for the existential theory of reals are impractical. One approach to approximate the LFP of the system $x = P(x)$ is to start with the 0 vector and apply repeatedly P to it; the vector $P^k(0)$ converges to the LFP q as $k \to \infty$, however the convergence is exponentially slow. A faster method that accelerates convergence is to use a decomposed version of Newton's method [23]: after a preprocessing 'cleaning' step, the system is decomposed into strongly connected components (SCC) and Newton is applied bottom up on the DAG of the SCCs; if we start from the 0 vector, then Newton is well defined (no singularity is encountered) and it converges monotonically to the LFP. This is a more practical approach; experiments with this method are reported in [43,55]. A similar Newton method can be applied more generally to monotone systems of polynomial equations, i.e. systems $x = P(x)$ where P is a vector of polynomials with positive rational coefficients; such a system may not have a fixed point, but if it does then it has a LFP and (decomposed) Newton starting at the 0 vector converges to it [23]. The rate of convergence of the method is investigated in [37,18]. They show that for strongly connected fixed point systems, Newton gains (at least) one bit of precision per iteration after some initial period, and some upper bounds are given for this initial period. In general however (for non-strongly connected systems) there are bad examples that require an exponential number of iterations to achieve a desired precision.

The analysis of more general properties of RMCs and pPDA is studied in [9,19,24,26]. Algorithms and lower bounds are given for linear time properties specified either by automata or by LTL (Linear Temporal Logic) formulas, and for branching time properties. The methods build on the termination analysis of the models as well as on methods for model checking of ordinary (nonrecursive) Markov chains. Results are given both for the general class of RMCs and pPDA, as well as for important subclasses (e.g., 1-RMCs and SCFGs, linear RMCs etc). Quantitative aspects of the executions of pPDA with a reward (cost) structure and checking of properties that involve these quantities are studied in [8,20]; these can be used for example to estimate expected termination time, stack length etc.

Recursive Markov Decision Processes and Stochastic Games are studied in [7,21,25,27,28]. For general multiexit RMDP's and RSGs, the qualitative (and quantitative) termination problems are undecidable, i.e., we cannot determine if a termination probability under optimal play is 1, and we cannot even approximate it [25]. For 1-exit RMDPs and games however, the termination problems (both qualitative and quantitative) are decidable and can be solved in PSPACE (same as for RMCs). These correspond to controlled and game versions of SCFGs and branching processes, for example, optimal control of a branching process to maximize or minimize the probability of extinction. In fact the qualitative problems for 1-RMDPs can be solved in polynomial time [27], and we can also compute the optimal and pessimal expected times to termination [21]. For simple 1-RSGs these problems are in NP∩co-NP and subsume the well-known open problem of Condon [11] of computing the value of simple stochastic games.

Many of the algorithms on probabilistic recursive models have been implemented in a tool called PReMo by Wojtczak and Etessami [55].

We gave in this paper a flavor of some of the recent work on probabilistic recursive models and their analysis. We only mentioned few of the techniques and the results; we refer to the papers for the detailed results. A comprehensive survey paper is being planned with Kousha Etessami [30], and we will defer to that for a thorough exposition.

Acknowledgement. Work partially supported by NSF Grant CCF-0728736.

References

1. Abney, S., McAllester, D., Pereira, F.: Relating probabilistic grammars and automata. In: Proc. 37th Ann. Meeting of Ass. for Comp. Linguistics, pp. 542–549. Morgan Kaufmann, San Francisco (1999)
2. Allender, E., Bürgisser, P., Kjeldgaard-Pedersen, J., Miltersen, P.B.: On the complexity of numerical analysis. In: 21st IEEE Computational Complexity Conference (2006)
3. Alur, R., Yannakakis, M.: Model checking of hierarchical state machines. ACM Trans. Prog. Lang. Sys. 23(3), 273–303 (2001)
4. Alur, R., Benedikt, M., Etessami, K., Godefroid, P., Reps, T.W., Yannakakis, M.: Analysis of recursive state machines. ACM Trans. Progr. Lang. Sys. 27, 786–818 (2005)
5. Bini, D., Latouche, G., Meini, B.: Numerical methods for Structured Markov Chains. Oxford University Press, Oxford (2005)
6. Bouajjani, A., Esparza, J., Maler, O.: Reachability analysis of pushdown automata: Applications to model checking. In: Mazurkiewicz, A., Winkowski, J. (eds.) CONCUR 1997. LNCS, vol. 1243, pp. 135–150. Springer, Heidelberg (1997)
7. Brázdil, T., Brozek, V., Forejt, V., Kučera, A.: Reachability in recursive Markov decision processes. In: Baier, C., Hermanns, H. (eds.) CONCUR 2006. LNCS, vol. 4137, pp. 358–374. Springer, Heidelberg (2006)
8. Brázdil, T., Kučera, A., Esparza, J.: Analysis and prediction of the long-run behavior of probabilistic sequential programs with recursion. In: Proc. of FOCS 2005, pp. 521–530 (2005)
9. Brázdil, T., Kučera, A., Stražovský, O.: Decidability of temporal properties of probabilistic pushdown automata. In: Diekert, V., Durand, B. (eds.) STACS 2005. LNCS, vol. 3404. Springer, Heidelberg (2005)
10. Canny, J.: Some algebraic and geometric computations in PSPACE. In: Proc. of 20th ACM STOC, pp. 460–467 (1988)
11. Condon, A.: The complexity of stochastic games. Inf. & Comp. 96(2), 203–224 (1992)
12. Courcoubetis, C., Yannakakis, M.: The complexity of probabilistic verification. Journal of the ACM 42(4), 857–907 (1995)
13. Courcoubetis, C., Yannakakis, M.: Markov decision processes and regular events. IEEE Trans. on Automatic Control 43(10), 1399–1418 (1998)
14. de Alfaro, L., Majumdar, R.: Quantitative solution of omega-regular games. J. Comp. Sys. Sc. 68(2), 374–397 (2004)
15. Durbin, R., Eddy, S.R., Krogh, A., Mitchison, G.: Biological Sequence Analysis: Probabilistic models of Proteins and Nucleic Acids. Cambridge U. Press (1999)
16. Esparza, J., Gawlitza, T., Kiefer, S., Seidl, H.: Approximative methods for motonone systems of min-max-polynomial equations. In: Proc. 35th ICALP (2008)
17. Esparza, J., Hansel, D., Rossmanith, P., Schwoon, S.: Efficient algorithms for model checking pushdown systems. In: Emerson, E.A., Sistla, A.P. (eds.) CAV 2000. LNCS, vol. 1855, pp. 232–247. Springer, Heidelberg (2000)
18. Esparza, J., Kiefer, S., Luttenberger, M.: Convergence thresholds of Newton's method for monotone polynomial equations. In: Proc. STACS (2008)
19. Esparza, J., Kučera, A., Mayr, R.: Model checking probabilistic pushdown automata. In: Proc. of 19th IEEE LICS 2004 (2004); Full version in Logical Methods in Computer Science 2(1) (2006)

20. Esparza, J., Kučera, A., Mayr, R.: Quantitative analysis of probabilistic pushdown automata: expectations and variances. In: Proc. of 20th IEEE LICS (2005)
21. Etessami, K., Wojtczak, D., Yannakakis, M.: Recursive Stochastic Games with Positive Rewards. In: Proc. 35th ICALP (2008)
22. Etessami, K., Wojtczak, D., Yannakakis, M.: Quasi-birth-death processes, tree-like QBDs, probabilistic 1-counter automata, and pushdown systems (submitted, 2008)
23. Etessami, K., Yannakakis, M.: Recursive Markov chains, stochastic grammars, and monotone systems of non-linear equations. In: Diekert, V., Durand, B. (eds.) STACS 2005. LNCS, vol. 3404, pp. 340–352. Springer, Heidelberg (2005), http://homepages.inf.ed.ac.uk/kousha/bib_index.html
24. Etessami, K., Yannakakis, M.: Algorithmic verification of recursive probabilistic state machines. In: Halbwachs, N., Zuck, L.D. (eds.) TACAS 2005. LNCS, vol. 3440, pp. 253–270. Springer, Heidelberg (2005)
25. Etessami, K., Yannakakis, M.: Recursive Markov Decision Processes and Recursive Stochastic Games. In: Caires, L., Italiano, G.F., Monteiro, L., Palamidessi, C., Yung, M. (eds.) ICALP 2005. LNCS, vol. 3580, pp. 891–903. Springer, Heidelberg (2005)
26. Etessami, K., Yannakakis, M.: Checking LTL Properties of Recursive Markov Chains. In: Proc. 2nd Intl. Conf. on Quantitative Evaluation of Systems. IEEE, Los Alamitos (2005)
27. Etessami, K., Yannakakis, M.: Efficient Qualitative Analysis of Classes of Recursive Markov Decision Processes and Simple Stochastic Games. In: Durand, B., Thomas, W. (eds.) STACS 2006. LNCS, vol. 3884, pp. 634–645. Springer, Heidelberg (2006)
28. Etessami, K., Yannakakis, M.: Recursive concurrent stochastic games. In: Bugliesi, M., Preneel, B., Sassone, V., Wegener, I. (eds.) ICALP 2006. LNCS, vol. 4052, pp. 324–335. Springer, Heidelberg (2006)
29. Etessami, K., Yannakakis, M.: On the complexity of Nash equilibria and other fixed points. In: Proc. of 48th IEEE FOCS (2007)
30. Etessami, K., Yannakakis, M.: Recursive Markov Processes (in preparation, 2008)
31. Fagin, R., Karlin, A., Kleinberg, J., Raghavan, P., Rajagopalan, S., Rubinfeld, R., Sudan, M., Tomkins, A.: Random walks with "back buttons" (extended abstract). In: ACM Symp. on Theory of Computing, pp. 484–493 (2000); Full version in Ann. of App. Prob., 11, pp 810–862 (2001)
32. Filar, J., Vrieze, K.: Competitive Markov Decision Processes. Springer, Heidelberg (1997)
33. Garey, M.R., Graham, R.L., Johnson, D.S.: Some NP-complete geometric problems. In: 8th ACM Symp. on Theory of Computing, pp. 10–22 (1976)
34. Haccou, P., Jagers, P., Vatutin, V.A.: Branching Processes: Variation, Growth, and Extinction of Populations. Cambridge U. Press (2005)
35. Harris, T.E.: The Theory of Branching Processes. Springer, Heidelberg (1963)
36. Jagers, P.: Branching Processes with Biological Applications. Wiley, Chichester (1975)
37. Kiefer, S., Luttenberger, M., Esparza, J.: On the convergence of Newton's method for monotone systems of polynomial equations. In: Proc. 39th Symp. on Theory of Computation (STOC), pp. 217–226 (2007)
38. Kimmel, M., Axelrod, D.E.: Branching processes in biology. Springer, Heidelberg (2002)
39. Kolmogorov, A.N., Sevastyanov, B.A.: The calculation of final probabilities for branching random processes. Dokl. Akad. Nauk SSSR 56, 783–786 (1947) (Russian)
40. Kwiatkowska, M.: Model checking for probability and time: from theory to practice. In: 18th IEEE LICS, pp. 351–360 (2003)

41. Latouche, G., Ramaswami, V.: Introduction to Matrix Analytic Methods in Stochastic Modeling. ASA-SIAM series on statistics and applied probability (1999)
42. Manning, C., Schütze, H.: Foundations of Statistical Natural Language Processing. MIT Press, Cambridge (1999)
43. Nederhof, M.J., Satta, G.: Using Newton's method to compute the partition function of a PCFG (unpublished manuscript, 2006)
44. Neyman, A., Sorin, S. (eds.): Stochastic Games and Applications. Kluwer, Dordrecht (2003)
45. Neuts, M.F.: Stuctured Stochastic Matrices of M/G/1 Type and their applications. Marcel Dekker, New York (1989)
46. Paz, A.: Introduction to Probabilistic Automata. Academic Press, London (1971)
47. Puterman, M.L.: Markov Decision Processes. Wiley, Chichester (1994)
48. Renegar, J.: On the computational complexity and geometry of the first-order theory of the reals, parts I-III. J. Symb. Comp. 13(3), 255–352 (1992)
49. Sakakibara, Y., Brown, M., Hughey, R., Mian, I.S., Sjolander, K., Underwood, R., Haussler, D.: Stochastic context-free grammars for tRNA modeling. Nucleic Acids Research 22(23), 5112–5120 (1994)
50. Sevastyanov, B.A.: The theory of branching processes. Uspehi Mathemat. Nauk 6, 47–99 (1951) (Russian)
51. Shapley, L.S.: Stochastic games. Proc. Nat. Acad. Sci. 39, 1095–1100 (1953)
52. Tiwari, P.: A problem that is easier to solve on the unit-cost algebraic RAM. Journal of Complexity, 393–397 (1992)
53. van Houdt, B., Blondia, C.: Tree structured QBD Markov chains and tree-like QBD processes. Stochastic Models 19(4), 467–482 (2003)
54. Vardi, M.: Automatic verification of probabilistic concurrent finite-state programs. In: Proc. of 26th IEEE FOCS, pp. 327–338 (1985)
55. Wojtczak, D., Etessami, K.: Premo: an analyzer for probabilistic recursive models. In: Grumberg, O., Huth, M. (eds.) TACAS 2007. LNCS, vol. 4424. Springer, Heidelberg (2007), http://groups.inf.ed.ac.uk/premo/

Concurrency, Synchronization, and Conflicts in Petri Nets

Hsu-Chun Yen[*]

Dept. of Electrical Engineering, National Taiwan University, Taipei, Taiwan, R.O.C.
Dept. of Computer Science, Kainan University, Taoyuan, Taiwan, R.O.C.
yen@cc.ee.ntu.edu.tw

Petri nets represent one of the most popular formalisms for specifying, modeling, and analyzing concurrent systems. In spite of their popularity, many interesting problems concerning Petri nets are either undecidable or of very high complexity. Lipton [7] and Rackoff [10] showed exponential space lower and upper bounds, respectively, for the boundedness problem. As for the containment and the equivalence problems, Rabin [1] and Hack [5], respectively, showed these two problems to be undecidable. The reachability problem is known to be decidable [8] and exponential-space-hard [7].

Studying Petri nets from the aspect of formal language has long been recognized as an important branch of research in Petri net theory. It has been shown that all Petri net languages are context-sensitive, assuming that a transition's label cannot be λ. Also, Petri net languages and context-free languages are incomparable, i.e., there are Petri net languages that are not context-free and vice versa. See [9,11]. It was shown in [4] that Petri net languages are exactly those that can be expressed by *concurrent regular expressions*, i.e., regular expressions augmented with *interleaving, interleaving closure, synchronization* and *renaming* operations. As *interleaving* (denoted by $\parallel$) is also known as *shuffle* in formal languages, it is of interest to take a closer look at various shuffle-related issues in the framework of Petri net languages.

A *Petri net* (PN, for short) is a 3-tuple (P, T, φ), where P is a finite set of *places*, T is a finite set of *transitions*, and φ is a *flow function* $\varphi : (P \times T) \cup (T \times P) \rightarrow N$. A *marking* is a mapping $\mu : P \rightarrow N$, specifying a PN's *configuration*. The computational power of PNs stems from the ability for their transitions to compete for resources as well as to synchronize and to execute concurrently in the course of a computation. Generally speaking, there are two sources of "resource sharing" in the computation of a PN. For $x \in P \cup T$, we define ${}^\bullet x = \{y \mid \varphi(y, x) > 0\}$ and $x^\bullet = \{y \mid \varphi(x, y) > 0\}$.

- *Place sharing*: $t_1, t_2 \in T$ and ${}^\bullet t_1 \cap {}^\bullet t_2 \neq \emptyset$.
  Transitions t_1 and t_2 "share" a common input place p in ${}^\bullet t_1 \cap {}^\bullet t_2$, in the sense that they compete for resources (tokens) kept in p.

[*] Research supported in part by *National Science Council* Grant NSC-96-2221-E-002-028 and *Excellent Research Projects of National Taiwan University*, 95R0062-AE00-05.

O.H. Ibarra and B. Ravikumar (Eds.): CIAA 2008, LNCS 5148, pp. 33–35, 2008.

- *Transition sharing*: $p_1, p_2 \in P$ and $p_1^\bullet \cap p_2^\bullet \neq \emptyset$.
  Places p_1 and p_2 "share" a common output transition t in $p_1^\bullet \cap p_2^\bullet$, in the sense that they synchronize with each other using transition t.

In this talk, we first survey some of the analytical techniques and results known for various restricted classes of PNs lacking the capabilities of synchronization and/or resource sharing. PNs without transition sharing are called *communication-free*[1] PNs. For PNs free from place sharing, a hierarchy of "conflict-free" PNs has been defined in the literature (see e.g., [2]). It is known that the reachability sets of communication-free PNs as well as various "conflict-free" PNs are effectively semilinear. (See [14] for a survey of complexity results concerning various restricted classes of PNs.)

To study PN languages, we consider labeled PNs of the form $(\mathcal{P}, \Sigma, \eta)$, where $\mathcal{P}$ is a PN, Σ is a finite set of *transition labels*, and η is a mapping $\eta : T \to \Sigma$. The *sequential language* (or simply *language*) $L_{seq}(\Gamma, \mu_0) = \{\eta(\sigma) \mid \mu_0 \overset{\sigma}{\to}, \sigma \in T^*\}$, a language over alphabet Σ, consists of the set of sequences of labels corresponding to transition sequences executable from the initial marking μ_0. We investigate the issue of *separability* in the theory of PN languages. Intuitively speaking, a PN is said to be k-separable if starting from a marking μ which is divisible by $k > 1$ (called k-marking), any computation sequence σ of the PN can be distributed to k sequences $\sigma_1, ..., \sigma_k$ executing on k identical copies of the PN, each begins with $\frac{\mu}{k}$ as its initial marking, such that (1) $\forall 1 \le i \le k$, $\frac{\mu}{k} \overset{\sigma_i}{\to}$, and (2) $\#_\sigma = \sum_{1 \le i \le k} \#_{\sigma_i}$, where $\#_\sigma$ (resp., $\#_{\sigma_i}$) denotes the transition count of σ (resp., σ_i). If the initial marking μ_0 is a k-marking, and $\mu_0 \overset{\sigma}{\to}$ implies σ is separable, then the PN (w.r.t. the initial marking μ_0) is called k-separable. It was shown in [2] that marked graphs are always k-separable. We are able to strengthen the result of [2] by showing the property of k-separability to hold for a wider class of PNs using a simpler technique. We also relate k-separability to the issue of shuffle decomposability, which is central to a number of intriguing problems in formal languages (see, e.g., [3,6]). A PN Γ being k-separable only guarantees that $\overbrace{L_{seq}(\Gamma, \frac{\mu}{k}) \| \cdots \| L_{seq}(\Gamma, \frac{\mu}{k})}^{k} \subseteq L_{seq}(\Gamma, \mu)$. It requires a stronger version of k-separability to capture the notion of "shuffle decomposability" in the framework of PN languages. We also present some open problems along this line.

Another issue addressed in this talk is with respect to PN languages under the *concurrent semantics*, as opposed to the traditional *interleaving semantics*. In this setting, each step $\mu \overset{X}{\Rightarrow}$ of a PN involves a set X of executable transitions that are concurrently enabled in marking μ. With respect to initial marking μ_0, the *concurrent language* of Γ is $L_{conc}(\Gamma, \mu_0) = \{\eta(\delta) \mid \mu_0 \overset{\delta}{\Rightarrow}, \delta \in (2^T)^*\}$ (a language over alphabet 2^Σ). Concurrent PN languages have only been scarcely studied in the literature in the past (e.g., [12], [13]). We present some known

---

[1] More precisely, PN $\mathcal{P} = (P, T, \varphi)$ is communication-free if $\forall t \in T, p \in P, |^\bullet t| \le 1$ and $\varphi(p, t) \le 1$.

results concerning concurrent PN languages, and also point out some problems remain to be answered.

References

1. Baker, H.: Rabin's proof of the undecidability of the reachability set inclusion problem of vector addition systems, Computation Structures Group Memo 79, Project MAC, MIT (July 1973)
2. Best, E., Esparza, J., Wimmel, H., Wolf, K.: Separability in conflict-free Petri nets. In: Virbitskaite, I., Voronkov, A. (eds.) PSI 2006. LNCS, vol. 4378, pp. 1–18. Springer, Heidelberg (2007)
3. Campeanu, C., Salomaa, K., Vagvolgyi, S.: Shuffle quotient and decompositions. In: Kuich, W., Rozenberg, G., Salomaa, A. (eds.) DLT 2001. LNCS, vol. 2295, pp. 223–226. Springer, Heidelberg (2002)
4. Garg, V., Raghunath, M.: Concurrent regular expressions and their relationship to Petri nets. Theoretical Computer Science 96, 285–304 (1992)
5. Hack, M.: The equality problem for vector addition systems is undecidable. C.S.C. Memo 121, Project MAC, MIT (1975)
6. Ito, M.: Shuffle decomposition of regular languages. Journal of Universal Computer Science 8(2), 257–259 (2002)
7. Lipton, R.: The reachability problem requires exponential space, Technical Report 62, Yale University, Dept. of CS (January 1976)
8. Mayr, E.: An algorithm for the general Petri net reachability problem. In: STOC, pp. 238–246 (1981)
9. Peterson, J.: Petri Net Theory and the Modeling of Systems. Prentice Hall, Englewood Cliffs (1981)
10. Rackoff, C.: The covering and boundedness problems for vector addition systems. Theoretical Computer Science 6, 223–231 (1978)
11. Reisig, W.: Petri Nets: An Introduction. Springer, New York (1985)
12. Wolfsthal, Y., Yoeli, M.: An equivalence theorem for labeled marked graphs. IEEE Trans. on Parallel and Distributed Systems 5(8), 886–891 (1994)
13. Yen, H.: Sequential versus concurrent languages of labeled conflict-free Petri nets. IEEE Trans. on Automatic Control 47(7), 1158–1162 (2002)
14. Yen, H.: Introduction to Petri net theory. In: Esik, Z., Martin-Vide, C., Mitrana, V. (eds.) Recent Advances in Formal Languages and Applications. Studies in Computational Intelligence, ch.14, vol. 25, pp. 343–373 (2006)

Automated Compositional Reasoning of Intuitionistically Closed Regular Properties*

Yih-Kuen Tsay[1] and Bow-Yaw Wang[2]

[1] Department of Information Management, National Taiwan University, Taiwan
[2] Institute of Information Science, Academia Sinica, Taiwan

Abstract. Analysis of infinitary safety properties with automated compositional reasoning through learning is discussed. We consider the class of intuitionistically closed regular languages and show that it forms a Heyting algebra and is finitely approximatable. Consequently, compositional proof rules can be verified automatically and learning algorithms for finitary regular languages suffice for generating the needed contextual assumptions. We also provide a semantic justification of an axiom to deduce circular compositional proof rules for such infinitary languages.

1 Introduction

Compositional reasoning is probably the best way to harness complexity in formal verification [7]. It reduces complexity by decomposing systems into components according to compositional proof rules. In the assume-guarantee paradigm, each component is verified separately with auxiliary contextual assumptions. With an adequate degree of automation, compositional reasoning is also seen by many as an effective technique to alleviate the state explosion problem in model checking. One approach to full automation based on learning has been proposed in [6,5]. In the approach, system behaviors and properties are restricted to regular languages and the needed contextual assumptions are generated by a learning algorithm. It is possible in theory to extend automated compositional reasoning based on learning to ω-regular languages [8]. However, it is not clear how this extension can be made practically usable. The learning algorithm in [8] generates ω-automata by posing membership and equivalence queries, the latter of which are computationally expensive for ω-regular languages.

A natural question to ask is whether automated compositional reasoning can be generalized to some subclass of ω-regular languages while maintaining practical feasibility. In particular, one may consider the class of closed ω-regular languages, which corresponds to the class of safety properties and is of fundamental importance in formal specification. Unfortunately, this subclass of ω-regular languages does not form a Boolean algebra [14]. Developing compositional proof

---

* The work is partly supported by NSC grant 96-3114-P-001-002-Y. The second author is also supported by NSC grant 95-2221-E-001-024-MY3 and the SISARL thematic project of Academia Sinica.

O.H. Ibarra and B. Ravikumar (Eds.): CIAA 2008, LNCS 5148, pp. 36–45, 2008.

rules for the subclass is more involved. Moreover, weakest contextual assumptions may not be generated by learning algorithms because they may not belong to the subclass. Automated compositional reasoning therefore may not work even if compositional proof rules are available [6].

In this paper, we extend automated compositional reasoning to the class of intuitionistically closed regular languages. An intuitionistically closed regular language contains all (finite) prefixes of ω-strings in its corresponding closed ω-regular language. Finite approximations in an intuitionistically closed regular language allow to characterize its ω-strings. Learning algorithms for regular languages suffice to generate contextual assumptions for the class efficiently. Furthermore, we are able to show the class of intuitionistically closed regular languages forms a Heyting algebra. Compositional proof rules can thus be deduced automatically [1,18]. Automated compositional reasoning is therefore generalized to the class of intuitionistically closed regular languages without any penalty.

The intuitionistic interpretation additionally admits circular compositional proof rules. Circularity in compositional reasoning has been observed in various models of reactive systems (see, for example, [3]). For intuitionistically closed regular languages, we are able to establish the same circular compositional proof rule in [1,18]. More circular compositional proof rules can be established syntactically. The combination of automata and proof theory hence relieves users from making tedious inductive proofs for circular reasoning.

It is practically impossible to enumerate all works related to compositional reasoning. Readers are referred to [7] for a thorough introduction. The learning algorithm L^* for regular languages was introduced in [4]. It generates the minimal finite state automaton for an unknown regular language with a polynomial number of membership and equivalence queries. Applying the L^* algorithm to compositional reasoning was first proposed in [6].

Introductions to infinitary languages can be found in [15,14]. Closed ω-regular languages were characterized by Landweber [10,17,14]. The learning algorithm L^ω for ω-regular languages in the intersection of Borel classes F_σ and G_δ was introduced in [12]. However, the algorithm L^ω requires asymptotically more queries than L^*. In [8], a learning algorithm for general ω-regular languages is introduced. It may make an exponential number of queries, though.

In [1], a finitary intuitionistic interpretation was proposed to derive proof rules in compositional reasoning. An effective version of the interpretation had been developed and applied in automated compositional reasoning [18]. An infinitary intuitionistic interpretation for linear temporal logic was introduced in [11]. None generalizes automated compositional reasoning to infinitary languages.

The paper is organized as follows. After the introduction, some backgrounds are given in Section 2. The following section presents the negative result for closed ω-regular languages. Infinitary regular languages under intuitionistic interpretation are introduced in Section 4. The correspondence between Landweber automata and intuitionistically closed regular languages is given in Section 5. Section 6 shows that the class of intuitionistically closed regular languages forms a Heyting algebra. Applications to automated compositional reasoning are presented in Section 7. We conclude this paper in Section 8.

2   Preliminaries

A *partially ordered set* $(P, \leq)$ consists of a set P and a reflexive, anti-symmetric, and transitive binary relation $\leq \subseteq P \times P$ [9]. A *lattice* $(L, \leq, \sqcup, \sqcap)$ is a partially ordered set where the *least upper bound* $a \sqcup b$ and the *greatest lower bound* $a \sqcap b$ with respect to $\leq$ exist for any pair of elements a, b in L. A *Boolean algebra* $(B, \leq, \sqcup, \sqcap, -, 0, 1)$ is a lattice such that (1) $0 \leq a$ and $a \leq 1$ for all $a \in B$; (2) $a \sqcup -a = 1$, $a \sqcap -a = 0$ for all $a \in B$; and (3) $a \sqcup (b \sqcap c) = (a \sqcup b) \sqcap (a \sqcup c)$ and $a \sqcap (b \sqcup c) = (a \sqcap b) \sqcup (a \sqcap c)$ for all $a, b, c \in B$. The Boolean domain $\mathbb{B} = \{\mathsf{false}, \mathsf{true}\}$ forms the Boolean algebra $(\mathbb{B}, \Rightarrow, \vee, \wedge, \overline{\bullet}, \mathsf{false}, \mathsf{true})$.

A *Heyting algebra* $(H, \leq, \sqcup, \sqcap, \Rightarrow, 0, 1)$ is a lattice where (1) $0 \leq a$ and $a \leq 1$ for all $a \in H$; and (2) for all $a, b \in H$, the *pseudo-complement of* a *relative to* b, $a \Rightarrow b$, satisfies

$$\text{for all } c \in H, c \leq (a \Rightarrow b) \text{ if and only if } c \sqcap a \leq b.$$

Let Σ be an *alphabet* consisting of a finite set of *symbols*. A *string* α is a finite sequence of symbols. We say α is a string of *length* n (denoted by $|\alpha| = n$) if $\alpha = \alpha(1)\alpha(2) \cdots \alpha(n)$. The *empty string* λ is the string of length zero. The set of all strings is denoted by Σ^*. An ω-*string* $\xi = \xi(1)\xi(2) \cdots \xi(i) \cdots$ is an infinite sequence of symbols with length $|\xi| = \omega$ by convention. We denote the set of all ω-strings by Σ^ω and define $\Sigma^\infty = \Sigma^* \cup \Sigma^\omega$. A *language* is a subset of Σ^*; an ω-*language* is a subset of Σ^ω; and an *intuitionistic language* is a subset of Σ^∞.

Let $\sigma, \tau \in \Sigma^\infty$. We say σ is a *prefix* of τ (written $\sigma \sqsubseteq \tau$) if $\tau = \sigma\nu$ for some $\nu \in \Sigma^\infty$, or $\sigma = \tau$. For any $\sigma \in \Sigma^\infty$, define $\mathbf{A}(\sigma) = \{\tau \in \Sigma^\infty : \tau \sqsubseteq \sigma\}$. It is routine to generalize the definition over any intuitionistic language X by taking $\mathbf{A}(X) = \{\tau \in \Sigma^\infty : \tau \sqsubseteq \sigma \text{ for some } \sigma \in X\}$. An intuitionistic language $X \subseteq \Sigma^\infty$ is *prefix-closed* if $\mathbf{A}(X) \subseteq X$.

Given an intuitionistic language $X \subseteq \Sigma^\infty$, define its *classical closure* $\mathbf{cl}_\omega(X)$ to be $\{\xi \in \Sigma^\omega : \mathbf{A}(\xi) \cap \Sigma^* \subseteq \mathbf{A}(X)\}$. For any ω-language L, we say it is *classically closed* if $\mathbf{cl}_\omega(L) = L$. The class of classically closed ω-languages is denoted by $\mathcal{F}_\omega$. It is known that classically closed ω-languages correspond to safety properties [2]. Similarly, define the *intuitionistic closure* $\mathbf{cl}_\infty(X) = \{\sigma \in \Sigma^\infty : \mathbf{A}(\sigma) \cap \Sigma^* \subseteq \mathbf{A}(X)\}$ for any intuitionistic language $X \subseteq \Sigma^\infty$. An intuitionistic language X is *intuitionistically closed* if $\mathbf{cl}_\infty(X) = X$. We write $\mathcal{F}_\infty$ for the class of intuitionistically closed languages. Note that $X \subseteq \mathbf{cl}_\infty(X)$ for $X \in \Sigma^\infty$ and $L \subseteq \mathbf{cl}_\omega(L)$ for $L \in \Sigma^\omega$. Moreover, $\mathbf{cl}_\infty(X) \subseteq X$ if $X \in \mathcal{F}_\infty$.

An intuitionistic language may not be intuitionistically closed even if its ω-strings form a classically closed ω-language. Consider $X = (01)^* \subseteq \Sigma^\infty$ where $\Sigma = \{0, 1\}$. $X \cap \Sigma^\omega = \emptyset$ is classically closed. But the completion of its strings $(01)^\omega$ is not in X. Hence X is not intuitionistically closed.

An *automaton* $M = (\Sigma, Q, q_0, \delta, F)$ consists of an alphabet Σ, a finite set of *states* Q, an *initial state* $q_0 \in Q$, a *transition relation* $\delta \subseteq Q \times \Sigma \times Q$, and a set of *accepting states* $F \subseteq Q$. For clarity, we write $q \xrightarrow{a} q'$ if $(q, a, q') \in \delta$. Moreover, we say the automaton M is *deterministic* if its transition relation is in fact a function from $Q \times \Sigma$ to Q. Given $\sigma \in \Sigma^\infty$ and an automaton M, a *run of M on σ* is a sequence of states $q_0 q_1 \cdots q_i \cdots$ such that $q_0 \xrightarrow{\sigma(1)} q_1 \cdots q_i \xrightarrow{\sigma(i+1)} q_{i+1} \cdots$. The set $Run_M(\sigma)$ contains runs of M on σ; it is a singleton if M is deterministic.

Let $M = (\Sigma, Q, q_0, \delta, F)$ be an automaton and $\alpha \in \Sigma^*$ with $|\alpha| = n$. A run $r = q_0 q_1 \cdots q_n \in Run_M(\alpha)$ satisfies the *finite acceptance condition* if $q_n \in F$. The automaton M *accepts* α if r satisfies the finite acceptance condition for some $r \in Run_M(\alpha)$. The set of strings accepted by M with finite acceptance condition forms a language $L_*(M)$. A language L in Σ^* is *regular* if $L = L_*(M)$ for some automaton M. The class of regular languages is denoted by $\mathcal{R}_*$.

Let $M = (\Sigma, Q, q_0, \delta, F)$ be an automaton, $\xi \in \Sigma^\omega$, and $r \in Run_M(\xi)$. Define $Inf_M(r) = \{q : q \text{ occurs infinitely often in } r\}$. We say r satisfies the *Büchi acceptance condition* if $Inf_M(r) \cap F \neq \emptyset$. Similarly, define $Rng_M(r) = \{q : q \text{ occurs in } r\}$. We say r satisfies the *Landweber acceptance condition* if $Rng_M(r) \subseteq F$. A *Büchi automaton* is an automaton $B = (\Sigma, Q, q_0, \delta, F)$ with the Büchi acceptance condition. It *accepts* the ω-language $L_\omega(B) = \{\xi \in \Sigma^\omega : Inf_B(r) \cap F \neq \emptyset \text{ for some } r \in Run_B(\xi)\}$. The class of ω-languages accepted by Büchi automata are denoted by $\mathcal{R}_\omega$. A *Landweber automaton* is a deterministic automaton $R = (\Sigma, Q, q_0, \delta, F)$ with the Landweber acceptance condition. It *accepts* the ω-language $L_\omega(R) = \{\xi \in \Sigma^\omega : Rng_R(r) \subseteq F \text{ for the } r \in Run_R(\xi)\}$.

Theorem 1. *[10,14] Let $L \subseteq \Sigma^\omega$. $L \in \mathcal{R}_\omega \cap \mathcal{F}_\omega$ if and only if $L = L_\omega(R)$ for some Landweber automaton R.*

Let M and P be automata. The *language containment problem* is to decide whether $L_\bullet(M) \subseteq L_\bullet(P)$. In the automata-theoretic approach to formal verification, system behaviors and requirements are specified by the languages accepted by automata M and P respectively. Hence the conformance of the system M with respect to the requirement P is reduced to the language containment problem [16]. Oftentimes, a system is specified by the composition of its components; its behaviors are defined as the intersection of those of its components [6,18]. The number of states therefore grows exponentially in compositions. An effective solution to the state explosion problem is compositional reasoning.

In compositional reasoning, compositional proof rules are used to deduce the correctness of a system by parts. A *compositional proof rule* is of the form

$$\ell \; \frac{\Gamma_0, \Gamma_1, \ldots, \Gamma_n}{\Delta} \; \mathcal{C}$$

where ℓ is its *label*, $\mathcal{C}$ is a *side condition*, $\Gamma_0, \Gamma_1, \ldots, \Gamma_n$, and Δ are instances of the language containment problem. The instances $\Gamma_0, \Gamma_1, \ldots, \Gamma_n$ are the *premises* of the compositional proof rule; Δ is the *conclusion*. A compositional proof rule is *sound* if its conclusion follows from its premises; it is *invertible* if all its premises are satisfiable provided its conclusion holds.

3   Compositional Reasoning of Classically Closed Languages

In the assume-guarantee paradigm of compositional reasoning, users are allowed to specify contextual assumptions in premises of compositional proof rules. If the compositional proof rule is sound and invertible, users are guaranteed to find proper assumptions to verify the system. Finding proper assumptions nevertheless is tedious and often requires clairvoyance. Automated compositional reasoning applies machine learning to generate assumptions for users automatically. Consider the following compositional proof rule, where system behaviors and property are formalized as regular languages J, K, and L respectively [5]:

$$R0 \ \frac{J \cap A \subseteq L \qquad K \subseteq A}{J \cap K \subseteq L}$$

Since regular languages are closed under Boolean operations, learning algorithms gradually converge to the weakest assumption $L \cup \overline{J}$ through a series of membership and equivalence queries. These queries are reduced to membership and language containment problems and then resolved automatically.

Extending the automated methodology to ω-regular languages does not look promising. The only learning algorithm for general ω-regular languages may make an exponential number of queries [8]. Moreover, the language containment problem for ω-regular languages is computationally harder than for regular languages. Even if one considers the subclass with efficient learning algorithms [12], resolving equivalence queries for ω-regular languages is still less efficient.

The outlook does not improve for the most important class of classically closed ω-regular languages. Consider again the compositional proof rule $R0$. Suppose now J, K, L are classically closed ω-regular languages. The weakest assumption $\overline{J} \cup L$ is not necessarily classically closed since the class of classically closed ω-regular languages is not closed under complementation. It is too restrictive to consider only the class of classically closed ω-regular languages. One wonders whether the weakest assumption is defined too liberally. If only assumptions in the class of classically closed ω-regular languages are considered, could the weakest assumption exist? Algebraically, the weakest assumption is but the pseudo-complement of J relative to L. It is however not hard to see that the weakest assumption does not always exist.

Proposition 1. *For some $K, L \in \mathcal{R}_\omega \cap \mathcal{F}_\omega$, there is no $C \in \mathcal{R}_\omega \cap \mathcal{F}_\omega$ such that for all $J \in \mathcal{R}_\omega \cap \mathcal{F}_\omega$, $J \cap K \subseteq L$ if and only if $J \subseteq C$.*

Proposition 1 suggests that automated compositional reasoning cannot be applied to classically closed ω-regular languages naïvely. In the following, we propose a new class of infinitary languages suitable for the automated technique.

4   Intuitionistic Regular Languages

To motivate the intuitionistic interpretation, consider the ω-languages $K = (01)^\omega$ and $L = \emptyset$. We would like to find the maximal classically closed ω-language

J such that $J \cap K \subseteq L$. Observe that the ω-language $J_i = (01)^i 0^\omega$ satisfies $J_i \cap K \subseteq \emptyset$ for $i \in \mathbb{N}$. Hence $J_i \subseteq J$ for $i \in \mathbb{N}$. But one would have $(01)^\omega \in J$ and $J \cap K \neq \emptyset$ for J is classically closed.

One way to circumvent the problem is to disallow J_i's. Notice that $\mathbf{A}(J_i) \cap \mathbf{A}(K) \neq \emptyset$ though $J_i \cap K = \emptyset$ for each i. Indeed, $\cup_{i\in\mathbb{N}}\mathbf{A}(J_i)$ and the closure property imply $(01)^\omega \in J$. If prefixes of ω-languages were taken into consideration, the embarrassing dilemma would disappear.

The idea is best illustrated automata-theoretically. Recall that automata for finitary and infinitary languages are indistinguishable structurally; only their acceptance conditions differ. We therefore generalize the language accepted by an automaton to the new interpretation.

Definition 1. *Let B be a Büchi automaton. Define*

$$L_\infty(B) = \{\sigma \in \Sigma^\infty : B \text{ accepts } \sigma \text{ by finite or Büchi acceptance condition}\}$$
$$\mathcal{R}_\infty = \{X \subseteq \Sigma^\infty : X = L_\infty(B) \text{ for some Büchi automaton } B\}.$$

Unlike classical ω-regular languages, intuitionistic regular languages do not form a Boolean algebra. To apply automated compositional reasoning, one could try to form a Heyting algebra over intuitionistic regular languages [18].

5   Landweber Automata and Intuitionistically Closed Regular Languages

Recall that the class of ω-languages accepted by Landweber automata coincides with the class of classically closed ω-regular languages (Theorem 1). We consider strings accepted by finite acceptance condition as well.

Definition 2. *Let R be a Landweber automaton. Define $L_\infty(R) = \{\sigma \in \Sigma^\infty : Rng_R(r) \subseteq F \text{ for the } r \in Run_R(\sigma)\}$.*

The following lemma states the intuitionistic language accepted by a Landweber automaton is indeed intuitionistically regular.

Lemma 1. *Let R be a Landweber automaton. $L_\infty(R) \in \mathcal{R}_\infty$.*

To show $L_\infty(R)$ is intuitionistically closed for any Landweber automaton R, consider the infinite run for any ω-string in $\mathbf{cl}_\infty(L_\infty(R))$. It only visits accepting states since all prefixes of the ω-string belong to $L_\infty(R)$. Hence only accepting states can occur in the infinite run. The ω-string belongs to $L_\infty(R)$ as well.

Lemma 2. *Let R be a Landweber automaton. $L_\infty(R)$ is intuitionistically closed.*

Recall that intuitionistic regular languages are defined by (non-deterministic) Büchi automata but intuitionistically closed regular languages are by (deterministic) Landweber automata. To show that any intuitionistically closed regular language is accepted by a Landweber automaton, one must close the gap between deterministic and non-deterministic computation. Since there is no gap in classically closed ω-regular languages (Theorem 1), one would not expect differently in our intuitionistic interpretation.

Lemma 3. *Let $X \in \mathcal{R}_\infty$. If X is intuitionistically closed, $X = L_\infty(B)$ for some deterministic Büchi automaton B.*

It is not hard to translate deterministic Büchi automata to Landweber automata. The correspondence between intuitionistically closed regular languages and intuitionistic languages accepted by Landweber automata is obtained.

Theorem 2. *For any $X \subseteq \Sigma^\infty$, $X \in \mathcal{R}_\infty \cap \mathcal{F}_\infty$ if and only if $X = L_\infty(R)$ for some Landweber automaton R.*

6   Intuitionistically Closed Regular Languages as Heyting Algebra

We first characterize pseudo-complements. Given $X, Y \in \Sigma^\infty$, the language $X \rightarrow Y$ consists of strings whose every prefixe, if in X, also belongs to Y.

Definition 3. *[11] Let $X, Y \in \Sigma^\infty$. $X \rightarrow Y = \{\sigma \in \Sigma^\infty : \mathbf{A}(\sigma) \cap X \subseteq Y\}$.*

We now show that $X \rightarrow Y$ is intuitionistically closed regular if both X and Y are. Since X and Y are intuitionistically closed regular languages, they are accepted by Landweber automata R and S respectively. We define a Landweber automaton $R \rightarrow S$ such that $L_\infty(R \rightarrow S) = L_\infty(R) \rightarrow L_\infty(S) = X \rightarrow Y$.

Definition 4. *Let $R = (\Sigma, P, p_0, \phi_R, F_R)$ and $S = (\Sigma, Q, q_0, \phi_S, F_S)$ be Landweber automata. Define the Landweber automaton $R \rightarrow S = (P \times Q \times \mathbb{B}, (p_0, q_0, b_0), \phi, F)$ as follows.*

- $b_0 = \mathsf{true}$ *if and only if $p_0 \in F_R$ implies $q_0 \in F_S$*
- $(p', q', b') = \phi((p, q, b), a)$ *if*
    - $p' = \phi_R(p, a)$, $q' = \phi_S(q, a)$, *and*
    - $b' = \mathsf{true}$ *if and only if $b = \mathsf{true}$, and $p' \in F_R$ implies $q' \in F_S$.*
- $F = \{(p, q, \mathsf{true}) : p \in P, q \in Q\}$.

By construction, the language $L_\infty(R \rightarrow S)$ is prefix-closed. Moreover, a string is in $L_\infty(R \rightarrow S)$ if all its finite prefixes belong to $L_\infty(R \rightarrow S)$ since $L_\infty(R \rightarrow S)$ is intuitionistically closed. We can now show $L_\infty(R \rightarrow S) = L_\infty(R) \rightarrow L_\infty(S)$.

Proposition 2. *Let R and S be Landweber automata. $L_\infty(R \rightarrow S) = L_\infty(R) \rightarrow L_\infty(S)$.*

To summarize, we have shown the language $K \rightarrow L$ is intuitionistically closed regular if both K and L are intuitionistically closed regular.

Corollary 1. *If $X, Y \in \mathcal{R}_\infty \cap \mathcal{F}_\infty$, $X \rightarrow Y \in \mathcal{R}_\infty \cap \mathcal{F}_\infty$.*

It is easy to verify $\emptyset$ and Σ^∞ are both intuitionistically closed regular. Moreover, $X \cup Y$, $X \cap Y$, and $X \rightarrow Y$ are intuitionistically closed regular if both X and Y are. Hence the class $\mathcal{R}_\infty \cap \mathcal{F}_\infty$ forms a Heyting algebra.

Theorem 3. $(\mathcal{R}_\infty \cap \mathcal{F}_\infty, \subseteq, \cup, \cap, \rightarrow, \emptyset, \Sigma^\infty)$ *is a Heyting algebra.*

A simple application of elementary proof theory allows to establish sound and invertible compositional proof rules [1,18].

Corollary 2. *If a compositional proof rule is provable by the system LJ, it is sound and invertible for intuitionistically closed regular languages.*

Particularly, the rule given in Section 3 is sound and invertible for $\mathcal{R}_\infty \cap \mathcal{F}_\infty$. Moreover, the weakest assumption $J \rightarrow L$ is in fact an intuitionistically closed regular language by Theorem 3. A learning algorithm for intuitionistically closed regular languages can generate a Landweber automaton accepting $J \rightarrow L$. The termination of automated compositional reasoning is thus ensured.

Circularity in compositional proof rules is always intriguing because it contradicts our intuition. Consider the following rule where $\mathcal{C}$ is a side condition [3].

$$\frac{J_0 \cap K_1 \subseteq K_0 \qquad K_0 \cap J_1 \subseteq K_1}{J_0 \cap J_1 \subseteq K_0 \cap K_1} \, \mathcal{C}$$

Circular reasoning arises because the premise $J_0 \cap K_1 \subseteq K_0$ assumes K_1 to establish K_0 and the other assumes K_0 to establish K_1. Circular reasoning is not sound for Heyting algebra in general. But the class $\mathcal{R}_\infty \cap \mathcal{F}_\infty$ admits such circularity conditionally. The following definition is needed to describe the condition.

Definition 5. *Let $X \subseteq \Sigma^\infty$ and $\Xi \subseteq \Sigma$. X is said to constrain Ξ (write $X \triangleright \Xi$) if $\alpha a \in X$ for any $\alpha \in X \cap \Sigma^*$ and $a \notin \Xi$.*

Definition 5 intuitively says that a language X is not interfered by the symbols not in Ξ if $X \triangleright \Xi$. If two languages are not interfering with each other, one can apply the following lemma to have circular compositional proof rules.

Lemma 4. *Let $X, Y \in \mathcal{F}_\infty$ with $X, Y \neq \emptyset$, and $\Xi_X, \Xi_Y \subseteq \Sigma$. If $X \triangleright \Xi_X$, $Y \triangleright \Xi_Y$, and $\Xi_X \cap \Xi_Y = \emptyset$, then $(X \rightarrow Y) \cap (Y \rightarrow X) \subseteq X$.*

Note that Lemma 4 is only applicable to non-empty intuitionistically closed languages. It is necessary since the pseudo-complement of the empty language is Σ^∞. Fortunately, the class of non-empty intuitionistically closed regular languages still forms a Heyting algebra with the minimal element $\{\lambda\}$. The circular compositional proof rule described above can thus be established by the system LJ and Lemma 4 (see also [1,18]).

7   Applications

An advantageous feature of intuitionistically closed regular languages is that they contain finite approximations and their completions. If one could infer more information from finite approximations, algorithms for automata with finite acceptance condition would suffice to solve problems for intuitionistically closed regular languages. In this section, we carry out the plan and obtain efficient automated compositional reasoning for intuitionistically closed regular languages.

Firstly, it is not hard to show the language containment problem for intuitionistically closed regular languages is equivalent to those for regular languages. Intuitively, if all finite approximations of an intuitionistically closed regular language are contained in another intuitionistically closed regular language, their completions belong to the latter as well.

Lemma 5. *Let R and S be Landweber automata. $L_*(R) \subseteq L_*(S)$ if and only if $L_\infty(R) \subseteq L_\infty(S)$.*

Next, we show that it is possible to deduce information about intuitionistically closed regular languages from their finite approximations.

Theorem 4. *Let R, S, and T be Landweber automata. Then $L_*(R) \odot L_*(S) \subseteq L_*(T)$ if and only if $L_\infty(R) \odot L_\infty(S) \subseteq L_\infty(T)$, where $\odot \in \{\cup, \cap, \rightarrow\}$.*

Consider the compositional proof rules $R0$ in Section 3, both premises are equivalent to the regular language containment problem by Theorem 4. That is, for any Landweber automata M_0, M_1, and P, we have

$$\text{R0'} \frac{L_*(M_0) \cap L_*(A) \subseteq L_*(P) \qquad L_*(M_1) \subseteq L_*(A)}{L_\infty(M_0) \cap L_\infty(M_1) \subseteq L_\infty(P)}$$

Since the premises $L_*(M_0) \cap L_*(A) \subseteq L_*(P)$ and $L_*(M_1) \subseteq L_*(A)$ are instances of the regular language containment problem, learning algorithms for regular languages suffice to generate the weakest assumption in the new rule. The most efficient learning algorithm for regular languages requires $O(kmn^2)$ and $n-1$ membership and equivalence queries respectively, where k is the size of alphabet, n is the number of states, and m is the length of the longest counterexample [13]. In comparison, the most efficient learning algorithm for any subclass of ω-regular languages requires $O(n^4)$ and $O(n^2)$ membership and equivalence queries respectively [12]. Since it is harder to resolve the containment problem for ω-regular languages, the compositional proof rule (R0') is definitely preferred.

8   Conclusion

The class of intuitionistically closed regular languages was introduced. We showed that the class forms a Heyting algebra and is finitely approximatable. It moreover admits circular compositional proof rules. Our results extend automated compositional reasoning to the class of intuitionistically closed regular languages most satisfactorily. Not only can compositional proof rules for the new class be deduced automatically, but also finding assumptions be done as efficiently as for regular languages. Given the negative result on classically closed ω-regular languages (Section 3), the present work is perhaps the best that one can hope for the compositional analysis of safety properties.

Our interpretation for intuitionistic languages differs from those in [11]. It would be interesting to investigate more properties about intuitionistic regular languages in our interpretation. Moreover, a correspondence between intuitionistic languages and automata in the interpretation of [11] could be useful to solve the model checking problem of intuitionistic linear temporal logic.

References

1. Abadi, M., Plotkin, G.D.: A logical view of composition. Theoretical Computer Science 114(1), 3–30 (1993)
2. Alpern, B., Schneider, F.: Defining liveness. Information Processing Letters 21, 181–185 (1985)
3. Alur, R., Henzinger, T.: Reactive modules. Formal Methods in System Design 15(1), 7–48 (1999)
4. Angluin, D.: Learning regular sets from queries and counterexamples. Information and Computation 75(2), 87–106 (1987)
5. Barringer, H., Giannakopoulou, D., Păsăreanu, C.S.: Proof rules for automated compositional verification through learning. In: Workshop on Specification and Verification of Component-Based Systems, pp. 14–21 (2003)
6. Cobleigh, J.M., Giannakopoulou, D.: Learning assumptions for compositional verification. In: Garavel, H., Hatcliff, J. (eds.) TACAS 2003. LNCS, vol. 2619, pp. 331–346. Springer, Heidelberg (2003)
7. de Roever, W.P., de Boer, F., Hanneman, U., Hooman, J., Lakhnech, Y., Poel, M., Zwiers, J.: Concurrency Verification: Introduction to Compositional and Noncompositional Methods. Cambridge Tracts in Theoretical Computer Science, vol. 54. Cambridge University Press, Cambridge (2001)
8. Farzan, A., Chen, Y.F., Clarke, E.M., Tsay, Y.K., Wang, B.Y.: Extending automated compositional verification to the full class of omega-regular languages. In: Ramakrishnan, C., Rehof, J. (eds.) TACAS. LNCS, vol. 4963, pp. 2–17. Springer, Heidelberg (2008)
9. Goldblatt, R.: Topoi: The Categorial Analysis of Logic, revised edn. Dover Publications (2006)
10. Landweber, L.: Decision problems for ω-automata. Mathematical Systems Theory 3, 376–384 (1969)
11. Maier, P.: Intuitionistic LTL and a new characterization of safety and liveness. In: Marcinkowski, J., Tarlecki, A. (eds.) CSL 2004. LNCS, vol. 3210, pp. 295–309. Springer, Heidelberg (2004)
12. Maler, O., Pnueli, A.: On the learnability of infinitary regular sets. Information and Computation 118(2), 316–326 (1995)
13. Rivest, R.L., Schapire, R.E.: Inference of finite automata using homing sequences. Information and Computation 103(2), 299–347 (1993)
14. Staiger, L.: ω-languages. In: Rozenberg, G., Salomaa, A. (eds.) Handbook of Formal Languages, vol. 3, pp. 339–387. Springer, Heidelberg (1997)
15. Thomas, W.: Automata on infinite objects. In: van Leeuwen, J. (ed.) Handbook of Theoretical Computer Science, vol. B, pp. 133–191. Elsevier Science Publishers, Amsterdam (1990)
16. Vardi, M.: Verification of concurrent programs: the automata-theoretic framework. In: Proceedings of the Second IEEE Symposium on Logic in Computer Science, pp. 167–176 (1987)
17. Wagner, K.: On ω-regular sets. Information and Control 43, 123–177 (1979)
18. Wang, B.Y.: Automatic derivation of compositional rules in automated compositional reasoning. In: Caires, L., Vasconcelos, V.T. (eds.) CONCUR. LNCS, vol. 4703, pp. 303–316. Springer, Heidelberg (2007)

Antimirov and Mosses's Rewrite System Revisited[*]

Marco Almeida, Nelma Moreira, and Rogério Reis

DCC-FC & LIACC, Universidade do Porto
R. do Campo Alegre 1021/1055, 4169-007 Porto, Portugal
{mfa,nam,rvr}@ncc.up.pt

Abstract. Antimirov and Mosses proposed a rewrite system for deciding the equivalence of two (extended) regular expressions. In this paper
we present a functional approach to that method, prove its correctness,
and give some experimental comparative results. Besides an improved
version of Antimirov and Mosses's algorithm, we present a version using
partial derivatives. Our preliminary results lead to the conclusion that,
indeed, these methods are feasible and, generally, faster than the classical
methods.

Keywords: regular languages, regular expressions, derivatives, partial
derivatives, regular expression equivalence, minimal automata, rewriting
systems.

1 Introduction

Although, because of their efficiency, finite automata are normally used for regular language manipulation, regular expressions (*re*) provide a particularly good
notation for their representation. The problem of deciding whether two *re* are
equivalent is PSPACE-complete [SM73]. This is normally solved by transforming
each *re* into an equivalent NFA, convert those automata to equivalent deterministic ones, and finally minimize both DFAs, and decide if the resulting automata
are isomorphic. The worst case complexity of the automata determinization process is exponential in the number of states.

Antimirov and Mosses [AM94] presented a rewrite system for deciding the
equivalence of extended *re* based on a new complete axiomatization of the extended algebra of regular sets. This axiomatization, or any other classical complete axiomatization of the algebra of regular sets, can be used to construct an
algorithm for deciding the equivalence of two *re*. Normally, however, these de-
duction systems are quite inefficient. This rewrite system is a refutation method
that normalizes regular expressions in such a way that testing their equivalence
corresponds to an iterated process of testing the equivalence of their derivatives.
Termination is ensured because the set of derivatives to be considered is finite,

[*] This work was partially funded by Fundação para a Ciência e Tecnologia (FCT) and
Program POSI, and by project ASA (PTDC/MAT/65481/2006).

O.H. Ibarra and B. Ravikumar (Eds.): CIAA 2008, LNCS 5148, pp. 46–56, 2008.

and possible cycles are detected using *memoization*. Antimirov and Mosses suggested that their method could lead to a better average-case algorithm than those based on the comparison of the equivalent minimal DFAs. In this paper we present a functional approach to that method, prove its correctness, and give some experimental comparative results. Besides an improved version of Antimirov and Mosses's algorithm, we present a new version using partial derivatives. Our preliminary results lead to the conclusion that indeed these methods are feasible and, quite often, faster than the classical methods.

The paper is organized as follows. Section 2 contains several basic definitions and facts concerning regular languages and *re*. In Section 3 we present our variant of Antimirov and Mosses's method for testing the equivalence of two *re*. An improved version using partial derivatives is also presented. Section 4 gives some experimental comparative results between classical methods and the one presented in Section 3. Finally, in Section 5 we discuss some open problems, as ongoing and future work.

2   Regular Expressions and Automata

Here we recall some definitions and facts concerning regular languages, regular expressions and finite automata. For further details we refer the reader to the works of Hopcroft *et al.* [HMU00], Kozen [Koz97] and Kuich and Salomaa [KS86].

Let Σ be an alphabet and Σ^* be the set of all *words* over Σ. The *empty word* is denoted by ϵ and the length of a word w is denoted by $|w|$. A language is a subset of Σ^*, and if L_1 and L_2 are two languages, then $L_1 \cdot L_2 = \{xy \mid x \in L_1 \text{ and } y \in L_2\}$. A *re* α over Σ represents a (regular) language $L(\alpha) \subseteq \Sigma^*$ and is inductively defined by: $\emptyset$ is a *re* and $L(\emptyset) = \emptyset$; ϵ is a *re* and $L(\epsilon) = \{\epsilon\}$; $a \in \Sigma$ is a *re* and $L(a) = \{a\}$; if α and β are *re*, $(\alpha + \beta)$, $(\alpha \cdot \beta)$ and $(\alpha)^*$ are *re*, respectively with $L((\alpha + \beta)) = L(\alpha) \cup L(\beta)$, $L((\alpha \cdot \beta)) = (L(\alpha) \cdot L(\beta))$ and $L((\alpha)^*) = L(\alpha)^*$. The operator $\cdot$ is often omitted. We adopt the usual convention that $\star$ has precedence over $\cdot$, and $\cdot$ has higher priority than $+$. Let RE be the set of *re* over Σ. The size of α is denoted by $|\alpha|$ and represents the number of symbols, operators, and parentheses in α. We denote by $|\alpha|_\Sigma$ the number of symbols in α. We define the *constant part* of α as $\varepsilon(\alpha) = \epsilon$ if $\epsilon \in L(\alpha)$, and $\varepsilon(\alpha) = \emptyset$ otherwise. Two *re* α and β are *equivalent*, and we write $\alpha \sim \beta$, if $L(\alpha) = L(\beta)$. The algebraic structure $(RE, +, \cdot, \emptyset, \epsilon)$, constitutes an idempotent semi-ring, and, with the unary operator $\star$, a Kleene algebra. There are several well-known complete axiomatizations of Kleene algebras [Sal66, Koz94], but we will essentially consider Salomaa's axiom system F_1 which, besides the usual axioms for an idempotent semi-ring, contains the following two axioms for the $\star$ operator:

$$\alpha^* \sim \epsilon + \alpha\alpha^*; \quad \alpha^* \sim (\epsilon + \alpha)^*.$$

As for rules of inference, system F_1 has the usual rule of substitution and the following rule of *solution of equations*:

$$\frac{\alpha \sim \beta\alpha + \gamma, \quad \varepsilon(\beta) = \emptyset}{\alpha \sim \beta^\star\gamma} \qquad (R_{se})$$

A *nondeterministic finite automaton* (NFA) A is a tuple $(Q, \Sigma, \delta, q_0, F)$ where Q is the finite set of states, Σ is the alphabet, $\delta \subseteq Q \times \Sigma \cup \{\epsilon\} \times Q$ the transition relation, q_0 the initial state and $F \subseteq Q$ the set of final states. A NFA without ϵ-transitions is *deterministic* (DFA) if, for each pair $(q, a) \in Q \times \Sigma$ there exists at most one q' such that $(q, a, q') \in \delta$. Two NFA are *equivalent* if they accept the same language. A DFA is called *minimal* if there is no equivalent DFA with fewer states. Minimal DFAs are unique up to isomorphism. DFAs, NFAs, and *re* represent the same set of languages, *i.e.*, regular languages.

2.1   Succinct Regular Expressions

Equivalent *re* do not need to have the same size. *Irreducible re* as defined by Ellul *et.al* [ESW02] have no redundant occurrences of $\emptyset$, ϵ, $\star$, and parentheses. A *re* α is *uncollapsible* if **none** of the following conditions hold:

- α contains the proper sub-expression $\emptyset$, and $|\alpha| > 1$;
- α contains a sub-expression of the form $\beta\gamma$ or $\gamma\beta$ where $L(\beta) = \{\epsilon\}$;
- α contains a sub-expression of the form $\beta+\gamma$ where $L(\beta) = \{\epsilon\}$ and $\epsilon \in L(\gamma)$.

A *re* α is *irreducible* if it is uncollapsible and **both** two conditions are true:

- α does not contain superfluous parentheses (we adopt the usual operator precedence conventions and omit outer parentheses);
- α does not contain a sub-expression of the form $\beta^{\star^\star}$.

The previous reductions rely on considering *re modulo* some algebraic properties of *re*: identity elements of $+$ and $.$, annihilator element for $\cdot$, and idempotence of $\star$. We also consider $\emptyset^\star = \epsilon$ and $\epsilon^\star = \epsilon$.

Let ACI be the set of axioms that includes the associativity, commutativity and idempotence of disjunction and let $ACIA$ be the set ACI plus the associativity of concatenation. In this work, besides where otherwise stated, we consider irreducible regular expressions modulo $ACIA$ (and denote them by RE). This allows a more succinct representation of *re*, and is essential for ensuring the termination of the algorithms described in the next section.

Our implementation of *re* follows the object-oriented model. We use a different class for each operator which assures that the *re* are kept irreducible modulo $ACIA$, while trying to make the overhead of these transformations negligible. ACI properties are ensured by representing disjunctions as sets, that are coded using hash tables. This allows for a very efficient way of ensuring idempotence (as repeated elements result in a hash value clash), prohibiting $\emptyset$ as an argument, and rending the use of parentheses needless. In a similar way, concatenations are implemented with ordered lists, and the idempotence of the Kleene star is assured by not allowing double stared *re* in the constructor.

2.2   Linear Regular Expressions

A *re* α is *linear* if it is of the form $a_1\alpha_1 + \cdots + a_n\alpha_n$ for $a_i \in \Sigma$ and $\alpha_i \in RE$. The set of all the linear *re* is denoted by RE_{lin}, and can be defined by the following (abstract syntax) context-free grammar, where A is the initial symbol, $L(B) = RE - \{\epsilon, \emptyset\}$ and $L(C) = \Sigma$:

$$A \rightarrow C \mid C \cdot B \mid A + A. \tag{G_1}$$

We say that an expression $a\beta$ has *head* $a \in \Sigma$ and *tail* β. We denote by head(α) and tail(α), respectively, the multiset of all heads and the multiset of all tails in a linear *re* α. A linear regular expression α is *deterministic* if no element of head(α) occurs more than once. We denote the set of all deterministic linear *re* by RE_{det}. Every *re* α can be written as a disjunction of its constant part and a (deterministic) linear *re* [Sal66]. A *re* is said to *pre-linear* if it belongs to the language generated by the following context-free grammar (abstract syntax) with initial symbol A', and A and B are as in G_1:

$$\begin{aligned} A' &\rightarrow \emptyset \mid D \\ D &\rightarrow A \mid D \cdot B \mid (D + D). \end{aligned} \tag{G_2}$$

The set of all pre-linear *re* is denoted by RE_{plin}.

2.3 Derivatives

The *derivative* [Brz64] of a *re* α with respect to a *symbol* $a \in \Sigma$, denoted $a^{-1}(\alpha)$, is defined recursively on the structure of α as follows:

$$a^{-1}(\emptyset) = \emptyset; \qquad\qquad a^{-1}(\alpha + \beta) = a^{-1}(\alpha) + a^{-1}(\beta);$$
$$a^{-1}(\epsilon) = \emptyset; \qquad\qquad a^{-1}(\alpha\beta) = a^{-1}(\alpha)\beta + \varepsilon(\alpha)a^{-1}(\beta);$$
$$a^{-1}(b) = \begin{cases} \epsilon, & \text{if } b = a; \\ \emptyset, & \text{otherwise}; \end{cases} \qquad a^{-1}(\alpha^\star) = a^{-1}(\alpha)\alpha^\star.$$

If α is a deterministic linear *re*, we have:

$$a^{-1}(\alpha) = \begin{cases} \beta, & \text{if } a \cdot \beta \text{ is a sub-expression of } \alpha; \\ \epsilon, & \text{if } \alpha = a; \\ \emptyset, & \text{otherwise}. \end{cases}$$

The *derivative* of a *re* α with respect to the *word* $w \in \Sigma^\star$, denoted $w^{-1}(\alpha)$, is defined recursively on the structure of w:

$$\epsilon^{-1}(\alpha) = \alpha; \quad (ua)^{-1}(\alpha)a^{-1}(u^{-1}(\alpha)), \text{ for any } u \in \Sigma^\star.$$

Considering *re* modulo the *ACI* axioms, Brzozowski [Brz64] proved that, for every *re* α, the set of its derivatives with respect to any word w is finite.

3   Regular Expression Equivalence

The classical approach to the problem of comparing two *re* α and β, *i.e.*, deciding if $L(\alpha) = L(\beta)$, typically consists of transforming each *re* into an equivalent NFA, convert those automata to equivalent deterministic ones, and minimize both DFAs. Because, for a given regular language, the minimal DFA is unique up to isomorphism, these can be compared using a canonical representation [RMA05], and thus checked if $L(\alpha) = L(\beta)$. In this section, we present two methods to verify the equivalence of two re. The first method is a variant of the rewrite system presented by Antimirov and Mosses [AM94], which provides an algebraic calculus for testing the equivalence of two re without the construction of the canonical minimal automata. It is a functional approach on which we always consider the re to be irreducible and not extended (with intersection). The use of irreducible re allows us to avoid the simplification step of Antimirov and Mosses's system with little overhead. The second method improves this first one by using the notion of partial derivative.

3.1 Regular Expression's Linearization

Let $a \in \Sigma$, and α, β, γ be arbitrary re. We define the functions $\text{lin} = \text{lin}_2 \circ \text{lin}_1$, and det as follows:

$$\text{lin}_1 : RE \to RE_{plin}$$
$$\text{lin}_1(\emptyset) = \emptyset;$$
$$\text{lin}_1(\epsilon) = \emptyset;$$
$$\text{lin}_1(a) = a;$$
$$\text{lin}_1(\alpha + \beta) = \text{lin}_1(\alpha) + \text{lin}_1(\beta);$$
$$\text{lin}_1(\alpha^*) = \text{lin}_1(\alpha)\alpha^*;$$
$$\text{lin}_1(a\alpha) = a\alpha;$$
$$\text{lin}_1((\alpha + \beta)\gamma) = \text{lin}_1(\alpha\gamma) + \text{lin}_1(\beta\gamma);$$
$$\text{lin}_1(\alpha^*\beta) = \text{lin}_1(\alpha)\alpha^*\beta + \text{lin}_1(\beta).$$

$$\text{lin}_2 : RE_{plin} \to RE_{lin} \cup \{\emptyset\}$$
$$\text{lin}_2(\alpha + \beta) = \text{lin}_2(\alpha) + \text{lin}_2(\beta);$$
$$\text{lin}_2((\alpha + \beta)\gamma) = \text{lin}_2(\alpha\gamma) + \text{lin}_2(\beta\gamma);$$
$$\text{lin}_2(\alpha) = \alpha. \quad \text{(Otherwise)}$$

$$\text{det} : RE_{lin} \cup \{\emptyset\} \to RE_{det} \cup \{\emptyset\}$$
$$\text{det}(a\alpha + a\beta + \gamma) = \text{det}(a(\alpha + \beta) + \gamma);$$
$$\text{det}(a\alpha + a\beta) = a(\alpha + \beta);$$
$$\text{det}(a\alpha + a) = a(\alpha + \epsilon);$$
$$\text{det}(\alpha) = \alpha. \quad \text{(Otherwise)}$$

The functions lin and lf linearize regular expressions. Function lin_1 corresponds to the function f of the original rewrite system which, contrary to what is claimed by Antimirov and Mosses, returns a pre-linear re, and not a linear one. We use the function lin for efficiency reasons because in a single pass returns a re in a form such that the derivative w.r.t. *any* symbol of the alphabet is readily available. To show that $\text{lin}(\alpha)$ returns either the linear part of α or $\emptyset$, it is enough to observe the following facts, which have straightforward proofs that can be found, along with all the missing proofs, in an extended version of the present paper.

- The function lin_1 is well defined.
- For $\alpha \in RE$, $\text{lin}_1(\alpha) \in L(G_2)$.
- For $\alpha \in RE_{plin}$, $\alpha \sim \text{lin}_2(\alpha)$.
- For $\alpha \in RE$, $\text{lin}(\alpha) \in L(G_1) \cup \{\emptyset\}$.
- For $\alpha \in RE_{lin} \cup \{\emptyset\}$, $\text{det}(\alpha) \in RE_{det}$ and $\alpha \sim \text{det}(\alpha)$.
- For $\alpha \in RE$, $L(\text{lin}(\alpha)) = \begin{cases} L(\alpha), & \text{if } \epsilon \notin L(\alpha); \\ L(\alpha) - \{\epsilon\}, & \text{if } \epsilon \in L(\alpha). \end{cases}$

Thus we have:

Theorem 1. *For any re α, $\alpha \sim \varepsilon(\alpha) + \mathrm{lin}(\alpha)$, and $\alpha \sim \varepsilon(\alpha) + \det(\mathrm{lin}(\alpha))$.*

Considering the definition of derivative (Subsection 2.3), we also have:

Theorem 2. *Let $a \in \Sigma$ and $\alpha \in RE$, then $a^{-1}(\alpha) = a^{-1}(\det(\mathrm{lin}(\alpha)))$.*

3.2 Regular Expression Equivalence

We now present the main functions of the comparison processes. The first one, the function derivatives, computes the set of the derivatives of a pair of deterministic linear *re* (α, β), with respect to each symbol of the alphabet. It is enough to consider only the symbols in $\mathrm{head}(\alpha) \cup \mathrm{head}(\beta)$, and we do that for efficiency reasons. The function is, then, defined as follows:

$$\begin{aligned}
\text{derivatives} \quad &: \quad (RE_{det} \cup \{\emptyset\}) \times (RE_{det} \cup \{\emptyset\}) \to \mathcal{P}(RE \times RE) \\
\text{derivatives}(\alpha, \beta) \quad &= \quad \{\, (a^{-1}(\alpha), a^{-1}(\beta)) \mid a \in \mathrm{head}(\alpha) \cup \mathrm{head}(\beta) \,\}.
\end{aligned}$$

The equiv function, applied to two *re* α and β, returns $True$ if and only if $\alpha \sim \beta$. It is defined in the following way:

$$\begin{aligned}
\text{equiv} \quad &: \quad \mathcal{P}(RE^2) \times \mathcal{P}(RE^2) \to \{True, False\} \\
\text{equiv}(\emptyset, H) \quad &= \quad True; \\
\text{equiv}(\{(\alpha, \beta)\} \cup S, H) \quad &= \quad \begin{cases} False, & \text{if } \varepsilon(\alpha) \neq \varepsilon(\beta); \\ \text{equiv}(S \cup S', H'), & \text{otherwise}; \end{cases}
\end{aligned}$$

where

$$\begin{aligned}
\alpha' &= \det(\mathrm{lin}(\alpha)); & S' &= \{\, p \mid p \in \text{derivatives}(\alpha', \beta'), \, p \notin H' \,\}; \\
\beta' &= \det(\mathrm{lin}(\beta)); & H' &= \{\, (\alpha, \beta) \,\} \cup H.
\end{aligned}$$

In each step the function equiv proceeds by rewriting a pair of *re* into a set S of pairs of derivatives. When either a disagreement pair is found, *i.e.*, a pair of derivatives such that their constant parts are different, or the set S is empty, the function returns. If $\alpha \sim \beta$ the call equiv($\{(\alpha, \beta)\}$) returns the value $True$, otherwise returns $False$. Comparing with the Antimirov and Mosses's rewrite system TR, we note that in each call to equiv(S, H), the set S contains only pairs of *re* which are not in H, thus rendering the rule (IND) of TR unnecessary. On the other hand, our data structures avoid the need of the rule (SIM) by assuring that the *re* are always irreducible.

Theorem 3. *The function* equiv *is terminating.*

Lemma 1. *Given $\alpha, \beta \in RE_{det} \cup \{\emptyset\}$, $\forall (\alpha', \beta') \in \text{derivatives}(\alpha, \beta)$, $\alpha \sim \beta \Rightarrow \alpha' \sim \beta'$.*

Theorem 4. *The call* equiv($\{(\alpha, \beta)\}, \emptyset$) *returns $True$ if and only if $\alpha \sim \beta$.*

3.3 Improved Equivalence Method Using Partial Derivatives

Antimirov [Ant96] introduced the notion of the partial derivatives set of a regular expression α and proved that its cardinality is bounded by the number of alphabetic symbols that occurs in α. He showed that this set can be obtained directly from a new linearization process of α. This new process can be easily implemented in our approach, as a variant of lin function, as we already consider disjunctions as sets. We now briefly review this notions and show how they can be used to improve the equiv algorithm.

Linear Forms. Let $\Sigma \times RE$ be the set of *monomials* over an alphabet Σ. Let $\mathcal{P}_{fin}(A)$ be the set of all finite parts of A. A linear *re* $a_1 \cdot \alpha_1 + \cdots + a_n \cdot \alpha_n$ can be represented by a finite set of monomials $l \in \mathcal{P}_{fin}(\Sigma \times RE)$, named *linear form*, and such that $l = \{(a_1, \alpha_1), \ldots, (a_n, \alpha_n)\}$. We define a function $\sum : \mathcal{P}_{fin}(\Sigma \times RE) \to RE_{lin}$ by $\sum(l) = a_1 \cdot \alpha_1 + \cdots + a_n \cdot \alpha_n$. Concatenation of a linear form l with a *re* β is defined by $l \cdot \beta = \{(a_1, \alpha_1 \cdot \beta), \ldots, (a_n, \alpha_n \cdot \beta)\}$. We can now define the linearization of a *re* α into a linear form as follows:

$$\text{lf} : RE \to \mathcal{P}_{fin}(\Sigma \times RE)$$

$$\text{lf}(\emptyset) = \emptyset; \qquad\qquad\qquad \text{lf}(\alpha^\star) = \text{lf}(\alpha) \cdot \alpha^\star;$$
$$\text{lf}(\epsilon) = \emptyset; \qquad\qquad\qquad \text{lf}(a \cdot \alpha) = \{(a, \alpha)\};$$
$$\text{lf}(a) = \{(a, \epsilon)\}; \qquad\qquad \text{lf}((\alpha + \beta) \cdot \gamma) = \text{lf}(\alpha \cdot \gamma) \cup \text{lf}(\beta \cdot \gamma);$$
$$\text{lf}(\alpha + \beta) = \text{lf}(\alpha) \cup \text{lf}(\beta); \qquad \text{lf}(\alpha^\star \cdot \beta) = \text{lf}(\alpha) \cdot \alpha^\star \cdot \beta \cup \text{lf}(\beta).$$

The following theorem relates the method of linearization presented in the Section 2.2 with linear forms.

Theorem 5. *For any re α, $\text{lin}(\alpha) = \sum(lf(\alpha))$.*

Partial Derivatives. Given a *re* α and a symbol $a \in \Sigma$, a *partial derivative* of α w.r.t. a is a *re* ρ such that $(a, \rho) \in \text{lf}(\alpha)$. The set of partial derivatives of α w.r.t. a is denoted by $\partial_a(\alpha)$. The notion of partial derivative of α can be extended to words $w \in \Sigma^\star$, sets of *re* $R \subseteq RE$, and sets of words $W \subseteq \Sigma^\star$, as follows:

$$\partial_\epsilon(\alpha) = \{\alpha\}; \qquad\qquad\qquad \partial_w(R) = \bigcup_{\alpha \in R} \partial_w(\alpha);$$

$$\partial_{ua}(\alpha) = \partial_a(\partial_u(\alpha)), \text{ for any } u \in \Sigma^\star; \qquad \partial_W(\alpha) = \bigcup_{w \in W} \partial_w(\alpha).$$

There is a strong connection between the sets of partial derivatives and the derivatives of a *re*. Trivially extending the notion of language represented by a *re* to sets of *re*, we have that $L(\partial_w(\alpha)) = L(w^{-1}(\alpha))$, for any $w \in \Sigma^\star$, $\alpha \in RE$. One of the advantages of using partial derivatives is that for any $\alpha \in RE$, $|PD(\alpha) = \partial_{\Sigma^\star}(\alpha)| \leq |\alpha|_\Sigma$, where $PD(\alpha)$ stands for the set of all the syntactically different partial derivatives.

Improving equiv by Using Partial Derivatives. Let us now consider a determinization process for linear forms. We say that a linear form is deterministic if, for each symbol $a \in \Sigma$, there is at most one element of the form (a, α). Let lfX be an extended version of the linearization function lf, defined as follows:

$$\mathrm{lfX}(\alpha) = \{(a, \sum_{(a,\alpha') \in \mathrm{lf}(\alpha)} \alpha') \mid a \in \Sigma\}.$$

We can replace the function composition det · lin with the deterministic linear form obtained with lfX. This new extended linear form allows us to use the previously defined equiv function with only two slight modifications. We redefine the derivatives function as follows:

$$\text{derivatives} \quad : \quad \mathcal{P}_{fin}^{det}(\Sigma \times RE) \times \mathcal{P}_{fin}^{det}(\Sigma \times RE) \to \mathcal{P}(RE \times RE)$$
$$\text{derivatives}(\alpha, \beta) = \{(\alpha', \beta') \mid (a, \alpha') \in \alpha, (a, \beta') \in \beta\}.$$

In the definition of equiv, we change $\alpha' = \mathrm{lfX}(\alpha)$ and $\beta' = \mathrm{lfX}(\beta)$. The new function will be called equivP in the next section.

4 Experimental Results

We will now present some experimental results. These are the running times for the two methods for checking the equivalence of regular expressions. One uses the equivalent minimal DFA, the other is the direct *re* comparison method, as described on the Section 3. All tests were performed on batches of $10,000$ pairs of uniformly random generated *re*, and the running times do not include the time necessary to parse each *re*. Each batch contains *re* of size 10, 50 or 100, with either 2, 5 or 10 symbols. For the uniform generation of random *re* we implemented the method described by Mairson [Mai94] for the generation of context-free languages. We used a grammar for almost irreducible *re* presented by Shallit [Sha04]. As the data sets were obtained with a uniform random generator, the size of each sample is sufficient to ensure a 95% confidence level within a 1% error margin. It is calculated with the formula $n = (\frac{z}{2\epsilon})^2$, where z is obtained from the normal distribution table such that $P(-z < Z < z)) = \gamma$, ϵ is the error margin, and γ is the desired confidence level.

We tested the equivalence of each pair of *re* using both the classical approach and the direct comparison method. We used Glushkov's algorithm to obtain the NFAs from the *re*, and the well-known subset construction to make each NFA deterministic. As for the DFA minimization process, we applied two different algorithms: Hopcroft and Brzozowski's. On one hand, Hopcroft's algorithm has the best known worst-case running time complexity analysis, $O(kn \log n)$. On the other, it is pointed out by Almeida *et. al* [AMR07] that when minimizing NFAs, Brzozowski's algorithm has a better practical performance. As for the direct comparison method, we compared both the original rewriting system (**AM**) and our variant of the algorithm both with (**equivP**) and without partial derivatives

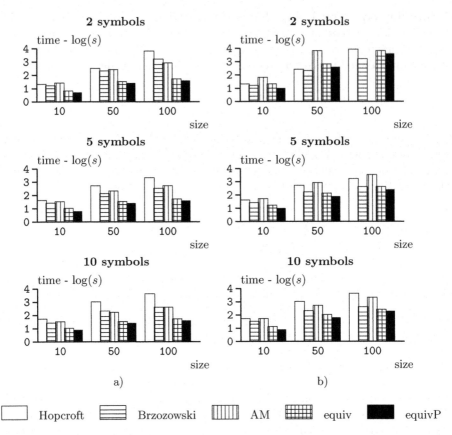

Fig. 1. Running times of three different methods for checking the equivalence of *re*. a) 10.000 pairs of random *re*; b) 10.000 pairs of syntactically equal random *re*. The missing column corresponds to a larger than reasonable observed runtime.

(**equiv**). Because the direct comparison methods try to compute a refutation, we performed a set of tests for the worst case scenario of these algorithms: the equivalence of two syntactically equal regular expressions.

As shown in Figure 1 (a), when comparing randomly generated *re*, any of the direct methods is always the fastest. Note also that Hopcroft's algorithm never achieves shorter running times than Brzozowski's. Figure 1 (b) shows the results of the application of each algorithm to pairs of syntactically equal random *re*. Except for the samples of *re* with size 50 or 100, over an alphabet of 2 symbols, the direct *re* comparison methods are still the fastest. Again, Brzozowki's algorithm always presents better running times than Hopcroft's. Among the direct comparison methods, **equivP** always performs better, with a speedup of 20% − 30%. It is important to state that, asymptotically, when using the minimal DFA approach, the minimization algorithm is the bottleneck of the entire process. It always takes over 50% of the total amount of time when the size of the *re* and/or the alphabet grows . To ensure the fairness of the comparison for the method using NFAs, we tried several algorithms for computing (small) NFAs from *re* (c.f Ilie and Yu [IY03]), but the size of the NFAs seems not to affect significantly the overall performance.

5   Conclusion

We presented a variant method based on a rewrite system for testing the equivalence of two *re*, that attempts to refute its equivalence by finding a pair of derivatives that disagree in their constant parts. While a good behaviour was expected for some non-equivalent *re*, experimental results point to a good average-case performance for this method, even when feeded with equivalent *re*. Some improvement was also achieved by using partial derivatives. Given the spread of multi-cores and grid computer systems, a parallel execution of the better behavioured classic method and our direct comparison method can lead to an optimized framework for testing *re* equivalence. A better theoretical understanding of relationships between the two approaches would be helpful towards the characterization of their average-case complexity. In particular, it will be interesting to compare our method with the one by Hopcroft and Karp [HK71].

References

[AM94]   Antimirov, V.M., Mosses, P.D.: Rewriting extended regular expressions. In: Rozenberg, G., Salomaa, A. (eds.) Developments in Language Theory, pp. 195–209. World Scientific, Singapore (1994)

[AMR07]   Almeida, M., Moreira, N., Reis, R.: On the performance of automata minimization algorithms. Technical Report DCC-2007-03, DCC - FC & LIACC, Universidade do Porto (June 2007)

[Ant96]   Antimirov, V.M.: Partial derivatives of regular expressions and finite automaton constructions. Theor. Comput. Sci. 155(2), 291–319 (1996)

[Brz64]   Brzozowski, J.A.: Derivatives of regular expressions. Journal of the Association for Computing Machinery 11(4), 481–494 (1964)

[ESW02]   Ellul, K., Shallit, J., Wang, M.: Regular expressions: New results and open problems. In: The DCFS 2002 conference, London, Ontario (2002)

[HK71]   Hopcroft, J., Karp, R.M.: A linear algorithm for testing equivalence of finite automata. Technical Report TR 71 -114, University of California, Berkeley, California (1971)

[HMU00]   Hopcroft, J., Motwani, R., Ullman, J.D.: Introduction to Automata Theory, Languages and Computation. Addison-Wesley, Reading (2000)

[IY03]   Ilie, L., Yu, S.: Follow automata. Inf. Comput. 186(1), 140–162 (2003)

[Koz94]   Kozen, D.C.: A completeness theorem for Kleene algebras and the algebra of regular events. Infor. and Comput. 110(2), 366–390 (1994)

[Koz97]   Kozen, D.C.: Automata and Computability. Undergrad. Texts in Computer Science. Springer, Heidelberg (1997)

[KS86]   Kuich, W., Salomaa, A.: Semirings, Automata, Languages, vol. 5. Springer, Heidelberg (1986)

[Mai94]   Mairson, H.G.: Generating words in a context-free language uniformly at random. Information Processing Letters 49, 95–99 (1994)

[RMA05] Reis, R., Moreira, N., Almeida, M.: On the representation of finite automata. In: Mereghetti, C., Palano, B., Pighizzini, G., Wotschke, D. (eds.) Proc. of DCFS 2005, Como, Italy, pp. 269–276 (2005)

[Sal66]   Salomaa, A.: Two complete axiom systems for the algebra of regular events. Journal of the Association for Computing Machinery 13(1), 158–169 (1966)

[Sha04]   Shallit, J.: Regular expressions, enumeration and state complexity. In: Domaratzki, M., Okhotin, A., Salomaa, K., Yu, S. (eds.) CIAA 2004. LNCS, vol. 3317. Springer, Heidelberg (2005)

[SM73]   Stockmeyer, L.J., Meyer, A.R.: Word problems requiring exponential time: Preliminary report. In: Conf. Record of 5th Annual ACM Symposium on Theory of Computing, Austin, Texas, USA, pp. 1–9. ACM, New York (1973)

Antichain-Based Universality and Inclusion Testing over Nondeterministic Finite Tree Automata*

Ahmed Bouajjani[1], Peter Habermehl[1,2], Lukáš Holík[3],
Tayssir Touili[1], and Tomáš Vojnar[3]

[1] LIAFA, CNRS and University Paris Diderot, France
{abou,haberm,touili}@liafa.jussieu.fr
[2] LSV, ENS Cachan, CNRS, INRIA
[3] FIT, Brno University of Technology, Czech republic
{holik,vojnar}@fit.vutbr.cz

Abstract. We propose new antichain-based algorithms for checking universality and inclusion of nondeterministic tree automata (NTA). We have implemented these algorithms in a prototype tool and our experiments show that they provide a significant improvement over the traditional determinisation-based approaches. We use our antichain-based inclusion checking algorithm to build an abstract regular tree model checking framework based entirely on NTA. We show the significantly improved efficiency of this framework through a series of experiments with verifying various programs over dynamic linked tree-shaped data structures.

1 Introduction

Tree automata are useful in numerous different areas, including, e.g., the implementation of decision procedures for various logics, XML manipulation, linguistics or formal verification of systems, such as parameterised networks of processes, cryptographic protocols, or programs with dynamic linked data structures. A classical implementation of many of the operations, such as minimisation or inclusion checking, used for dealing with tree automata in the different application areas often assumes that the automata are deterministic. However, as our own practical experience discussed later in the paper shows, the determinisation step may yield automata being too large to be handled although the original nondeterministic automata are quite small. It may even be the case that the corresponding minimal deterministic automata are small, but they cannot be computed as the intermediary automata resulting from determinisation are too big.

As the situation is similar for other kinds of automata, recently, a lot of research has been done to implement efficiently operations like minimisation (or at least reduction) and universality or inclusion checking on nondeterministic word, Büchi, or tree automata. We follow this line of work and propose and experimentally evaluate new *efficient algorithms* for *universality and inclusion checking* on *nondeterministic* (bottom-up) *tree automata*. Instead of the classical subset construction, we use *antichains of sets*

---

* This work was supported by the French projects ANR-06-SETI-001 AVERISS and RNTL AVERILES, the Czech Grant Agency (projects 102/07/0322, 102/05/H050), the Barrande project 17356TD, and the Czech Ministry of Education by the project MSM 0021630528 *Security-Oriented Research in Information Technology*.

O.H. Ibarra and B. Ravikumar (Eds.): CIAA 2008, LNCS 5148, pp. 57–67, 2008.

of states of the considered automata and extend some of the antichain-based algorithms recently proposed for universality and inclusion checking over finite word automata [12] to tree automata (while also showing that the others are not practical for them).

To evaluate the proposed algorithms, we have implemented them in a prototype tool over the Timbuk tree automata library [9] and tested them in a series of experiments showing that they provide a significant advantage over the traditional determinisation-based approaches. The experiments were done on randomly generated automata with different densities of transitions and final states like in [12] as well as within an important complex application of tree automata. Indeed, our antichain-based inclusion checking algorithm for tree automata fills an important hole in the tree automata technology enabling us to implement an *abstract regular tree model checking* (ARTMC) framework based entirely on nondeterministic tree automata. ARTMC is a generic technique for automated formal verification of various kinds of infinite-state and parameterised systems. In particular, we consider its use for verification of *programs manipulating dynamic tree-shaped data structures*, and we show that the use of nondeterministic instead of deterministic tree automata improves significantly the efficiency of the technique.

Related Work. In [12], antichains were used for dual forward and backward algorithms for universality and inclusion testing over finite word automata. In [8], antichains were applied for Büchi automata. Here, we show how the forward algorithms from [12] can be extended to finite (bottom-up) tree automata (using algorithms computing upwards). We also show that the backward computation from word automata is not practical for tree automata (where it corresponds to a downward computation). The regular tree model checking framework was studied in, e.g., [11,6,2], and its abstract version in [4,5]—in all cases using deterministic tree automata. When implementing a framework for abstract regular tree model checking based on nondeterministic tree automata, we exploit the recent results [1] on simulation-based reduction of tree automata.

2   Preliminaries

An alphabet Σ is ranked if it is endowed with a mapping $rank : \Sigma \to \mathbb{N}$. For $k \geq 0$, $\Sigma_k = \{f \in \Sigma \mid rank(f) = k\}$ is the set of symbols of rank k. The set T_Σ of terms over Σ is defined inductively: if $k \geq 0$, $f \in \Sigma_k$, and $t_1, \ldots, t_k \in T_\Sigma$, then $f(t_1, \ldots, t_k)$ is in T_Σ. We abbreviate the so-called *leaf terms* of the form $a()$, $a \in \Sigma_0$, by simply a. A (nondeterministic, bottom-up) *tree automaton* (NTA) is a tuple $\mathcal{A} = (Q, \Sigma, F, \delta)$ where Q is a finite set of states, Σ is a ranked alphabet, $F \subseteq Q$ is a set of final states, and δ is a set of rules of the form $f(q_1, \ldots, q_n) \to q$ where $n \geq 0$, $f \in \Sigma_n$, and $q_1, \ldots, q_n, q \in Q$. We abbreviate the *leaf rules* of the form $a() \to q$, $a \in \Sigma_0$, as $a \to q$. Let t be a term over Σ. A bottom-up run of $\mathcal{A}$ on t is obtained as follows: first, we assign a state to each leaf according to the leaf rules in δ, then for each internal node, we collect the states assigned to all its children and associate a state to the node itself according to the non-leaf δ rules. Formally, if during the state assignment process subterms $t_1, \ldots, t_n$ are labelled with states $q_1, \ldots, q_n$, and if a rule $f(q_1, \ldots, q_n) \to q$ is in δ, which we will denote by $f(q_1, \ldots, q_n) \to_\delta q$, then the term $f(t_1, \ldots, t_n)$ can be labelled with q. A term t is accepted if $\mathcal{A}$ reaches its root in a final state. The language accepted by the automaton $\mathcal{A}$ is the set of terms that it accepts: $\mathcal{L}(\mathcal{A}) = \{t \in T_\Sigma \mid t \xrightarrow{*}_\delta q(t) \text{ and } q \in F\}$.

A tree automaton is *complete* if for all $n \geq 0$, $f \in \Sigma_n$, $q_1, ..., q_n \in Q$, there is at least one $q \in Q$ such that $f(q_1, ..., q_n) \rightarrow_\delta q$. A tree automaton may in general be *nondeterministic*—we call it *deterministic* if there is at most one $q \in Q$ such that $f(q_1, ..., q_n) \rightarrow_\delta q$ for any $n \geq 0$, $f \in \Sigma_n$, $q_1, ..., q_n \in Q$.

3   Universality Checking

Lattices and Antichains. The following definitions are similar to the corresponding ones in [12]. Let Q be a finite set. An *antichain* over Q is a set $S \subseteq 2^Q$ s.t. $\forall s, s' \in S : s \not\subseteq s'$, i.e., a set of pairwise incomparable subsets of Q. We denote by L the set of antichains. A set $s \in S \subseteq 2^Q$ is minimal in S iff $\forall s' \in S : s' \not\subset s$. Given a set $S \subseteq 2^Q$, $\lfloor S \rfloor$ denotes the set of minimal elements of S. We define a partial order on antichains: for two antichains $S, S' \in L$, let $S \sqsubseteq S'$ iff $\forall s' \in S' \exists s \in S : s \subseteq s'$. Given two antichains $S, S' \in L$, the $\sqsubseteq$-lub (least upper bound) is the antichain $S \sqcup S' = \lfloor \{s \cup s' \mid s \in S \wedge s' \in S'\} \rfloor$ and the $\sqsubseteq$-glb (greatest lower bound) is the antichain $S \sqcap S' = \lfloor \{s \mid s \in S \vee s \in S'\} \rfloor$. We extend these definitions to lub and glb of arbitrary subsets of L in the obvious way, giving the operators $\bigsqcup$ and $\bigsqcap$. Then, we get a complete lattice $(L, \sqsubseteq, \sqcup, \sqcap, \{\emptyset\}, \emptyset)$, where $\{\emptyset\}$ is the minimal element and $\emptyset$ the maximal one.

Upward Universality Checking Using Antichains. To check universality of a tree automaton, the standard approach is to make it complete, determinise it, complement it, and check for emptiness. As determinisation is expensive, we propose here an algorithm for checking universality without determinisation. The main idea is to try to find at least one term not accepted by the automaton. For this, we perform a kind of symbolic simulation of the automaton to cover all runs necessarily leading to non-accepting states.

In the following, $q, q_1, q_2, ...$ denote states of NTA, $s, s_1, s_2, ...$ denote sets of such states, and $S, S_1, S_2, ...$ denote antichains of sets of states. We assume dealing with complete automata and first give some definitions. For $f \in \Sigma_n$, $n \geq 0$, $Post_f^\delta(s_1, ..., s_n) = \{q \mid \exists q_i \in s_i, 1 \leq i \leq n : f(q_1, ..., q_n) \rightarrow_\delta q\}$. We omit δ if no confusion arises. Note that, for $a \in \Sigma_0$, $Post_a(\emptyset) = \{q \mid a \rightarrow_\delta q\}$ is the set of states that may be assigned to the leaf a, and $Post_f(\emptyset) = \emptyset$ for $f \in \Sigma_n$, $n \geq 1$. Let $Post(S) = \lfloor \{Post_f(s_1, ..., s_n) \mid n \geq 0, s_1, ..., s_n \in S, f \in \Sigma_n\} \rfloor$. Clearly, $Post$ is monotonic wrt. $\sqsubseteq$.

Let $Post_0(S) = S$ and for all $i > 0$, $Post_i(S) = Post(Post_{i-1}(S)) \sqcap S$. Intuitively, $Post_i(S)$ contains the $\sqsubseteq$-smallest sets $s \subseteq Q$ of states into which the automaton can nondeterministically get after processing a term of height up to i starting from the states in the elements of S. Using only the minimal sets is enough as we just need to know if there is a term on which the given automaton runs exclusively into non-final states. This makes universality checking easier than determinisation using the general subset construction.

Clearly, $Post_1(S) = Post(Post_0(S)) \sqcap S \sqsubseteq S = Post_0(S)$. Moreover, for $i > 0$, if $Post_i(S) \sqsubseteq Post_{i-1}(S)$, then due to the monotonicity of $Post$, $Post(Post_i(S)) \sqsubseteq Post(Post_{i-1}(S))$, $Post(Post_i(S)) \sqcap S \sqsubseteq Post(Post_{i-1}(S)) \sqcap S$, and therefore $Post_{i+1}(S) \sqsubseteq Post_i(S)$. Altogether, we get (1) $\forall S \in L \; \forall i \geq 0 : Post_{i+1}(S) \sqsubseteq$

$Post_i(S)$. Since we work on a finite lattice, this implies that for all S there exists j_S such that $Post_{j_S}(S) = Post_{j_S+1}(S)$. We let $Post^*(S) = Post_{j_S}(S)$.

Lemma 1. *Let $\mathcal{A} = (Q, \Sigma, F, \delta)$ be a tree automaton and t a term over Σ. Let $s = \{q \mid t \xrightarrow{*}_\delta q\}$, then $Post^*(\emptyset) \sqsubseteq \{s\}$.*

Proof. We proceed by structural induction on t. For the *basic case*, let $t = a \in \Sigma_0$. Then, $s = \{q \mid a \rightarrow_\delta q\} = Post_a(\emptyset)$, and thus there is $s' \in Post(\emptyset)$ s.t. $s' \subseteq s$ since $Post$ is obtained by taking the minimal elements. Furthermore, because of (1), there is also $s'' \subseteq s'$ such that $s'' \in Post^*(\emptyset)$. For the *induction step*, let $t = f(t_1, ..., t_n)$. Let $s_i = \{q \in Q \mid t_i \xrightarrow{*}_\delta q\}$ for $i \in \{1, ..., n\}$. Let $s = \{q \mid t \xrightarrow{*}_\delta q\}$. Then, $s = \{q \mid \exists q_1 \in s_1, ..., q_n \in s_n : f(q_1, ..., q_n) \rightarrow_\delta q\}$. By induction, there exists $s'_i \subseteq s_i$ s.t. $s'_i \in Post^*(\emptyset)$. Let $s' = Post_f(s'_1, ..., s'_n)$. Then, by definition of $Post_f$, we have $s' \subseteq s$, and by definition of $Post^*$, there exists $s'' \subseteq s'$ with $s'' \in Post^*(\emptyset)$. $\square$

Lemma 2. *Let $\mathcal{A} = (Q, \Sigma, F, \delta)$ be an automaton and let $s \in Post^*(\emptyset)$. Then there exists a term t over Σ such that $s = \{q \mid t \xrightarrow{*}_\delta q\}$.*

Proof. Let $i \geq 1$ be the smallest index s.t. $s \in Post_i(\emptyset)$. We proceed by induction on i. For the *basic case*, $i = 1$. Then, there is $a \in \Sigma_0$ s.t. $s = Post_a(\emptyset) = \{q \mid a \xrightarrow{*}_\delta q\}$, $t = a$. For the *induction step*, let $i > 1$. There exists $f \in \Sigma_n$ and $s_1, ..., s_n \in Post_{i-1}(\emptyset)$ with $s = Post_f(s_1, ..., s_n)$. By induction, there exists $t_1, ..., t_n$ s.t. for $j \in \{1, ..., n\}$, $s_j = \{q \mid t_j \xrightarrow{*}_\delta q\}$. Let $t = f(t_1, ...t_n)$. By definition of $Post_f$, $s = \{q \mid t \xrightarrow{*}_\delta q\}$. $\square$

We can now give a theorem allowing to decide universality *without determinisation*.

Theorem 1. *A tree automaton $\mathcal{A}=(Q, \Sigma, F, \delta)$ is not universal iff $\exists s \in Post^*(\emptyset).s \subseteq \overline{F}$.*

Proof. Let $\mathcal{A}$ be not universal. Let t be a term not accepted by $\mathcal{A}$ and $s = \{q \mid t \xrightarrow{*}_\delta q\}$. As t is not accepted by the automaton, $s \subseteq \overline{F}$. By Lemma 1, there is $s' \in Post^*(\emptyset)$ s.t. $s' \subseteq s \subseteq \overline{F}$. Suppose now that there exists $s \in Post^*(\emptyset)$ s.t. $s \subseteq \overline{F}$. By Lemma 2, there exists a term t with $s = \{q \mid t \xrightarrow{*}_\delta q\}$. Since $s \subseteq \overline{F}$, t is not accepted by $\mathcal{A}$. $\square$

Experiments with Upward Universality Checking Using Antichains. We have implemented the above approach for testing universality of tree automata in a prototype based on the Timbuk tree automata library [9]. We give the results of our experiments run on an Intel Xeon processor at with 2.7GHz and 16GB of memory in Fig. 1. We ran our tests on randomly generated automata and on automata obtained from abstract regular tree model checking applied in verification of several pointer-manipulating programs.

In the random tests, we first used automata with 20 states and varied the *density of their transitions* (the average number of different right-hand side states for a given left-hand side of a transition rule, i.e., $|\delta|/|\{f(q_1, ..., q_n) \mid \exists q \in Q : f(q_1, ..., q_n) \rightarrow_\delta q\}|$) and the *density of their final states* (i.e., $|F|/|Q|$). Fig. 1(a) shows the probability of such automata being universal, and Fig. 1(b) the average times needed for checking their universality using our antichain-based approach. The difficult instances are naturally those where the probability of being universal is about one half. In Fig. 1(c), we show how the running times change for some selected instances of the problem (in terms of some

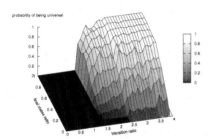
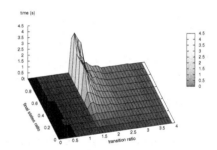

(a) Probability that a tree automaton (TA) with 20 states and some density of transitions and final states is universal

(b) Average times of antichain-based universality checking on TA with 20 states and some density of transitions and final states

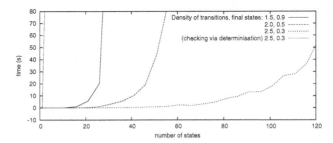

(c) Universality checking via determinisation and antichains on TA with selected densities of transitions and final states

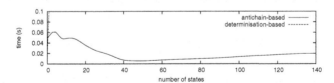

(d) Determinisation-based and antichain-based universality checking on TA from abstract regular tree model checking

Fig. 1. Experiments with universality checking on tree automata

chosen densities of transitions and final states, including those for which the problem is the most difficult) when the number of states of the automata grows. We also show the time needed when universality is checked using determinisation, complement, and emptiness checking. We see that the antichain-based approach behaves in a significantly better way. The same conclusion can also be drawn from the results of Fig. 1(d) obtained on automata from experimenting with abstract regular tree model checking applied for verifying various procedures manipulating trees presented in Section 5.

Downward Universality Checking with Antichains. The *upward universality checking* introduced above for tree automata conceptually corresponds to the *forward* universality checking of finite word automata of [12]. In [12], a dual *backward* universality checking is also introduced. It is based on computing the *controllable predecessors* of the set of non-final states. Controllable predecessors are the predecessors that can be forced by an input symbol to continue into a given set of states. Then, the automaton is non-universal iff the controllable predecessors of the non-final states cover the set of initial states.

Downward universality checking for tree automata as a dual approach to upward universality checking is problematic since the controllable predecessors of a set of states $s \subseteq Q$ of an NTA $\mathcal{A} = (Q, \Sigma, F, \delta)$ do not form a set of states, but a set of *tuples* of states, i.e., $CPre(s) = \{(q_1, ..., q_n) \mid n \in \mathbb{N} \wedge \exists f \in \Sigma \, \forall q \in Q : f(q_1, ..., q_n) \to_\delta q \Rightarrow q \in s\}$. Note that if we flatten the set $CPre(s)$ to the set $FCPre(s)$ of states that appear in some of the tuples of $CPre(s)$ and check that starting from leaf rules the computation can be forced into some subset of $FCPre(s)$, then this does not imply that the computation can be forced into some state from s. That is because for any rule $f(q_1, ..., q_n) \to_\delta q$, $q \in s$, not all of the states q_1, ..., q_n may be reached. Moreover, it is too strong to require that starting from leaf rules, it must be possible to force the computation into all states of $FCPre_f(s)$. Clearly, it is enough if the computation starting from leaf rules can be forced into s via some of the vectors in $CPre(s)$, not necessarily all of them. Also, if we keep $CPre(s)$ for $s \subseteq Q$ as a set of vectors, we also have to define the notion of controllable predecessors for sets of vectors of states, which is a set of vectors of vectors of states, etc. Clearly, such an approach is not practical.

4   Inclusion Checking

Let $\mathcal{A} = (Q, \Sigma, F, \delta)$ and $\mathcal{B} = (Q', \Sigma, F', \delta')$ be two tree automata. We want to check if $\mathcal{L}(\mathcal{A}) \subseteq \mathcal{L}(\mathcal{B})$. The traditional approach computes the complement of $\mathcal{B}$ and checks if it has an empty intersection with $\mathcal{A}$. This is costly as computing the complement necessitates determinisation. Here we show how to check inclusion without determinisation.

As before, the idea is to find at least one term accepted by $\mathcal{A}$ and not by $\mathcal{B}$. For that, we simultaneously simulate the runs of the two automata using pairs (p, s) with $p \in Q$ and $s \subseteq Q'$ where p memorises the run of $\mathcal{A}$ and s all the possible runs of $\mathcal{B}$. If t is a term accepted by $\mathcal{A}$ and not by $\mathcal{B}$, the simultaneous run of the two automata on t reaches the root of t at a pair of the form (p, s) with $p \in F$ and $s \subseteq \overline{F'}$. Notice that s must represent *all* the possible runs of $\mathcal{B}$ on t to make sure that no run of $\mathcal{B}$ can accept the term t. Therefore, s must be a set of states.

Formally, an *antichain* over $Q \times 2^{Q'}$ is a set $\mathcal{S} \subseteq Q \times 2^{Q'}$ such that for every $(p, s), (p', s') \in \mathcal{S}$, if $p = p'$, then $s \not\subset s'$. We denote by L_I the set of all antichains over $Q \times 2^{Q'}$. Given a set $\mathcal{S} \in Q \times 2^{Q'}$, an element $(p, s) \in \mathcal{S}$ is *minimal* if for every $s' \subset s$, $(p, s') \notin \mathcal{S}$. We denote by $\lfloor \mathcal{S} \rfloor$ the set of minimal elements of $\mathcal{S}$. Given two antichains $\mathcal{S}$ and $\mathcal{S}'$, we define the order $\sqsubseteq_I$, the least upper bound $\sqcup_I$, and the greatest lower bound $\sqcap_I$ as follows: $\mathcal{S} \sqsubseteq_I \mathcal{S}'$ iff for every $(p, s') \in \mathcal{S}'$, there is $(p, s) \in \mathcal{S}$ s.t. $s \subseteq s'$; $\mathcal{S} \sqcup_I \mathcal{S}' = \lfloor \{(p, s \cup s') \mid (p, s) \in \mathcal{S} \wedge (p, s') \in \mathcal{S}'\} \rfloor$; and $\mathcal{S} \sqcap_I \mathcal{S}' = \lfloor \{(p, s) \mid (p, s) \in \mathcal{S} \vee (p, s) \in \mathcal{S}'\} \rfloor$. These definitions can be extended to arbitrary sets in the usual way leading to the operators $\bigsqcup_I$ and $\bigsqcap_I$, yielding a complete lattice as in Section 3.

Given $f \in \Sigma_n, n \geq 0$, we define $IPost_f((p_1, s_1), ..., (p_n, s_n)) = \{(p, s) \mid f(p_1, ..., p_n) \to_\delta p \wedge s = Post_f^{\delta'}(s_1, ..., s_n)\}$. Let $\mathcal{S}$ be an antichain over $Q \times 2^{Q'}$. Then, let $IPost(\mathcal{S}) = \lfloor \{IPost_f((p_1, s_1), ..., (p_n, s_n)) \mid n \geq 0, (p_1, s_1), ..., (p_n, s_n) \in$

$S, f \in \Sigma_n\}]$. Let $IPost_0(S) = S$ and $IPost_i(S) = IPost(IPost_{i-1}(S)) \sqcap_I S$. As before, we can show that $\forall S \in L_I \ \forall i \geq 0 : IPost_{i+1}(S) \sqsubseteq_I IPost_i(S)$, and that for every antichain S, there exists a J such that $IPost_{J+1}(S) = IPost_J(S)$. Let $IPost^*(S) = IPost_J(S)$. Note that, like in the case of $Post_a(\emptyset)$ in Section 3, $IPost_a(\emptyset) = \{(q, Post_a^{\delta'}(\emptyset)) \mid a \to_\delta q\}$ for $a \in \Sigma_0$, and $IPost_f(\emptyset) = \emptyset$ for $f \in \Sigma_n$, $n \geq 1$. Then, we get the following lemma. The proof is similar to the one of Lemma 1.

Lemma 3. *Let $\mathcal{A} = (Q, \Sigma, F, \delta)$ and $\mathcal{B} = (Q', \Sigma, F', \delta')$ be two tree automata, and let t be a term over Σ. Let $p \in Q$ such that $t \xrightarrow{*}_\delta p$, and $s = \{q \in Q' \mid t \xrightarrow{*}_{\delta'} q\}$. Then, $IPost^*(\emptyset) \sqsubseteq_I \{(p, s)\}$.*

We can also show the following lemma. Its proof is similar to the one of Lemma 2.

Lemma 4. *Let $\mathcal{A} = (Q, \Sigma, F, \delta)$ and $\mathcal{B} = (Q', \Sigma, F', \delta')$ be two tree automata, and let $(p, s) \in IPost^*(\emptyset)$. Then there is a term t over Σ s.t. $t \xrightarrow{*}_\delta p$ and $s = \{q \mid t \xrightarrow{*}_{\delta'} q\}$.*

Then, we can decide inclusion *without determinising the automata* as follows:

Theorem 2. *Let $\mathcal{A} = (Q, \Sigma, F, \delta)$ and $\mathcal{B} = (Q', \Sigma, F', \delta')$ be two tree automata. Then, $\mathcal{L}(\mathcal{A}) \subseteq \mathcal{L}(\mathcal{B})$ iff for every $(p, s) \in IPost^*(\emptyset)$, $p \in F \Rightarrow s \not\subseteq \overline{F'}$.*

Proof. Suppose that $(p, s) \in IPost^*(\emptyset)$ with $p \in F$ and $s \subseteq \overline{F'}$. Using Lemma 4 there is a term t with $t \xrightarrow{*}_\delta p$ and $s = \{q \mid t \xrightarrow{*}_{\delta'} q\}$. As $p \in F$ and $s \subseteq \overline{F'}$, t is accepted by $\mathcal{A}$ and not by $\mathcal{B}$, i.e., $\mathcal{L}(\mathcal{A}) \not\subseteq \mathcal{L}(\mathcal{B})$. Suppose now $\mathcal{L}(\mathcal{A}) \not\subseteq \mathcal{L}(\mathcal{B})$. Let t be a term accepted by $\mathcal{A}$ and not by $\mathcal{B}$. Let $p \in F$ such that $t \xrightarrow{*}_\delta p$, and let $s = \{q \mid t \xrightarrow{*}_{\delta'} q\}$. Then, $s \subseteq \overline{F'}$. Lemma 3 implies that $IPost^*(\emptyset)$ contains a pair (p, s') s.t. $s' \subseteq s \subseteq \overline{F'}$. $\square$

Experiments with Checking Inclusion Via Antichains. We have implemented the proposed antichain-based approach for inclusion checking on tree automata again on top of the Timbuk library and performed similar tests as with universality checking in Section 3 (see [3] for details). The results show that the antichain-based approach is again significantly faster than the usual approach of checking $\mathcal{L}(\mathcal{A}_1) \subseteq \mathcal{L}(\mathcal{A}_2)$ as $\mathcal{L}(\mathcal{A}_1) \cap \overline{\mathcal{L}(\mathcal{A}_2)} = \emptyset$, requiring determinisation of $\mathcal{A}_2$. This holds both for randomly generated automata and for those encountered in the experiments with abstract regular tree model checking (ARTMC) described below. In fact, the antichain-based inclusion checking allowed us to implement an ARTMC framework entirely based on NTA which is significantly more efficient than the framework based on deterministic automata.

5   Regular Tree Model Checking

Regular tree model checking (RTMC) [11,6,2,4] is a general and uniform framework for verifying infinite-state systems. In RTMC, configurations of a system being verified are encoded by trees, sets of the configurations by tree automata, and transitions of the verified system by a term rewriting system (usually given as a tree transducer or a set of tree transducers). Then, verification problems based on performing reachability analysis correspond to computing closures of regular languages under rewriting systems, i.e., given a rewriting system τ and a regular tree language I, one needs to compute $\tau^*(I)$, where τ^* is the reflexive-transitive closure of τ. This computation is impossible in general. Therefore, the main issue in RTMC is to find accurate and powerful fixpoint acceleration techniques helping the convergence of computing language closures.

Abstract regular tree model checking (ARTMC) [4] is an efficient acceleration technique for RTMC. It is based on interleaving the application of τ when computing $\tau^*(I)$ via the union $\bigcup_{i \geq 0} \tau^i(I)$ with an application of an abstraction function α on the tree automata encoding the so-far computed sets of reachable configurations. If α is *finitary* (i.e., its domain is finite), the abstract reachability computation reaches a fixpoint in a finite number of steps. Moreover, if α is *overapproximating* (i.e., if $\mathcal{L}(\mathcal{A}) \subseteq L(\alpha(\mathcal{A}))$ for each tree automaton $\mathcal{A}$), the computation stops with an automaton $\mathcal{A}$ such that $\tau^*(I) \subseteq \mathcal{L}(\mathcal{A})$. If $\mathcal{A}$ does not intersect the bad configurations, the system is proved safe. Otherwise, a (concrete) backward reachability computation based on τ^{-1} checks if the system is really erroneous, or if a spurious error was reached due to a too coarse abstraction. In the latter case, the abstraction is refined and the computation repeats.

In [4], two automata abstractions based on *automata state equivalences* are given. The *finite height* equivalence relates states accepting equal languages of trees up to some finite height, and the *predicate* equivalence relates states whose languages have non-empty intersections with the same "predicate" tree languages out of a given set of such languages. When abstracting an automaton, its states are split into equivalence classes, and all states of each class are collapsed into one. Hence, both of the mentioned abstractions are overapproximating. They are automatically refined by refining the state equivalence classes (for details see [4]).

Nondeterministic Abstract Regular Tree Model Checking. Originally, ARTMC was defined for and tested on minimal deterministic tree automata (DTA). However, the various experiments done showed that the determinisation step is a significant bottleneck. To avoid it and to implement ARTMC using NTA, we need the following operations over NTA: (1) application of the transition relation τ, (2) union, (3) abstraction and its refinement, (4) intersection with the set of bad configurations, (5) emptiness, and (6) inclusion checking (needed for testing if the abstract reachability computation has reached a fixpoint). Finally, (7) a method to reduce the size of the computed NTA is also desirable. An implementation of Points (1), (2), (4), and (5) is easy. Moreover, concerning Point (3), the abstraction mechanisms of [4] can be lifted to work on NTA in a straightforward way while preserving their guarantees to be finitary, overapproximating, and the ability to exclude spurious counterexamples. Furthermore, the recent work [1] gives efficient algorithms for reducing NTA based on computing suitable simulation equivalences on their states, which covers Point (7). Hence, the last obstacle for implementing nondeterministic ARTMC was Point (6), i.e., efficient inclusion checking on NTA. The approach of Section 4 solves this problem, allowing us to implement a prototype nondeterministic ARTMC framework and test it on suitable examples. We now give the first very encouraging results that we achieved.

Experiments with Nondeterministic ARTMC. We have implemented the nondeterministic ARTMC framework using the Timbuk tree library [9] and compared it with an ARTMC implementation based on the same library, but using DTA. In particular, the

Table 1. Running times (in sec.) of det. and nondet. ARTMC applied for verification of various tree manipulating programs ($\times$ denotes a too long run or a failure due to a lack of memory).

	DFT		RB-delete (null,undef)		RB-insert (null,undef)	
	det.	nondet.	det.	nondet.	det.	nondet.
full abstr.	5.2	2.7	$\times$	$\times$	33	15
restricted abstr.	40	3.5	$\times$	60	145	5.4

	RB-delete (RB preservation)		RB-insert (RB preservation)		RB-insert (gen., test.)	
	det.	nondet.	det.	nondet.	det.	nondet.
full abstr.	$\times$	$\times$	$\times$	$\times$	$\times$	$\times$
restricted abstr.	$\times$	57	$\times$	89	$\times$	978

deterministic ARTMC framework uses determinisation and minimisation after computing the effect of each forward or backward step to try to keep the automata as small as possible and to allow for easy fixpoint checking, which is not based on inclusion but identity checking on the obtained automata (due to the fact that the computed sets are only growing and minimal DTA are canonical). For NTA, the size reduction from [1], which we use, does not yield canonical automata, and antichain-based inclusion checking is really needed.

We have applied the framework to verify several procedures manipulating dynamic tree-shaped data structures linked by pointers. The trees being manipulated are encoded directly as the trees handled in ARTMC, each node is labelled by the data stored in it and the pointer variables currently pointing to it. All program statements are encoded as (possibly non-structure preserving) tree transducers. The encoding is fully automated. The only allowed destructive pointer updates (i.e., pointer manipulating statements changing the shape of the tree) are tree rotations [7] and addition of new leaf nodes.

We have in particular considered verification of the depth-first tree traversal and the standard procedures for rebalancing red-black trees after insertion or deletion of a leaf node [7]. We verified that the programs do not manipulate undefined and null pointers in a faulty way. For the procedures on red-black trees, we also verified that their result is a red-black tree (not taking into account the non-regular balancedness condition). In general, the set of possible input trees for the verified procedures as well as the set of correct output trees were given as tree automata. In the case of rebalancing red-black trees after insertion, we also used a generator program preceding the tested procedure which generates random red-black trees and a tester program which tests the output trees being correct. Here, the set of input trees contained just an empty tree, and the verification was reduced to checking that a predefined error location is unreachable. The size of the programs ranges from 10 to about 100 lines of pure pointer manipulations.

The results of our experiments on an Intel Xeon processor at 2.7GHz with 16GB of available memory (as in Section 3) are summarised in Table 1. The predicate abstraction proved to give much better results (hence we do not consider the finite-height abstraction here). The abstraction was either applied after firing each statement of the program ("full abstr.") or just when reaching a loop point in the program ("restricted abstr."). Our results are very encouraging and show a significant improvement in the efficiency of ARTMC based on NTA. Indeed, the ARTMC framework based on DTA has either been significantly slower (up to 25-times) or has completely failed (a too long running time or a lack of memory)—the latter case being quite frequent.

6 Conclusion

We have proposed new antichain-based algorithms for universality and inclusion checking on (nondeterministic) tree automata. The algorithms have been thoroughly tested both on randomly generated automata and on automata obtained from various verification runs of the ARTMC framework. The new algorithms are significantly more efficient than the classical determinisation-based approaches to universality and inclusion checking. Moreover, using the proposed inclusion checking algorithm together with some other recently published results, we have implemented a complete ARTMC framework based on NTA and tested it on verification of several real-life pointer-intensive procedures. The results show a very encouraging improvement in the capabilities of the framework. In the future, we would like to implement the antichain-based universality and inclusion checking algorithms (as well as other recently proposed algorithms for dealing with NTA, such as the simulation-based reduction algorithms) on automata symbolically encoded as in the MONA tree automata library [10]. We hope that this will yield another significant improvement in the tree automata technology allowing for a new generation of tools using tree automata (including, e.g., the ARTMC framework).

References

1. Abdulla, P.A., Bouajjani, A., Holík, L., Kaati, L., Vojnar, T.: Computing Simulations over Tree Automata: Efficient Techniques for Reducing TA. In: TACAS 2008. LNCS, vol. 4963. Springer, Heidelberg (2008)
2. Abdulla, P.A., Legay, A., d'Orso, J., Rezine, A.: Simulation-Based Iteration of Tree Transducers. In: Halbwachs, N., Zuck, L.D. (eds.) TACAS 2005. LNCS, vol. 3440, pp. 30–44. Springer, Heidelberg (2005)
3. Bouajjani, A., Habermehl, P., Holík, L., Touili, T., Vojnar, T.: Antichain-based Universality and Inclusion Testing over Nondeterministic Finite Tree Automata. Technical Report FIT-TR-2008-1, FIT, Brno University of technology, Czech Republic (2008)
4. Bouajjani, A., Habermehl, P., Rogalewicz, A., Vojnar, T.: Abstract Regular Tree Model Checking. ENTCS 149, 37–48 (2006)
5. Bouajjani, A., Habermehl, P., Rogalewicz, A., Vojnar, T.: Abstract Regular Tree Model Checking of Complex Dynamic Data Structures. In: Yi, K. (ed.) SAS 2006. LNCS, vol. 4134, pp. 52–70. Springer, Heidelberg (2006)
6. Bouajjani, A., Touili, T.: Extrapolating Tree Transformations. In: Brinksma, E., Larsen, K.G. (eds.) CAV 2002. LNCS, vol. 2404. Springer, Heidelberg (2002)
7. Cormen, T.H., Leiserson, C.E., Rivest, R.L.: Introduction to Algorithms. MIT Press, Cambridge (1990)
8. Doyen, L., Raskin, J.-F.: Improved Algorithms for the Automata-based Approach to Model Checking. In: Grumberg, O., Huth, M. (eds.) TACAS 2007. LNCS, vol. 4424, pp. 451–465. Springer, Heidelberg (2007)
9. Genet, T.: Timbuk: A Tree Automata Library,
http://www.irisa.fr/lande/genet/timbuk

10. Klarlund, N., Møller, A.: MONA Version 1.4 User Manual, BRICS, Department of Computer Science, University of Aarhus, Denmark (2001)
11. Shahar, E.: Tools and Techniques for Verifying Parameterized Systems. PhD thesis, Faculty of Mathematics and Computer Science, The Weizmann Inst. of Science, Rehovot, Israel (2001)
12. De Wulf, M., Doyen, L., Henzinger, T.A., Raskin, J.-F.: Antichains: A New Algorithm for Checking Universality of Finite Automata. In: Ball, T., Jones, R.B. (eds.) CAV 2006. LNCS, vol. 4144, pp. 17–30. Springer, Heidelberg (2006)

Testing Whether a Binary and Prolongeable Regular Language L Is Geometrical or Not on the Minimal Deterministic Automaton of *Pref*(L)

J.-M. Champarnaud, J.-Ph. Dubernard, and H. Jeanne

LITIS, University of Rouen, France
{jean-marc.champarnaud,jean-philippe.dubernard}@univ-rouen.fr,
hadrien.jeanne@etu.univ-rouen.fr

Abstract. Our aim is to present an efficient algorithm that checks whether a binary and prolongeable regular languge is geometrical or not, based on specific properties of its minimal deterministic automaton. Geometrical languages have been introduced in the framework of off-line temporal validation of real-time softwares. Actually, validation can be achieved through both a model based on regular languages and a model based on discrete geometry. Geometrical languages are intended to develop a link between these two models. The regular case is of practical interest regarding to implementation features, which motivates the design of an efficient geometricity test addressing the family of regular languages.

Keywords: Finite automata, regular languages, minimal automaton, geometrical language, geometricity test, temporal validation.

1 Introduction

Geometrical languages have been first introduced in [1,2]. The main motivation was the modelization of real-time task systems in the framework of off-line temporal validation. Computing the feasibility of a real-time software [9,3] consists in checking whether there exists a scheduling sequence that leads all tasks to reach their deadlines. This can be achieved through a model based on regular languages [5]. Thanks to specific properties of the languages involved in temporal validation, a model based on discrete geometry [7,8] can also be designed, which drastically reduces the computing time. Geometrical languages are intended to develop a link between these two models. The challenge is the following: if we are able to interpret in terms of languages those properties that make the geometrical objects be so efficient, then we can expect to design new automata-based algorithms with improved complexities.

We start from a natural definition for a geometrical figure in a d-dimension space associated with an alphabet $\Sigma = \{a_1, \ldots, a_d\}$: a geometrical figure is a set of points of $\mathbb{N}^d$ including the origin of the reference and such that, for any point in the figure, there exists a trajectory (from the origin) to this point. A geometrical figure can be seen as a (non necessarily finite) automaton: each point of the figure is a state, the origin of the reference is the initial state, every state is final and there is an implicit transition with label a_i from $P = (x_j)_{1 \leq j \leq d}$ to $P' = (x'_j)_{1 \leq j \leq d}$ as soon as $\forall j \neq i$, $x'_j = x_j$ and

O.H. Ibarra and B. Ravikumar (Eds.): CIAA 2008, LNCS 5148, pp. 68–77, 2008.

$x_i' = x_i + 1$. Hence we can define the language of a geometrical figure and also the geometrical figure of a language. Finally, a language is said to be geometrical if and only if the language of its prefixes is equal to the language of its geometrical figure. Studying the properties of the (non necessarily regular) geometrical languages turn to be of both theoretical and practical interest as reported in [1,2].

In this paper, we focus on the family of geometrical regular languages. A method checking whether a given regular language L is geometrical or not is described in [2]. Unfortunately, it was shown that it only works for a restricted family of regular languages. Moreover it involves numerous conversions of an automaton into an equivalent expression and thus it has an exponential worst case time complexity. In this paper we present an original approach, directly based on the minimal automaton of the language $Pref(L)$, which yields a polynomial complexity.

The two following sections recall fundamental notions concerning languages, automata and geometrical languages. In Section 4, geometrical properties are stated in terms of automata. The last two sections are devoted to the two-dimension case. A polynomial algorithm for checking the geometricty of a prolongeable regular language is presented in Section 5 and the general case is sketched in Section 6.

2   Preliminaries

Let us first review basic notions concerning finite automata. For a comprehensive treatment of this domain, references [4,13] can be consulted.

Let Σ be a non-empty finite set of symbols, called the *alphabet*. A *word* over Σ is a finite sequence of symbols, usually written $x_1 x_2 ... x_n$. The length of a word u, denoted by $|u|$, is the number of symbols in u. The empty word, denoted by ε, has a length equal to zero. We also denote by $|u|_a$ the number of occurrences of the symbol a in the word u. If $u = x_1 ... x_n$ and $v = y_1 ... y_m$ are two words over the alphabet Σ, their concatenation $u \cdot v$, usually written uv, is the word $x_1 ... x_n y_1 ... y_m$. Let Σ^* be the set of words over Σ. We say that u in Σ^* is a prefix of w in Σ^* ($u \in Pref(w)$) if there exists v in Σ^* such that $uv = w$. A *language* L over Σ is a subset of Σ^*. We denote by $Pref(L)$ the set of prefixes of the words of the language L. We denote by $w^{-1}L$ and we call left residual of L w.r.t. w the set $\{u \in \Sigma^* \mid wu \in L\}$. The set of regular languages is the set containing the empty set and the single element sets of the symbols, and that is closed under finite concatenation, finite union and star. Any regular language can be denoted by a regular expression formed by the atoms $\emptyset$, $a \in \Sigma$, and the operations of finite concatenation ($\cdot$), finite union ($+$) and star ($*$).

An *automaton* is a 5-tuple $\mathcal{A} = (Q, \Sigma, \delta, I, T)$ where Q is the set of states, δ is a subset of $Q \times \Sigma \times Q$ whose elements are called transitions and where I and T are subsets of Q, whose elements are respectively called initial states and final states. An automaton $\mathcal{A}$ is said to be finite if Q is finite. It is said to be complete if for any $q \in Q$ and any $a \in \Sigma$, $|\delta(q, a)| \geq 1$. An automaton can be made complete if necessary by adding a sink state. An automaton $\mathcal{A}$ is said to be deterministic if it has a unique initial state and if for any $q \in Q$ and any $a \in \Sigma$, $|\delta(q, a)| \leq 1$. If the automaton is deterministic, the notation $p.a$ can be used instead of $\delta(p, a)$. A path of length n in $\mathcal{A}$ is a sequence of n transitions: $(q_0, a_1, q_1), (q_1, a_2, q_2), ..., (q_{n-1}, a_n, q_n)$. The word $a_1 a_2 ... a_n$

is called the label of this path. A path is said to be successful if $q_0 \in I$ and $q_n \in T$. The language recognized by $\mathcal{A}$ is the set $L(\mathcal{A})$ of words that are labels of successful paths. Kleene's theorem [6] states that a language is recognized by a finite automaton if and only if it is regular. We will say DFA for a deterministic finite automaton and NFA for a non-deterministic finite automaton.

The left language of a state q is the set of words w such that there exists a path in $\mathcal{A}$ whose first state is initial, whose last state is q, and whose label is w. The right language of a state q is the set of words w such that there exists a path in $\mathcal{A}$ whose first state is q, whose last state is final, and whose label is w. We denote by $\overleftarrow{L}_q^{\mathcal{A}}$ the left language of q in $\mathcal{A}$, and by $\overrightarrow{L}_q^{\mathcal{A}}$ its right language. A DFA $\mathcal{A}$ is said to be minimal if and only if any two distinct states of $\mathcal{A}$ have distinct right languages. The theorem of Myhill-Nerode [10,11] states that any regular language has a unique minimal DFA up to an isomorphism.

Let us recall the notion of *prefix tree* of a DFA. Let Σ be an alphabet of size d. In order to define the d-ary prefix tree of a DFA, we assume that Σ and Σ^* are equipped with a total order. From now on we will consider that Σ^* is equipped with the graded lexicographic order (denoted by $\prec$), that corresponds to a breadth-first construction of the prefix tree and fits with our purpose. Let $\mathcal{A} = (Q, \Sigma, \delta, p_0, T)$ be a DFA. We consider the mapping $\varphi : Q \to \Sigma^*$ such that $\varphi(q) = min_\prec \{u \in \Sigma^* \mid p_0.u = q\}$, *i.e.* $\varphi(q)$ is the smallest label of a path from p_0 to q. The set $\varphi(Q)$ is a prefix set of Σ^*. The labeled tree $T_{\mathcal{A}} = (V, U, \Sigma)$ with $V = \varphi(Q)$ and $U = \{(\varphi(p), a, \varphi(q)) \mid (p, a, q) \in \delta\}$ is called the *prefix tree* of $\mathcal{A}$. The mapping φ is a one-to-one mapping from Q to the set V of vertices of $T_{\mathcal{A}}$; it is called the canonical labeling of the automaton $\mathcal{A}$.

3   Geometrical Languages

Let us now review basic definitions and properties of geometrical languages, as introduced in [1,2]. Let d be a positive integer. Let $1 \leqslant k \leqslant d$. We denote by $\boldsymbol{u}_k$ the coordinate vector $(0, 0, ..., 1, ...0)$ of dimension d, where 1 is in the k-th position. We denote by $\mathcal{O}$ the point with coordinate $(0, 0, ..., 0)$. In what follows, we will write P instead of $\overrightarrow{\mathcal{O}P}$, for instance $P = (3, 2)$. Let F be a set of points with coordinates in $\mathbb{N}^d$. A *trajectory* t of length n in F is a sequence $(P_i)_{0 \leqslant i \leqslant n}$ of points of F, such that $P_0 = \mathcal{O}$ and for all $i, 0 \leqslant i \leqslant n - 1$, there exists $k, 1 \leqslant k \leqslant d$ such that $P_{i+1} = P_i + \boldsymbol{u}_k$. The *set of trajectories* of F is denoted by $Traj(F)$.

Definition 1. *A geometrical figure F of dimension d is either the empty set or a set of points in $\mathbb{N}^d$ where every point belongs to some trajectory of F.*

For instance, $F_1 = \{(0, 0), (0, 1), (1, 0), (1, 1)\}$ is a 2-dimension geometrical figure (Figure 1).

Let $\Sigma = \{a_1, a_2, ..., a_d\}$ be a finite alphabet where the symbol a_i corresponds to the dimension i. Then, the word $w = w_1 w_2 \cdots w_n$ associated with a trajectory $t = (P_i)_{0 \leqslant i \leqslant n}$ of a figure F is defined by: $\forall i, 0 \leqslant i \leqslant n - 1, w_{i+1} = a_k$, where $P_{i+1} = P_i + \boldsymbol{u}_k$. The word associated with a trajectory t is denoted by $word(t)$. Reciprocally the (set of points in the) trajectory associated with a word w is denoted by $traj(w)$.

Fig. 1. $F_1 = \{(0,0),(0,1),(1,0),(1,1)\}$

We denote by $c : \Sigma^* \longrightarrow \mathbb{N}^d$ the Parikh mapping [12] that maps a word w to its coordinate vector $(|w|_{a_1}, |w|_{a_2}, ..., |w|_{a_d})$. The geometrical figure $\mathcal{F}(L)$ associated with a language $L \subseteq \Sigma^*$ is defined by $\mathcal{F}(L) = \bigcup_{w \in Pref(L)} traj(w)$. Reciprocally, the language $\mathcal{L}(F)$ associated with a geometrical figure $F \subseteq \mathbb{N}^d$ is defined by $\mathcal{L}(F) = \{word(t) \mid t \in Traj(F)\}$. Finally, a language is said to be *geometrical* if the set of its prefixes is equal to the set of words having a trajectory in the associated figure.

Definition 2. *The language L is said to be geometrical if and only if $Pref(L) = \mathcal{L}(\mathcal{F}(L))$.*

For every language L, $Pref(L) \subseteq \mathcal{L}(\mathcal{F}(L))$. But some languages are such that $\mathcal{L}(\mathcal{F}(L)) \not\subseteq Pref(L)$. It is the case of $\{a, ba\}$ that is not geometrical, whereas $\{ab, ba\}$ is geometrical. Notice that these two languages have the same geometrical figure, the figure F_1 of Figure 1.

Definition 3. *A language L is semi-geometrical if and only if $\forall u, v \in Pref(L)$ such that $c(u) = c(v)$, we have $u^{-1}Pref(L) = v^{-1}Pref(L)$.*

Proposition 1. *[2] If a language is geometrical then it is semi-geometrical.*

Proposition 2. *[2] Let $\Sigma = \{a_1, a_2, ..., a_d\}$ and $L \subseteq \Sigma^*$. The two following conditions are equivalent:*

(1) *L is geometrical.*
(2) $\forall u, v \in Pref(L), \underbrace{\exists k, 1 \leq k \leq d, c(u) + \boldsymbol{u}_k = c(v)}_{(*)} \Rightarrow u \cdot a_k \in Pref(L)$

Let us take the example of the language $L = \{a, ba, bb\}$ over the alphabet $\Sigma = \{a, b\}$. Then the words $u = a$ and $v = ba$ are such that $c(u) + (0, 1) = c(v)$ (condition $(*)$). Proposition 2 tells that, if L was geometrical, then ab would be in $Pref(L)$. We conclude that L is not geometrical.

4   Characterization of Geometrical Regular Languages in Terms of Automata (Arbitrary Dimension)

Geometrical properties (Definition 2, Definition 3 and Proposition 2) are defined in terms of languages. We now state them in terms of automata. In the following, L is a regular language and $F = \mathcal{F}(L)$ is the geometrical figure of L.

Definition 4. *Let $\mathcal{D} = (Q, \Sigma, \delta, p_0, T)$ be a DFA such that $L(\mathcal{D}) = Pref(L)$ and s be the sink state of $\mathcal{A}$ (if it exists). For all $P \in \mathbb{N}^2$, we set $States_Q(P) = \{p \in Q \mid \exists u \in \Sigma^*$ such that $p = p_0.u$ and $c(u) = P\}$ if P is in F and $States_Q(P) = \{s\}$ otherwise.*

Definition 5. *Let $P = (x_1, \ldots, x_d)$ be a point of $\mathbb{N}^d$. We set $Parents(P) = \{P - c(a_i) \mid a_i \in \Sigma\} \cap \mathbb{N}^d$. We also set $level(P) = x_1 + \ldots + x_d$.*

Definition 6. *Two points P and P' of a geometrical figure G are said to be adjacent if there exists a point P'' such that $\{P, P'\} \subset Parents(P'')$.*

Definition 7. *Let $\mathcal{D} = (Q, \Sigma, \delta, p_0, T)$ be a DFA such that $L(\mathcal{D}) = Pref(L)$ and φ be the canonical labeling of $\mathcal{D}$. The geometrical figure $F_Q = \{c(v) \mid v \in \varphi(Q)\}$ is the set of points associated with the states of Q.*

Proposition 3. *Let $\mathcal{D} = (Q, \Sigma, \delta, p_0, T)$ be a DFA such that $L(\mathcal{D}) = Pref(L)$. The three following conditions are equivalent:*

(1) The language L is semi-geometrical.
(2) $\forall P \in F, \forall u \in \Sigma^* \mid c(u) = P, u^{-1}Pref(L)$ is uniquely defined.
(3) $\forall P \in F, \forall p \in States_Q(P), \overrightarrow{L}_p^{\mathcal{D}}$ is uniquely defined.

Corollary 1. *Let $\mathcal{A} = (Q, \Sigma, \delta, p_0, T)$ be the minimal DFA of $Pref(L)$. The two following conditions are equivalent:*

(1) The language L is semi-geometrical.
(2) $\forall P \in F, |States_Q(P)| = 1$.

From now on we will consider the minimal automaton $\mathcal{A} = (Q, \Sigma, \delta, p_0, T)$ of $Pref(L)$. For all P in F, the unique element of $States_Q(P)$ will be denoted by $state(P)$.

Corollary 2. *Let $\mathcal{A} = (Q, \Sigma, \delta, p_0, T)$ be the minimal DFA of $Pref(L)$ and φ be the canonical labeling of $\mathcal{A}$. A necessary condition for the language L to be semi-geometrical is that the Parikh mapping be injective from $\varphi(Q)$ to F_Q.*

Proposition 4. *Let $\mathcal{A} = (Q, \Sigma, \delta, p_0, T)$ be the minimal DFA of $Pref(L)$. The three following conditions are equivalent:*

(1) The language L is geometrical.
(2) $\forall P \in \mathbb{N}^d, \forall a_i \in \Sigma \mid P - c(a_i) \in F$, we have:
– either $\forall u \mid c(u) = P - c(a_i), ua_i \in Pref(L)$,
– or $\forall u \mid c(u) = P - c(a_i), ua_i \notin Pref(L)$.
(3) $\forall P \in \mathbb{N}^d, \forall a_i \in \Sigma \mid P - c(a_i) \in F, state(P - c(a_i)).a_i = state(P)$.

5   Case of Prolongeable Regular Languages (Case $d = 2$)

The language L is not necessarily finite, neither is the figure $\mathcal{F}(L)$. Therefore a stepwise procedure straightforwardly deduced from Proposition 4 and based on a development of the figure level by level does not yield an algorithm for checking the geometricity of the language L.

The trick is that geometricity only depends on a simple property, based on classical geometrical arguments, that must be satisfied by each state of the minimal automaton $\mathcal{A} = (Q, \Sigma, \delta, p_0, T)$ of $Pref(L)$. This can be illustrated as follows (for $d = 2$). We assume that there exists a conflict involving the point P at level k in F and its two parents $P_2 = P - c(a)$ and $P_1 = P - c(b)$ that belong to F and are such that: $state(P_1).b \neq state(P_2).a$. Let us examine level $k - 2$. A particularly simple case is when there exists a point P' in F such that $P' \in Parents(P_1) \cap Parents(P_2)$. Let us set $p' = state(P')$. The conflict comes from the fact that $p'.ba \neq p'.ab$ and thus it only depends on the state p'. Let P'' be the point in F_Q whose associated state is p'. The conflict can be detected as soon as the figure is developed from P''.

This section is devoted to the study of this state property in a restricted frame. First, since geometrical arguments are used we will only investigate the two-dimension problem. Second we will focus on the case where the language L is prolongeable, that is $\forall u \in L, \exists a \in \Sigma \mid u.a \in L$. The general case will be sketched in the last section.

5.1 A Necessary and Sufficient Condition of Geometricity

Let L be a prolongeable language over $\Sigma = \{a, b\}$ and $F = \mathcal{F}(L)$ be the geometrical figure of L. We consider the minimal automaton $\mathcal{A} = (Q, \Sigma, \delta, p_0, T)$ of $Pref(L)$. Since L is prolongeable, then either $\mathcal{A}$ has no sink state or it holds: $\forall p \in Q, p.a \neq s \vee p.b \neq s$, where s is the sink state of $\mathcal{A}$. The automaton $\mathcal{A}$ is said to be essential. We first introduce some notation that fits with the case $d = 2$. For two points $P = (x, y)$ and $P' = (x', y')$ at the same level of a geometrical figure G we say that (P, P') is a pair of adjacent points (we write $P < P'$) if and only if $x' = x - 1$ and $y' = y + 1$.

Definition 8. *Let P and P' be two points of a geometrical figure G. We say that there is a conflict (P, P') if $P < P'$ and $state(P).b \neq state(P').a$.*

By Proposition 4, a regular language is geometrical if and only if there exists no conflict in its geometrical figure. In the following, given a word $u \in \Sigma^\omega$, we will denote by $\hat{u}_k$ the prefix of length k of u.

Definition 9. *Let $\mathcal{A} = (Q, \Sigma, \delta, p_0, T)$ be the minimal DFA of $Pref(L)$. Let $P \in F$ and $p = state(P)$.*

(1) We consider the word $u = u_1 \ldots u_k \ldots$ defined by $u_{k+1} = b$ if $p.(\hat{u}_k b) \neq s$ and $u_{k+1} = a$ otherwise. The trajectory $traj(u)$ is said to be the rightmost trajectory from the point P.
(2) We consider the word $v = v_1 \ldots v_k \ldots$ defined by $v_{k+1} = a$ if $p.(\hat{v}_k a) \neq s$ and $v_{k+1} = b$ otherwise. The trajectory $traj(v)$ is said to be the leftmost trajectory from the point P.

Since L is prolongeable, the trajectories $traj(u)$ and $traj(v)$ are well defined and have an infinite length. They can intersect or not and this feature will be studied later.

Definition 10. *Let $\mathcal{A} = (Q, \Sigma, \delta, p_0, T)$ be the minimal DFA of $Pref(L)$. Let $P \in F_Q$ and $p = state(P)$. Assume that the points $P + c(a)$ and $P + c(b)$ are in F. Let $traj(u)$ be the rightmost trajectory of $P + c(a)$ and $traj(v)$ be the leftmost trajectory of*

$P + c(b)$. *The hole of the state p is the region of $\mathbb{N}^2$ delimited by the trajectories traj(u) and traj(v).*

For any $p \in Q$, there exists no point of F in the hole of p. Let $h_p = min\{k \geq 0 \mid P + c(a\hat{u}_k) = P + c(b\hat{v}_k)\}$. We say that h_p is the depth of the hole of p. The depth of a hole is infinite if the trajectories *traj(u)* and *traj(v)* do not intersect. We now define the "hole property" for a state in Q.

Definition 11. *Let $\mathcal{A} = (Q, \Sigma, \delta, p_0, T)$ be the minimal DFA of Pref(L). Let $P \in F_Q$ and $p = state(P)$. The state p is said to satisfy the hole property if and only if either $(P + c(a) \notin F \lor P + c(b) \notin F)$ or for all $k \mid 0 \leq k < h_p$, the pair of points $(P + c(a\hat{u}_k), P + c(b\hat{v}_k))$ is not a conflict.*

Definition 12. *(1) The reverse rightmost trajectory from a point P is a finite sequence $(P_i)_{1 \leq i \leq m}$ such that: $P_1 = P$, $P_m = \mathcal{O}$, and for all $1 \leq i < m$, $P_{i+1} = P_i - c(a)$ if $P_i - c(a) \in F$ and $P_{i+1} = P_i - c(b)$ otherwise.*
(2) The reverse leftmost trajectory from a point P is a finite sequence $(P_i)_{1 \leq i \leq m}$ such that: $P_1 = P$ and $P_m = \mathcal{O}$ and for all $1 \leq i < m$, $P_{i+1} = P_i - c(b)$ if $P_i - c(b) \in F$ and $P_{i+1} = P_i - c(a)$ otherwise.

Lemma 1. *Assume that P is in F and that its two parents $P - c(a)$ and $P - c(b)$ are in F. Then the reverse rightmost trajectory of $P - c(b)$ and the reverse leftmost trajectory of $P - c(a)$ necessarily intersect.*

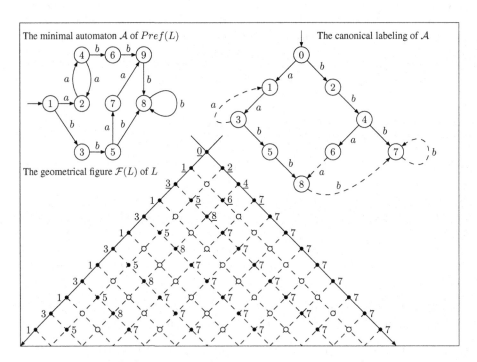

Fig. 2. Checking the hole condition for the states of $\mathcal{A}$

Notice that the rightmost and leftmost trajectories are defined from the transitions in the automaton, while the reverse versions are defined from the implicit transitions in the figure.

Proposition 5. *Let L be a prolongeable language and $\mathcal{A} = (Q, \Sigma, \delta, p_0, T)$ be the minimal DFA of Pref(L). The two following conditions are equivalent:*

(1) *The language L is geometrical.*
(2) *For all state in Q the hole property is satisfied.*

Let us comment the Figure 2. The geometrical figure F_Q (i.e. the set of points associated with the state labels $\underline{0}, \underline{1}, \ldots, \underline{8}$) can be drawn while computing the canonical labeling of the automaton $\mathcal{A}$. The hole of the state 0 is delimited by the rightmost trajectory from the point $(1, 0)$, that is the sequence $((1, 0), (2, 0), (2, 1), (2, 2), (2, 3))$, and by the leftmost trajectory from the point $(0, 1)$, that is $((0, 1), (0, 2), (1, 2), (2, 2), (3, 2))$, that intersect in $(2, 2)$.

Since $state(1, 0).b = state(0, 1).a = s$ and $state(2, 1).b = state(1, 2).a = 8$, the state 0 satisfies the hole property The states 3 and 4 also satisfy the hole property and their holes are infinite.

5.2   A Polynomial Algorithm for Checking Geometricity

We show that the hole property for a state can be checked in polynomial time.

Lemma 2. *Let $\mathcal{A} = (Q, \Sigma, \delta, p_0, T)$ be the minimal DFA of Pref(L). Let $n = |Q|$ and u be the word associated with the rightmost trajectory from $P + c(a)$. There exist two words u' and u'' such that $u = u'u''^{\omega}$, with $|u'| + |u''| < n$.*

Similarly the word v associated with the leftmost trajectory from $P + c(b)$ is such that there exist two words v' and v'' that satisfy $v = v'v''^{\omega}$, with $|v'| + |v''| < n$.

We consider the points $A_0 = P + c(a)$, $A_1 = P + c(au')$ and $A_2 = P + c(au'u'')$. As a corollary of Lemma 2, the rightmost trajectory from $P + c(a)$ is made of an initial piece from A_0 to A_1, followed by an infinite repetition of the piece going from A_1 to A_2. Let D be the line connecting A_1 to A_2. The slope of D is $\alpha = |u''|_b / |u''|_a$ if $|u''|_a \neq 0$ and ∞ otherwise. Similarly, we consider the points $B_0 = P + c(b)$, $B_1 = P + c(bv')$ and $B_2 = P + c(bv'v'')$. Let E be the line connecting B_1 to B_2. The slope of E is $\beta = |v''|_b / |v''|_a$ if $|v''|_a \neq 0$ and ∞ otherwise.

Without loss of generality we will assume that $|u'| = |v'|$. which implies that *level* $(A_1) = level(B_1)$. Let $A_1 = (x_a, y_a)$ and $B_1 = (x_b, y_b)$. We say that there is a gap $\delta = x_a - x_b$ between A_1 and B_1. We will also only consider finite slopes.

We examine the number of conflict tests that should be performed in order to check the hole property of a state, according to the relative values of the slopes α and β and to the value of the gap δ between A_1 and B_1.

Proposition 6. *Let L be a prolongeable language and $\mathcal{A} = (Q, \Sigma, \delta, p_0, T)$ be its minimal automaton. Whether a state $p \in Q$ satisfies the hole property or not can be checked in $O(n^3)$ time.*

Corollary 3. *Whether a prolongeable regular language L is geometrical or not can be checked in $O(n^4)$ time on the minimal automaton of Pref(L).*

6   Case of an Arbitrary Transition Function

We now sketch the general case, when the regular language L is not necessarily prolongeable. Let $\mathcal{A} = (Q, \Sigma, \delta, p_0, T)$ be the minimal automaton of $Pref(L)$. If $\mathcal{A}$ has a sink state s we denote by s' the unique state (if it exists) such that $s'.a = s'.b = s$.

Let $P \in F_Q$ and $p = state(P)$. Assume that the points $P + c(a)$ and $P + c(b)$ are in F. Consider the word u as defined in Definition 9. In the general case, u is either an infinite word $u = u'u''^{\omega}$ or a finite word $u = u_1u_2 \ldots u_m$ with $m < n$ and $p.(au_1u_2 \ldots u_{m-1}) = s'$. In the latter case the trajectory from $A_0 = P + c(a)$ is made of a piece A_0A_1, with $A_1 = P + c(au)$ and $state(A_1) = s'$. Let $A_1 = (x, y)$. Let $A_2 = (x', y')$ be the leftmost son of A_1 that is $x' = x + i$, $y' = y - i + 1$ with $i = max\{j \mid 2 \leq j \leq x + y + 2 \wedge (x + j, y - j + 1) \in F\}$ (we assume that outside $(x, -1)$ points are added to the figure so that their rightmost trajectory is parallel to the a-axis). Now we can compute the rightmost trajectory from A_2, and once again it can be either infinite or a piece A_2A_3.

Finally we have two possible cases. The first case is when the successive pieces $A_{2q}A_{2q+1}$ have a finite length. Since the number of states of $\mathcal{A}$ is finite, there exist two integers m and t such that $0 \leq m < t < n$ and $state(A_{2t}) = state(A_{2m})$. Hence we may consider an infinite rightmost trajectory from A_0 made of an initial sequence of pieces $A_{2q}A_{2q+1}$, for $0 \leq q \leq m - 1$, followed by an infinite repetition of the sequence of pieces $A_{2q}A_{2q+1}$, for $m \leq q \leq t - 1$. The second case is when there exists $0 \leq q < n$ such that the piece from A_{2q} is infinite.

The definition of the hole of a state p extends to the general case as well as the hole property. Our claim is that it is possible to design a polynomial algorithm addressing the case of regular languages in the same way we did for prolongeable languages. However this part is quite technical and it will not be developed here.

7   Conclusion

We have presented an $O(n^4)$ algorithm for checking whether a prolongeable regular language L is geometrical or not, on the minimal automaton of $Pref(L)$, as well as tools for studying the general case of a regular language. These results address the two-dimension case. First investigations of higher dimensions are encouraging.

References

1. Blanpain, B.: Automates, Langages et Géométrie, Mémoire de DEA, Université de Rouen (2006)
2. Blanpain, B., Champarnaud, J.-M., Dubernard, J.-P., Geniet, D.: Geometrical Languages. In: LATA 2007, Proceedings, Report 35/07, GRLMC Universitat Rovira I Virgili, pp. 127–138 (2007)
3. Baruah, S.K., Rosier, L.E., Howell, R.R.: Algorithms and Complexity Concerning the Preemptive Scheduling of Periodic, Real-Time Tasks on one Processor. Real-Time Systems, vol. 2, pp. 301–324. Kluwer Academic Press, Dordrecht (1990)
4. Eilenberg, S.: Automata, Languages and Machines, Vol. A & B. Academic Press, London (1976)

5. Geniet, D., Largeteau, G.: WCET free time analysis of hard real-time systems on multiprocessors: A regular language-based model. Theor. Comput. Sci. 388(1-3), 26–52 (2007)
6. Kleene, S.C.: Representation of events in nerve nets and finite automata, Automata Studies, pp. 2–42. Princeton Univ. Press, Princeton (1956)
7. Largeteau, G., Geniet, D., Andres, E.: Discrete Geometry Applied in Hard Real-Time Systems Validation. In: Andrès, É., Damiand, G., Lienhardt, P. (eds.) DGCI 2005. LNCS, vol. 3429, pp. 23–33. Springer, Heidelberg (2005)
8. Largeteau, G., Geniet, D.: Quantification du taux d'invalidité d'applications temps-réel à contraintes strictes, Techniques et Sciences Informatiques (to appear)
9. Liu, C.L., Layland, J.W.: Scheduling Algorithms for multiprogramming in real-time environment. Journal of the ACM, 46–61 (1973)
10. Myhill, J.: Finite automata and the representation of events, Wright Patterson Air Force Base, Ohio, USA, WADC TR-57-624 (1957)
11. Nerode, A.: Linear automata transformations. Proceedings of American Mathematical Society 9, 541–544 (1958)
12. Parikh, R.J.: On context-free languages. Journal of the Association for Computing Machine 13(4), 570–581 (1966)
13. Sakarovitch, J.: Eléments de théorie des automates. Vuibert Informatique (2003)

Hopcroft's Minimization Technique: Queues or Stacks?

Andrei Păun[1,2,3], Mihaela Păun[4], and Alfonso Rodríguez-Patón[3]

[1] Bioinformatics Department, National Institute of Research and Development for
Biological Sciences, Splaiul Independenţei, Nr. 296, Sector 6, Bucharest, Romania
[2] Department of Computer Science, Louisiana Tech University, Ruston
PO Box 10348, Louisiana, LA-71272 USA
apaun@latech.edu
[3] Departamento de Inteligencia Artificial, Facultad de Informática,
Universidad Politécnica de Madrid,
Campus de Montegancedo s/n, Boadilla del Monte
28660 Madrid, Spain
arpaton@fi.upm.es
[4] Department of Mathematics and Statistics, Louisiana Tech University, Ruston
PO Box 10348, Louisiana, LA-71272 USA
mpaun@latech.edu

Abstract. We consider the absolute worst case time complexity for
Hopcroft's minimization algorithm applied to unary languages (or a modification of this algorithm for cover automata minimization). We show
that in this setting the worst case is reached only for deterministic automata or cover automata following the structure of the de Bruijn words.
We refine a previous result by showing that the Berstel/Carton example
reported before is actually the absolute worst case time complexity in the
case of unary languages for deterministic automata. We show that the
same result is valid also when considering the setting of cover automata
and an algorithm based on the Hopcroft's method used for minimization
of cover automata. We also show that a LIFO implementation for the
splitting list is desirable for the case of unary languages in the setting of
deterministic finite automata.

1   Introduction

This work is in part a continuation of the result reported by Berstel and Carton
in [2] regarding the number of steps required for minimizing a unary language
through Hopcroft's minimization technique. The second part of the paper considers the same problem in the setting of Cover Automata. This new type of automata was introduced by Prof. Dr. Sheng Yu and Drs. Sântean and Câmpeanu
in [6] and since then was investigated by several authors such as in [4], [8], [14],
[16], [19], etc.

In the first part of the paper we will analyze and extend the result by Bestel
and Carton from [2]. There it was shown that Hopcroft's algorithm for minimizing unary languages requires O(n log n) steps when considering the example

O.H. Ibarra and B. Ravikumar (Eds.): CIAA 2008, LNCS 5148, pp. 78–91, 2008.

of automata following the structure induced by de Bruijn words (see [3]) as input and when making several "bad" implementation decisions. The setting of the paper [2] is for languages over an unary alphabet, considering the automata associated to the language(s) having the number of states a power of 2 and choosing "in a specific way" which set to become a splitting set in the case of ties. In this context, the previous paper showed that the algorithm needs $O(n \ log \ n)$ steps for the algorithm to complete, which is reaching the theoretical asymptotic worst case time complexity for the algorithm as reported in [9,10,11,13] etc.

We were initially interested in investigating further the complexity of an algorithm described by Hopcroft, specifically considering the setting of unary languages, but for a stack implementation in the algorithm. Our effort has led to the observation that when considering the worst case for the number of steps of the algorithm (which in this case translates to the largest number of states appearing in the splitting sets), a LIFO implementation indeed outperforms a FIFO strategy as suggested by experimental results on random automata as reported in [1].

One major **observation/clarification** that is needed is the following: we do not consider the asymptotic complexity of the run-time, but the actual number of steps. For the setting of the current paper when comparing $n \ log \ n$ steps and $n \ log(n-1)$ or $\frac{n}{2} \ log \ n$ steps we will say that $n \ log \ n$ is worse than both $n \ log(n-1)$ and $\frac{n}{2} \ log \ n$, even though when considering them in the framework of the asymptotic complexity (big-O) they have the same complexity, i.e. $n \ log(n-1) \in \Theta(n \ log \ n)$ and $\frac{n}{2} \ log \ n \in \Theta(n \ log \ n)$.

In Section 2 we give some definitions, notations and previous results, then in Section 3 we give a brief description of the algorithm discussed and its features. Section 4 describes the properties for the automaton that reaches worst possible case in terms of steps required for the algorithm (as a function of the initial number of states of the automaton). We then briefly consider the case of cover automata minimization with a modified version of the Hopcroft's algorithm in Section 6 and conclude by giving some final remarks in the Section 7.

2   Preliminaries

We assume the reader is familiar with the basic notations of formal languages and finite automata, see for example the excellent work by Yu [20]. In the following we will be denoting the cardinality of a finite set T by $|T|$, the set of words over a finite alphabet Σ is denoted Σ^*, and the empty word is λ. The length of a word $w \in \Sigma^*$ is denoted with $|w|$. For $l \geq 0$ we define the following sets of words:

$$\Sigma^l = \{w \in \Sigma^* \mid |w| = l\}, \Sigma^{\leq l} = \bigcup_{i=0}^{l} \Sigma^i, \text{ and for } l > 0 \text{ we define } \Sigma^{<l} = \bigcup_{i=0}^{l-1} \Sigma^i.$$

A deterministic finite automaton (DFA) is a quintuple $A = (\Sigma, Q, \delta, q_0, F)$ where Σ is a finite set of symbols, Q is a finite set of states, $\delta : Q \times \Sigma \longrightarrow Q$ is the transition function, q_0 is the start state, and F is the set of final states.

We can extend δ from $Q \times \Sigma$ to $Q \times \Sigma^*$ by $\overline{\delta}(s, \lambda) = s$, $\overline{\delta}(s, aw) = \overline{\delta}(\delta(s, a), w)$. We will usually denote the extension $\overline{\delta}$ of δ by δ when there is no danger of confusion.

The language recognized by the automaton A is $L(A) = \{w \in \Sigma^* \mid \delta(q_0, w) \in F\}$. In what follows we assume that δ is a total function, i.e., the deterministic automaton is also complete.

For a DFA $A = (\Sigma, Q, \delta, q_0, F)$, we can always assume, without loss of generality, that $Q = \{0, 1, \ldots, |Q| - 1\}$ and $q_0 = 0$. Throughout this paper we will assume that the states are labeled with numbers from 0 to $|Q| - 1$. If L is finite, $L = L(A)$ and A is complete, there is at least one state, called the sink state or dead state, for which $\delta(sink, w) \notin F$, for any $w \in \Sigma^*$. If L is a finite language, we denote by l the maximum among the lengths of all words in L.

For the following definitions we assume that L is a finite language over the alphabet Σ and l is the length of the longest word(s) in L.

Definition 1. *Cover Language. A language L' over Σ is called a cover language for the finite language L if $L' \cap \Sigma^{\leq l} = L$. A deterministic finite cover automaton (DFCA) for L is a deterministic finite automaton (DFA) A, such that the language accepted by A is a cover language of L.*

Definition 2. *State equivalence. Let $A = (\Sigma, Q, \delta, 0, F)$ be a DFA. We say that $p \equiv_A q$ (state p is equivalent to q in A) if for every $w \in \Sigma^*$, $\delta(p, w) \in F$ iff $\delta(q, w) \in F$.*

Definition 3. *Level. Let $A = (\Sigma, Q, \delta, 0, F)$ be a DFA (or a DFCA for L). We define, for each state $q \in Q$, $level(q) = \min\{|w| \mid \delta(0, w) = q\}$.*

The right language of a state $p \in Q$ and for a DFCA $A = (Q, \Sigma, \delta, q_0, F)$ for L is $R_p = \{w \mid \delta(p, w) \in F, |w| \leq l - level_A(p)\}$.

Definition 4. *Word similarity. Let $x, y \in \Sigma^*$. We define the following similarity relation in the following way: $x \sim_L y$ if for all $z \in \Sigma^*$ such that $xz, yz \in \Sigma^{\leq l}$, $xz \in L$ iff $yz \in L$, and we write $x \nsim_L y$ if $x \sim_L y$ does not hold.*

Definition 5. *State similarity. Let $A = (\Sigma, Q, \delta, 0, F)$ be a DFCA for L. We consider two states p, $q \in Q$ and $m = \max\{level(p), level(q)\}$. We say that p is similar with q in A, denoted by $p \sim_A q$, if for every $w \in \Sigma^{\leq l-m}$, $\delta(p, w) \in F$ iff $\delta(q, w) \in F$. We say that two states are dissimilar if they are not similar (the above does not hold).*

If the automaton is understood, we may omit in the following the subscript A when writing the similarity of two states in a DFCA A.

Lemma 1. *Let $A = (\Sigma, Q, \delta, 0, F)$ be a DFCA for a finite language L. Let $p, q \in Q$, with $level(p) = i$, $level(q) = j$, and $m = \max\{i, j\}$. If $p \sim_A q$, then $R_p \cap \Sigma^{\leq l-m} = R_q \cap \Sigma^{\leq l-m}$.*

Proof. See the proof given in [6].

Definition 6. *A DFCA A for a finite language is a minimal DFCA if and only if any two distinct states of A are dissimilar.*

Once two states have been detected as similar, one can merge the higher level one into the lower level one by redirecting transitions. We refer the interested reader to [6] for the merging theorem and other properties of cover automata.

3 Hopcroft's State Minimization Algorithm

In [11], an elegant algorithm for state minimization of DFAs was described. This algorithm was proven to be of the order $O(n \ log \ n)$ in the worst case (asymptotic evaluation). We will study further the complexity of the algorithm by considering the various implementation choices of the algorithm. We will show that by implementing the list of the splitting sets as a queue, one will be able to reach the absolute worst possible case with respect to the number of steps required for minimizing an automaton. We will also show that by changing the implementation strategy from a queue to a stack, we will never be able to reach that absolute worst case in the number of steps for minimizing automata, thus, at least from this perspective, the programmers should implement the list S from the following algorithm as a stack (LIFO).

The algorithm uses a special data structure that makes the set operations of the algorithm fast. We will give in the following the description of the minimization algorithm working on the automaton $(\Sigma, Q, \delta, q_0, F)$ that has an arbitrary alphabet Σ and later we will restrict the discussion to the case of unary languages.

1: $P = \{F, \ Q - F\}$
2: for all $a \in \Sigma$ do
3:     Add$((\min(F, \ Q - F), a), S)$ (min w.r.t. the number of states)
4: while $S \neq \emptyset$ do
5:     get (C, a) from S (we extract (C, a) according to the
      strategy associated with the list S: FIFO/LIFO/...)
6:     for each $B \in P$ that is split by (C, a) do
7:       B', B'' are the sets resulting from splitting of B w.r.t. (C, a)
8:       Replace B in P with both B' and B''
9:       for all $b \in \Sigma$ do
10:         if $(B, b) \in S$ then
11:           Replace (B, b) by (B', b) and (B'', b) in S
12:         else
13:           Add$((\min(B', B''), b), S)$

where the splitting of a set B by the pair (C, a) (the line 6) means that $\delta(B, a) \cap C \neq \emptyset$ and $\delta(B, a) \cap (Q - C) \neq \emptyset$. We have denoted above by $\delta(B, a)$ the set $\{q \mid q = \delta(p, a), \ p \in B\}$. The B' and B'' from line 7 are defined as the following two subsets of B: $B' = \{b \in B \mid \delta(b, a) \in C\}$ and $B'' = B - B'$.

It is useful to explain briefly the working of the algorithm: we start with the partition $P = \{F, Q - F\}$ and one of these two sets is then added to the splitting sequence S. The algorithm proceeds by breaking the partition into smaller sets according to the current splitting set retrieved from S. With each splitting of a set in P the number of sets stored in S grows (either through instruction 11 or instruction 13). When all the splitting sets from S are processed, and S becomes empty, then the partition P shows the state equivalences in the input automaton: all the states contained in a same set B in P are equivalent. Knowing all equivalences, one can easily minimize the automaton by merging all the states found in the same set in the final partition P at the end of the algorithm.

We note that there are three levels of "nondeterminism" in the implementation of the algorithm. All these three choices influence the algorithm by changing the number of steps performed for a specific input automaton. We describe first the three implementation choices, and later we show the worst case scenario for each of them.

The "most visible" implementation choice is the choice of the strategy for processing the list stored in S: as a queue, as a stack, etc. The second and third such choices in implementation of the algorithm appear when a set B is split into B' and B''. If B is not present in S, then the algorithm is choosing which set B' or B'' to be added to S, choice that is based on the minimal number of states in these two sets (line 13). In the case when both B' and B'' have the same number of states, then we have the second implementation choice (the choosing of the set that will be added to S). The third such choice appears when the split set (B, a) is in the list S; then the algorithm mentions the replacement of (B, a) by (B', a) and (B'', a) (line 11). This is actually implemented in the following way: (B'', a) is replacing (B, a) and (B', a) is added to the list S (or vice-versa). Since we saw that the processing strategy of S matters, then also the choice of which B' or B'' is added to S and which one replaces the previous location of (B, a) matters in the actual run-time of the algorithm.

In the original paper [11] and later in [9], and [13], when describing the complexity of the minimization method, the authors showed that the algorithm is influenced by the number of states that appear in the sets processed in S. Intuitively, that is why the smaller of the (add) B' and B'' is inserted in S in line 13; and this is what makes the algorithm sub-quadratic. In the following we will focus on exactly this issue of the number of states appearing in sets processed in S.

4   Worst Case Scenario for Unary Languages

Let us start the discussion by making several observations and preliminary clarifications: we are discussing about languages over an unary alphabet. To make the proof easier, we restrict our discussion to the automata having the number of states a power of 2. The three levels of implementation choices are clarified/set in the following way: we assume that the processing of S is based on a FIFO approach, we also assume that there is a strategy of choosing between two sets that have been just splitted. These two sets have the same number of elements in such a way that the one that is added to the queue S makes the third implementation nondeterminism irrelevant. In other words, no splitting of a set already in S will take place (line 11 will not be executed).

Let us assume that such an automaton with 2^n states is given as input for the minimization algorithm described in the previous section. We note that since we have only one letter in the alphabet, the states (C, a) from the list S can be written without any problems as C, thus the list S (for the particular case of unary languages) becomes a list of sets of states. So let us assume that the automaton $A = (\{a\}, Q, \delta, q_0, F)$ is given as the input of the algorithm, where $|Q| = 2^n$. The algorithm proceeds by choosing the first splitter set to be added to S. The first such set will be chosen between F and $Q - F$ based on their number of states. Since we are interested in the worst case scenario for the algorithm, and the algorithm run-time is influenced by the total number of states that will appear in the list S throughout the running of the algorithm (as shown in [11], [9], [13] and mentioned in [2]), it is clear that we want to maximize the sizes of the sets that are added to S. It is time to give a Lemma that will be useful in the following.

Lemma 2. *For deterministic automata over unary languages, if a set R with $|R| = m$ is the current splitter set, then R cannot add to the list S sets containing all together more than m states (line 13).*

Proof. We can rephrase the Lemma as: for all the sets B_i from the current partition P such that $\delta(B_i, a) \cap R \neq \emptyset$ and $\delta(B_i, a) \cap (Q - R) \neq \emptyset$. Then $\sum_{\forall i} |B'_i| \leq m$, where B'_i is the smaller of the two sets that result from the splitting of the set $B_i \in P$ with respect to R.

We have only one letter in the alphabet, thus the number of states q such that $\delta(q, a) \in R$ is at most m. Each B'_i is chosen as the set with the smaller number of states when splitting B_i thus $|B'_i| \leq |\delta(B_i, a) \cap R|$ which implies that $\sum_{\forall i} |B'_i| \leq \sum_{\forall i} |\delta(B_i, a) \cap R| = |(\bigcup_{\forall i} \delta(B_i, a)) \cap R| \leq |R|$ (because all B_i are disjoint).

Thus we proved that if we start splitting according to a set R, then the new sets added to S contain at most $|R|$ states.   □

Coming back to our previous setting, we will start with the automaton $A = (\{a\}, Q, \delta, q_0, F)$ (where $|Q| = 2^n$) given as input to the algorithm and we have to find the smaller set between F and $Q - F$. In the worst case (according to Lemma 2) we have that $|F| = |Q - F|$, as otherwise, fewer than 2^{n-1} states will be contained in the set added to S and thus less states will be contained in the sets added to S in the second stage of the algorithm, and so on. So in the worst case we have that the number of final states and the number of non-final states is the same. To simplify the discussion we will give some notations. We denote by S_w, $w \in \{0, 1\}^*$ the set of states $p \in Q$ such that $\delta(p, a^{i-1}) \in F$ iff $w_i = 1$ for $i = 1..|w|$, where $\delta(p, a^0)$ denotes p. As an example, $S_1 = F$, S_{110} contains all the final states that are followed by a final state and then by a non-final state and S_{00000} denotes the states that are non-final and are followed in the automaton by four more non-final states.

With these notations we have that at this initial step of the algorithm, either $F = S_1$ or $Q - F = S_0$ can be added to S as they have the same number of states. Either one that is added to the queue S will split the partition P in the worst case scenario in the following four possible sets $S_{00}, S_{01}, S_{10}, S_{11}$, each with 2^{n-2} states. This is true as by splitting the sets F and $Q - F$ in sets with sizes other than 2^{n-2}, then according to Lemma 2 we will not reach the worst possible number of states in the queue S and also splitting only F or only $Q - F$ will add to S only one set of 2^{n-2} states not two of them.

All this means that half of the non-final states go to a final state ($|S_{01}| = 2^{n-2}$) and the other half go to a non final state (S_{00}). Similarly, for the final states we have that 2^{n-2} of them go to a final state (S_{11}) and the other half go to a non-final state. The current partition at this step 1 of the algorithm is $P = \{S_{00}, S_{01}, S_{10}, S_{11}\}$ and the splitting sets are one of the S_{00}, S_{01} and one of the S_{10}, S_{11}. Let us assume that it is possible to chose the splitting sets to be added to the queue S in such a way so that no splitting of another set in S will happen, (chose in this case for example S_{10} and S_{00}). We want to avoid splitting of other sets in S since if that happens, then smaller sets will be added to the queue S by the splitted set in S (see such a choice of splitters described also in [2]).

We have arrived at step 2 of the algorithm. Since the first two sets from S are now processed, in the worst case they will be able to add to the queue S at most 2^{n-2} states each by each splitting two of the four current sets in the partition P. Of course, to reach the worst case, we need them to split different sets, thus we obtain eight sets in the partition P corresponding to all the possibilities of words of length 3 on a binary alphabet: $P=\{S_{000}, S_{001}, S_{010}, S_{011}, S_{100}, S_{101}, S_{110}, S_{111}\}$ having 2^{n-3} states each. Thus four of these sets will be added to the queue S. And we could continue our reasoning up until the i-th step of the algorithm:

We now have 2^{i-1} sets in the queue S, each having 2^{n-i} states, and the partition P contains 2^i sets S_w corresponding to all the words w of the length i. Each of the sets in the splitting queue is of the form $S_{x_1 x_2 \ldots x_i}$, then a set $S_{x_1 x_2 x_3 \ldots x_i}$ can only split at most two other sets $S_{0 x_1 x_2 x_3 \ldots x_{i-1}}$ and $S_{1 x_1 x_2 x_3 \ldots x_{i-1}}$ from the partition P. To reach the worst case for the algorithm, no set (of level i) from the splitting queue should be splitting a set already in the queue, and also, it should split 2 distinct sets in the partition P, making the partition at step $i+1$ the set $P = \{S_w \mid |w| = i+1\}$. Furthermore, each such S_w should have exactly 2^{n-i-1} states. In this way the process continues until we arrive at the n-th step. If the process would terminate before the step n, of course we would not reach the worst possible number of states passing through S.

We will now describe the properties/restrictions of an automaton that would obey a processing through the Hopcroft's algorithm as described above (for the worst case scenario). We started with 2^n states, out of which we have 2^{n-1} final and also 2^{n-1} non-final. Out of the final states, we have 2^{n-2} that precede another final state (S_{11}), and also 2^{n-2} non-final states that precede other non-final states for S_{00}, etc. The strongest restrictions are found in the final partition sets S_w, with $|w| = n$, each have exactly one element, which means that all the words of length n over the binary alphabet can be found in this automaton by following the transitions between states and having 1 for a final state and 0 for a non-final state. It is clear that the automaton needs to be circular and following the pattern of de Bruijn words, [3]. Such an automaton for $n = 3$ was depicted in [2] as in the following Figure 1.

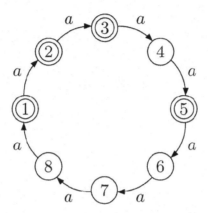

Fig. 1. A cyclic automaton of size 8 for the de Bruijn word 11101000, containing all words of size 3 over the binary alphabet {0, 1}

It is easy to see now that a stack implementation for the list S will not be able to reach the maximum as smaller sets will be processed before considering larger sets. This fact will lead to splitting of sets already in the list S. Once this happens for a set with j states, then the number of states that will appear in S is decreased by at least j because the splitted sets will not be able to add as many states as a FIFO implementation was able to do. We conjecture that in such a setting the LIFO strategy could prove the algorithm linear with respect to the size of the input. We reference [15] for previous work in this direction. If the aforementioned third level of implementation choice is set to add the smaller set of B', B'' to the stack and B to be replaced by the larger one. We proved the following result:

Theorem 1. *The absolute worst case run-time complexity for the Hopcroft's minimization algorithm for unary languages is reached when the splitter list S in the algorithm is following a FIFO strategy and only for automata having a structure induced by de Bruijn words of size n. In that setting the algorithm will pass through the queue S exactly $n2^{n-1}$ states for the input automaton of size 2^n. Thus for m states of the input automaton we have exactly $\frac{m}{2}\log_2 m$ states passing through S.*

Proof. Due to the previous discussion we now know that the absolute maximum for the complexity of the Hopcroft's algorithm is reached in the case of the FIFO strategy for the splitter list S. The maximum is reached when the input automaton is following the structure of the *de Bruijn* words for a binary alphabet.

What remains to be proven is the actual number of states that pass through the queue S: in the first stage exactly half of all states are added to S through one of the sets S_0 or S_1, in the second stage half of the states are again added to S through two of the four sets $S_{00}, S_{01}, S_{10}, S_{11}$. At the third stage half of states are added to S because four of the following eight sets $S_{000}, S_{001}, S_{010}, S_{011}, S_{100}, S_{101}, S_{110}, S_{111}$ are added to S, each having exactly 2^{n-3} states. We continue this process until the last stage of the algorithm, stage n: when still 2^{n-1} states are added to S through the fact that exactly 2^{n-1} sets, each containing exactly one state, are added to the splitting queue. Of course, at this stage we have the partitioning into $\{S_w \mid |w| = n\}$ and half of these sets will be added to S through the instruction at line 13. It should be now clear that we have exactly n stages in this execution of the algorithm, each with 2^{n-1} states added to S, hence the result.

5   Stacks

In this section we will consider the case of the LIFO implementation for the splitting sequence S used in the algorithm. Let us assume that we start with a minimal automaton having 2^n states.

Following the steps of the procedure and lemma 2 one can easily see that in the list S we can have in the worst case scenario the following number of states: $2^{n-1} \mid 2^{n-2}, 2^{n-2} \mid 2^{n-3}, 2^{n-3}, 2^{n-2} \mid 2^{n-4}, 2^{n-4}, 2^{n-3}, 2^{n-2} \mid \ldots$ and finally $2, 2, 2^2, 2^3, 2^4, \ldots, 2^{n-4}, 2^{n-3}, 2^{n-2}$

In this way one reaches in n steps a set in S that contains exactly one state. At this moment this single state will be partitioning all the states that lead to this single state in the automaton, thus if the state is on the loop of the automaton in exactly another n steps all the states will be in their own partitions and the algorithm finishes. The worst case scenario is when this first partitioned state is actually the start state and this state does not have any incoming transitions, thus it does not split any other state. This case is still not reaching the $O(n2^n)$ states in S because at the next step another single state will be in its own partition set in P. To be in the worst case, this state has to be very near of the start state of the automaton (otherwise all the states that precede it will be split and added to the partition P). We will have an increasing number of states that are partitioned by much smaller states which is bringing down the number of the states that pass through S. Another observation is the following: the first $n-1$ sets that appear in S are actually coming from specific splittings; if one considers that the first single state in a set in S is $S_{x_1 x_2 x_3 \ldots x_n}$ then it comes from the splitting of $S_{x_1 x_2 \ldots x_{n-1}}$ through $S_{x_2 x_3 \ldots x_{n-1} Y}$. Through a careful analysis we notice that the restrictions on words do not allow an "explosion" of the number of states that can be added to the list S, so in linear time we obtain the most refined partition P.

When considering the start automaton (still unary) non-minimal, the procedure is changed a little as the actual discussion is delayed by at most $log_2 a$ where a is the period of the loop. The main observation is that even though the procedure will choose the set by the smallest number of states in the set, that set could actually contain more "minimal states" than the set that was not added to S, thus the "lag" in the algorithm amounts to $log_2 a$ with a being the maximal number of states that are in an equivalence class in the automaton. The discussion proceeds in a similar fashion, still in at most $n + log_2 a$ steps we reach the first state in the minimal automaton, and after that stage the stack implementation makes the order of consideration of the splitting of partition in such a way that it is linear.

Following this discussion we showed in a sketched way that the Hopcroft's algorithm with stack implementation applied for unary automata has a linear time requirement for completion.

6   Cover Automata

In this section we discuss briefly about an extension to Hopcroft's algorithm to cover automata. Körner reported at CIAA'02 and also in [14] a modification of the Hopcroft's algorithm so that the resulting sets in the partition P will give the similarities between states with respect to the input finite language L.

To achieve this, the algorithm is modified as follows: each state will have its level computed at the start of the algorithm; each element added to the list S will have three components: the set of states, the alphabet letter and the current length considered. We start with $(F, a, 0)$ for example. Also the splitting of a set B by (C, a, l_1) is defined as before with the extra condition that we ignore during the splitting the states that have their level$+l_1$ greater than l (l being the longest word in the finite language L). Formally we can define the sets $X = \{p \mid \delta(p, a) \in C, \ level(p) + l_1 \leq l\}$ and $Y = \{p \mid \delta(p, a) \notin C, \ level(p) + l_1 \leq l\}$. Then a set B will be split only if $B \cap X \neq \emptyset$ and $B \cap Y \neq \emptyset$.

The actual splitting of B ignores the states that have levels higher than or equal to $l - l_1$. This also adds a degree of implementation nondeterminism to the algorithm when such states appear because the programmer can choose to add these sets in either of the two splitted sets obtained from B. The worst implementation choice would be to put the states with level higher than $l - l_1$ in such a way that they balance the number of states in both B' and B'' (where $B' = X \cup Z'$ and $B'' = Y \cup Z''$ and $Z' \cap Z'' = \emptyset$, and $Z' \cup Z'' = B - (X \cup Y)$ are all the states of level higher than or equal to $l - l_1$). We note that this is an obviously "bad" implementation choice, thus we assume that the programmer would avoid it. We will make in this case the choice to have the states split as in the case of DFA, according to whether $\delta(p, a) \in C$, then $p \in X$, otherwise, $p \in Y$. This choice will make the Lemma 2 valid also for the Cover automata case, with the modifications to the algorithm mentioned above.

The algorithm proceeds as before to add the smaller of the newly splitted sets to the list S together with the value $l_1 + 1$.

Let us now consider the same problem as in [2], but in this case for the case of DFCA minimization through the algorithm described in [14]. We will consider the same example as before, the automata based on de Bruijn words as the input to the algorithm (we note that the modified algorithm can start directly with a DFCA for a specific language, thus we can have as input even cyclic automata). We need to specify the actual length of the finite language that is considered and also the starting state of the de Bruijn automaton (since the algorithm needs to compute the levels of the states). We can choose the length of the longest word in L as $l = 2^n$ and the start state as $S_{111...1}$. For example, the automaton in figure 1 would be a cover automaton for the language $L = \{0, 1, 2, 4, 8\}$ with $l = 8$ and the start state $q_0 = 1$. Following the same reasoning as in [2] but for the case of the new algorithm with respect to the modifications, we can show that also for the case of DFCA a queue implementation (as specifically given in [14]) is a worse choice than a stack implementation for S. We note that the discussion is not a straight-forward extension of the work reported by Berstel in [2] as the new dimension added to the sets in S, the length and also the levels of states need to be discussed in detail. We will give the details of the construction and the step-by-step discussion of this fact in the following:

We start as before with an automaton with 2^n states working on a unary language given as: $A = (\{a\}, Q, \delta, q_0, F)$ where $|Q| = 2^n$. Let us take a look at the possible levels of the states in deterministic automata over unary languages: Such an automaton is formed by a line followed by a loop. The line or the loop can be possibly empty: if the loop is empty (or containing only non-final states), then the automaton accepts only a finite set of numbers, if the loop contains at least one state that is final, it accepts an infinite set. In either case the levels of the states is $0, 1, 2, 3, ..., n - 2, n - 1$. One can see that the highest level in such a unary DFA is at most $n - 1$.

Following the variant of Lemma 2 for DFCA it is clear that the worst possible case is when $|F| = |Q - F|$. Let us consider that S starts with the pair $(F, 0)$ or $(Q - F, 0)$, in either case at the second stage of the algorithm the partition P will be split in the following four possible sets (similarly as in the case of DFA): $S_{00}, S_{01}, S_{10}, S_{11}$. To continue with the worst possible case, each of these sets need to contain exactly 2^{n-2} states (otherwise, according to Lemma 2 for the DFCA case, a set with less states is added to S and also in the next steps less states will be added to S). Also in this case it is necessary to make a "bad" choice of the sets that will be added next to S (one from the S_{00}, S_{01} and one from S_{10}, S_{11}). We will use the same choosing strategy as before. The difference is that these sets will be added to S and with the length 1: for example, at the next step S will contain $(S_{00}, 1)$ and $(S_{10}, 1)$. At the next stage of the algorithm we will observe a difference from the DFA case: one of the states at the next stage will not be splitted from the set because of its high level. Considering that we have a state of level $l - 1$, at this step this high-level state will not be considered for splitting, thus can be added to either one or the other of the halves of the state containing it. For the final automaton, considering that the state $S_{11..1}$ is the start state, the high level state is $S_{011..1}$.

We continue the process in a similar fashion until the i-th stage of the algorithm by carefully choosing the splitting sets, and by having at each stage yet another state that would not be considered in the splitting due to its high level. But because the forth implementation choice, the number of states in each set remains the same. At this moment we will have 2^{i-1} pairs in the queue S, each formed between a set containing 2^{n-i} states and the value $i-1$. Thus we will compute the splitter sets X and Y as given before in the case of DFA with the extra condition that the sets p satisfying the condition also satisfy the fact that $level(p) + i - 1 \leq l$.

At this moment the partition P has exactly 2^i components that are in the worst case exactly the sets S_w for all $w \in \{0,1\}^i$. In the worst case all the level i states from the splitting queue S will not break a set already in the queue S, but at the same time will split two other sets in the partition P. This is achieved by the careful choosing of the order in which these sets arrive in the queue (one of these "worst" additions to S strategies was described in [2]). In this way, at the end of the stage i in the algorithm we will have the partition P containing all the sets S_w with $w \in \{0,1\}^{i+1}$ and each of them having 2^{n-i-1} states. In the queue S there will be 2^i pairs of states with the number i. These splitting pairs will be used in the next stage of the algorithm.

This process will continue until the $n-1$-th stage as before (otherwise we will not be in the worst possible case) and at the n-th stage exactly $n-2$ sets will not be added to the queue S (as opposed to the DFA case), thus only $2^{n-1} - n + 2$ singleton sets will be added.

This makes the absolute worst case for the run-time of the minimization of DFCA based on Hopcroft's method have exactly $n2^{n-1}-n+2$ states pass through S. The input automaton still follows the structure induced by de Bruijn words; and when considering the start state as $S_{11...1}$, the states that will be similar with other states are the $n-2$ states of highest levels: $S_{011...1}, S_{001..1}, ..., S_{00...011}$. In fact we will have several similarities between these high level states and other states in the automaton, more precisely, for an automaton with 2^n states (following the structure of de Bruijn words containing all the subwords of size n) we have the following pattern of similarities: the state $S_{011...1}$ will have exactly $2^{n-2} - 1$ similarities with other states in the automaton (because the level of this state is $2^n - 1$, thus only the pattern 01 is making the difference to other states), for $S_{001...1}$ we will have $2^{n-3} - 1$ similarities (as for its level $2^n - 2$ the pattern making the difference is 001), and so on, until $S_{000...01}$ will actually have $2^{n-(n-1)} - 1 = 2 - 1 = 1$ similarities (since its level is $2^n - n + 2$ and the pattern making the difference is 000...01). These values are obtained from considering the fact that the structure of the automaton will have all the sub-words of size n, thus we can compute how many times a particular pattern appears in the automaton.

This shows that a result similar to Theorem 1 holds also for the case of DFCA with the only difference in the counting of states passing through S: $n2^{n-1}-n+2$ rather than $n2^{n-1}$. It should be clear now that a stack implementation for the list

S is more efficient, at least for the case of unary languages and when considering the absolute worst possible run-time of the algorithm.

7   Final Remarks

We showed that at least in the case of unary languages, a stack implementation is more desirable than a queue for keeping track of the splitting sets in Hopcroft's algorithm. This is the first instance when it was shown that the stack is out-performing the queue. Thus at least for the special case of unary languages we know that it is better to have the implementation of S in the algorithm as a stack rather than the intuitive implementation as a queue.

It remains open whether these results can be extended to languages containing more than one letter in the alphabet.

For the case of cover automata one should settle the extra implementation choice (the forth implementation choice as mentioned in the text) as follows: rather than balancing the number of states in the two splitted sets, actually try to un-balance them by adding all the high level states to the bigger set. These remarks should achieve a reasonable speed-up for the algorithm.

References

1. Baclet, M., Pagetti, C.: Around Hopcroft's Algorithm. In: Ibarra, O.H., Yen, H.-C. (eds.) CIAA 2006. LNCS, vol. 4094, pp. 114–125. Springer, Heidelberg (2006)
2. Berstel, J., Carton, O.: On the complexity of Hopcrofts state minimization algorithm. In: Domaratzki, M., Okhotin, A., Salomaa, K., Yu, S. (eds.) CIAA 2004. LNCS, vol. 3317, pp. 35–44. Springer, Heidelberg (2005)
3. de Bruijn, N.G.: A Combinatorial Problem. Koninklijke Nederlandse Akademie v. Wetenschappen 49, 758–764 (1946)
4. Câmpeanu, C., Păun, A., Yu, S.: An Efficient Algorithm for Constructing Minimal Cover Automata for Finite Languages. International Journal of Foundations of Computer Science 13(1), 83–97 (2002)
5. Câmpeanu, C., Salomaa, K., Yu, S.: Tight Lower Bound for the State Complexity of Shuffle of Regular Languages. Journal of Automata, Languages and Combinatorics 7(3), 303–310 (2002)
6. Câmpeanu, C., Sântean, N., Yu, S.: Minimal Cover-Automata for Finite Languages. In: Champarnaud, J.-M., Maurel, D., Ziadi, D. (eds.) WIA 1998. LNCS, vol. 1660, pp. 32–42. Springer, Heidelberg (1999); Theoretical Computer Science 267, 3–16 (2001)
7. Champarnaud, J.M., Maurel, D.: Automata Implementation. In: Champarnaud, J.-M., Maurel, D., Ziadi, D. (eds.) WIA 1998. LNCS, vol. 1660. Springer, Heidelberg (1999)
8. Domaratzki, M., Shallit, J., Yu, S.: Minimal Covers of Formal Languages. In: Kuich, W., Rozenberg, G., Salomaa, A. (eds.) DLT 2001. LNCS, vol. 2295, pp. 319–329. Springer, Heidelberg (2002)
9. Gries, D.: Describing an algorithm by Hopcroft. Acta Informatica 2, 97–109 (1973)
10. Hopcroft, J.E., Ullman, J.D., Motwani, R.: Introduction to Automata Theory, Languages and Computation. Addison-Wesley, Reading (2001)

11. Hopcroft, J.E.: An $n \ log \ n$ algorithm for minimizing states in a finite automaton. In: Kohavi, Z., Paz, A. (eds.) Theory of Machines and Computations, pp. 189–196. Academic Press, London (1971)

12. Ilie, L., Yu, S.: Follow automata. Inf. Comput. 186(1), 140–162 (2003)

13. Knuutila, T.: Re-describing an algorithm by Hopcroft. Theoretical Computer Science 250(1-2), 333–363 (2001)

14. Körner, H.: A Time and Space Efficient Algorithm for Minimizing Cover Automata for Finite Languages. International Journal of Foundations of Computer Science 14(6), 1071–1086 (2003)

15. Paige, R., Tarjan, R.E., Bonic, R.: A Linear Time Solution to the Single Function Coarsest Partition Problem. Theoretical Computer Science 40, 67–84 (1985)

16. Păun, A., Santean, N., Yu, S.: An $O(n^2)$ Algorithm for Constructing Minimal Cover Automata for Finite Languages. In: Yu, S., Păun, A. (eds.) CIAA 2000. LNCS, vol. 2088, pp. 243–251. Springer, Heidelberg (2001)

17. Salomaa, A.: Formal Languages. Academic Press, London (1973)

18. Salomaa, K., Wu, X., Yu, S.: Efficient Implementation of Regular Languages Using Reversed Alternating Finite Automata. Theor. Comput. Sci. 231(1), 103–111 (2000)

19. Sântean, N.: Towards a Minimal Representation for Finite Languages: Theory and Practice. MSc Thesis, Department of Computer Science, The University of Western Ontario (2000)

20. Yu, S.: Regular Languages. In: Rozenberg, G., Salomaa, A. (eds.) Handbook of Formal Languages, pp. 41–110. Springer, Heidelberg (1998)

21. Yu, S.: State Complexity of Finite and Infinite Regular Languages. Bulletin of the EATCS 76, 142–152 (2002)

22. Yu, S.: State Complexity: Recent Results and Open Problems. Fundam. Inform. 64(1-4), 471–480 (2005)

23. Yu, S.: On the State Complexity of Combined Operations. In: Ibarra, O.H., Yen, H.-C. (eds.) CIAA 2006. LNCS, vol. 4094, pp. 11–22. Springer, Heidelberg (2006)

24. Wood, D., Yu, S.: Automata Implementation. In: Proceedings of Second International Workshop on Implementing Automata. LNCS, vol. 1436. Springer, Heidelberg (1998)

25. The Grail + Project. A symbolic computation environment for finite state machines, regular expressions, and finite languages,
http://www.csd.uwo.ca/research/grail/

Learning Regular Languages Using Nondeterministic Finite Automata[*]

Pedro García[1], Manuel Vázquez de Parga[1], Gloria I. Álvarez[2], and José Ruiz[1]

[1] DSIC, Universidad Politécnica de Valencia. Valencia (Spain)
[2] Pontificia Universidad Javeriana. Cali, Colombia

Abstract. A new general method for inference of regular languages using nondeterministic automata as output has recently been developed and proved to converge. The aim of this paper is to describe and analyze the behavior of two implementations of that method and to compare it with two well known algorithms for the same task. A complete set of experiments has been carried out and the results of the new algorithms improve the existing ones both in recognition rates as in sizes of the output automata.

1 Introduction

The first ideas in the field of regular languages inference focused the description of the target languages using deterministic finite automata (*DFAs*). Many of the algorithms and heuristics proposed in this field use the technique of merging supposedly-equivalent states as a way to generalize the input. The starting point is the *prefix tree acceptor* (*PTA*), which is a tree-shaped automaton that recognizes the sample. The first of these algorithms (1973) is due to Trakhtembrot and Barzdin [12]. It is described as a contraction procedure in a finite tree that represents the words up to a certain length of a regular language. If the given data contains a certain characteristic set of the target language, it finds out the smallest *DFA* that recognizes the language.

The *RPNI* algorithm [10] starts from the *PTA* of the sample also. The merges are done in canonical order (two levels of ordering: length and alphabetical) controlled by the negative samples. The main ideas to improve the performance of *RPNI* have dealt with the order in which the states are merged. The algorithm *EDSM* [9] led to a control strategy called blue-fringe in which one of the states to merge is in the root of a tree. This algorithm, known as RedBlue is considered the state of art of DFAs inference by means of state merging. In [1] a new measure to order the merges called shared evidence is proposed. Using the concept of inclusion between the residuals of states, an extension of *RPNI* that enlarges the training set while learning has been proposed in [6].

These methods, which output *DFAs*, do not behave well sometimes when the target language has been obtained using randomly generated automata or

---

[*] Work partially supported by Spanish Ministerio de Educación y Ciencia under project TIN2007-60769.

O.H. Ibarra and B. Ravikumar (Eds.): CIAA 2008, LNCS 5148, pp. 92–101, 2008.

regular expressions. This reason led to researchers to develop algorithms that output *NFAs*. Note that *NFAs* are generally smaller descriptions for a regular language than its equivalent *DFAs*. One of those is the *DeLeTe2* algorithm [5], which output an special type of *NFA* called Residual Finite State Automaton *(RFSA)*. A *RFSA* is an automaton with its states being residuals of the language it accepts.

A subclass of the class of *NFAs* called *unambiguous finite automata* (*UFA*) has been defined and inferred in [4]. One of the properties of *UFA* is that the same target language will be achieved independently of the order in which states are merged. Some algorithms that use the same strategy that *RPNI* but output *NFAs* have been proposed [2]. The first attempt to use the *maximal automata* of the positive sample instead of the *PTA* is done in [13], where every positive sample is considered independently.

Finally, in [7] a general inference method based in states merging has been developed and proved to converge. It has been named *OIL* (order independent learning). It starts building the maximal automaton that recognizes the positive samples and one of its main features is that the convergence is achieved independently from the order in which states are merged. The convergence is proved using the concept of *Universal Automaton* of a language.

This latter fact about order-independent merging convergence opens up new possibilities of learning algorithms. In this paper two new algorithms based on the previous method are proposed. They will be referred to as *MOIL* (minimal order independent learning) and *VOIL* (voting order...). Both have in common that they canonically order the positive samples, and in an incremental way, build the maximal automata of the sample and merge the states in a random order to obtain an irreducible automata, controlled by the negative samples. Running the algorithm several times with different orders, different automata may be obtained. The difference between *MOIL* and *VOIL* is that the former outputs the smallest of the obtained automata, whereas the later keeps all of them and classifies the test samples by a majority vote. The proposed algorithms also use some evidence measure: as sometimes a state in the current automaton could be merged to several previous states, it chooses the merge that makes the resulting automaton to accept more positive samples.

2   Definitions and Notation

2.1   Languages and Automata

A language L is any subset of A^*, the free monoid generated by a finite alphabet A. The elements $x \in A^*$ are called *words* and the neutral element is denoted λ. The complement of L is denoted $\overline{L}$. The residual of L with respect to the word x is $x^{-1}L = \{y \in A^* : xy \in L\}$.

A (non deterministic) *finite automaton* (*NFA*) is a 5-tuple $\mathcal{A} = (Q, A, \delta, I, F)$, where Q is a finite set of states, A is an alphabet, $I, F \subseteq Q$ are respectively the set of initial and final states and $\delta : Q \times A \rightarrow 2^Q$ is the transition function, also be denoted as $\delta \subseteq Q \times A \times Q$ and is extended to $Q \times A^*$ as usual. The language accepted by $\mathcal{A}$ is $L(\mathcal{A}) = \{x \in A^* : \delta(I, x) \cap F \neq \emptyset\}$. The *left language* of a state q with respect to $\mathcal{A}$ is $L_q = \{x \in A^* : q \in \delta(I, x)\}$.

A *sub-automaton* of a NFA $\mathcal{A} = (Q, A, \delta, I, F)$ is any finite automaton $\mathcal{A}' = (Q', A, \delta', I', F')$ where $Q' \subseteq Q$, $I' \subseteq I \cap Q'$, $F' \subseteq F \cap Q'$ and $\delta' \subseteq \delta \cap Q' \times A \times Q'$. If $\mathcal{A}'$ is a sub-automaton of $\mathcal{A}$ then $L(\mathcal{A}') \subseteq L(\mathcal{A})$.

Let $D \subset A^*$ finite. The *maximal automaton* for D is the NFA $MA(D) = (Q, A, \delta, I, F)$ where $Q = \cup_{x \in D}\{(u, v) \in A^* \times A^* : uv = x\}$, $I = \{(\lambda, x) : x \in D\}$, $F = \{(x, \lambda) : x \in D\}$ and for $(u, av) \in Q$, $\delta((u, av), a) = (ua, v)$. So defined $L(MA(D)) = D$.

Let $\mathcal{A} = (Q, A, \delta, I, F)$ be an automaton and let π be a partition of Q. Let $B(q, \pi)$ be the class of π that contains q. The *quotient automaton* of π in $\mathcal{A}$ is $\mathcal{A}/\pi = (Q', A, \delta', I', F')$, where $Q' = Q/\pi = \{B(q, \pi) : q \in Q\}$, $I' = \{B \in Q' : B \cap I \neq \emptyset\}$, $F' = \{B \in Q' : B \cap F \neq \emptyset\}$ and the transition function is $B' \in \delta'(B, a)$ if and only if $\exists q \in B, \exists q' \in B'$ with $q' \in \delta(q, a)$.

The *merge* of states p and q in a finite automaton $\mathcal{A}$, denoted $merge(\mathcal{A}, p, q)$ is a particular quotient in which one of the blocks of the partition is the set $\{p, q\}$ and the rest are singletons.

An automaton $\mathcal{A}$ is *irreducible* in L if and only if $L(\mathcal{A}) \subseteq L$ and for any non trivial partition π of the states of $\mathcal{A}$, $L(\mathcal{A}/\pi) - L \neq \emptyset$. $\mathcal{A}$ is irreducible if it is irreducible in $L(\mathcal{A})$.

Given a regular language L, let U be the finite set of all the possible intersections of residuals of L with respect to the words of A^*, that is, $\mathsf{U} = \{u_1^{-1}L \cap ... \cap u_k^{-1}L : k \geq 0, u_1, ..., u_k \in A^*\}$. The *universal automaton (UA)* [3,11] for L is $\mathcal{U} = (\mathsf{U}, A, \delta, I, F)$ where $I = \{q \in \mathsf{U} : q \subseteq L\}$, $F = \{q \in \mathsf{U} : \lambda \in q\}$ and the transition function is such that $q \in \delta(p, a)$ iff $q \subseteq a^{-1}p$.

The *UA* for a language L does not have any mergible states. A theorem [3] states that every automata that recognizes a subset of a language L can be projected into the *UA* for L by a homomorphism.

2.2   Grammatical Inference

Regular language learning is the process of learning an unknown regular language from a finite set of labeled examples. A positive (resp. negative) sample of L is any finite set $D_+ \subseteq L$ (resp. $D_- \subseteq \overline{L}$). If it contains positive and negative words it will be denoted as (D_+, D_-) and called a *complete sample*. A *complete presentation* of $L \subseteq \Sigma^*$ is a sequence of all the words of A^* labelled according to their membership to L.

An *inference algorithm* is an algorithm that on input of any sample outputs a representation of a language called hypothesis. The algorithm is *consistent* if the output contains D_+ and is disjoint with D_-. For the family of regular languages, the set of hypotheses, $\mathcal{H}$, can be the set of *NFAs*.

The type of convergence that we will use in our algorithms was defined by Gold [8] and is called *identification in the limit*. It is a framework proposed in order to analyze the behavior of different learning tasks in a computational way.

An algorithm $\mathcal{IA}$ identifies a class of languages $\mathcal{L}$ by means of hypotheses in $\mathcal{H}$ *in the limit* if and only if for any $L \in \mathcal{L}$, and any presentation of L, the infinite sequence of hypotheses output by $\mathcal{IA}$ converges to $h \in \mathcal{H}$ such that $L(h) = L$, that is, there exists t_0 such that $(t \geq t_0 \Rightarrow h_t = h_{t_0} \wedge L(h_{t_0}) = L)$, where h_t denotes the hypothesis output by $\mathcal{IA}$ after processing t examples.

Most of the regular language inference algorithms output *DFAs* but recently, an algorithm called DeLeTe2 was proposed in [5]. It converges to an *RFSA* of size in between the sizes of the canonical *RFSA* and of the minimal *DFA* of the target language. It has the inconvenience that it generally outputs non consistent hypotheses. To overcome this difficulty, a program, also called DeLeTe2, has been proposed which obtains the best recognition rates -so far- when the languages to infer are obtained from random *NFAs* or regular expressions.

The generalizing process of the learning algorithms we propose in this paper is based in merging the states of the the maximal automaton of the positive samples in a random order, under the control of the negative samples. They are instances of the general method called OIL, which has been proposed in [7] by the same authors of the current paper.

3   Two Algorithms of the OIL Scheme

A general method was described in [7] which, on input of a set of blocks of positive and negative samples for a target regular language L, obtains an automaton that recognizes L in the limit. The method is called **OIL** (Order Independent Learning) and is described in Algorithm 1.

The method starts building the maximal automata for the first set of positive words $D_+^{(1)}$ and obtains a partition of the set of states such that the quotient automaton is irreducible in $\overline{D_-^{(1)}}$.

For every new block which is not consistent with the previous automaton (otherwise this new block is just deleted), it has to consider the following possibilities:

1. If the new set of negative samples is consistent with the current automaton,
   - It deletes the positive words accepted by the current hypothesis.
   - It builds the maximal automata $MA(D_+^{(i)})$ for the new set of positive words and adds to the set of negative ones the new block, obtaining D_-.
   - It finds a partition of the states of the disjoint union of the previous automaton with $MA(D_+^{(i)})$ such that the quotient automaton is irreducible in $\overline{D_-}$.

2. Otherwise it steps back and runs the algorithm starting with the first set of words, but considering the whole set of negative samples presented so far.

The convergence of the method was proved in [7] using the concepts of *irreducible automaton in a language* and of *universal sample*. To keep this paper self-contained, we recall these definitions and give a brief description of the proof of the convergence of the method.

Algorithm 1. OIL

Require: A sequence of blocks$\langle(D_+^{(1)}, D_-^{(1)}), (D_+^{(2)}, D_-^{(2)}), ..., (D_+^{(n)}, D_-^{(n)})\rangle$.
Ensure: An irreducible automaton consistent with the sample (recognizes the target language in the limit).
1: **STEP** 1:
2: Build $MA(D_+^{(1)})$;
3: $D_- = D_-^{(1)}$;
4: Find a partition π of the states of $MA(D_+^{(1)})$ such that $MA(D_+^{(1)})/\pi$
     is irreducible in $\overline{D_-}$.
5: **STEP** $i + 1$:
6: Let $\mathcal{A} = (Q, A, \delta, I, F)$ be the output of the algorithm after processing the first i
     blocks, for $i \geq 1$.
7: $D_- = D_- \cup D_-^{(i+1)}$.
8: **if** $\mathcal{A}$ is consistent with $(D_+^{(i+1)}, D_-^{(i+1)})$ **then**
9:     Go to **Step** $i + 2$.
10: **end if**
11: **if** $\mathcal{A}$ is consistent with $D_-^{(i+1)}$ **then**
12:     $D_+^{(i+1)'} = D_+^{(i+1)} - L(\mathcal{A})$;
13:     Build $MA(D_+^{(i+1)'})$; $//MA(D_+^{(i+1)'}) = (Q', A, \delta', I', F')//$
14:     $\mathcal{A}' = (Q \cup Q', A, \delta \cup \delta', I \cup I', F \cup F')$;
15:     Find a partition π of $Q \cup Q'$ such that $\mathcal{A}'/\pi$ is irreducible in $\overline{D_-}$.
16:     $\mathcal{A} = \mathcal{A}'/\pi$; Go to **Step** $i + 2$.
17: **end if**
18: **if** $\mathcal{A}$ is not consistent with $D_-^{(i+1)}$ **then**
19:     **Run OIL** with input $\langle(D_+^{(1)}, D_-), (D_+^{(2)}, D_-), \ldots, (D_+^{(i+1)}, D_-)\rangle$
20:     Go to **Step** $i + 2$.
21: **end if**
22: Return $\mathcal{A}$

A universal sample for L is a finite set $D_+ \subseteq L$ such that if π is any partition of the states of $MA(D_+)$, such that $MA(D_+)/\pi$ is irreducible in L, then $L(MA(D_+)/\pi) = L$. The proof of its existence (and its finiteness) can be seen in [7].

The following facts are also proved in [7]:

1. If $D_+ \subseteq L$ is finite and π is a partition of the states of $MA(D_+)$ such that $MA(D_+)/\pi$ is irreducible in L, then $MA(D_+)/\pi$ is isomorphic to a subautomaton of $\mathcal{U}$ (the universal automaton of L). If D_+ is a universal sample, then $MA(D_+)/\pi$ accepts L.
2. If D_+ is a universal sample, there exists a finite set $D_- \subseteq \overline{L}$ such that if π is a partition that makes $MA(D_+)/\pi$ to be irreducible in $\overline{D_-}$, then $MA(D_+)/\pi$ is irreducible in L and accepts L.

Based in those facts, the convergence of algorithm **OIL** is proved straight forward. In fact, if $(D_+^{(1)}, D_-^{(1)}), (D_+^{(2)}, D_-^{(2)}), ...$ is a complete presentation of a regular language L, there exists a value of n such that $D_+ = \bigcup_{i=1}^{n} D_+^{(i)}$ is universal for L. In this case,

- If $\bigcup_{i=1}^{n} D_-^{(i)}$ is enough to guarantee a correct partition of the set of states, OIL will return a correct hypothesis that will not change (line 9).
- Otherwise, there will exist $m > n$ such that $D_- = \bigcup_{i=1}^{m} D_-^{(i)}$ will avoid any erroneous merging when the first n blocks of positive samples are processed considering always D_- as the control set.

In both cases **OIL** will converge to a correct hypothesis.

3.1 The Algorithms MOIL and VOIL

Based on the previous method we propose two algorithms. They are particular instances of the OIL scheme in which the way to obtain an irreducible automaton (lines 4 and 15 of the method) is specified. So those lines have to be changed by the function described in Algorithm 2. The function Run (**Common Part OIL**) of line 3 of both algorithms means to run the OIL scheme with the specific way of obtaining the partition established by Algorithm 2.

Both algorithms have in common that:

- they canonically order the set of positive samples and consider that every block contains just a single word, so $D_+ = \{x_1, x_1, \ldots, x_n\}$ with $x_i \ll x_j$ if $i < j$ and consider every block of positive samples as having one word, that is, $D_+^{(i)} = \{x_i\}$.
- they consider the whole set of negative samples from the beginning, so $D_-^{(1)} = D_-$ and $D_-^{(i)} = \emptyset$ if $i > 1$.
- if the current state has several candidates to be merged with, it chooses the state that makes the resulting automaton to accept more positive samples.
- they run the method k times (this can be done since the merges are done randomly and thus, several automata can be obtained).

They differ in how the output is considered. The first algorithm, called **MOIL** (Minimal OIL) outputs the smallest of the k hypotheses, that is, the automaton having smallest number of states. It is described in Algorithm 3.

The second, called **VOIL** (Voting OIL), keeps the k hypotheses and classifies the test sample voting among those hypotheses. It is described in Algorithm 4.

This way of obtaining the partition does not affect to the convergence of the process, so both algorithms converge and they run in time $O(n^2 m)$, where n is the sum of the lengths of the positive samples and m the sum of the lengths of the negative ones.

4 Experimental Results

We present the results -both in recognition rates and in size of the inferred automata- of the algorithms MOIL and VOIL and compare them with the results

---

Algorithm 2. FindPartition($\mathcal{A}, x, D_+, D_-$)

Require: A sequence of words (D_+, D_-), $x \in D_+$ and an automaton $\mathcal{A}$ with states randomly ordered.
Ensure: An irreducible automaton $\mathcal{A}$ consistent with the current sample ($\{x_i : x_i \ll x\}$).
1: Build $MA(x)$; //states of $MA(x)$ randomly ordered after those of $\mathcal{A}$//
2: $\mathcal{A} = \mathcal{A} \cup MA(x)$; //disjoint union//
3: **for** every state q_i of $MA(x)$ in order **do**
4:    $\mathcal{A} = $ merge $(\mathcal{A}, q_i, q_k)$ where q_k is any previous state such that:
5:    (1) merge $(\mathcal{A}, q_k, q_i)$ is consistent with D_-
6:    (2) merge $(\mathcal{A}, q_k, q_i)$ recognizes more words of D_+ than any other merge $(\mathcal{A}, q, q_i)$
7: **end for**
8: Return $(\mathcal{A})$

Algorithm 3. MOIL

1: size $= \infty$; output $= \emptyset$;
2: **for** $i = 1$ to k **do**
3:    $\mathcal{A} = $ Run (**Common Part OIL**);
4:    **if** size$(\mathcal{A}) < $ size **then**
5:       size $= size(\mathcal{A})$; output $= \mathcal{A}$;
6:    **end if**
7: **end for**
8: Return (output)

Algorithm 4. VOIL

1: output $= \emptyset$;
2: **for** $i = 1$ to k **do**
3:    $\mathcal{A} = $ Run (**Common Part OIL**);
4:    output $= Append(output, \mathcal{A})$;
5: **end for**
6: Return ($output$)

---

obtained by the algorithms RedBlue [9] and DeLeTe2 [5] for the same task. These algorithms constitute the state of art in regular languages inference. The former behaves better when the source comes from random DFAs whereas the latter works better when the source comes from NFAs or from regular expressions.

4.1 Corpora

The regular languages we use in the experiments come from the corpora used to run the algorithms DeLeTe2 [5] and UFA [4]. The target languages in them are randomly generated from three different sources: regular expressions (RE), deterministic (DFA) and nondeterministic (NFA) automata. Once we eliminate repetitions we keep 102 RE, 120 NFAs and 119 DFAs.

We generate 500 different training samples and divide them in five incremental sets of size 100, 200, 300, 400 and 500. We also generate 1000 test samples, different from the training ones. The length of the samples randomly varies from zero to 18. The samples are labeled by every automaton, obtaining 15 different sets (5 for each of RE, DFA and NFA). The percentage of positive and negative samples in each of the training sets is not controlled.

4.2 Experiments

We have done two basic experiments to compare the behavior of the new algorithms with the previous DeLeTe2 and RedBlue:

1. We run five times the basic method and thus we obtain five (may be) different automata for which we measure:
   (a) The average size and recognition rate of the five automata.
   (b) The size and recognition rate of the smallest automata (MOIL).
   (c) We label the test set according to the majority vote between the five automata measuring this way the recognition rate (VOIL).
2. We fix the training corpus (we use the sets re_100 and nfa_100) and run k times the method, being k an odd number varying from 3 to 15 and proceed as in (1)(c).

The results obtained by the algorithms are summarize in Table 1. We can see that both strategies -choosing the smallest hypothesis and voting among the five output hypotheses- present better recognition rates than those obtained by the algorithm DeLeTe2 and Red Blue when the source comes from random regular expressions or from NFAs. Note that those better recognition rates are obtained with hypotheses which are much smaller than those obtained by the algorithm DeLeTe2.

The size of the output is not reported when the labels come from voting, as in this case several hypotheses participate in the decision and the size can not be compared to the other outputs.

On the other hand the recognition rates of MOIL and VOIL algorithms when the source comes from random DFAs are as poor as they are when one uses the algorithm DeLeTe2 and they are far away of the rates obtained by Red Blue. For the case of DeLeTe2, this fact has been explained saying that the inference methods based on the detection of inclusion relations do not behave well when the target automata do not have those inclusion relations between states. Denis et al. [5] have experimentally shown that this was the case for randomly generated DFAs.

For the case of the algorithms we present, we conjecture that the reason of this behavior is that the size of minimal NFAs (hypotheses) which are equivalent to relatively small DFAs (targets) may be very similar to the size of the DFAs, so the algorithms that narrow the search space to DFAs tend to behave better. On the other hand, relatively small NFAs may have substantially greater equivalent DFAs.

The second experiment is done over the sets of samples er_100 and nfa_100 and the value of k indicating the number of automata output by the algorithm varies from 3 to 15, following the odd numbers. Of course it was expected that the size

Table 1. Recognition rates and average size of the smallest hypothesis and recognition rates voting for $k = 5$ compared to those of DeLeTe2 and RedBlue algoritms

Id.	Smallest A. Rate	Smallest A. Size	Vote Rate	DeLeTe2 Rate	DeLeTe2 Size	RedBlue Rate	RedBlue Size
er_100	93.79	8.27	93.32	91.65	30.23	87.94	10
er_200	97.83	7.80	97.27	96.96	24.48	94.81	9.97
er_300	98.77	7.68	98.68	97.80	31.41	96.46	11.05
er_400	99.20	7.55	99.10	98.49	27.40	97.74	10.43
er_500	99.66	6.82	99.53	98.75	29.85	98.54	10.47
nfa_100	75.00	21.46	76.42	73.95	98.80	68.15	18.83
nfa_200	78.05	35.23	79.94	77.79	220.93	72.08	28.80
nfa_300	81.27	45.81	82.94	80.86	322.13	74.55	36.45
nfa_400	83.87	52.40	85.58	82.66	421.30	77.53	42.58
nfa_500	85.64	58.81	87.06	84.29	512.55	80.88	47.54
dfa_100	60.17	28.01	60.34	62.94	156.89	69.12	18.59
dfa_200	63.05	49.63	63.54	64.88	432.88	77.18	25.83
dfa_300	66.01	65.17	67.41	66.37	706.64	88.53	25.10
dfa_400	69.12	78.66	70.53	69.07	903.32	94.42	21.36
dfa_500	72.29	88.30	73.66	72.41	1027.42	97.88	18.75

Table 2. Recognition rates for different values of k over the set of samples er_100 and nfa_100

k	er_100 Smallest H. Rec.	er_100 Smallest H. Size	er_100 Vote Rec.	nfa_100 Smallest H. Rec.	nfa_100 Smallest H. Size	nfa_100 Vote Rec.
3	92.15	9.79	92.17	74.23	22.77	75.41
5	93.79	8.27	93.32	75.00	21.46	76.42
7	94.90	7.51	93.59	75.32	20.30	77.46
9	94.63	7.42	93.83	75.67	19.90	77.65
11	94.82	7.49	93.82	75.85	19.67	77.83
13	95.01	7.18	93.95	76.32	19.51	77.78
15	95.14	7.10	94.32	76.23	19.10	78.00

of the smallest automaton becomes smaller as k gets larger, so this experiment wanted to measure how the variation of k affects to the recognition rates both average and of the smallest output.

The results are summarized in Table 2. Note that the recognition rates increase as k gets bigger, which would indicate that for this algorithm, the smallest hypothesis output tends to be the best.

5   Conclusions

The general scheme proposed in [7] opens up new possibilities of inference algorithms. Two implementations of this method have been proposed and measured its performance, both in recognition rates as in size of the output. The results are very promising as they beat -both in recognition rates as in size of output- the algorithm DeLeTe2, which is considered the state of art when samples are taken from random NFAs or regular expressions. In the case of samples taken from random DFAs, the proposed algorithms and DeLeTe2 are far away of the results obtained by the RedBlue.

References

1. Abela, J., Coste, F., Spina, S.: Mutually Compatible and Incompatible Merges for the Search of the Smallest Consistent DFA. In: Paliouras, G., Sakakibara, Y. (eds.) ICGI 2004. LNCS (LNAI), vol. 3264, pp. 28–39. Springer, Heidelberg (2004)
2. Alvarez, G.I., Ruiz, J., Cano, A., García, P.: Nondeterministic Regular Positive Negative Inference NRPNI. In: Díaz, J.F., Rueda, C., Buss, A. (eds.) XXXI CLEI 2005, pp. 239–249 (2005)
3. Conway, J.H.: Regular algebra and finite machines. Chapman and Hall, Boca Raton (1971)
4. Coste, F., Fredouille, D.: Unambiguous automata inference by means of state merging methods. In: Lavrač, N., Gamberger, D., Todorovski, L., Blockeel, H. (eds.) ECML 2003. LNCS (LNAI), vol. 2837, pp. 60–71. Springer, Heidelberg (2003)
5. Denis, F., Lemay, A., Terlutte, A.: Learning regular languages using RFSAs. Theoretical Computer Science 313(2), 267–294 (2004)
6. García, P., Ruiz, J., Cano, A., Alvarez, G.: Inference Improvement by Enlarging the Training Set while Learning DFAs. In: Sanfeliu, A., Cortés, M.L. (eds.) CIARP 2005. LNCS, vol. 3773, pp. 59–70. Springer, Heidelberg (2005)
7. García, P., Vazquez de Parga, M., Alvarez, G., Ruiz, J.: Universal Automata and NFA learning. Theoretical Computer Science (to appear, 2008)
8. Gold, E.M.: Language identification in the limit. Information and Control 10, 447–474 (1967)
9. Lang, K., Perarlmutter, B., Price, R.: Results of the abbadingo one DFA learning competition and a new evidence-driven state merging algorithm. In: Honavar, V.G., Slutzki, G. (eds.) ICGI 1998. LNCS (LNAI), vol. 1433, pp. 1–12. Springer, Heidelberg (1998)
10. Oncina, J., García, P.: Inferring Regular Languages in Polynomial Updated Time. In: de la Blanca, P., Sanfeliú, Vidal (eds.) Pattern Recognition and Image Analysis. World Scientific, Singapore (1992)
11. Polák, L.: Minimalizations of NFA using the universal automaton. In: Domaratzki, M., Okhotin, A., Salomaa, K., Yu, S. (eds.) CIAA 2004. LNCS, vol. 3317, pp. 325–326. Springer, Heidelberg (2005)
12. Trakhtenbrot, B., Barzdin, Y.: Finite Automata: Behavior and Synthesis. North Holland Publishing Company, Amsterdam (1973)
13. Vázquez de Parga, M., García, P., Ruiz, J.: A family of algorithms for non deterministic regular languages inference. In: Parsons, S., Maudet, N., Moraitis, P., Rahwan, I. (eds.) ArgMAS 2005. LNCS (LNAI), vol. 4049, pp. 265–275. Springer, Heidelberg (2006)

Multi-Return Macro Tree Transducers

Kazuhiro Inaba[1], Haruo Hosoya[1], and Sebastian Maneth[2,3]

[1] University of Tokyo
{kinaba,hahosoya}@is.s.u-tokyo.ac.jp
[2] National ICT Australia
sebastian.maneth@nicta.com.au
[3] University of New South Wales, Sydney

Abstract. An extension of macro tree transducers is introduced with the capability of states to return multiple trees at the same time. Under call-by-value semantics, the new model is strictly more expressive than call-by-value macro tree transducers, and moreover, it has better closure properties under composition.

1 Introduction

Macro tree transducers (mtts) [1,2] are a finite-state machine model for tree translation. They are motivated by compilers and syntax-directed semantics and more recently have been applied to XML transformations and query languages [3,4]. An mtt processes the input tree top-down, starting in its initial state at the root node. Depending on its state and the label of the current input node, it produces an output subtree which possibly contains recursive state calls to children of the current node. State calls may appear at internal nodes of the output and can thus be nested. Technically speaking, this means that a (state, current label)-rule is parameterized by a sequence of arbitrary output trees. The number of such "accumulating parameters" is fixed for each state of the transducer. The initial state has zero parameters, because we are interested in tree-to-tree, not (tuple of trees)-to-tree translations. If every state has zero parameters, then we obtain an ordinary top-down tree transducer [5,6], in which all state calls appear at leaves of output rule trees. It is well-known that accumulating parameters add power: mtts realize strictly more translations than top-down tree transducers (for instance, top-down tree transducers have at most exponential size increase while mtts can have double-exponential increase). However, mtts have the asymmetry that, while each state can propagate multiple output trees in a top-down manner in its accumulating parameters, it cannot do it in a bottom-up manner because it is still restricted to return only a single output tree and such a tree cannot be decomposed once created.

This paper introduces an extension of mtts called *multi-return macro tree transducer* (mr-mtt) that addresses this asymmetry. In an mr-mtt, states may return multiple trees (but a fixed number for each state, with the initial state returning exactly one tree). As an example, consider a nondeterministic translation *twist* that takes as input monadic trees of the form $s(s(\ldots s(z)\ldots))$ and produces output trees of the form $root(t_1, t_2)$ where t_1 is a monadic tree over a's and b's (and a leaf e), and t_2 is a monadic tree over A's and B's such that t_2 is the reverse of t_1, and both have the same size as the input. For instance, $root(a(a(b(e))), B(A(A(E))))$ is a possible output tree for the input

O.H. Ibarra and B. Ravikumar (Eds.): CIAA 2008, LNCS 5148, pp. 102–111, 2008.
© Springer-Verlag Berlin Heidelberg 2008

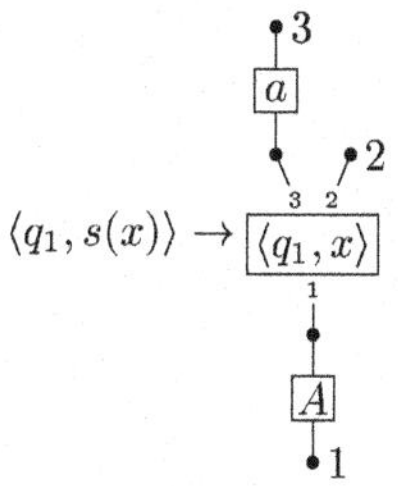

$$\langle q_0, \mathtt{s}(x)\rangle() \rightarrow \mathtt{let}\ (z_1, z_2) = \langle q_1, x\rangle(\mathtt{A}(\mathtt{E}))\ \mathtt{in\ root}(\mathtt{a}(z_1), z_2)$$
$$\langle q_0, \mathtt{s}(x)\rangle() \rightarrow \mathtt{let}\ (z_1, z_2) = \langle q_1, x\rangle(\mathtt{B}(\mathtt{E}))\ \mathtt{in\ root}(\mathtt{b}(z_1), z_2)$$
$$\langle q_0, \mathtt{z}\rangle() \rightarrow \mathtt{root}(\mathtt{e}, \mathtt{E})$$
$$\langle q_1, \mathtt{s}(x)\rangle(y_1) \rightarrow \mathtt{let}\ (z_1, z_2) = \langle q_1, x\rangle(\mathtt{A}(y_1))\ \mathtt{in}\ (\mathtt{a}(z_1), z_2)$$
$$\langle q_1, \mathtt{s}(x)\rangle(y_1) \rightarrow \mathtt{let}\ (z_1, z_2) = \langle q_1, x\rangle(\mathtt{B}(y_1))\ \mathtt{in}\ (\mathtt{b}(z_1), z_2)$$
$$\langle q_1, \mathtt{z}\rangle(y_1) \rightarrow (\mathtt{e}, y_1)$$

Fig. 1. Rules of the multi-return mtt realizing *twist*

$\mathtt{s}(\mathtt{s}(\mathtt{s}(\mathtt{z})))$. Such a translation can be realized by an mr-mtt with the rules of Fig. 1. The state q_1 is "multi-return"; it generates pairs of trees. The first component is generated in a top-down manner: at each input $\mathtt{s}$-node, an $\mathtt{a}$-labeled output node is generated which has below it the first component (z_1) of the recursive q_1-call at the child of the current input node. This is the left branch of the whole output tree. The right branch is obtained by the second component and is generated in a bottom-up manner through the accumulating parameter of q_1. As we will show, the above translation *twist*, cannot be realized by any conventional mtt. The proof of inexpressibility is technically involved and uses special normal forms of *twist* in order to derive a contradiction. In general it is very difficult to prove that a given translation cannot be realized by a tree transducer class, because hardly any tools exist for showing inexpressibility. Note that multi-return mtts have the same size increase as mtts.

In the case of deterministic and total deterministic transducers, mr-mtts are equally powerful as mtts. For the total deterministic case this already follows from the fact that tree generating top-down tree-to-graph transducers (trgen-tg) realize the same translations as total deterministic mtts [7]. Mr-mtts can be seen as particular trgen-tgs; e.g., the forth rule of *twist* is depicted as trgen-tgs rule in the left of Fig. 1.

Besides an increase in expressive power, mr-mtts have better closure properties than mtts: they are closed under left *and* right composition with total deterministic top-down tree transducers (D_tTs). This is rather surprising, because ordinary call-by-value mtts are not closed under composition with D_tTs. The latter was already shown in [1] for the case of left-composition. The case of right-composition is proved in this paper (using *twist*). In fact, our proof can even be "twisted" to the call-by-name semantics of mtts to show that call-by-name mtts are also not closed under right-composition with D_tT. Thus, the two main classes of mtts, call-by-value and call-by-name are both not closed under right-composition with D_tT, while call-by-value multi-return mtts are closed.

2 Definitions

A set Σ with a mapping *rank* : $\Sigma \rightarrow \mathbb{N}$ is called a *ranked set*. We often write $\sigma^{(k)}$ to indicate that $rank(\sigma) = k$. The *product* of a ranked set A and a set B is the ranked set $A \times B = \{\langle a, b\rangle^{(k)} \mid a^{(k)} \in A, b \in B\}$. The set T_Σ of *trees* t over a ranked set Σ is defined by the BNF $t ::= \sigma(t_1, \ldots, t_k)$ for $\sigma^{(k)} \in \Sigma$. We often omit parentheses for rank-0 and rank-1 symbols and write them as strings. For example, we write abcd instead of $\mathtt{a}(\mathtt{b}(\mathtt{c}(\mathtt{d}())))$.

When $x_1^{(0)}, \ldots, x_m^{(0)} \in \Sigma$ and $t, t_1, \ldots, t_m \in T_\Sigma$, *(simultaneous) substitution* of $t_1, \ldots, t_m$ for $x_1, \ldots, x_m$ in t is written $t[x_1/t_1, \ldots, x_m/t_m]$ (or sometimes $t[\vec{x}/\vec{t}]$ for brevity) and defined to be a tree where every occurrence of x_i ($i = 1, \ldots, m$) in t is replaced by the corresponding t_i. For a ranked set Σ and rank-0 symbol $\square \notin \Sigma$, a tree $\mathcal{C} \in T_{\Sigma \cup \{\square\}}$ that contains exactly one occurrence of $\square$ is called a *one-hole Σ-context*. We write $\mathcal{C}[t]$ as a shorthand for $\mathcal{C}[\square/t]$.

Macro Tree Transducers. Throughout the paper, we fix the sets of input variables $X = \{x_1, x_2, \ldots\}$ and accumulating parameters $Y = \{y_1, y_2, \ldots\}$ which are all of rank 0 and assume any other ranked set to be disjoint with X and Y. The set X_i is defined as $\{x_1, \ldots, x_i\}$, and Y_i is defined similarly.

A *macro tree transducer* (mtt) is specified as $M = (Q, q_0, \Sigma, \Delta, R)$, where Q, Σ, and Δ are finite ranked sets. We call Q the set of *states*, $q_0 \in Q$ the *initial state* of rank 0, Σ the *input alphabet*, Δ the *output alphabet*, and R the finite set of translation *rules* of the form $\langle q^{(m)}, \sigma^{(k)}(x_1, \ldots, x_k)\rangle(y_1, \ldots, y_m) \to r$ where the right-hand side r is a tree from $T_{\Delta \cup (Q \times X_k) \cup Y_m}$. Rules of this form are called $\langle q, \sigma\rangle$-rules. An mtt is *deterministic* (*total*, respectively) if there exists at most (at least) one $\langle q, \sigma\rangle$-rule for every $\langle q, \sigma\rangle \in Q \times \Sigma$. Also, an mtt is *linear* if the right-hand side of every rule in R contains at most one occurrence of x_i for each $x_i \in X$. We define the ranked set $\Lambda_M = \Delta \cup (Q \times T_\Sigma)$ and call trees in T_{Λ_M} the *sentential forms* of M. The translation realized by M is defined in terms of the rewrite relation $\Rightarrow_M$ over sentential forms. The "one-step derivation" relation that we use, is the *call-by-value* (also known as *IO-mode*) derivation relation. Let $u, u' \in T_{\Lambda_M}$. Then $u \Rightarrow_M u'$ if there is a $\langle q, \sigma\rangle$-rule in R with right-hand side r, a one-hole Λ_M-context $\mathcal{C}$, input trees $s_1, \ldots, s_k \in T_\Sigma$, and output trees $t_1, \ldots, t_m \in T_\Delta$, such that $u = \mathcal{C}[\langle q, \sigma(\vec{s})\rangle(\vec{t})]$ and $u' = \mathcal{C}[r[\vec{x}/\vec{s}, \vec{y}/\vec{t}]]$. We define $u\downarrow_M = \{t \in T_\Delta \mid u \Rightarrow_M^* t\}$ and the translation $\tau(M)$ realized by M as $\{\langle s, t\rangle \in T_\Sigma \times T_\Delta \mid t \in \langle q_0, s\rangle\downarrow_M\}$. The class of translations realized by mtts is denoted by *MT*. The restricted class of translations realized by deterministic (total, or linear) transducers is denoted by prefix D ($_t$, or L, respectively). An mtt with all its states of rank-0 (i.e., without accumulation parameters) is called *top-down tree transducer* and abbreviated as tt; the corresponding class of translations is denoted by T. As a special case, a linear total deterministic tt with one state only is also called *linear tree homomorphism* and the corresponding class of translations is denoted by *LHOM*.

The operator ; denotes sequential composition. That is, $\tau_1 ; \tau_2 = \{(s, t) \mid \exists w.(s, w) \in \tau_1, (w, t) \in \tau_2\}$ for two translations τ_1 and τ_2, and $A_1 ; A_2 = \{\tau_1 ; \tau_2 \mid \tau_1 \in A_1, \tau_2 \in A_2\}$ for two classes of translations A_1 and A_2.

Multi-return Macro Tree Transducers. The multi-return macro tree transducer extends mtt by construction and deconstruction (via let expressions) of tuples of return values. Each state now has a "dimension" which is the number of trees it returns. In addition to X and Y, we fix the set $Z = \{z_1, z_2, \ldots\}$ of let-variables, of rank 0, and assume it to be disjoint with any other ranked set.

Definition 1. A *multi-return macro tree transducer* (mr-mtt) of dimension $d \geq 1$ is a tuple $(Q, q_0, \Sigma, \Delta, R, D)$, where Q, q_0, Σ, and Δ are as for mtts, D is a mapping from Q to $\{1, \ldots, d\}$ such that $D(q_0) = 1$, and R is a set of rules of the form

$\langle q^{(m)}, \sigma^{(k)}(x_1, \ldots, x_k)\rangle(y_1, \ldots, y_m) \to r$ where $r \in rhs^{D(q)}$ and, for $e \geq 1$ the set rhs^e is defined as:

$$r ::= l_1 \ldots l_n \, (u_1, \ldots, u_e) \qquad\qquad\qquad (n \geq 0)$$

$$l ::= \text{let} \, (z_{j+1}, \ldots, z_{j+D(q')}) = \langle q'^{(k)}, x_i\rangle(u_1, \ldots, u_k) \text{ in} \qquad (x_i \in X_k)$$

with $u_1, u_2, \ldots \in T_{\Delta \cup Y_m \cup Z}$. We usually omit parentheses around tuples of size one, i.e., write like let $z_j = \cdots$ in u_1. We require any rule to be well-formed, that is, the leftmost occurrence of any variable z_i must appear at a "binding" position (between 'let' and '='), and the next occurrence (if any) must appear after the 'in' corresponding to the binding occurence. *Total*, *deterministic*, and *linear* mr-mtts are defined as for mtts.

As for mtts, the call-by-value semantics of mr-mtts is defined in terms of rewriting over sentential forms. Note that the target of rewriting is always the state call in the very first let expression of a given sentential form (this expression cannot have let-variables). Let $M = (Q, q_0, \Sigma, \Delta, R, D)$ be an mr-mtt. The set K_M of sentential forms κ of M is defined by the following BNF

$$\kappa ::= l_1 \ldots l_n \, u_1$$

$$l ::= \text{let} \, (z_{j+1}, \ldots, z_{j+D(q)}) = \langle q^{(k)}, s\rangle(u_1, \ldots, u_k) \text{ in}$$

where $s \in T_\Sigma$ and $u_1, u_2, \ldots \in T_{\Delta \cup Z}$. Again, we require the sentential forms to be well-formed in the same sense as for the right-hand sides of rules. Let $\kappa_1, \kappa_2 \in K_M$. Then $\kappa_1 \Rightarrow_M \kappa_2$ if κ_1 has the form let $(z_{j+1}, \ldots, z_{j+D(q)}) = \langle q^{(m)}, \sigma^{(k)}(s_1, \ldots, s_k)\rangle$ $(t_1, \ldots, t_m)$ in κ where $s_i \in T_\Sigma$ and $t_i \in T_\Delta$, and there is a $\langle q, \sigma\rangle$-rule in R with the right-hand side $l_1 \ldots l_n \, (u_1, \ldots, u_{D(q)})$ and κ_2 has the form $l'_1 \ldots l'_n \kappa'$ where

$$l'_i = l_i[x_1/s_1, \ldots, x_k/s_k, y_1/t_1, \ldots, y_m/t_m] \qquad (i = 1, \ldots, n)$$

$$u'_k = u_k[y_1/t_1, \ldots, y_m/t_m] \qquad\qquad (k = 1, \ldots, D(q))$$

$$\kappa' = \kappa[z_{j+1}/u'_1, \ldots, z_{j+D(q)}/u'_{D(q)}].$$

Here, we adopt the standard convention that substitution automatically avoids inappropriate variable capture by silently renaming let-variables.

We define $\kappa{\downarrow}_M = \{t \in T_\Delta \mid \kappa \Rightarrow^*_M t\}$. The translation $\tau(M)$ realized by M is defined as $\{(s, t) \in T_\Sigma \times T_\Delta \mid t \in (\text{let } z = \langle q_0, s\rangle \text{ in } z){\downarrow}_M\}$. The class of translations realized by mr-mtts is denoted by *MM*. By *d-MM* with $d \geq 1$, we denote the class of translations realized by mr-mtts of dimension d. The prefixes D, $_t$, and L are used in the same way as for mtts. Note that $MT \subseteq$ *1-MM* (by replacing each nested state call of the mtt by a let-binding), with determinism and totality being preserved.

For technical convenience, we sometimes regard rhs^d as a subset of $T_{\Delta \cup (Q \times X_k) \cup Y_m}$ $\cup Z \cup L^d_{mr}$ where $L^d_{mr} = \{\text{let}^{(4)}_1, \ldots, \text{let}^{(3+d)}_d, \text{tup}^{(1)}_1, \ldots, \text{tup}^{(d)}_d\}$, which should be understood as the abstract syntax tree of its textual representation.

3   Simulation of Multi-Return MTTs by MTTs

This section shows that any mr-mtt can be decomposed into a three-fold composition of simpler transducers, namely, a pre-processor for dealing with let-bindings, an mtt doing the essential translation, and a post-processor for dealing with tuples.

Tuple Return Values. Following the well-known (Mezei-Wright-like [8]) tupling-selection technique, we use special symbols to represent tuples and selection. For $n \geq 2$, define $L^n_{tup} = \{\tau_2^{(2)}, \ldots, \tau_n^{(n)}, \pi_1^{(1)}, \ldots, \pi_n^{(1)}\}$. Intuitively, τ_i means "construct a tuple of i elements" and π_i means "select the i-th element of". We define the transducer $tups^n_\Delta$ whose purpose is to recursively convert subtrees of the form $\pi_i(\tau_k(t_1, \ldots, t_k))$ into t_i. The *tupling-and-selection transducer $tups^n_\Delta$* is the linear deterministic total top-down tree transducer with input alphabet $\Delta \cup L^n_{tup}$, output alphabet Δ, set of states $\{q_1, \ldots, q_n\}$, initial state q_1, and the following rules for each q_i:

$$\langle q_i, \pi_k(x_1) \rangle \rightarrow \langle q_k, x_1 \rangle$$
$$\langle q_i, \tau_k(x_1, \ldots, x_k) \rangle \rightarrow \langle q_1, x_i \rangle \text{ if } 1 \leq i \leq k$$
$$\rightarrow \langle q_1, x_1 \rangle \text{ otherwise}$$
$$\langle q_i, \delta(x_1, \ldots, x_m) \rangle \rightarrow \delta(\langle q_1, x_1 \rangle, \ldots, \langle q_1, x_m \rangle) \text{ for } \delta^{(m)} \in \Delta, m \geq 0.$$

Lemma 2. $MM \subseteq 1\text{-}MM ; LD_tT$. *Totality, determinism, and numbers of rules and parameters are preserved.*

Proof. Let $M = (Q, \Sigma, \Delta, q_0, R, D)$ be an mr-mtt of dimension d. We define another mr-mtt $M' = (Q, \Sigma, \Delta \cup L^d_{tup}, q_0, R', D')$, where $D'(q) = 1$ for all $q \in Q$ and $R' = \{\langle q, \sigma(\vec{x}) \rangle (\vec{y}) \rightarrow et(r) \mid \langle q, \sigma(\vec{x}) \rangle (\vec{y}) \rightarrow r \in R\}$. The *explicit-tupling* function et is inductively defined as follows:

$$et(u_1) = u_1$$
$$et((u_1, \ldots, u_e)) = \tau_e(u_1, \ldots, u_e) \qquad\qquad \text{if } e > 1$$
$$et(\text{let } z_1 = \langle q, x \rangle (\vec{u}) \text{ in } r') = \text{let } z_1 = \langle q, x \rangle (\vec{u}) \text{ in } et(r')$$
$$et(\text{let } (z_1, \ldots, z_m) = \langle q, x \rangle (\vec{u}) \text{ in } r') =$$
$$\text{let } z_1 = \langle q, x \rangle (\vec{u}) \text{ in } et(r'[z_1/\pi_1(z_1), \ldots, z_m/\pi_m(z_1)])) \quad \text{if } m > 1.$$

We also apply et to sentential forms in K_M, and $tups^d_\Delta$ to sentential forms in $K_{M'}$. Then for all $\kappa_1, \kappa_2 \in K_M$ and $\kappa'_1, \kappa'_2 \in K_{M'}$ such that $et(\kappa_1) = \tau(tups^d_\Delta)(\kappa'_1)$, $\kappa_1 \Rightarrow_M \kappa_2$, and $\kappa'_1 \Rightarrow_{M'} \kappa'_2$ assuming that the two derivations are done by corresponding rules, we have $et(\kappa_2) = \tau(tups^d_\Delta)(\kappa'_2)$. By induction on the number of derivation steps, we have that $t' \in \tau(M')(s)$ if and only if $\tau(tups^d_\Delta)(t') \in \tau(M)(s)$. Thus, $\tau(M) = \tau(M') ; \tau(tups^d_\Delta)$ which proves the lemma. $\qquad\square$

Let-Bindings. Even without multiple return values, let-bindings still provide some additional power with respect to ordinary mtts. For example, the right-hand side of an mr-mtt rule let $z = \langle q, x \rangle$ in $\delta(z, z)$ is not necessarily equivalent to the mtt one $\delta(\langle q, x \rangle, \langle q, x \rangle)$. In the former rule, the two children of δ must be the same tree that is returned by a single state call $\langle q, x \rangle$. On the other hand, in the latter rule, two state calls $\langle q, x \rangle$ may return different trees due to nondeterminism. Thus, for simulating let-bindings we must first fully evaluate state calls to an output tree and *then* copy them if required. Basically, such order of evaluation can be simulated using accumulating parameters and state calls, since we adopt call-by-value semantics. For instance, the above example of mr-mtt rule is equivalent to the mtt rule $\langle p, x \rangle (\langle q, x \rangle)$ using an auxiliary state p and a set of auxiliary rules $\langle p, \sigma(\vec{x}) \rangle (y) \rightarrow \delta(y, y)$ for every $\sigma \in \Sigma$.

However, this approach does not work for nested let-bindings. The problem is that the calls of auxiliary states to simulate copying must be applied to some child of the current node. Consider the following rule:

$$\langle q, \sigma(x_1, \dots, x_n)\rangle \rightarrow \text{let } z_1 = \langle q_1, x_1\rangle \text{ in}$$
$$\text{let } z_2 = \langle q_2, x_2\rangle(z_1) \text{ in}$$
$$\vdots$$
$$\text{let } z_n = \langle q_n, x_n\rangle(z_1, \dots, z_{n-1}) \text{ in } \delta(z_1, \dots, z_n).$$

To simulate the first let-binding, we need an auxiliary state call like $\langle p, x_i\rangle(\langle q_1, x_1\rangle)$, and we do the rest of the work in the $\langle p, \sigma\rangle$-rules. But this time, we have to generate other state calls such as $\langle q_2, x_2\rangle(z_1)$ in the auxiliary rule, which is impossible since in $\langle p, x_i\rangle$ we are only able to apply states to the *children* of x_i, while x_2 is a *sibling* of x_i.

One possible solution is to insert auxiliary nodes of rank 1 above each node of the input tree, similar as done for the removal of stay moves in [9]. We can then run the auxiliary states on the inserted nodes in order to simulate the let-bindings. For instance, the first two lets of the above rule can be simulated by

$$\langle q, \bar{\sigma}_1(x_1)\rangle \rightarrow \langle p, x_1\rangle(\langle\langle q_1, 1\rangle, x_1\rangle, \alpha)$$
$$\langle p, \bar{\sigma}_2(x_1)\rangle(y_1, y_2) \rightarrow \langle p, x_1\rangle(y_1, \langle\langle q_2, 2\rangle, x_1\rangle(y_1)),$$

where α is an arbitrary output symbol of rank 0. The new auxiliary state $\langle q', i\rangle$ "skips" the next barred nodes and calls q' at the i-th child of the next σ-node. For $n \in \mathbb{N}$, we define mon_Σ^n ("*monadic insertion*") as the linear tree homomorphism which, for each $\sigma^{(k)} \in \Sigma$, has the rule $\langle q, \sigma(x_1, \dots, x_k)\rangle \rightarrow \bar{\sigma}_1(\bar{\sigma}_2(\cdots\bar{\sigma}_n(\sigma(\langle q, x_1\rangle, \dots, \langle q, x_k\rangle))\cdots))$.

Lemma 3. *1-MM $\subseteq$ LHOM ; MT. Totality and determinism are preserved. If the mr-mtt has n states of rank $\leq k$, r rules, $\leq l$ let-bindings per rule, and m input symbols of rank $\leq b$, then the mtt has at most $n + r + nb$ states, $k + l$ parameters, and $(r + nb)(l + 1)$ (or $(r + nb)(m + l + 1)$ in the case of totality) rules.*

Proof. Let the mr-mtt be $(Q, \Sigma, \Delta, q_0, R, D)$. The state set of the simulating mtt is $Q \cup \{p_r^{(k+m)} \mid r \in R, m = \text{number of let-bindings in } r, k = \text{rank of the state of } r\} \cup (Q \times \{1, \dots, b\})$. Suppose the mr-mtt has a rule $r \in R$ of the form (where $q^{(k)} \in Q$) $\langle q, \sigma(\vec{x})\rangle(y_1, \dots, y_k) \rightarrow \text{let } z_1 = \langle q_1, x_{i_1}\rangle(\vec{u}_1) \text{ in } \dots \text{let } z_m = \langle q_m, x_{i_m}\rangle(\vec{u}_m) \text{ in } u$. Let ζ be the substitution $[z_1/y_{k+1}, \dots, z_m/y_{k+m}]$. The simulating mtt has the following rules each corresponding to one let-binding:

$$\langle q, \bar{\sigma}_1(x_1)\rangle(y_1, \dots, y_k) \rightarrow \langle p_r, x\rangle(y_1, \dots, y_k, \langle\langle q_1, i_1\rangle, x_1\rangle(\vec{u}_1), \alpha, \dots, \alpha)$$
$$\langle p_r, \bar{\sigma}_2(x_1)\rangle(y_1, \dots, y_{k+m}) \rightarrow \langle p_r, x\rangle(y_1, \dots, y_{k+1}, \langle\langle q_2, i_2\rangle, x_1\rangle(\vec{u}_2\zeta), \alpha, \dots, \alpha)$$
$$\vdots$$
$$\langle p_r, \bar{\sigma}_m(x_1)\rangle(y_1, \dots, y_{k+m}) \rightarrow \langle p_r, x\rangle(y_1, \dots, y_{k+m-1}, \langle\langle q_m, i_m\rangle, x_1\rangle(\vec{u}_m\zeta))$$
$$\langle p_r, \bar{\sigma}_{m+1}(x_1)\rangle(y_1, \dots, y_{k+m}) \rightarrow \langle p_r, x\rangle(y_1, \dots, y_{k+m})$$
$$\vdots$$
$$\langle p_r, \bar{\sigma}_l(x_1)\rangle(y_1, \dots, y_{k+m}) \rightarrow \langle p_r, x\rangle(y_1, \dots, y_{k+m})$$
$$\langle p_r, \sigma(\vec{x})\rangle(y_1, \dots, y_{k+m}) \rightarrow u\zeta$$

where α is an arbitrary rank-0 output symbol. These dummy arguments are passed just for supplying exactly m arguments and will never appear in output trees.

The states $\langle q, j \rangle \in Q \times \{1, \ldots, b\}$ are used to remember the correct child number j where to apply q. The rules for $\langle q, j \rangle$ are:

$$\langle \langle q, j \rangle, \bar{\sigma}_i(x_1) \rangle (\vec{y}) \rightarrow \langle \langle q, j \rangle, x_1 \rangle (\vec{y}) \text{ for each } \sigma \in \Sigma \text{ and } 1 \leq i \leq l$$
$$\langle \langle q, j \rangle, \sigma(\vec{x}) \rangle (\vec{y}) \rightarrow \langle q, x_j \rangle (\vec{y}) \text{ for each } \sigma \in \Sigma \text{ of rank } \geq j.$$

It should be clear that this mtt preceded by mon_Σ^l realizes the same translation as the original mr-mtt. Let us take a look at totality and determinism. The original state q remains total (or deterministic, respectively) for a symbol $\bar{\sigma}_1$ if and only if it is total (deterministic) for σ in the original rule set. Newly added states p_r are deterministic if the original state q was. Newly added states $\langle q, j \rangle$ are deterministic. For the remaining undefined part (q-rules for $\bar{\sigma}_2, \ldots, \bar{\sigma}_l$ and σ and $\langle q, j \rangle$-rules for σ with rank $< j$), we add dummy rules to regain totality if the original mr-mtt was total. □

By combining Lemmas 2 and 3, we obtain the main result of this section.

Lemma 4. $MM \subseteq LHOM ; MT ; LD_tT.$

Since, by Theorem 7.6 of [1], DMT and D_tMT are both closed under left- and- right-composition with D_tT, we obtain the following corollary.

Corollary 5. $DMM = DMT \quad and \quad D_tMM = D_tMT.$

The right part of Corollary 5 follows also from the result of [7], that total deterministic tree generating top-down tree-to-graph transducers (trgen-tg) are equivalent to D_tMT, because as mentioned in the Introduction, mr-mtts are a special case of trgen-tgs.

4   Simulation of MTTs by Multi-Return MTTs

We now show that MM is closed under right-composition with D_tT. The idea is to construct the simulating mr-mtt by *running* the tt on the right-hand side of each rule of the original mr-mtt. Let $\{p_1, \ldots, p_n\}$ be the set of states of the tt. We construct the rules so that if a state q returns a tuple $(t_1, \ldots, t_d)$, then the corresponding state q' of the simulating mr-mtt returns $(\langle p_1, t_1 \rangle \downarrow, \ldots, \langle p_1, t_d \rangle \downarrow, \ldots, \langle p_n, t_1 \rangle \downarrow, \ldots, \langle p_n, t_d \rangle \downarrow)$.

Lemma 6. $MM ; D_tT \subseteq MM$. *Totality and determinism are preserved. The number of parameters and the dimension of the resulting mr-mtt are n times larger the original ones, where n is the number of states of the tt. The number of states increases by 1, and the number of rules is at most twice as that of the original one.*

Proof. Let $M = (Q, \Sigma, \Delta, q_0, R_M, D)$ be an mr-mtt and $N = (P, \Delta, \Gamma, p_1, R_N)$ be a D_tT with $P = \{p_1, \ldots, p_n\}$. We define the mr-mtt $M' = (Q', \Sigma, \Gamma, \hat{q}, R', D')$, where $Q' = \{q'^{(kn)} \mid q^{(k)} \in Q\} \cup \{\hat{q}^{(0)}\}$, $D'(q') = n \cdot D(q)$, $D'(\hat{q}) = 1$, and

$$R' = \{\langle q', \sigma(\vec{x}) \rangle (y_1, \ldots, y_{kn}) \rightarrow runN(r) \mid \langle q, \sigma(\vec{x}) \rangle (y_1, \ldots, y_k) \rightarrow r \in R_M\}$$
$$\cup \{\langle \hat{q}, \sigma(\vec{x}) \rangle \rightarrow runN_0(r) \mid \langle q_0, \sigma(\vec{x}) \rangle \rightarrow r \in R_M\}$$

where *runN* and *runN*$_0$ are defined inductively as follows. Recall from the Definitions the "tree view" of the right-hand side of our mr-mtt (with *tup* and *let* node).

$$runN_0(\mathsf{tup}_1(u_1)) = \mathsf{tup}_1(\langle p_1, u_1 \rangle \downarrow_{N'})$$
$$runN_0(\mathsf{let}_e(z_{s+1},\ldots, z_{s+e}, \langle q, x \rangle (u_1,\ldots, u_k), \kappa) = \mathsf{let}_{en}(\mathbf{z}_{s,e}, \langle q, x \rangle (\mathbf{pu}_k), runN_0(\kappa))$$
$$runN(\mathsf{tup}_e(u_1, \ldots, u_e)) = \mathsf{tup}_{en}(\mathbf{pu}_e)$$
$$runN(\mathsf{let}_e(z_{s+1},\ldots, z_{s+e}, \langle q, x \rangle (u_1,\ldots, u_k), \kappa) = \mathsf{let}_{en}(\mathbf{z}_{s,e}, \langle q, x \rangle (\mathbf{pu}_k), runN(\kappa))$$

where $\mathbf{z}_{s,e} = z_{sn+1}, \ldots, z_{sn+en}$, $\mathbf{pu}_m = \langle p_1, u_1 \rangle \downarrow_{N'}, \ldots, \langle p_1, u_m \rangle \downarrow_{N'}, \ldots, \langle p_n, u_1 \rangle$ $\downarrow_{N'}, \ldots, \langle p_n, u_m \rangle \downarrow_{N'}$ and N' is N extended by the rules $\langle p_j, y_i \rangle \rightarrow y_{(i-1)n+j}$ and $\langle p_j, z_i \rangle \rightarrow z_{(i-1)n+j}$ for $1 \leq i \leq \mu, 1 \leq j \leq n$, where μ is the maximum of the number of parameters and the number of let-bindings appearing in R_M. Then, by induction on the number of derivation steps, we can show that $\langle p_j, \langle q, t \rangle (\vec{u}) \downarrow_M \rangle \downarrow_{N'}$ is equal to the corresponding subtuples of $\langle q', t \rangle (\mathbf{pu}_k) \downarrow_{M'}$, which proves the lemma.   □

Note that the proof of Lemma 6 relies on the *totality* of N. It simulates all p_i-translations, some of which may not contribute to the final output. If N is not total, this try-and-discard strategy does not work. Undefined calls that are to be discarded will stop the whole translation, since we are considering call-by-value evaluation. The proof relies also on the *determinism* of N. If p_j is nondeterministic, multiple calls of $p_j(y_i)$ may generate different outputs and thus replacing them by the same single variable $y_{(i-1)n+j}$ yields incorrect results.

Next, we investigate the case of left-composition. The idea is, again, to simulate the composition $D_tT; MT$ by constructing an mr-mtt by running the mtt on the rules of tt. Note that we crucially use let-bindings here for simulating parameter copying of the original mtt. Suppose we have a tt rule $\langle q, \mathsf{e}(x_1) \rangle \rightarrow \mathsf{a}(\mathsf{b}, \langle q, x_1 \rangle)$ and mtt rules:

$$\langle p, \mathsf{a}(x_1, x_2) \rangle (y_1) \rightarrow \langle p, x_1 \rangle (\langle p, x_2 \rangle (y_1))$$
$$\langle p, \mathsf{b} \rangle (y_1) \rightarrow \mathsf{d}(y_1, y_1).$$

Using a let-binding, we construct a rule of the simulating transducer $\langle \langle p, q \rangle, \mathsf{e}(x_1) \rangle (y_1)$ $\rightarrow \mathsf{let}\ z = \langle \langle p, q \rangle, x_1 \rangle (y_1)$ in $\mathsf{d}(z, z)$ which correctly preserves the original semantics that the left and right child of the d node are equal. Note that without let-bindings, we cannot avoid duplicating a state call; at best we will have the rule $\langle \langle p, q \rangle, \mathsf{e}(x_1) \rangle (y_1) \rightarrow$ $\mathsf{d}(\langle \langle p, q \rangle, x_1 \rangle (y_1), \langle \langle p, q \rangle, x_1 \rangle (y_1))$, which is incorrect because the duplicated state calls may nondeterministically yield different outputs, which is not originally intended.

Lemma 7. $D_tT; MT \subseteq 1\text{-}MM$. *Totality and determinism are preserved. The number of states is n times larger, where n is the number of states of the D_tT. The number of parameters remains the same. The number of rules may be double exponential with respect to the depth of right-hand sides of the D_tT.*

Proof. Let $M_1 = (Q, \Sigma, \Gamma, q_0, R_1)$ be a D_tT and $M_2 = (P, \Gamma, \Delta, p_0, R_2)$ an mtt. Define $M_\times = (P \times Q, \Sigma, \Delta, \langle p_0, q_0 \rangle, R, D)$ with $R = \{\langle \langle p, q \rangle, \sigma(\vec{x}) \rangle (\vec{y}) \rightarrow \kappa \mid \kappa \in f_z(\langle p, r \rangle (\vec{y}), z), r$ is the right-hand side of the unique $\langle q, \sigma \rangle$-rule of $R_1\}$. Intuitively, a state $\langle p, q \rangle$ denotes the translation by q followed by p. The relation f_z is very similar to the derivation relation of M_2 (thus, $f_z(\langle p, r \rangle (\vec{y}), z)$ should be intuitively read as

$\langle p, r \rangle(\vec{y}) \downarrow_{M_2}$). However, to "factor out" let-bindings for avoiding incorrect duplication of state calls, we define it slightly differently. For the sake of simplicity, we define f_z as a nondeterministic function as follows:

$$f_z(y, u) = u[z/y] \qquad\qquad y \in Y \cup Z$$
$$f_z(\delta(t_1, \ldots, t_k), u) = f_{z_1}(t_1, \ldots f_{z_k}(t_k, u[z/\delta(z_1, \ldots, z_k)]) \cdots) \qquad \delta \in \Delta$$
$$f_z(\langle p, \langle q, x_i \rangle \rangle(t_1, \ldots, t_k), u) = f_{z_1}(t_1, \ldots f_{z_k}(t_k,$$
$$\text{let } z = \langle \langle p, q \rangle, x_i \rangle(z_1, \ldots, z_k) \text{ in } u) \ldots)$$
$$f_z(\langle p, \gamma(\vec{s}) \rangle(t_1, \ldots, t_k), u) = f_{z_1}(t_1, \ldots f_{z_k}(t_k, f_z(\kappa[\vec{x}/\vec{s}, \vec{y}/\vec{z}], u) \cdots)$$
$$\text{for every right-hand side } \kappa \text{ of any } \langle p, \gamma \rangle\text{-rule}, \gamma \in \Gamma.$$

The last argument u of f_z denotes a context where the translated right-hand side of the rule should be placed. By induction on the structure of the input tree s, we can prove $\langle p, \langle q, s \rangle \downarrow_{M_1}\rangle(\vec{t}) \downarrow_{M_2} = \langle \langle p, q \rangle, s \rangle(\vec{t}) \downarrow_{M_\times}$ for $p \in P$, $q^{(k)} \in Q$, $\vec{t} \in T_\Delta^k$, and $s \in T_\Sigma$, which proves the lemma. $\qquad\square$

We can now generalize the lemma in two directions: the second translation from MT to MM, and the first translation from total to partial.

Lemma 8. $D_t T ; MM \subseteq MM$. *Totality and determinism are preserved.*

Proof. By Lemma 4, $D_t T ; MM \subseteq D_t T ; LHOM ; MT ; LD_t T$. By Lemma 6.9 of [6], which says that $D_t T$ is closed under composition, the latter is in $D_t T ; MT ; LD_t T$. By Lemma 7 this is included in $MM ; LD_t T$, which is in MM by Lemma 6. $\qquad\square$

Lemma 9. $DT ; MM \subseteq MM$.

Proof. We have $DT \subseteq DT\text{-}FTA ; D_t T$ (Lemma 5.22 of [1]) where $DT\text{-}FTA$ is the class of partial identity translations recognized by deterministic top-down tree automata, Lemma 8, and $DT\text{-}FTA ; MM \subseteq MM$ (can be proved by the same construction as for Lemma 5.21 of [1]; for every rule of the initial state, we add one let-binding that carries out the run of the automaton). These three lemmas prove $DT ; MM \subseteq MM$. $\qquad\square$

Using the lemmas proved up to here, we obtain the two main theorems: the characterization of mr-mtts in terms of mtts and its closure properties.

Theorem 10. $MM = LHOM ; MT ; LD_t T$. *Determinism and totality are preserved.*

Theorem 11. $DT ; MM \subseteq MM$ *and* $MM ; D_t T \subseteq MM$.

5 Expressiveness

First we show that mr-mtts of dimension 1 are already more powerful than normal mtts even without tuple-returning capability. On page 123 of [1], a counterexample to show $MT \subsetneq LHOM ; MT$ is given without proof. (The difficult part of their counterexample to be realized in MT is the generation of two *identical* pairs of a nondeterministic relabeling of the input, which is similar to our *twist* translation that generates *mutually reverse* pair of nondeterministic relabelings.) By this example and Lemma 7, we have the following proposition, which shows that binding intermediate trees by let-expressions itself adds expressiveness.

Proposition 12. $MT \subsetneq 1\text{-}MM$.

Moreover, mr-mtts that return pairs of trees are strictly more powerful than single return ones. Here we only give a sketch of the proof. For more detail, see [10] (which proves the unrealizability in MT, but it also works for $1\text{-}MM$ and call-by-name mtts).

Theorem 13. $1\text{-}MM \subsetneq 2\text{-}MM$.

Proof (Sketch). A translation realized in $2\text{-}MM$, namely, the *twist* translation of the Introduction is shown not to be realizable by any mr-mtt with dimension 1. The proof is by contradiction. Note that the number of outputs of *twist* is exponential with respect to the size of the input, that is, $|twist(\mathsf{s}^n\mathsf{z})| = 2^n$. We first assume an mr-mtt M of dimension 1 to realize *twist*, and then by giving two normal forms of sentential forms (a weak normal form that contains no let-variables under output symbols, and a strong normal form that is the weak normal form with at most one let-binding), we can show that $|\tau(M)(\mathsf{s}^n\mathsf{z})| = O(n^2)$, which is a contradiction. $\square$

Note that the composition $MT; D_tT$ can realize *twist*. We can construct an mtt (both in call-by-value and call-by-name semantics) that nondeterministically translates the input $\mathsf{s}^n\mathsf{z}$ into all monadic trees of the form $(\mathsf{a}|\mathsf{b})^n(\mathsf{A}|\mathsf{B})^n\mathsf{E}$ such that the lower-part is the reverse of the upper-part. Then we split such monadic trees to lower- and upper-parts by a D_tT transducer, so that the composition of these two translations realizes *twist*. Thus, together with the proof of Theorem 13, we have the following theorem.

Theorem 14. $MT; D_tT \not\subseteq MT$ and $MT_{OI}; D_tT \not\subseteq MT_{OI}$, where MT_{OI} denotes the class of translations realized by call-by-name mtts.

Acknowledgements. We like to thank Joost Engelfriet for his comment that mr-mtts can be simulated by simpler transducers, which led us to the results in Sections 3 and 4. This work was partly supported by Japan Society for the Promotion of Science.

References

1. Engelfriet, J., Vogler, H.: Macro tree transducers. JCSS 31, 71–146 (1985)
2. Fülöp, Z., Vogler, H.: Syntax-Directed Semantics: Formal Models Based on Tree Transducers. Springer, Heidelberg (1998)
3. Maneth, S., Berlea, A., Perst, T., Seidl, H.: XML type checking with macro tree transducers. In: Principles of Database Systems (PODS), pp. 283–294 (2005)
4. Perst, T., Seidl, H.: Macro forest transducers. IPL 89, 141–149 (2004)
5. Rounds, W.C.: Mappings and grammars on trees. MST 4, 257–287 (1970)
6. Thatcher, J.W.: Generalized sequential machine maps. JCSS 4, 339–367 (1970)
7. Engelfriet, J., Vogler, H.: The translation power of top-down tree-to-graph transducers. JCSS 49, 258–305 (1994)
8. Mezei, J., Wright, J.B.: Algebraic automata and context-free sets. Inf. Contr. 11, 3–29 (1967)
9. Engelfriet, J., Maneth, S.: A comparison of pebble tree transducers with macro tree transducers. Acta Informatica 39, 613–698 (2003)
10. Inaba, K., Hosoya, H.: Multi-return macro tree transducers. In: PLAN-X (2008)

Computing Convex Hulls by Automata Iteration

François Cantin[1], Axel Legay[2], and Pierre Wolper[1]

[1] Université de Liège, Institut Montefiore, Liège, Belgium
{cantin,pw}@montefiore.ulg.ac.be
[2] Carnegie Mellon University, Computer Science Department, Pittsburgh, PA
alegay@cs.cmu.edu

Abstract. This paper considers the problem of computing the real convex hull of a finite set of n-dimensional integer vectors. The starting point is a finite-automaton representation of the initial set of vectors. The proposed method consists in computing a sequence of automata representing approximations of the convex hull and using extrapolation techniques to compute the limit of this sequence. The convex hull can then be directly computed from this limit in the form of an automaton-based representation of the corresponding set of real vectors. The technique is quite general and has been implemented. Also, our result fits in a wider scheme whose objective is to improve the techniques for converting automata-based representation of constraints to formulas.

1 Introduction

Automata-based representations for sets of integer and real vectors have been a subject of growing interest in recent years [1,3,13,17,19]. While usually not optimal for specific problems, they provide much stronger generality and canonicity than other representations. For instance, in this context, combining real and integer constraints is very simple once the right framework has been set up [4]. The benefit of using automata-based representations for arithmetic sets could be even greater if one could, whenever appropriate, freely move between this and other representations such as explicit constraints. Going from constraints to automata has long been successfully studied [9,2,7], but going in the other direction is substantially more difficult. Nevertheless, it has been shown that it is possible [18] to construct constraint formulas from automata representing sets of integer vectors and that, under some restrictions, this can be done quite effectively [16].

One case that is not well handled though is that of finite sets of integer vectors. Indeed, imagine that a finite set of integers is represented by constraints and that an automaton representing this set is built from these. Since the set is finite, this acyclic automaton lacks the structure needed to construct the corresponding constraints. One is thus stuck with the automaton or with an enumerative representation of the set it defines, which is far from satisfactory. The work presented here was motivated by this problem with the idea of solving it along the following lines. The first step is to compute, as an automaton, a minimal dense set of

O.H. Ibarra and B. Ravikumar (Eds.): CIAA 2008, LNCS 5148, pp. 112–121, 2008.
© Springer-Verlag Berlin Heidelberg 2008

real-vectors that contains the finite set of integers. On this automaton, techniques similar to those of [16,18] could then be applied to obtain constraints.

This paper proposes a solution for the first step in the form of a purely automata-based technique for computing the real convex hull (*i.e.* the convex hull over $\mathbb{R}^n$) of a finite automaton-represented finite set of integers. Note that, beyond the motivation outlined above, this is also a worthwhile challenge of independent interest in the area of automata-based representations. In simple terms, our approach proceeds as follows. We start with an automata-based representation of a finite set of integer vectors. We then repeatedly apply a transformation to this automaton that adds to the set the vectors that are mid-way between those it includes. This yields an infinite sequence of automata-represented sets. The limit of this infinite sequence is then computed as an automaton, using the extrapolation-based techniques of [5]. This limit is not quite the convex closure since we prove that it will only contain convex combinations of the initial vectors with coefficients that are multiples of a negative power of 2. This limit thus needs to be "completed" in order to obtain the convex hull and we show that this can be done by computing its topological closure. Bar a technical point due to the fact that some reals have two encodings in our framework, the computation of the topological closure is quite an easy step. This being done, the closure is obtained.

The extrapolation-based techniques of [5], which have so far only been applied in the context of "regular model checking" [8], are semi-algorithms that tackle the undecidable problem of computing the limit of an infinite sequence by extrapolating finite prefixes of the sequence. For the procedure above to work correctly, we thus depend on the result of the extrapolation being exact, which is not guaranteed a priori. Nevertheless, this can be checked as described in [5], but one interesting twist is that checking safety (enough is obtained) can be done much more easily (and just as correctly) after computing the topological closure. This is due to the fact that taking the topological closure yields an automaton that falls within an easier to handle class. Checking preciseness (nothing is added) with the techniques of [5] is probably not practical, but in the present situation one can exploit the properties of the extrapolation and make this check just as simple as the safety check.

Our approach has been implemented and the implementation has actually served as a guide to hone our results. The implementation has been tested and performs well, within the bounds allowed by the automata manipulations needed for the computation of the limit of the sequence of approximations. We certainly do not claim to outperform more traditional methods when they apply, our goal being to establish the basis of a different approach with interesting characteristics, performance gains not being part of our initial agenda. Also note that complexity analysis would not yield useful information since, at the heart of our approach, lies the extrapolation procedure which is only a semi-amgorithm.

Related Work. Computing convex hulls is of course a well studied problem of independent interest. There are quite a few known techniques for computing convex hulls of a set of vectors in a non automata-theoretic setting. Among these a long series of algorithms specialized to the 2D and 3D case and widely used and studied in computational geometry. Algorithms for the general case (any dimensions) have also been studied [12]. All those algorithms, which are generally more efficient than an automata-based approach, require an enumeration of the set, which we avoid here. In [14], Finkel and Leroux show that the convex hull of a (possibly infinite) set of integer vector represented by an automaton is a computable polyhedron. The algorithm in [14] can be applied to infinite sets and is guaranteed to terminate. On the other hand, this algorithm, may require to enumerate the set represented by the automaton and is restricted to work in $\mathbb{Z}^n$.

Some proofs had to be omitted due to space constraints. A self-contained long version of this paper is available at [11].

2   Automata-Theoretic Background

2.1   Automata on Infinite Words

An infinite word (or ω-word) w over an alphabet Σ is a mapping $w : \mathbb{N} \to \Sigma$ from the natural numbers to Σ. The length-k prefix of an infinite word w, i.e. the finite-word $w(0), w(1), \ldots, w(k-1)$, will be denoted by $pref_k(w)$.

A *Büchi automaton* on infinite words is a five-tuple $A = (Q, \Sigma, \delta, q_0, F)$, where Q is a finite set of states, Σ is the input alphabet, $\delta : Q \times \Sigma \to 2^Q$ is a *transition function* ($\delta : Q \times \Sigma \to Q$ if the automaton is deterministic), q_0 is the initial state, and F is a set of accepting states. A *run* π of a Büchi automaton $A = (Q, \Sigma, \delta, q_0, F)$ on an ω-word w is a mapping $\pi : \mathbb{N} \to Q$ such that $\pi(0) = q_0$ and for all $i \geq 0$, $\pi(i+1) \in \delta(\pi(i), w(i))$ (nondeterministic automata) or $\pi(i+1) = \delta(\pi(i), w(i))$ (deterministic automata). Let $inf(\pi)$ be the set of states that occur infinitely often in a run π. A run π is said to be accepting if $inf(\pi) \cap F \neq \emptyset$. An ω-word w is accepted by a Büchi automaton if that automaton has some accepting run on w. The language $L_\omega(A)$ of infinite words defined by a Büchi automaton A is the set of ω-words it accepts.

We will also use the notion of *weak* automata [21]. Roughly speaking, a weak automaton is a Büchi automaton such that each of the strongly connected components of its graph contains either only accepting or only non-accepting states. Not all omega-regular languages can be accepted by weak deterministic Büchi automata, nor even by weak nondeterministic automata. However, there are algorithmic advantages to working with weak automata. Indeed, weak deterministic automata can be complemented simply by inverting their accepting and non-accepting states, while the complementation operation for Büchi automata requires intricate algorithms that not only are worst-case exponential, but are also hard to implement and optimize [24]. There exists a simple determinization procedure for weak automata [22], which produces Büchi automata that are deterministic, but not necessarily weak. However, we will be working in a context in which the obtained automata are always easily transformed into weak auatomata [4]. A final advantage of weak deterministic Büchi automata is that they admit a normal form, which is unique up to isomorphism [20].

2.2 Automata-Based Representations of Sets of Integers and Reals

In this section, we briefly introduce the representation of sets of integer and real vectors by finite automata. Details are only given for the case of real vectors, the case of integer vectors being a simplification of the former where automata on finite words replace automata on infinite words. A survey on this topic can be found in [7].

In order to make a finite automaton recognize numbers, one needs to establish a mapping between these and words. Our encoding scheme corresponds to the usual notation for reals and relies on an arbitrary integer base $r > 1$. We encode a number x in base r, most significant digit first, by words of the form $w_I \star w_F$, where w_I encodes the integer part x_I of x as a finite word over $\{0, \ldots, r-1\}$, the special symbol "$\star$" is a separator, and w_F encodes the fractional part x_F of x as an infinite word over $\{0, \ldots, r-1\}$. Negative numbers are represented by their r's complement. The length p of $|w_I|$, which we refer to as the *integer-part length* of w, is not fixed but must be large enough for $-r^{p-1} \leq x_I < r^{p-1}$ to hold.

According to this scheme, each number has an infinite number of encodings, since their integer-part length can be increased unboundedly. In addition, the rational numbers whose denominator has only prime factors that are also factors of r have two distinct encodings with the same integer-part length. For example, in base 10, the number $11/2$ has the encodings $005 \star 5(0)^\omega$ and $005 \star 4(9)^\omega$, "ω" denoting infinite repetition. We call these respectively the *high* and *low* encodings and refer collectively to them as *dual* encodings.

To encode a vector of real numbers, we represent each of its components by words of identical integer-part length. This length can be chosen arbitrarily, provided that it is sufficient for encoding the vector component with the highest magnitude. An encoding of a vector $\mathbf{x} \in \mathbb{R}^n$ can indifferently be viewed either as a n-tuple of words of identical integer-part length over the alphabet $\{0, \ldots, r - 1, \star\}$, or as a single word w over the alphabet $\{0, \ldots, r-1\}^n \cup \{\star\}^1$.

Real vectors being encoded by infinite words, a set of vectors can be represented by an infinite-word automaton accepting the corresponding encodings. Since a real vector has an infinite number of possible encodings, we have to choose which of these the automata will recognize. A natural choice is to accept all encodings. This leads to the following definition.

Definition 1. *Let $n > 0$ and $r > 1$ be integers. A base-r n-dimension* Real Vector Automaton (RVA) *[6] is a Büchi automaton $\mathcal{A} = (Q, \Sigma, \delta, Q_0, F)$ over the alphabet $\Sigma = \{0, \ldots, r-1\}^n \cup \{\star\}$, such that (1) Every word accepted by $\mathcal{A}$ is an encoding in base r of a vector in $\mathbb{R}^n$, and (2) For every vector $\mathbf{x} \in \mathbb{R}^n$, $\mathcal{A}$ accepts either all the encodings of $\mathbf{x}$ in base r, or none of them.*

An RVA is said to *represent* the set of vectors encoded by the words that belong to its accepted language. In [4], it is shown that if the set represented by the

---

[1] In practice, one reads the bits of the vector components in a round robin way, which avoids an exponential-size alphabet. However, for presentation purposes, it is easier to view all same-position bits of the vector components as being read simultaneously.

RVA can be defined in the first-order theory of linear constraints, then this RVA can be transformed into an equivalent weak deterministic Büchi automata. If not explicitly mentioned, we assume that the RVAs we manipulate are minimal weak deterministic Büchi automata. Also, since our implementation works with a base 2 representation, we will present all our results in this context, knowing that they can be generalized to other bases.

3   Convex Hulls and Topological Concepts

We recall a few notations and definitions that are used throughout the paper.

Let $\mathbb{Z}$, $\mathbb{Q}$, and $\mathbb{R}$ be respectively the sets of integers, rational, and reals, and let $\mathbb{Z}^n$, $\mathbb{Q}^n$, and $\mathbb{R}^n$ denote the usual n-dimensional Euclidean vector spaces. Vectors are written in boldface, e.g. $\mathbf{x}$, and scalars without emphasis, e.g. a. The *ith* component of a vector $\mathbf{x} \in \mathbb{R}^n$ is denoted by $\mathbf{x}[i]$. We say that a set $E \in \mathbb{R}^n$ is *convex* iff for each $\mathbf{x_1}, \mathbf{x_2} \in E$, we have $\{\alpha\mathbf{x_1} + (1 - \alpha)\mathbf{x_2} \mid \alpha \in [0,1]\} \subseteq E$. We will also use the following usual definitions.

Definition 2. *Given a set $E \subseteq \mathbb{R}^n$, the* convex hull *of E is the set $Conv(E) \subseteq \mathbb{R}^n$ defined by*

$$Conv(E) = \{\mathbf{x} \mid \exists\mathbf{x_1}, \ldots, \mathbf{x_k} \in E \; \exists\lambda_1, \ldots, \lambda_k \in [0,1] \; \mathbf{x} = \sum_{i=1}^{k} \lambda_i\mathbf{x}_i \; \wedge \sum_{i=1}^{k} \lambda_i = 1\}$$

The *Euclidean distance* between two vectors $\mathbf{x}, \mathbf{x}' \in \mathbb{R}^n$, denoted by $|\mathbf{x} - \mathbf{x}'|$ is the real number $\sqrt{\sum_{i=1}^{n}(\mathbf{x}[i] - \mathbf{x}'[i])^2}$. The *open ball* centered in $\mathbf{x} \in \mathbb{R}^n$ with a radius $\epsilon > 0$ is the subset $B_{(\mathbf{x},\epsilon)} = \{\mathbf{x}' \mid |\mathbf{x} - \mathbf{x}'| < \epsilon\}$. A set $E \subseteq \mathbb{R}^n$ is said to be *open* if for any $\mathbf{x} \in E$ there exists $\epsilon > 0$ such that $B_{(\mathbf{x},\epsilon)} \subseteq E$. A *closed* set E is a subset of $\mathbb{R}^n$ such that $\mathbb{R}^n \setminus E$ is an open set. A *compact* set in $\mathbb{R}^n$ is a bounded and closed set. We use the concept of *topological closure* of a set.

Definition 3. *Given a set $E \subseteq \mathbb{R}^n$, the* topological closure *$TC(E)$ of E is the smallest closed set that contains E.*

When dealing with infinite words, we will be working with the topology on words induced by the distance defined by

$$d(w, w') = \begin{cases} \frac{1}{|common(w,w')|+1} & \text{if } w \neq w' \\ 0 & \text{if } w = w', \end{cases}$$

where $common(w, w')$ denotes the longest common prefix of w and w'. Notice that, among words that validly encode vectors, words that are topologically close encode vectors that are close according to the Euclidean distance, the reverse also being true except for the cases where dual encodings can appear.

4   Computing Convex Hulls

In this section, we describe a technique to compute the convex hull over $\mathbb{R}^n$ of a *finite* set $E = \{\mathbf{x_1}, \mathbf{x_2}, \ldots, \mathbf{x_k}\}$ defined over $\mathbb{Z}^n$.

The technique proceeds by constructing a sequence of approximations of the convex hull by adding the vectors that are mid-way between those obtained so far. This is quite an obvious way to proceed, but in order to exploit it, we need to formalize its exact properties. We use the following definitions.

Definition 4. *The median sequence of E is the* infinite *sequence $E_0, E_1, E_2, \ldots$ such that (1) $E_0 = E$ and (2) $E_{i+1} = E_i \cup \{(\mathbf{x_1} + \mathbf{x_2})/2 \mid \mathbf{x_1}, \mathbf{x_2} \in E_i\}$ for each $i \in \mathbb{N}$.*

The *limit* of the median sequence of E, denoted by E^*, is defined by $\bigcup_{i=0}^{\infty} E_i$. It is easy to see that each vector $\mathbf{v}$ of E^* is also a vector of $Conv(E)$. However, E^* is not the complete convex hull, but can be characterized using the following definition.

Definition 5. *The 2-chopped convex hull of a finite subset $E=\{\mathbf{x_1}, \mathbf{x_2}, \ldots, \mathbf{x_k}\}$ of $\mathbb{Z}^n$ is the* maximal *subset $Conv_{2^*}(E)$ of $Conv(E)$, where for each $\mathbf{v} \in Conv_{2^*}(E)$, $\mathbf{v} = \sum_{i=1}^{k} \lambda_i \mathbf{x_i}$ with $\lambda_i \in [0,1]$, $\sum_{i=1}^{k} \lambda_i = 1$, and $\lambda_i = \frac{k_i}{2^{m_i}}$ for $k_i, m_i \in \mathbb{N}$ and $i \in [1, \ldots, k]$.*

Theorem 1. *For any finite subset $E = \{\mathbf{x_1}, \mathbf{x_2}, \ldots, \mathbf{x_k}\}$ of $\mathbb{Z}^n$, the limit of its median sequence and its 2-chopped convex hull coincide, i.e $E^* = Conv_{2^*}(E)$.*

Even though the 2-chopped convex hull of a set E is not quite its real convex hull, it contains vectors that are arbitrarily close to any element of the full convex closure. In fact, the convex hull of E is included in the topological closure of its 2-chopped hull. The following theorem states that these two sets coincide.

Theorem 2. *For any finite subset $E = \{\mathbf{x_1}, \mathbf{x_2}, \ldots, \mathbf{x_k}\}$ of $\mathbb{Z}^n$, we have that $TC(Conv_{2^*}(E)) = Conv(E)$.*

Computing the real convex hull of a finite set of integer vectors can thus be reduced to compute the topological closure of the limit of its median sequence. We now investigate how to compute $Conv_{2^*}(E)$ and $TC(E)$ for a set E described by an *RVA*.

5   Algorithmic Issues

We consider a finite subset $E = \{\mathbf{x_1}, \mathbf{x_2}, \ldots, \mathbf{x_k}\}$ of $\mathbb{Z}^n$ that is represented by a (weak deterministic) RVA A_E. Our goal is to compute an RVA that represents the convex hull over $\mathbb{R}^n$ of E. According to the results in Section 4, this can be done by computing an RVA A_{E^*} representing the limit E^* of the median sequence of E, and then computing an RVA representing the topological closure of E^*. We now show how these two problems can be tackled by automata-based semi-algorithms.

5.1   Computing an RVA for the 2-Chopped Hull

Computing the elements of the median sequence. We notice that since E is finite and represented by a weak deterministic RVA, each element in its median sequence can also be represented in the same way (see [11] for details).

Computing the limit of the median sequence. Computing A_{E^*} amounts to computing the limit of an infinite sequence of weak deterministic automata. To finitely compute this limit, we obviously need some form of "speed-up" technique. We will use the extrapolation-based technique proposed in [5]. A rough description of the technique is as follows. The technique proceeds by comparing successive automata in a prefix of the sequence, trying to identify the difference between these in the form of an "increment", and extrapolating the repetition of this increment by adding loops to the last automaton of the prefix. If the extrapolation is *correct*, then the limit is computed, else, one has to lengthen the prefix and restart the extrapolation process. Checking correctness of the extrapolation is a non trivial procedure whose description is, for technical reasons, postponed to Section 5.3. The technique has been implemented in a tool called T(O)RMC [23]. The tool relies on the LASH package [15] for automata manipulation procedures, but implements the specific algorithms given in [5]. There is no guarantee that T(O)RMC will produce a result since the general problem of computing the limit of a sequence of automata is undecidable.

It is worth mentioning that the automata produced by T(O)RMC are weak, but not necessarily deterministic [5]. Furthermore, if one tries to determinize these automata, one might end up combining accepting and non accepting connected components, which leads to an automaton that is not weak. This situation actually occurred systematically in our experiment, which is not surprising since the 2-chopped convex hull of a set of integer vectors is not definable in $\langle \mathbb{R}, +, \leq, Z \rangle$ and thus falls outside the guaranteed reach of weak deterministic automata given in [4].

5.2   Computing the Topological Closure of an RVA-Represented Set

In this section, we explicitly consider RVAs that may not be weak deterministic. Consider a set $E \subseteq \mathbb{R}^n$ represented by an RVA A_E. Our goal is to compute an RVA $A_{TC(E)}$ that represents the topological closure of E. The intuition behind the computation is that we need to add to the language accepted by A_E, all words that are arbitrarily close to words of this language. This is fairly straightforward to do since we only need to add words that have arbitrarily long common prefixes with accepted words. A simple step to do this is to make accepting all states of the fractional part of the automaton. Of course, this will compute the topological closure within the topology on infinite words, but this also almost computes the vector Euclidean topological closure as it is shown by the following result.

Theorem 3. *Let A_E be a RVA representing a vector set E. Let $\overline{A}_E$ be A_E with all states of its fractional part made accepting, and let $W(\mathbf{v}, n)$ be the set of all the encodings of a vector $\mathbf{v} \in \mathbb{R}^n$. For each vector $\mathbf{v} \in \mathbb{R}^n$, $W(\mathbf{v}, n) \cap L(\overline{A}_E) \neq \emptyset$ if and only if $\mathbf{v} \in TC(E)$.*

Theorem 3 guarantees that $\overline{A}_E$ contains at least one encoding for each vector in $TC(E)$. However the automaton $\overline{A}_E$ is not necessarily $A_{TC(E)}$. Indeed, there is no guarantee that $\overline{A}_E$ will contain *all* the encodings of each vector included in the topological closure. We thus need an extra step that adds all missing encodings. To do this, we use the fact that an automaton that recognizes words that are dual encodings of the same numbers can be built with simple automata-based operations (see [10] for the detailed algorithm).

5.3   Correctness Criterion

After having constructed the extrapolation A_E^* of a finite sequence $A_E^{i_1}$, $A_E^{i_2}$, ..., $A_E^{i_l}$ of automata representing elements in the median sequence of a set E, it remains to check whether it accurately corresponds to what we really intend to compute, i.e., A_{E^*}. This is done by first checking that the extrapolation is *safe*, in the sense that it captures all words accepted by A_{E^*} ($L(A_{E^*}) \subseteq L(A_E^*)$), and then checking that it is *precise*, i.e. that it accepts no more words than A_{E^*} ($L(A_E^*) \subseteq L(A_{E^*})$). To lighten the presentation, we will often use the notations and operations defined for sets of vectors directly on the automata that represent them.

Safety. We first investigate how to check whether A_E^* is safe. The idea is simply to perform one more mid-point adding step on A_E^* and to check that this does not change the accepted language. Given a set E, let $C_2(E)$ be the set $\{\mathbf{y} \mid \mathbf{y} = (\mathbf{x_1} + \mathbf{x_2})/2 \mid \mathbf{x_1}, \mathbf{x_2} \in E\}$. We have the following theorem.

Theorem 4. *Let A_E^* and A_{E^*} be respectively the extrapolation of a median automata sequence for a set E and a representation of the actual limit of this sequence. We have that, if $L(C_2(A_E^*)) \subseteq L(A_E^*)$, then $L(A_{E^*}) \subseteq L(A_E^*)$.*

The required computation step is thus to check that $L(C_2(A_E^*)) \subseteq L(A_E^*)$. This is simple except for the fact that, the result of the extrapolation is representable by an automaton which is weak but not necessarily deterministic (see Section 5.1), and hence testing inclusion requires to complement a Büchi automaton. The problem can be solved by first applying the topological closure step to A_E^* and then performing the safety check given by Lemma 4.

It is easy to see that doing this has no impact on the result of the test. However it has an impact on its efficiency since the strongly connected component added by T(O)RM are made uniformly accepting status by the procedure that computes the topological closure. This ensures that we only need to complement weak deterministic automata.

Preciseness. Checking preciseness could be performed with the techniques proposed in [5]. However, this solution (which involves counter automata) is computationally demanding and not really practical. In the present situation, one can however propose a much more efficient scheme that exploits the properties of the extrapolation. Due to space limitation, we only sketch the procedure here, details can be found in [11].

Definition 6. *Let $E \in \mathbb{R}$ be a convex set. The set of extreme points of E, denoted $S(E)$, is defined as $\{\mathbf{x} \in E \mid (\neg \exists (\mathbf{x_1}, \mathbf{x_2}) \in E)(\mathbf{x_1} \neq \mathbf{x_2} \wedge \mathbf{x} = (\mathbf{x_1} + \mathbf{x_2})/2)\}$.*

By extension we will also use the notation $S(A)$ on automata representing vector sets. We now present our preciseness check. Instead of checking whether $L(A_E^*) \subseteq L(A_{E^*})$, we check $L(TC(A_E^*)) \subseteq L(Conv(A_E))$. This is enough to ensure that we do not compute an overapproximation of the hull.

Theorem 5. *Let A_E^* be an RVA that represents a safe extrapolation of the limit of the median sequence of a finite set of integer vectors represented by the RVA A_E. If $L(S(TC(A_E^*))) \subseteq L(A_E)$, then $L(TC(A_E^*)) \subseteq L(Conv(A_E))$.*

In summary, to check the preciseness of an RVA A_E^* that represents a safe extrapolation of the limit of the median sequence of a finite set $E \subseteq \mathbb{Z}^n$, we first compute an RVA $TC(A_E^*)$ for the topological closure of the set represented by A_E^*. We then compute an automaton for $S(TC(A_E^*))$, which is easily done by computing the difference between $TC(A_E^*)$ and $C_2(TC(A_E^*))$. Finally, one checks whether the language of the resulting automaton is included in that of A_E. Again, all complementation operations are only applied to weak deterministic Büchi automata.

Infinite Sets. It is worth mentioning that our results do not extend as such to the computation of the real convex hull of an infinite set of integer vectors. Indeed, by relying on the computation of a topological closure, our methodology produces convex hulls which are closed sets. However there are infinite sets of integer vectors whose convex hull is not closed.

6   A Brief Note on the Experimental Results

The approach presented in this paper has been tested on several examples using a prototype implementation that relies on T(O)RMC. We computed the convex hull over $\mathbb{R}^n$ of finite convex sets in $\mathbb{Z}^n$, of the difference/union of finite convex sets in $\mathbb{Z}^n$, and of arbitrary finite sets of points in $\mathbb{Z}^n$. Some experiments that validate the fact that our approach performs well for sets for which the representation by automata remains manageable are reported in [11].

References

1. Bartzis, C., Bultan, T.: Construction of efficient bdds for bounded arithmetic constraints. In: Garavel, H., Hatcliff, J. (eds.) TACAS 2003. LNCS, vol. 2619, pp. 394–408. Springer, Heidelberg (2003)
2. Boigelot, B.: Symbolic Methods for Exploring Infinite State Spaces. Collection des publications de la Faculté des Sciences Appliquées, Liège (1999)
3. Boigelot, B., Herbreteau, F.: The power of hybrid acceleration. In: Ball, T., Jones, R.B. (eds.) CAV 2006. LNCS, vol. 4144, pp. 438–451. Springer, Heidelberg (2006)
4. Boigelot, B., Jodogne, S., Wolper, P.: An effective decision procedure for linear arithmetic over the integers and reals. ACM Transactions on Computational Logic 6(3), 614–633 (2005)

5. Boigelot, B., Legay, A., Wolper, P.: Omega-regular model checking. In: Jensen, K., Podelski, A. (eds.) TACAS 2004. LNCS, vol. 2988, pp. 561–575. Springer, Heidelberg (2004)

6. Boigelot, B., Rassart, S., Wolper, P.: On the expressiveness of real and integer arithmetic automata. In: Larsen, K.G., Skyum, S., Winskel, G. (eds.) ICALP 1998. LNCS, vol. 1443, pp. 152–163. Springer, Heidelberg (1998)

7. Boigelot, B., Wolper, P.: Representing arithmetic constraints with finite automata: An overview. In: Stuckey, P.J. (ed.) ICLP 2002. LNCS, vol. 2401, pp. 1–19. Springer, Heidelberg (2002)

8. Bouajjani, A., Jonsson, B., Nilsson, M., Touili, T.: Regular model checking. In: Emerson, E.A., Sistla, A.P. (eds.) CAV 2000. LNCS, vol. 1855, pp. 403–418. Springer, Heidelberg (2000)

9. Boudet, A., Comon, H.: Diophantine equations, presburger arithmetic and finite automata. In: Proc of ICALP. LNCS, vol. 1159, pp. 30–43. Springer, Heidelberg (1996)

10. Cantin, F.: Techniques d'extrapolation d'automates: Application au calcul de la fermeture convexe. Master's thesis, University of Liège, Belgium (2007)

11. Cantin, F., Legay, A., Wolper, P.: Computing convex hulls by automata iteration. Technical report, University of Liège (2008), http://www.montefiore.ulg.ac.be/~legay/papers/ciaa08rep.pdf

12. Chazelle, B.: An optimal convex hull algorithm in any fixed dimension. Discrete & Computational Geometry 10, 377–409 (1993)

13. Eisinger, J., Klaedtke, F.: Don't care words with an application to the automata-based approach for real addition. In: Ball, T., Jones, R.B. (eds.) CAV 2006. LNCS, vol. 4144, pp. 67–80. Springer, Heidelberg (2006)

14. Finkel, A., Leroux, J.: The convex hull of a regular set of integer vectors is polyhedral and effectively computable. IPL (96-1), 30–35 (2005)

15. The Liège Automata-based Symbolic Handler (LASH), http://www.montefiore.ulg.ac.be/~boigelot/research/lash/

16. Latour, L.: From automata to formulas: Convex integer polyhedra. In: Proc. of LICS, pp. 120–129. IEEE Computer Society, Los Alamitos (2004)

17. Leroux, J.: Algorithmique de la vérification des systèmes à compteurs. Approximation et accélération. Implémentation de l'outil FAST. PhD thesis, Cachan (2004)

18. Leroux, J.: A polynomial time presburger criterion and synthesis for number decision diagrams. In: Proc of LICS, pp. 147–156. IEEE Computer Society, Los Alamitos (2005)

19. Leroux, J., Sutre, G.: Flat counter automata almost everywhere! In: Peled, D.A., Tsay, Y.-K. (eds.) ATVA 2005. LNCS, vol. 3707, pp. 489–503. Springer, Heidelberg (2005)

20. Löding, C.: Efficient minimization of deterministic weak automata. IPL (79-3), 105–109 (2001)

21. Muller, D.E., Saoudi, A., Schupp, P.E.: Alternating automata, the weak monadic theory of the tree and its complexity. In: Proc of ICALP, Rennes, pp. 275–283. Springer, Heidelberg (1986)

22. Safra, S.: Exponential determinization for ω-automata with strong-fairness acceptance condition. In: Proc. of POPL, Victoria (May 1992)

23. The T(O)RMC toolset, http://www.montefiore.ulg.ac.be/~legay/TORMC/index-tormc.html

24. Vardi, M.: The büchi complementation saga. In: Thomas, W., Weil, P. (eds.) STACS 2007. LNCS, vol. 4393, pp. 12–22. Springer, Heidelberg (2007)

A Translation from the HTML DTD into a Regular Hedge Grammar

Takuya Nishiyama and Yasuhiko Minamide

Department of Computer Science, University of Tsukuba
{nishiyama,minamide}@score.cs.tsukuba.ac.jp

Abstract. The PHP string analyzer developed by the second author approximates the string output of a program with a context-free grammar. By developing a procedure to decide inclusion between context-free and regular hedge languages, Minamide and Tozawa applied this analysis to checking the validity of dynamically generated XHTML documents. In this paper, we consider the problem of checking the validity of dynamically generated HTML documents instead of XHTML documents.

HTML is not specified by an XML schema language, but by an SGML DTD, and we can omit several kinds of tags in HTML documents. We formalize a subclass of SGML DTDs and develop a translation into regular hedge grammars. Thus we can validate dynamically generated HTML documents. We have implemented this translation and incorporated it in the PHP string analyzer. The experimental results show that the validation through this translation works well in practice.

1 Introduction

The PHP string analyzer was developed by the second author to check various properties of PHP programs [Min05]. It approximates the string output of a program with a context-free grammar. Minamide and Tozawa applied the analysis to checking the validity of XHTML documents generated dynamically by a server-side program [MT06]. They developed a decision procedure that checks inclusion between a context-free and regular hedge languages. The validity is checked by applying the procedure to the context-free and regular hedge grammars obtained from a program and the XHTML DTD.

In this paper, we consider the problem of checking the validity of dynamically generated HTML documents instead of XHTML documents. HTML is not based on XML, but on SGML [Gol90], and its specification is given as an SGML DTD. Unlike XML documents, we can omit several kinds of tags in HTML documents according to the HTML DTD [Wor99]. Models of XML schema languages have been studied based on the theory of formal languages. Murata proposed a regular hedge grammar as a foundation of XML schemas [Mur99], and XML DTDs were modeled as a subclass of context-free grammars called XML-grammars by Berstel and Boasson [BB02]. However, the presence of tag omission makes it harder to model an SGML DTD as a formal language. As far as we know, there is no formal model of SGML DTD.

O.H. Ibarra and B. Ravikumar (Eds.): CIAA 2008, LNCS 5148, pp. 122–131, 2008.

In this paper, we formalize a subclass of SGML DTDs and develop a translation from the subclass into regular hedge grammars. The subclass is expressive enough to include the HTML DTD, making it possible to validate dynamically generated HTML documents based on the decision procedure of Minamide and Tozawa.

Even though it seems rather difficult to formalize general SGML DTDs and represent them with regular hedge grammars, we found that the following two properties hold for the HTML DTD. (a) It is possible to check whether an end tag can be omitted or not by looking at the next element of an SGML document, and (b) the number of direct nestings of tag omissions is bounded by a fixed number determined by the DTD.

We can write an HTML document like the following.

    `<p> <p> <p>` ...

It seems that p elements can be nested any number of times. However, according to the HTML DTD, a p element cannot appear as a child of p. Thus, the string above is interpreted as the following string by inserting `</p>` symbols.

    `<p> </p><p> </p><p> </p>` ...

Thus, p elements are not nested in the string.

Based on these observations, we first formalize the language of an SGML DTD satisfying the first condition as an image of a regular hedge language under a transducer, omitting end tags from a valid string not including tag omissions. Furthermore, we show that if an SGML DTD satisfies both conditions, the image is also a regular hedge language, and we develop a translation from the subclass of SGML DTDs into regular hedge grammars. We have implemented this translation and incorporated it in the PHP string analyzer. The experimental results show that the validation through the translation works well in practice.

This paper is organized as follows. In Section 2, we review SGML and SGML DTD. We formalize the subset of SGML DTDs by modeling end-tag omission with a transducer in Section 3. Section 4 introduces a further restricted class of SGML DTD and gives a translation from a DTD into a regular hedge grammar. The translation is extended to support the exclusion feature of SGML DTD in Section 5. Finally, we show our experimental results.

2   SGML and SGML DTD

SGML is a predecessor of XML, and a markup language for structured documents such as XML. One of the essential differences between SGML and XML is that we can omit tags in SGML documents. In SGML, a document type is specified with the schema language DTD. Although it is quite similar to the DTD for XML, it has more features to specify the type of documents: tag omission, inclusion, and exclusion are the features used in the HTML DTD that are specific to SGML DTD.

Let us consider the following SGML DTD.

```
<!DOCTYPE friends [
 <!ELEMENT friends O O (person)* >
 <!ELEMENT person  - O (name, phone?) >
 <!ELEMENT name    - O (#PCDATA) >
 <!ELEMENT phone   - O (#PCDATA) >
 ] >
```

This declaration specifies content-models of five elements. For example, inside the **friends** element any sequence of **person** elements can appear, as specified by the regular expression **(person)***.

This declaration also specifies tag omission for each element, namely whether or not the start and end tags of the element are optional, by two characters between the element name and the content-model. If the first character is "O", then the start tag of the element can be omitted. Otherwise, it is mandatory. The second character indicates the same for the end tag of the element. For the DTD above, only the start tag of the element **friends** and the end tags of the elements **friends**, **person**, **name**, and **phone** can be omitted. We call elements with optional end tags end-tag omittable elements.

However, tags cannot be omitted everywhere even if it is specified so in a DTD. A tag in a document can only be omitted if the structure of the document can be uniquely determined without the tag. Warmer and van Egmond clarified the condition in the specification as follows [WvE89]. An end tag can be omitted only if it is followed by the end tag of another open element, or by the start tag of another element or an SGML character that is not allowed in the element's content-model.

Let us clarify the condition with the following example.

```
<!DOCTYPE a [
 <!ELEMENT a - - (b|c|d)* >
 <!ELEMENT b - O (c,d)+ >
 <!ELEMENT c - - (#PCDATA) >
 <!ELEMENT d - - (#PCDATA) >
 ] >
```

The end tag **</b>** is specified to be omittable in this DTD and the following document is valid.

```
<a><b><c>A</c><d>B</d><c>C</c></a>
```

It is interpreted as the following by inserting **</b>** before the second **<c>**. This is because c,d,c is not allowed in the content model **(c,d)+** of the element **b**.

```
<a><b><c>A</c><d>B</d></b><c>C</c></a>
```

On the other hand, **</b>** in the following document cannot be omitted because c,d,c,d is allowed in b.

```
<a><b><c>A</c><d>B</d></b><c>C</c><d>D</d></a>
```

As this example shows, to decide whether an end tag can be omitted, it is necessary to look ahead to an unbounded number of elements in general.

3   Formalization of SGML DTD

As stated above, an SGML specific feature that is often used in HTML documents is the omission of end tags. Although start tags of several elements including HTML, HEAD, and BODY are specified as optional in the HTML DTD, it is rather rare to omit them (at least in a server-side program). Thus, in this paper, we formalize a subset of SGML DTDs that allow omission only of end tags. Furthermore, to simplify our formalization, we introduce a subclass of SGML DTDs that makes it possible to check whether an end tag can be omitted or not by looking only at the next element of an SGML document. The class is expressive enough to deal with the HTML DTD as we discussed in the introduction.

To formalize SGML documents and DTDs, we consider SGML documents as strings over a paired alphabet. Let Σ be a base alphabet corresponding to the set of element names. We introduce a paired alphabet consisting of two sets $\acute{\Sigma}$ and $\grave{\Sigma}$:

$$\acute{\Sigma} = \{\acute{a} \mid a \in \Sigma\} \qquad \grave{\Sigma} = \{\grave{a} \mid a \in \Sigma\}$$

where $\acute{\Sigma}$ and $\grave{\Sigma}$ correspond to the set of start tags and the set of end tags, respectively. For example, the following document is described as $\acute{a}\acute{b}\acute{c}\grave{c}\grave{b}\acute{b}\grave{b}\grave{a}$.

```
<a><b><c></c></b><b></b></a>
```

If we omit the end tag of c, we obtain an unbalanced string, $\acute{a}\acute{b}\acute{c}\grave{b}\acute{b}\grave{b}\grave{a}$. We discuss the validity of SGML documents based on this representation, and thus ignore the attributes and the text parts of a document.

Definition 1. *We formalize SGML DTD as a 4-tuple* $D = (\Sigma_e, \Sigma_m, M, r)$.

- Σ_e *is the finite set of symbols corresponding to element names.*
- $\Sigma_m(\subseteq \Sigma_e)$ *is the set of symbols with omittable end tags.*
- M *is a function from* Σ_e *to regular languages over* Σ_e. *The regular language* $M(a)$ *corresponds to the content-model of* a.
- $r \in \Sigma_e$ *is the root element.*

We restrict the content-models for end-tag omittable elements: to the regular languages of the form $(a_1|a_2|\cdots|a_n)^*$ or $(a_1|a_2|\cdots|a_n)^+$ where a_i are symbols. This makes it possible to decide whether or not an end tag can be omitted by looking one symbol ahead. We say that an SGML DTD is *simple* if it satisfies this condition.

Let us consider the following simple DTD.

```
<!DOCTYPE a [
  <!ELEMENT a - - (x, b?)* >
  <!ELEMENT x - O (b)* >
  <!ELEMENT b - - (x)+ >
] >
```

This DTD is represented as $D = (\{a, x, b\}, \{x\}, M, a)$ where $M(a) = (xb?)^*$, $M(x) = b^*, M(b) = x^+$. The string $\acute{a}\acute{x}\grave{x}\acute{b}\acute{x}\grave{b}\grave{a}$ is valid with respect to D. On the other hand, $áx̂x̂b̀b̀à$ is not valid, because this string does not have the x element that should appear inside the b element.

For simple DTDs, we formalize the language of a DTD D as follows.

1. Construct the regular hedge grammar $G_0(D)$ that generates all the valid balanced strings, in turn the valid strings without any tag omission.
2. Construct the finite transducer $T(D)$ that outputs all the valid strings obtained by omitting tags from a valid balanced string.

The language of D is the image of $G_0(D)$ under $T(D)$.

Regular hedge grammars (RHGs) were introduced by Murata as a model of XML schemas [Mur99]. Let us introduce a string version of RHGs.

Definition 2. *An RHG is a 5-tuple $(\Sigma_2, \Sigma_1, N, P, S)$ where Σ_2, Σ_1, and N are a base of a paired alphabet, the set of local symbols, and the set of nonterminals respectively. Each production rule in P has the following form:*

$$X \to áRà$$

where $X \in N$ and R is a regular language over $N \cup \Sigma_1$. $S \in N$ is a start symbol [1].

An RHG defines a language over $\acute{\Sigma}_2 \cup \grave{\Sigma}_2 \cup \Sigma_1$. We denote elements of Σ_2 and Σ_1 by a, b, c and x, y, z, respectively. In this paper, without loss of generality we assume that each nonterminal of an RHG has exactly one production rule.

For the construction of the RHG $G_0(D)$, we consider that all element names are base symbols and introduce a nonterminal X_a for each element name $a \in \Sigma_e$. Then, $G_0(D)$ is defined as $(\Sigma_e, \emptyset, N, P, X_r)$ where $N = \{X_a \mid a \in \Sigma_e\}$ and P has the following rule for each $a \in \Sigma_e$.

$$X_a \to áM(a)à$$

This is basically the same as the interpretation used for XML DTDs by Berstel and Boasson [BB02].

Example 1. Let us consider the DTD D_1 below.

```
<!DOCTYPE a [
 <!ELEMENT a - - (x, b) >
 <!ELEMENT b - - (b)* >
 <!ELEMENT x - O (y | a)* >
 <!ELEMENT y - O (b)* >
] >
```

$G_0(D_1) = (\{a, b, x, y\}, \emptyset, \{X_a, X_b, X_x, X_y\}, P, X_a)$ where P has the following production rules.

$$X_a \to áX_x X_b à \quad X_b \to b́X_b^* b̀ \quad X_x \to x́(X_y | X_a)^* x̀ \quad X_y \to ýX_b^* ỳ$$

This RHG generates all valid balanced strings of the DTD.

---

[1] The original definition of RHGs allows us to use a regular expression instead of a single nonterminal to describe starting points of derivation.

To formalize end-tag omission, we introduce the finite transducer $T(D)$ that takes the valid balanced strings of the DTD D. The transducer produces all possible strings that can be obtained by omitting end tags according to D.

Let us first review a subclass of finite transducers called a generalized sequential machine (GSM). We adopt in this paper the definition of GSMs without final states.

Definition 3. *A GSM T is a 5-tuple $(Q, \Sigma, \Delta, \sigma, q_0)$ where Q is the finite set of states, Σ is the input alphabet, Δ is the output alphabet, σ is the transition-and-output function from $Q \times \Sigma$ to $2^{Q \times \Delta^*}$, and $q_0 \in Q$ is the initial state.*

For a simple DTD, the end tag of $a \in \Sigma_m$ can be omitted if the next symbol is an end tag $\grave{b}$ such that $b \neq a$, or a start tag $\acute{b}$ such that b does not appear in $M(a)$. Although the condition related to start tag differs from the original one in Section 2, they coincide for a simple DTD, because $M(a)$'s form is restricted to enable this.

We simplify presentation of $T(D)$ by describing it as taking a reversed string and outputting all the reversed valid strings obtained by end-tag omission. The transducer memorizes the last outputted symbol as its state and decides whether an end tag can be omitted or not. The reversed string of a valid string $\alpha_1 \alpha_2 \cdots \alpha_n$ is $\check{\alpha}_n \cdots \check{\alpha}_2 \check{\alpha}_1$ where $\check{\grave{a}} = \grave{a}$ and $\check{\acute{a}} = \acute{a}$. The GSM $T(D)$ is formalized as follows.

Definition 4. *Let $D = (\Sigma_e, \Sigma_m, M, r)$ be a simple SGML DTD. We define the GSM $T(D)$ as $(Q, \Sigma_T, \Sigma_T, \sigma_T, q_0)$ where $\Sigma_T = \acute{\Sigma}_e \cup \grave{\Sigma}_e$ and $Q = \{q_0\} \cup \{q_\alpha \mid \alpha \in \Sigma_T\}$. The GSM has the following transitions and outputs.*

$(q_\alpha, \alpha) \in \sigma_T(q, \alpha)$ *if* $\alpha \in \Sigma_T$ *and* $q \in Q$.
$(q_0, \epsilon) \in \sigma_T(q_0, \acute{x})$ *if* $x \in \Sigma_m$.
$(q_{\acute{a}}, \epsilon) \in \sigma_T(q_{\acute{a}}, \acute{x})$ *if* $x \in \Sigma_m$, $a \in \Sigma_e$, *and* $a \neq x$.
$(q_{\grave{a}}, \epsilon) \in \sigma_T(q_{\grave{a}}, \acute{x})$ *if* $x \in \Sigma_m$, $a \in \Sigma_e$, *and* a *does not appear in* $M(x)$.

Then, The language of a simple DTD D is formalized as $(T(D)(L(G_0(D))^R))^R$.

It should be noted that the language cannot be represented by a regular hedge language in general. Let us consider the following DTD [2].

```
<!DOCTYPE a [
  <!ELEMENT a - 0 (a)? >
] >
```

The language of this DTD is $\{\acute{a}^m \grave{a}^n \mid 0 < m \wedge 0 \leq n \leq m\}$ and cannot be represented as an RHG.

4   A Translation from a DTD into an RHG

We consider a subclass of simple DTDs where the number of direct nestings of omittable elements is bounded and translate a DTD in this class into an RHG

---

[2] Although this DTD is not simple, the language can be formalized by slightly extending the definition of $T(D)$.

by considering tags of omittable elements as local symbols. This class includes the HTML DTD and thus enables validation of dynamically generated HTML documents with the decision algorithm of Minamide and Tozawa [MT06].

Let us consider the graph $\{(x,y) \in \Sigma_m \times \Sigma_m \mid y$ appears in $M(x)\}$ where Σ_m is the set of end-tag omittable elements. We say that a DTD is *acyclic* if its graph is acyclic. This requirement corresponds to requiring that the number of direct nestings of omittable elements is bounded. For an acyclic simple DTD, we develop a translation into an RHG. It consists of the three steps.

First, we construct the RHG $G_0'(D)$ that generates the same language as $G_0(D)$ by taking advantage of the acyclicity of DTDs. It is done by recursively expanding all nonterminals X_a for $a \in \Sigma_m$.

Example 2. For the DTD D_1, we obtain $G_0'(D_1) = (\Sigma_e', \acute{\Sigma}_m \cup \grave{\Sigma}_m, \{X_c \mid c \in \Sigma_e'\}, P', X_a)$ where $\Sigma_e' = \Sigma_e \setminus \Sigma_m$ and P' has the following production rules.

$$X_a \to \acute{a}\acute{x}(\acute{y}X_b^*\grave{y}\mid X_a)^*\grave{x}X_b\grave{a} \qquad X_b \to \acute{b}X_b^*\grave{b}$$

Hereafter in this section, we consider that the symbols in $\acute{\Sigma}_m \cup \grave{\Sigma}_m$ are local: $\Sigma_2 = \Sigma_e \setminus \Sigma_m$ and $\Sigma_1 = \acute{\Sigma}_m \cup \grave{\Sigma}_m$.

Second, we lift the GSM $T(D)$ over $\acute{\Sigma}_e \cup \grave{\Sigma}_e$ to $T_a(D)$ over $\{X_b \mid b \in \Sigma_e \setminus \Sigma_m\} \cup \acute{\Sigma}_m \cup \grave{\Sigma}_m$ for each $a \in \Sigma_e \setminus \Sigma_m$. Namely, we lift the GSM operating on the terminal symbols to $\Sigma_1 \cup N$. This lifting is possible if a GSM is *surface local*. A surface local GSM, as we define it, is a GSM that operate essentially on the surface of balanced string.

Definition 5. *Let* $\Sigma = \acute{\Sigma}_2 \cup \grave{\Sigma}_2 \cup \Sigma_1$ *and* $T = (Q, \Sigma, \Sigma, \sigma, s)$ *be a GSM. We say that* T *is surface local if the following conditions hold.*

1. *For each* $a \in \Sigma_2$, *there exist states* $q_{\acute{a}}$ *and* $q_{\grave{a}}$ *such that* $\sigma(q, \acute{a}) = \{(q_{\acute{a}}, \acute{a})\}$ *and* $\sigma(q, \grave{a}) = \{(q_{\grave{a}}, \grave{a})\}$ *for all* $q \in Q$.
2. *For all* $b \in \Sigma_1$, $(q', w) \in \sigma(q, b)$ *implies* $w \in \Sigma_1^*$.

It is clear from the definition that the GSM $T(D)$ for a simple SGML DTD D is surface local. A surface local GSM can be lifted as follows.

Definition 6. *Let* Σ *be* $\acute{\Sigma}_2 \cup \grave{\Sigma}_2 \cup \Sigma_1$, $T = (Q, \Sigma, \Sigma, \sigma, s)$ *be a surface local GSM, and* $G = (\Sigma_2, \Sigma_1, N, P, S)$ *be an RHG.*

We introduce a lifted GSM $T_a = (Q, \Sigma_1 \cup N, \Sigma_1 \cup N, \sigma', q_{\grave{a}})$ *for each* $a \in \Sigma_2$. *The transition-output function* σ' *is defined as follows:*

$$\sigma'(q, x) = \sigma(q, x) \quad (q \in Q \text{ and } x \in \Sigma_1)$$
$$\sigma'(q, X) = \{(q_{\acute{b}}, X)\} \quad (q \in Q \text{ and } G \text{ has a rule of the form } X \to \acute{b}R\grave{b}).$$

Finally, we construct the RHG $G(D)$ that represents the language of D, by composing $T_a(D)$ and each production rule of $G_0'(D)$.

Theorem 1. *Let* G *and* T *be an RHG and a surface local GSM. We construct an RHG* G' *as follows:*

$$X \to \acute{a}T_a(R)\grave{a}$$

for a production rule $X \to \acute{a}R\grave{a}$. *Then,* $T(L(G)) = L(G')$.

In the previous section, we have defined the language of an SGML DTD as $(T(D)(L(G_0(D))^R))^R$. Let G' be an RHG constructed as in the theorem for $G_0'(D)^R$ and $T(D)$. Then we have $G' = T(D)(L(G_0(D))^R)$. Thus, the language of D can be described by the RHG G'^R.

Example 3. The grammar that generates the language of D_1 can be described as follows:

$$X_a \to \acute{a}\acute{x}(\acute{y}X_b^*\acute{y}?|X_a)^*\acute{x}X_b\grave{a} \mid \acute{a}\acute{x}((\acute{y}X_b^*\acute{y}?|X_a)^*(\acute{y}X_b^*\acute{y}|X_a))?X_b\grave{a}$$
$$X_b \to \acute{b}X_b^*\grave{b}$$

where X_a is the start symbol. The production rule for X_a can be read as follows. If $\acute{x}$ is omitted then the last $\grave{y}$ cannot be omitted, and vice versa.

5 Exclusion and Inclusion in SGML DTD

In contrast to XML DTD, SGML DTD can specify non-local constraints on elements with inclusion and exclusion. They are used to allow or disallow some elements appearing as a descendant of an element.

We have extended our translation from an SGML DTD to an RHG to support the exclusions appearing in the HTML DTD. To simplify translation, the support of exclusion is restricted so that exclusion is specified only for non-omittable elements. The HTML DTD satisfies this restriction.

Let us consider the following DTD to explain the extended translation.

```
<!DOCTYPE a [
 <!ELEMENT a - - (b|c)*      >
 <!ELEMENT b - - (a,c)   -(b)>
 <!ELEMENT c - - (a)?    -(c)>
] >
```

The parts -(b) and -(c) are the specifications of exclusion. The former means b cannot appear as a descendant of b, even if it is specified as being allowed to do so. The latter indicates the same for c in c.

This DTD is translated into an RHG by introducing a nonterminal X_a^S for each element name a and the set of excluded elements S as follows:

$$X_a^\emptyset \to \acute{a}(X_b^\emptyset|X_c^\emptyset)^*\grave{a} \quad X_a^{\{b\}} \to \acute{a}(X_c^{\{b\}})^*\grave{a} \quad X_a^{\{b,c\}} \to \acute{a}\grave{a}$$
$$X_b^\emptyset \to \acute{b}X_a^{\{b\}}X_c^{\{b\}}\grave{b} \quad X_b^{\{b\}} \to \acute{b}X_a^{\{b\}}X_c^{\{b\}}\grave{b}$$
$$X_c^\emptyset \to \acute{c}X_a^{\{c\}}\grave{c} \quad\quad X_c^{\{b\}} \to \acute{c}X_a^{\{b,c\}}\grave{c}$$

where $X_b^{\{b,c\}}$ is not included because it generates no terminal strings.

The transducer $T(D)$ for the DTD D can be constructed in the exactly same manner under the condition that exclusion is specified only for non-omittable elements.

One problem with this translation is that it may increase the size of the grammar exponentially. In our experiments, we could obtain an RHG for the HTML DTD even if we enabled exclusion. However, we failed to minimize the RHG and to use it directly for HTML validation.

6   Experimental Results

We have implemented a parser for SGML DTD and the translation from DTDs into RHGs given above. We conducted our experiments on the HTML 4.01 Transitional DTD, which contains declarations for 109 elements. To simulate unsupported features of DTDs appearing in the HTML DTD, we modified the DTD as follows.

– The TABLE element is defined as follows. The start and end tags of TBODY can be omitted and they usually are omitted.

```
<!ELEMENT TABLE - -
    (CAPTION?, (COL*|COLGROUP*), THEAD?, TFOOT?, (TBODY)+)>
<!ELEMENT TBODY    O O (TR)+              -- table body -->
```

To support the omission, we have replaced the (TBODY)+ part of the content-model of the TABLE with (TBODY|TR)+ and conducted our experiments.
– The inclusion feature of the SGML DTD is used in the definition of the header of HTML documents. We have simulated it by expanding the element declarations with included elements. Although the inclusion feature is also used for the INS and DEL elements, we ignored them because the programs we considered do not use the INS and DEL elements.

In the implementation, we represent an RHG as a grammar with production rules of the forms $X \rightarrow \acute{a}Y\grave{a}Z$ or $X \rightarrow bY$ or $X \rightarrow \epsilon$, where $a \in \Sigma_2$ and $b \in \Sigma_1$. A grammar in this form can be considered as a tree automaton and algorithms such as determinization and minimization for tree automata can be applied to it. An RHG can be converted into a grammar in this form, and vice versa. In our implementation, a minimized RHG is converted into an algebra called a binoid to decide CFL-RHL inclusion [PQ68].

When we ignored exclusions we obtained the RHG that has 187 nonterminals and 7471 production rules. After minimizing it, the grammar has 56 nonterminals and 6758 production rules and the binoid converted from the RHG has 2381 elements. The RHG obtained with exclusion enabled translation has 3213 nonterminals and 115647 production rules. As we noted earlier, the translation to support exclusion may increase the size of the RHG exponentially. Although the RHG is only one order of magnitude larger, the determinization and minimization of the RHG and the generation of the binoid failed because the RHG is too large.

The implementation was incorporated into the PHP string analyzer developed by Minamide [Min05]. The analyzer generates a CFG that conservatively approximates the string output of a PHP program. It is available from http://www.score.cs.tsukuba.ac.jp/~minamide/phpsa/. In our experiments, we checked the validity of Web pages generated by a PHP program against the HTML DTD. To reduce the size of the binoid obtained by the translation, we first extract the set of element names appearing in a CFG obtained by the analyzer and delete the elements from the DTD that do not appear in the set.

Table 1. HTML validation

Programs	Element names	RHG (minimized) Nonterminals	Productions	Binoid	Bugs	Execution time (s)
webchess	20	20	439	375	1	3.37
faqforge	19	16	315	106	16	1.19
phpwims	18	16	268	39	3	1.65

Table 1 shows the results of our experiments. The column 'elements' shows the number of element names that may appear in generated HTML documents. The columns 'RHG' and 'binoid' show their sizes. We found several bugs through our experiments and corrected them. The numbers of bugs found are also shown. The column 'time' shows the execution time spent to generate binoids from the DTD and check the CFL-RHL inclusion. These times do not include the time spent to generate a CFG from a PHP program by the analyzer.

References

[BB02]   Berstel, J., Boasson, L.: Formal properties of XML grammars and languages. Acta Informatica 38(9), 649–671 (2002)

[Gol90] Goldfarb, C.F.: The SGML Handbook. Oxford University Press, Oxford (1990)

[Min05] Minamide, Y.: Static approximation of dynamically generated Web pages. In: Proceedings of the 14th International World Wide Web Conference, pp. 432–441. ACM Press, New York (2005)

[MT06]   Minamide, Y., Tozawa, A.: XML validation for context-free grammars. In: Kobayashi, N. (ed.) APLAS 2006. LNCS, vol. 4279, pp. 357–373. Springer, Heidelberg (2006)

[Mur99] Murata, M.: Hedge automata: a formal model for XML schemata (1999), http://www.xml.gr.jp/relax/hedge_nice.html

[PQ68]   Pair, C., Quere, A.: Définition et étude des bilangages réguliers. Information and Control 13(6), 565–593 (1968)

[Wor99] World Wide Web Consortium. HTML 4.01 Transitional DTD (1999), http://www.w3.org/TR/html401/loose.dtd

[WvE89] Warmer, J., van Egmond, S.: The implementation of the Amsterdam SGML Parser. Electronic Publishing 2(2), 65–90 (1989)

Tree-Series-to-Tree-Series Transformations

Andreas Maletti*

International Computer Science Institute
1947 Center Street, Suite 600, Berkeley CA-94704, USA
maletti@icsi.berkeley.edu

Abstract. We investigate the tree-series-to-tree-series (ts-ts) transformation computed by tree series transducers. Unless the used semiring is complete, this transformation is, in general, not well-defined. In practice, many used semirings are not complete (like the probability semiring). We establish a syntactical condition that guarantees well-definedness of the ts-ts transformation in arbitrary commutative semirings. For positive (*i. e.*, zero-sum and zero-divisor free) semirings the condition actually characterizes the well-definedness, so that well-definedness is decidable in this scenario.

1 Introduction

Tree series transducers [1,2] are a generalization of tree transducers [3,4,5,6,7]. The framework TIBURON [8] implements a generalization of top-down tree series transducers [2] using various weight structures such as the BOOLEAN semiring ($\{0, 1\}, \vee, \wedge$) and the probability semiring ($\mathbb{R}, +, \cdot$). Such tree series transducers compute both a tree-to-tree-series (t-ts) and a tree-series-to-tree-series (ts-ts) transformation, where a tree series is a mapping assigning a weight to each tree. The t-ts transformation is always well-defined, but the ts-ts transformation is well-defined only for complete semirings [9,10] such as the BOOLEAN semiring. However, for the probability semiring the ts-ts transformation need not be well-defined because infinite sums might occur. Of course, some incomplete semirings (*e. g.*, positive semirings) can be extended by a new element ∞, which is the result of all nontrivial infinite sums. However, such a definition is clearly not practical and does not work for the probability semiring.

A standard application of the ts-ts transformation is the computation of the image of a recognizable tree series [11,12,13,14]. This is, for example, used to translate a language model (parses of an input sentence) to a language model (resp., parses of output sentences) in another language. For some tree series transducers the image is again a recognizable tree series [15,16]. In fact, the image operation is implemented in TIBURON for the BOOLEAN semiring. However, in the probability semiring, the image operation is only meaningful if the ts-ts transformation is well-defined.

---

* This work was supported by a fellowship within the Postdoc-Programme of the German Academic Exchange Service (DAAD).

O.H. Ibarra and B. Ravikumar (Eds.): CIAA 2008, LNCS 5148, pp. 132–140, 2008.

In this contribution we investigate for which tree series transducers the ts-ts transformation is well-defined following the approach of [17,18] for weighted finite-state transducers. To this end, we develop a general notion of convergence that can serve as a baseline for all semirings. More refined notions for particular semirings can be derived in the same manner. Thereafter we present a syntactical condition, which in general, guarantees that the ts-ts transformation is well-defined (using the baseline notion of convergence mentioned). In fact, the condition is such that we obtain a characterization for certain tree series transducers over positive (*i. e.*, zero-sum and zero-divisor free) semirings. This yields that well-definedness of the ts-ts transformation is decidable for certain tree series transducers over positive semirings. This also applies to tree series transducers over the BOOLEAN semiring (*i. e.*, tree transducers).

2   Preliminaries

The nonnegative integers are denoted by $\mathbb{N}$ and $\mathbb{N}_+ = \mathbb{N} \setminus \{0\}$. We use $[k, n]$ for $\{i \mid k \leqslant i \leqslant n\}$ where the i are either integers or reals depending on the context. In the former case, we abbreviate $[1, n]$ to $[n]$. An *alphabet* is a finite set of *symbols*. A *ranked alphabet* is an alphabet Σ together with a mapping $\mathrm{rk} \colon \Sigma \to \mathbb{N}$, which assigns to each symbol a *rank*. The set of symbols of rank k is denoted by Σ_k. For convenience we assume fixed sets $\mathrm{X} = \{\mathrm{x}_i \mid i \in \mathbb{N}_+\}$ and $\mathrm{Z} = \{\mathrm{z}_i \mid i \in \mathbb{N}_+\}$ of *variables*. For $k \in \mathbb{N}$ we use $\mathrm{X}_k = \{\mathrm{x}_i \mid i \in [k]\}$ and $\mathrm{Z}_k = \{\mathrm{z}_i \mid i \in [k]\}$. Given $V \subseteq \mathrm{X} \cup \mathrm{Z}$, the set $T_\Sigma(V)$ of *Σ-trees indexed by V* is the smallest set T such that $V \subseteq T$ and for every $\sigma \in \Sigma_k$ and $t_1, \dots, t_k \in T$ also $\sigma(t_1, \dots, t_k) \in T$. We generally assume that $\mathrm{X} \cup \mathrm{Z}$ is disjoint with any considered ranked alphabet, so we usually write α instead of $\alpha()$ whenever $\alpha \in \Sigma_0$. Moreover, we also use T_Σ for $T_\Sigma(\emptyset)$. Let $t, t_1, \dots, t_k \in T_\Sigma(\mathrm{Z})$. We denote by $t[t_1, \dots, t_k]$ the tree obtained from t by replacing for every $i \in [k]$ every z_i-leaf in t by the tree t_i. The tree t is *nondeleting* (resp., *linear*) in $V \subseteq \mathrm{Z}$, if each $v \in V$ occurs at least (resp., at most) once in t. The set of variables occurring in t is $\mathrm{var}(t)$ and the *size* of t (*i. e.*, the number of nodes in t) is $\mathrm{size}(t)$. Finally, the *height* of a tree is inductively defined by $\mathrm{height}(v) = 1$ for every $v \in V$ and $\mathrm{height}(\sigma(t_1, \dots, t_k)) = 1 + \max\{\mathrm{height}(t_i) \mid i \in [k]\}$ for every $\sigma \in \Sigma_k$ and $t_1, \dots, t_k \in T_\Sigma(V)$.

An algebraic structure $(A, +)$ is a *monoid* if $+$ is an associative (binary) operation on A that permits a neutral element. A *(commutative) semiring* $(A, +, \cdot)$ consists of two commutative monoids $(A, +)$ and $(A, \cdot)$ such that $\cdot$ distributes over $+$ and the neutral element 0 of $(A, +)$ is absorbing with respect to $\cdot$ (*i. e.*, $a \cdot 0 = 0 = 0 \cdot a$ for every $a \in A$). The neutral element of an additive operation is usually denoted by 0 and that of multiplicative operation by 1. We also use the summation $\sum_{i \in I} a_i$ for an index set I and a family $(a_i \mid i \in I)$ of semiring elements. Such a summation is *well-defined* if $a_i = 0$ for almost all $i \in I$. The actual sum is then defined in the obvious way. A semiring $\mathcal{A} = (A, +, \cdot)$ is *zero-sum free*, whenever $a + b = 0$ implies that $a = 0$ for every $a, b \in A$, and *zero-divisor free*, whenever $a \cdot b = 0$ implies that $0 \in \{a, b\}$. A zero-sum and zero-divisor free semiring is *positive*.

Let $\mathcal{A} = (A, +, \cdot)$ be a semiring. Every mapping $\varphi \colon T \to A$ for some $T \subseteq T_\Sigma(V)$ is a *tree series*. We denote the set of those by $\mathcal{A}\langle\!\langle T\rangle\!\rangle$. We usually write the *coefficient* $\varphi(t)$ *of* t *in* φ as (φ, t). Moreover, we write φ as the formal sum $\sum_{t \in T} (\varphi, t)\, t$. We extend both operations of $\mathcal{A}$ componentwise to tree series, i. e., $(\varphi + \psi, t) = (\varphi, t) + (\psi, t)$ for every $\varphi, \psi \in \mathcal{A}\langle\!\langle T\rangle\!\rangle$ and $t \in T$. The *support* of φ is $\mathrm{supp}(\varphi) = \{t \mid (\varphi, t) \neq 0\}$. The set of tree series with finite support is denoted by $\mathcal{A}\langle T\rangle$. For every $a \in A$, the tree series $\widetilde{a}$ is such that $(\widetilde{a}, t) = a$ for every $t \in T$. The tree series φ is *nondeleting* (resp., *linear*) in V, if every $t \in \mathrm{supp}(\varphi)$ is nondeleting (resp., linear) in V. We use $\mathrm{var}(\varphi)$ as a shorthand for $\bigcup_{t \in \mathrm{supp}(\varphi)} \mathrm{var}(t)$.

Let $\varphi \in \mathcal{A}\langle T_\Delta(Z)\rangle$ and $\psi_1, \dots, \psi_k \in \mathcal{A}\langle T_\Delta(Z)\rangle$. The *pure substitution* [19,2] of $(\psi_1, \dots, \psi_k)$ into φ is defined by

$$\varphi \leftarrow (\psi_1, \dots, \psi_k) = \sum_{t, t_1, \dots, t_k \in T_\Delta(Z)} (\varphi, t)(\psi_1, t_1) \cdots (\psi_k, t_k)\, t[t_1, \dots, t_k] \ .$$

Let $\mathcal{A}$ be a semiring, Σ and Δ be ranked alphabets, and Q a finite set. A *(polynomial) representation* [2] is a family $\mu = (\mu_k \mid k \in \mathbb{N})$ of $\mu_k \colon \Sigma_k \to \mathcal{A}\langle T_\Delta(Z)\rangle^{Q \times (Q \times X_k)^*}$ such that for every $\sigma \in \Sigma_k$ and $q \in Q$

(i) $\mu_k(\sigma)_{q,w} \in \mathcal{A}\langle T_\Delta(Z_{|w|})\rangle$ for every $w \in (Q \times X_k)^*$ and
(ii) $\mu_k(\sigma)_{q,w} = \widetilde{0}$ for almost all $w \in (Q \times X_k)^*$.

A *(polynomial) tree series transducer* [1,2] is a tuple $(Q, \Sigma, \Delta, \mathcal{A}, I, \mu)$ such that μ is a representation and $I \subseteq Q$. It is *top-down* (resp., *bottom-up*) [2] if $\mu_k(\sigma)_{q,w}$ is nondeleting and linear in $Z_{|w|}$ [resp., if there exist $q_1, \dots, q_k \in Q$ such that $w = (q_1, x_1) \cdots (q_k, x_k)$] for every $\sigma \in \Sigma_k$, $q \in Q$, and $w \in (Q \times X_k)^*$ such that $\mu_k(\sigma)_{q,w} \neq \widetilde{0}$. Let $h_\mu \colon T_\Sigma \to \mathcal{A}\langle\!\langle T_\Delta\rangle\!\rangle^Q$ be defined for every $\sigma \in \Sigma_k$, $t_1, \dots, t_k \in T_\Sigma$, and $q \in Q$ by

$$h_\mu\big(\sigma(t_1, \dots, t_k)\big)_q = \sum_{\substack{w \in (Q \times X_k)^*, \\ w = (q_1, x_{i_1}) \cdots (q_n, x_{i_n})}} \mu_k(\sigma)_{q,w} \leftarrow \big(h_\mu(t_{i_1})_{q_1}, \dots, h_\mu(t_{i_n})_{q_n}\big) \ .$$

The transducer M computes the *tree-to-tree-series transformation* (t-ts transformation) $\tau_M \colon T_\Sigma \to \mathcal{A}\langle\!\langle T_\Delta\rangle\!\rangle$ defined by $\tau_M(t) = \sum_{q \in I} h_\mu(t)_q$ for every $t \in T_\Sigma$. Both h_μ and the t-ts transformation τ_M are well-defined. Finally, the *tree-series-to-tree-series transformation* (ts-ts transformation) computed by M is $\tau_M(\varphi) = \sum_{t \in T_\Sigma} (\varphi, t) \cdot \tau_M(t)$ for every $\varphi \in \mathcal{A}\langle\!\langle T_\Sigma\rangle\!\rangle$, whenever this sum is well-defined. We say that τ_M is well-defined whenever $\tau_M(\varphi)$ is well-defined for every $\varphi \in \mathcal{A}\langle\!\langle T_\Sigma\rangle\!\rangle$.

3   Convergence

In this section, we will explore when the ts-ts transformation of a tree series transducer $M = (Q, \Sigma, \Delta, \mathcal{A}, I, \mu)$ is well-defined. Roughly speaking, it is well-defined if every output tree $u \in T_\Delta$ can be generated [i. e., $u \in \mathrm{supp}(\tau_M(t))$] by only finitely many input trees $t \in T_\Sigma$. Note that our definition of well-definedness works in any semiring; for particular semirings like $(\mathbb{R}, +, \cdot, 0, 1)$ other notions of well-definedness (or equivalently, convergence) might be more realistic. However, those more refined notions typically include our notion of well-definedness (i. e., any sum that is well-defined according to our definition is also well-defined in the refined setting and the sums coincide), so that our approach can be seen as a general baseline. We first show that τ_M is well-defined if and only if $\tau_M(\widetilde{1})$ is well-defined. Thus, subsequent investigations need not consider the actual input tree series.

Proposition 1. *The ts-ts transformation τ_M is well-defined if and only if $\tau_M(\widetilde{1})$ is well-defined.*

Proof. Let $\varphi \in A\langle\!\langle T_\Sigma \rangle\!\rangle$ and $u \in T_\Delta$. One direction is trivial. In the other direction, the sum $\tau_M(\widetilde{1})$ is well-defined by assumption. Hence, $(\tau_M(t), u) = 0$ for almost all $t \in T_\Sigma$. Thus, $\tau_M(\varphi)$ is well-defined. □

Let us take a closer look at $\tau_M(\widetilde{1})$. By definition, it is $\sum_{t \in T_\Sigma} \tau_M(t)$. This is well-defined if it is not possible to transform large (with respect to the size) input trees to small output trees. Let us introduce the notion of convergence [18] that we will use. For every $\varphi \in A\langle\!\langle T_\Delta(Z) \rangle\!\rangle$ let $\|\varphi\| = \max_{t \in \mathrm{supp}(\varphi)} \mathrm{size}(t)^{-1}$. We call $\|\varphi\|$ the *norm of* φ. Intuitively, the norm of φ is the inverse of the size of a smallest tree in the support of φ. Thus, the norm of $\widetilde{0}$ is 0.

Proposition 2. *For every $\varphi, \psi \in A\langle\!\langle T_\Delta(Z) \rangle\!\rangle$*

(i) $\|\varphi\| = 0$ if and only if $\varphi = \widetilde{0}$.
(ii) $\|\varphi + \psi\| \leqslant \|\varphi\| + \|\psi\|$.

Actually, it can be shown that $\|\cdot\|$ is a monoid-homomorphism from $(A\langle\!\langle T_\Delta(Z) \rangle\!\rangle, +)$ to $([0,1], \max)$ if A is zero-sum free. We derive the distance $d_{\|\cdot\|}$ on $A\langle\!\langle T_\Delta(Z) \rangle\!\rangle$, which is given by $d_{\|\cdot\|}(\varphi, \psi) = |\,\|\varphi\| - \|\psi\|\,|$ for every $\varphi, \psi \in A\langle\!\langle T_\Delta(Z) \rangle\!\rangle$.

Proposition 3. *The distance $d_{\|\cdot\|}$ defines a pseudometric on $A\langle\!\langle T_\Delta(Z) \rangle\!\rangle$.*

With the help of this pseudometric, we can now introduce the usual notion of CAUCHY-convergence for sequences of tree series.

Definition 4. *Let $\Psi = (\psi_i \mid i \in \mathbb{N})$ be a family of $\psi_i \in A\langle\!\langle T_\Delta(Z) \rangle\!\rangle$. It converges (using the pseudometric $d_{\|\cdot\|}$) if*

$$(\exists \psi \in A\langle\!\langle T_\Delta(Z) \rangle\!\rangle)(\forall \epsilon > 0)(\exists j_\epsilon \in \mathbb{N})(\forall j \geqslant j_\epsilon) : d_{\|\cdot\|}(\psi_j, \psi) < \epsilon \ .$$

If Ψ converges, then ψ in the above display is a limit *of Ψ and we say that Ψ converges to ψ or symbolically $\Psi \to \psi$.*

Convergence to $\widetilde{0}$ will play a central role. In fact, Ψ converges to $\widetilde{0}$ if

$$(\forall n \in \mathbb{N})(\exists j_n \in \mathbb{N})(\forall j \geqslant j_n) : \min_{t \in \mathrm{supp}(\psi_j)} \mathrm{size}(t) > n \ .$$

Let $T = (t_i \mid i \in \mathbb{N})$ be a family of $t_i \in T_\Sigma$. It is an *enumeration* of T_Σ if for every $t \in T_\Sigma$ there exists exactly one $i \in \mathbb{N}$ such that $t_i = t$, and it is *size-compliant* if $\text{size}(t_i) \leqslant \text{size}(t_j)$ for all $i \leqslant j$. We write $\tau_M(T)$ for the family $(\tau_M(t_i) \mid i \in \mathbb{N})$. Next we characterize when $\tau_M(\widetilde{1})$ is well-defined in terms of size-compliant enumerations.

Theorem 5. *The following are equivalent:*

(i) τ_M *is well-defined.*
(ii) $\tau_M(T) \to \widetilde{0}$ *for every size-compliant enumeration T of T_Σ.*
(iii) $\tau_M(T) \to \widetilde{0}$ *for some size-compliant enumeration T of T_Σ.*

Proof. The existence of at least one size-compliant enumeration of T_Σ is self-evident, so (ii) clearly implies (iii). Let us assume that there exists a size-compliant enumeration $T = (t_i \mid i \in \mathbb{N})$ such that $\tau_M(T)$ converges to $\widetilde{0}$. We know that for every $n \in \mathbb{N}$ there exists a $j_n \in \mathbb{N}$ such that for all $j \geqslant j_n$ we have that $\min_{u \in \text{supp}(\tau_M(t_j))} \text{size}(u) > n$, or equivalently, $u \notin \text{supp}(\tau_M(t_j))$ for all $u \in T_\Delta$ with $\text{size}(u) \leqslant n$. In particular, for every $u \in T_\Delta$ there exists $n_u \in \mathbb{N}$ such that $u \notin \text{supp}(\tau_M(t_n))$ for all $n \geqslant n_u$. Thus, $\tau_M(\widetilde{1})$ and by Proposition 1 also τ_M are well-defined.

Conversely, suppose that τ_M and hence $\tau_M(\widetilde{1})$ are well-defined (see Proposition 1). There exists a finite subset $S_u \subseteq T_\Sigma$ for every tree $u \in T_\Delta$ such that $u \notin \text{supp}(\tau_M(t))$ for every $t \notin S_u$. Let $n \in \mathbb{N}$ and $T = (t_i \mid i \in \mathbb{N})$ be a size-compliant enumeration of T_Σ. Let $U_n = \{u \in T_\Delta \mid \text{size}(u) \leqslant n\}$ and $S_n = \bigcup_{u \in U_n} S_u$. Clearly, U_n and thus also S_n are finite. Finally, let $m_n = \max_{t \in S_n} \text{size}(t) + 1$ and j_n be an index such that $\text{size}(t_{j_n}) \geqslant m_n$. It remains to prove that $\min_{u \in \text{supp}(\tau_M(t_j))} \text{size}(u) > n$ for every $j \geqslant j_n$. Suppose that $u \in \text{supp}(\tau_M(t_j))$ and $\text{size}(u) \leqslant n$. Thus $u \in U_n$. By this, we obtain that $t_j \in S_u$ and $t_j \in S_n$. It follows that $m_n \geqslant \text{size}(t_j) + 1$. By the size-compliance condition, $\text{size}(t_j) \geqslant \text{size}(t_{j_n}) \geqslant m_n$. With the previous inequality, we obtain $\text{size}(t_j) \geqslant \text{size}(t_j) + 1$. Thus, there exists no $u \in \text{supp}(\tau_M(t_j))$ with $\text{size}(u) \leqslant n$, which proves that $\tau_M(T) \to \widetilde{0}$. $\square$

The previous theorem is clear if $\mathcal{A}$ is zero-sum free, but in other cases one might be tempted to assume that the theorem only holds because of our peculiar (or even deficient) definition of well-defined sums. Let us show on an example that this is indeed not the case. Let $\Sigma = \Delta = \{\gamma^{(1)}, \alpha^{(0)}\}$ and $\mathcal{A} = \mathbb{Z}$. Moreover, let $\tau_M(t) = (-1)^{|t|_\gamma} \alpha$. Now one might argue that $\tau_M(\widetilde{1})$ is well-defined and equal to $\widetilde{0}$ because $\tau_M(\gamma^n(\alpha)) + \tau_M(\gamma^{n+1}(\alpha)) = \widetilde{0}$ for every even n. However, the last property also holds for each odd n, which yields $\tau_M(\widetilde{1}) = \tau_M(\alpha) + \sum_{t \in T_\Sigma \setminus \{\alpha\}} \tau_M(t) = \tau_M(\alpha)$. Thus, we argued for two different results of the sum, which shows that it is not well-defined.

4   Towards a Syntactical Property

Next, we present a syntactic condition that guarantees that the ts-ts transformation computed by a tree series transducer is well-defined. Let

$M = (Q, \Sigma, \Delta, \mathcal{A}, I, \mu)$ be a tree series transducer. Note that we could reduce the problem to unweighted tree transducers, but we avoid this for two reasons: (i) It is rather unintuitive that $\bigvee_{i \in \mathbb{N}} 1$ is not well-defined in the BOOLEAN semiring $(\{0, 1\}, \vee, \wedge)$ and (ii) we lack the space to introduce them (using the standard set notation). We generally follow the approach of [17,18] by the analysis is slightly more complicated by the tree structure. First we introduce some important notions like the dependency relations $P, R \subseteq Q \times Q$. For every $p, q \in Q$, let $(p, q) \in P$ (resp., $(p, q) \in R$) if $z_i \in \mathrm{supp}(\mu_k(\sigma)_{p,w})$ (resp., $\mathrm{supp}(\mu_k(\sigma)_{p,w}) \neq \emptyset$) for some $\sigma \in \Sigma_k$ and $w \in (Q \times X_k)^*$ such that $w_j = (q, x_i)$ for some $1 \leqslant j \leqslant |w|$. Let $\sqsubset$ and $\sqsubseteq$ (resp., $\prec$ and $\preceq$) be the transitive and reflexive, transitive closure of P (resp., of R), respectively. Note that in general $\sqsubseteq$ and $\preceq$ are not partial orders. Then the following definitions are natural (note that our reading is top-down).

Definition 6. *Let $q \in Q$.*

- *If $q \sqsubset q$ (resp., $q \prec q$), then q is* circular *(resp.,* self-replicating*).*
- *If there exists $p \in I$ such that $p \preceq q$, then q is* accessible*.*
- *If there exist $p \in Q$ and $\alpha \in \Sigma_0$ such that $\mu_0(\alpha)_{p,\varepsilon} \neq \widetilde{0}$ and $q \preceq p$, then q is* co-accessible*.*

The tree series transducer M is reduced *if every state is accessible and co-accessible. Finally, M is* non-circular *if no state $q \in Q$ is circular.*

Note that τ_M is trivially well-defined if M has no self-replicating state (the latter can easily be checked). In the sequel, we assume that M has at least one self-replicating state. It is also obvious that we can construct a reduced tree series transducer M' that is equivalent to M. We simply remove all states that are not accessible or not co-accessible. It should be clear that this procedure does not change the computed tree series.

Proposition 7. *There exists a reduced tree series transducer M' such that $\tau_M = \tau_{M'}$.*

Next, we introduce an essential notion: *deletion points*. A deletion point is a pair (p, q) of states such that one of the transitions into p deletes a subtree potentially processed in q.

Definition 8. *We say that $(p, q) \in Q^2$ is a* deletion point *if there exist $\sigma \in \Sigma_k$, $w \in (Q \times X_k)^*$, $u \in \mathrm{supp}(\mu_k(\sigma)_{p,w})$, and $i \in [k]$ such that*

- *there does not exist $1 \leqslant j \leqslant |w|$ and $r \in Q$ such that $w_j = (r, x_i)$, or*
- *$z_j \notin \mathrm{var}(u)$ for some $1 \leqslant j \leqslant |w|$ such that $w_j = (q, x_i)$.*

The conditions could be called input- *and* output-deleting, *respectively.*

Note that top-down and bottom-up tree series transducers have a deletion point if and only if they are deleting [2]. Note that if a top-down tree transducer has the deletion point (p, q), then it also has the deletion point (p, r) for every $r \in Q$. Let us illustrate the notion on a small example.

Example 9. Let $M = (\{\star, \bot\}, \Sigma, \Sigma, \mathbb{N}, \{\star\}, \mu)$ be the tree series transducer with $\Sigma = \{\sigma^{(2)}, \alpha^{(0)}\}$ and

$$\mu_0(\alpha)_{p,\varepsilon} = 1\,\alpha \qquad\qquad \mu_2(\sigma)_{\perp,(\perp,x_1)(\perp,x_2)} = 1\,\sigma(z_1,z_2)$$
$$\mu_2(\sigma)_{\star,(\star,x_1)(\perp,x_2)} = 1\,\sigma(z_1,\alpha) \qquad \mu_2(\sigma)_{\star,(\perp,x_1)(\star,x_2)} = 1\,\sigma(\alpha,z_2)$$

for every $p,q \in \{\star,\perp\}$. Then only $(\star,\perp)$ is a deletion point.

Definition 10 (see, e. g., [18]). *The tree series transducer M is* regulated *if it is non-circular and there exists no deletion point (p,q) such that $q \preceq r$ for some self-replicating $r \in Q$.*

Note that it is clearly decidable whether a tree series transducer is regulated. A regulated top-down tree series transducer is nondeleting [2]. This is due to the fact that a deleting top-down tree series transducer has a deletion point (p,q) and thus also the deletion point (p,r) where r is a self-replicating state.

Theorem 11. *Let M be a regulated tree series transducer. Then τ_M is well-defined.*

Proof. Let $M = (Q,\Sigma,\Delta,\mathcal{A},I,\mu)$. By Theorem 5, it is sufficient to show that for an arbitrary size-compliant enumeration $T = (t_i \mid i \in \mathbb{N})$ the family $\tau_M(T)$ converges to $\widetilde{0}$. Let $\mathrm{mx} = \max\{k \mid \Sigma_k \neq \emptyset\}$ and $n = \mathrm{card}(Q)$. We will prove that $\lfloor \mathrm{height}(t)/n \rfloor - n \leqslant \mathrm{height}(u)$ for every $t \in T_\Sigma$ and $u \in \mathrm{supp}(\tau_M(t))$. Consider a maximal path in t (which defines the height). Since M is non-circular, it may erase at most $n-1$ input symbols along this path before it produces output. It might also decide to delete the translation incurred along a suffix of the path. However, the length of such a suffix is limited by n because otherwise M has a deletion point that leads to a self-replicating state. Note that if M is a top-down tree series transducer, then it may not delete (because regulated implies nondeletion). Thus, in this case the bound could be improved to $\lfloor \mathrm{height}(t)/n \rfloor \leqslant \mathrm{height}(u)$. The formal proof of both bounds is straightforward and hence omitted. With the given lower bound, it is clear that $\tau_M(T)$ converges to $\widetilde{0}$ because $\mathrm{height}(u) \leqslant \mathrm{size}(u)$ for every $u \in T_\Delta$ and $\mathrm{size}(t) \leqslant \mathrm{mx}^{\mathrm{height}(t)}$ for every $t \in T_\Sigma$. Thus, τ_M is well-defined. □

We will show the converse only for positive semirings. The main benefit of this approach is that the problem can essentially be reduced to unweighted transducers. We need an additional notion. The tree series transducer M is *input-linear* if for every $q \in Q$, $\sigma \in \Sigma_k$, and $w \in (Q \times X_k)^*$ such that $\mu_k(\sigma)_{q,w} \neq \widetilde{0}$ there exists at most one $1 \leqslant j \leqslant |w|$ such that $w_j = (p,x)$ for every $x \in X_k$. Note that bottom-up implies input-linear. The following lemma shows that every tree series transducer can be turned into an input-nondeleting one (see Definition 8). In fact, we will only need it for input-linear tree series transducers.

Lemma 12 (see [20, Lemma 1(1)]). *If M is input-linear, then there exists a bottom-up tree series transducer M' such that $\tau_{M'} = \tau_M$.*

Proof. It follows directly by reconsidering the proof of [20, Lemma 1(1)]. The top-down tree series transducer constructed in this proof will be the identity if M is input-linear (as already noted before [20, Theorem 4]). Finally, note that the completeness-assumption is not necessary in our case because our tree series transducers are always polynomial [20]. □

Consequently, we will only deal with bottom-up tree series transducers. For those there exists a decomposition result [2, Lemma 5.6], which states that every bottom-up tree series transducer can be decomposed into a relabeling tree series transducer and a $\{0, 1\}$-weighted homomorphism tree series transducer (see [2] for the definitions of those notions). Roughly speaking, the relabeling tree series transducer annotates each node of the input tree by an applicable entry of μ. Such relabeled input trees are called runs. The homomorphism then simply evaluates the run thereby creating the output tree. We use this decomposition in the following informal argument.

Lemma 13. *Let M be a reduced bottom-up tree series transducer over a positive semiring. If τ_M is well-defined, then M is regulated.*

Proof. Suppose that $M = (Q, \Sigma, \Delta, \mathcal{A}, I, \mu)$ is not regulated. Since $\mathcal{A}$ is positive, we restrict ourselves to the unweighted (*i. e.*, BOOLEAN-semiring weighted) bottom-up tree transducer M' obtained by replacing every nonzero semiring coefficient in μ by 1. By a minor extension of [21, Corollary 3] we have supp$(\tau_{M'}(t))$ = supp$(\tau_M(t))$ for every $t \in T_\Sigma$. We will identify M and M' in the following discussion. If M has a deletion point (p, q), then there exists a subtree u of a run, which is deleted by the evaluation homomorphism, because p is accessible and co-accessible. Note that we can replace u by any run that arrives in the state p at the root. If there exists a self-replicating state r such that $p \preceq r$, then it is immediately clear that there exist infinitely many such runs, and consequently, infinitely many suitable input trees. Since the subrun is deleted all those input trees can be transformed to the same output tree. On the other hand, if M is circular, then we can transform infinitely many input trees into the same output tree by using the circle any number of times. The formal proof is again straightforward and omitted. $\square$

Theorem 14. *Let M be a reduced input-linear tree series transducer over a positive semiring. Then τ_M is well-defined if and only if M is regulated.*

Proof. It follows from Theorem 11 and Lemmata 12 and 13. $\square$

References

1. Kuich, W.: Tree transducers and formal tree series. Acta Cybernet 14(1), 135–149 (1999)
2. Engelfriet, J., Fülöp, Z., Vogler, H.: Bottom-up and top-down tree series transformations. J. Autom.Lang.Combin. 7(1), 11–70 (2002)
3. Rounds, W.C.: Mappings and grammars on trees. Math. Systems Theory 4(3), 257–287 (1970)
4. Thatcher, J.W.: Generalized^2 sequential machine maps. J. Comput. System Sci. 4(4), 339–367 (1970)
5. Thatcher, J.W.: Tree automata—an informal survey. In: Currents in the Theory of Computing, pp. 143–172. Prentice Hall, Englewood Cliffs (1973)
6. Engelfriet, J.: Bottom-up and top-down tree transformations—a comparison. Math. Systems Theory 9(3), 198–231 (1975)

7. Engelfriet, J.: Top-down tree transducers with regular look-ahead. Math. Systems Theory 10(1), 289–303 (1977)
8. May, J., Knight, K.: Tiburon: A weighted tree automata toolkit. In: Ibarra, O.H., Yen, H.-C. (eds.) CIAA 2006. LNCS, vol. 4094, pp. 102–113. Springer, Heidelberg (2006)
9. Hebisch, U., Weinert, H.J.: Semirings—Algebraic Theory and Applications in Computer Science. World Scientific, Singapore (1998)
10. Golan, J.S.: Semirings and their Applications. Kluwer Academic, Dordrecht (1999)
11. Bozapalidis, S., Louscou-Bozapalidou, O.: The rank of a formal tree power series. Theoret. Comput. Sci. 27(1–2), 211–215 (1983)
12. Bozapalidis, S.: Equational elements in additive algebras. Theory Comput. Systems 32(1), 1–33 (1999)
13. Kuich, W.: Formal power series over trees. In: Proc.3rd Int.Conf. Developments in Language Theory, Aristotle University of Thessaloniki, pp. 61–101 (1998)
14. Borchardt, B., Vogler, H.: Determinization of finite state weighted tree automata. J. Autom. Lang. Combin. 8(3), 417–463 (2003)
15. Kuich, W.: Full abstract families of tree series I. In: Jewels Are Forever, pp. 145–156. Springer, Heidelberg (1999)
16. Maletti, A.: Pure and o-substitution. Int. J. Found. Comput. Sci. 18(4), 829–845 (2007)
17. Salomaa, A., Soittala, M.: Theoretic Aspects of Formal Power Series. Springer, Heidelberg (1978)
18. Kuich, W., Salomaa, A.: Semirings, Automata, Languages. Monographs in Theoretical Computer Science. An EATCS Series, vol. 5. Springer, Heidelberg (1986)
19. Bozapalidis, S.: Context-free series on trees. Inform. and Comput. 169(2), 186–229 (2001)
20. Maletti, A.: The power of tree series transducers of type I and II. In: De Felice, C., Restivo, A. (eds.) DLT 2005. LNCS, vol. 3572, pp. 338–349. Springer, Heidelberg (2005)
21. Maletti, A.: Hierarchies of tree series transformations revisited. In: Ibarra, O.H., Dang, Z. (eds.) DLT 2006. LNCS, vol. 4036, pp. 215–225. Springer, Heidelberg (2006)

Automata-Theoretic Analysis of Bit-Split Languages for Packet Scanning

Ryan Dixon, Ömer Eğecioğlu, and Timothy Sherwood

Department of Computer Science
University of California, Santa Barbara
{rsd,omer,sherwood}@cs.ucsb.edu

Abstract. Bit-splitting breaks the problem of monitoring traffic payloads to detect the occurrence of suspicious patterns into several parallel components, each of which searches for a particular bit pattern. We analyze bit-splitting as applied to Aho-Corasick style string matching. The problem can be viewed as the recovery of a special class of regular languages over product alphabets from a collection of homomorphic images. We use this characterization to prove correctness and to give space bounds. In particular we show that the NFA to DFA conversion of the Aho-Corasick type machine used for bit-splitting incurs only linear overhead.

1 Introduction

Increasingly, routers are asked to play a role in scanning for, logging, and even preventing network based attacks. Signature based schemes rely on a set of signatures to describe malicious or suspicious data. While a wide variety of signature types are possible, depending on the exact nature of the intrusion detection or prevention method, a signature usually consists of at least a type of packet to search, a sequence of bytes to match, and a location where that sequence is to be searched for.

In an ideal case a signature includes a sequence of bytes which are always transmitted during a specific attack. The SQLSlammer worm, for example, sends 376 bytes to UDP port 1434 and can be detected in part by searching for the invariant framing byte 0x04 [4]. It is not uncommon to have thousands of signatures, each 4 to 40 bytes long. Searching through every byte of the payload of every packet for one of a large number of signatures quickly becomes a significant computational challenge.

One implementation concern is storage. A single state of a DFA must have 256 next-pointers each of which can address one of 10,000 states. At 448 bytes per state, the entire rule set of the intrusion detection system Snort [5] would require of 6 MB of on-chip storage.

To address these problems, bit-split Aho-Corasick machines have been proposed to reduce the storage requirements by a factor of 10, and enable scanning throughput on the order of 10 Gb/s (see [6]). While this work has demonstrated

O.H. Ibarra and B. Ravikumar (Eds.): CIAA 2008, LNCS 5148, pp. 141–150, 2008.

that bit-splitting works in the specific case of Aho-Corasick machines built over the Snort rule set, correctness or efficiency in the general case has not been shown. In this paper we analyze bit-splitting as applied to Aho-Corasick based string matching and prove that it works correctly in general. In addition, we prove that this approach avoids a potential combinatorial explosion observed in the simulation of NFA by DFA.

String matching in this context can be viewed as the problem of efficiently recognizing languages of the form

$$\Sigma^*(p_1 + p_2 + \cdots + p_m) \tag{1}$$

where $P = \{p_1, p_2, \ldots, p_m\}$ is a finite set of patterns (keywords). This corresponds to locating the first index in the given packet (text) where a signature (pattern) starts.

Some intrusion detection techniques make use of context free grammars to define a language of signatures, such as the $LL(k)$ parser at the heart of STATL [3]. The majority of intrusion detection systems are far more restrictive. The set P of patterns that Snort searches is a finite language. However, because Snort needs to find any member of P at any offset it is essentially a recognizer for languages of finite suffixes as in (1).

For some of the recent approaches to packet scanning techniques we refer the reader to [2, 6, 7] and the references therein.

2   The General Case of Two Alphabets

Our starting point is *bit-splitting* as described in [6] where a set of binary machines that run in parallel from a given Aho-Corasick machine M are constructed. Each machine searches for one bit of the input at a time, and a match occurs only when all of the machines agree. Since the split machines have exactly two possible next states they are far easier to compact into a small amount of memory. Also they are loosely coupled, and they can be run independently of one another.

The alphabet of M can be thought of as being $\Sigma = \{0, 1\}^8$. The correctness and performance of bit-splitting has to do with languages defined over alphabets which are Cartesian products of other alphabets, binary or otherwise.

Consider a DFA where the input alphabet is a Cartesian product of two alphabets. Such an automaton is a finite state machine $M = (Q, \Sigma, \delta, q_1, F)$ where $Q = \{q_1, q_2, \ldots, q_m\}$ is a set of states, q_1 is the start state, and $\delta : Q \times \Sigma \to Q$ is the transition function and $F \subseteq Q$ is the set of final states.

Suppose $\Sigma = A \times B$ for $A = \{\alpha_1, \alpha_2, \ldots, \alpha_r\}$ and $B = \{\beta_1, \beta_2, \ldots, \beta_s\}$. We further assume that $r, s \geq 2$.

Let $\mathcal{L} = \mathcal{L}(M)$ denote the language accepted by M. Each $w \in \mathcal{L}$ is of the form $w = a_1 b_1 \, a_2 b_2 \cdots a_n b_n$ for some $n \geq 0$ and $a_i \in A, b_i \in B$ for $i = 1, 2, \ldots, n$.

M can be "bit-split" to construct two nondeterministic finite state machines M_A and M_B. This is done by changing the alphabet and the transition function of M, but not the set of states, the initial state, or the set of final states, in the following manner.

Definition 1. *Given a DFA* $M = (Q, \Sigma, \delta, q_1, F)$ *where* $\Sigma = A \times B$ *with* $A = \{\alpha_1, \alpha_2, \ldots, \alpha_r\}$ *and* $B = \{\beta_1, \beta_2, \ldots, \beta_s\}$, *define*

$$M_A = (Q, A, \delta_A, q_1, F) \text{ where } \forall a \in A, q \in Q, \quad \delta_A(q, a) = \bigcup_{j=1}^{s} \delta(q, a\beta_j) \ ,$$

$$M_B = (Q, B, \delta_B, q_1, F) \text{ where } \forall b \in A, q \in Q, \quad \delta_B(q, b) = \bigcup_{i=1}^{r} \delta(q, \alpha_i b) \ .$$

M_A *and* M_B *are called* bit-split automata *or* projection automata *obtained from* M. $\mathcal{L}_A = \mathcal{L}(M_A)$ *and* $\mathcal{L}_B = \mathcal{L}(M_B)$ *denote the languages accepted by* M_A *and* M_B, *respectively.*

M_A and M_B can be described in a number of ways. Probably the easiest visualization is as follows: To construct the transition diagram of M_A, make a copy of M and erase the second letter in every transition in the transition diagram of M. M_B is constructed similarly. Since $r, s \geq 2$, M_A and M_B are both nondeterministic. The final step in bit-splitting is to take M_A and M_B and construct an equivalent DFA DM_A to M_A and an equivalent DFA DM_A to M_B. This final step is very important from an implementation standpoint, both because DFA are the only models that can be implemented on real machines and at the same time, the construction from NFA to DFA in general has the potential to increase the number of states exponentially.

The languages $\mathcal{L}_A$ and $\mathcal{L}_B$ are easily seen to be homomorphic images of $\mathcal{L}$. For example, if we define the homomorphism $h_A : \Sigma \to A$ by setting $h_A(\alpha_i\beta_j) = \alpha_i$ for every letter $\alpha_i\beta_j \in \Sigma$ for $i = 1, 2, \ldots, r$, $j = 1, 2, \ldots, s$, then $\mathcal{L}_A = h_A(\mathcal{L})$. In particular, given a regular expression R denoting $\mathcal{L}$, a regular expression for $\mathcal{L}_A$ is obtained from R by replacing each occurrence of the letter $\alpha_i\beta_j$ by α_i, and a regular expression for $\mathcal{L}_B$ is obtained from R by replacing each occurrence of $\alpha_i\beta_j$ by β_j.

Example: When $\Sigma = A \times B$ with $A = \{0, 1\}$ and $B = \{a, b\}$, the language $\mathcal{L}$ over Σ denoted by the regular expression $(0a + 0b + 1a + 1b)^*0b$ results in the languages $\mathcal{L}_A$ over A and $\mathcal{L}_B$ over B denoted by the regular expressions $(0+1)^*0$ and $(a + b)^*b$, respectively. The transition diagrams of M, M_A and M_B are as shown in Figure 1.

Definition 2. *Given* $\mathcal{L}_A$ *over* A *and* $\mathcal{L}_B$ *over* B, *the language* $Alt(\mathcal{L}_A, \mathcal{L}_B)$ *over* $A \times B$ *is defined by*

$$Alt(\mathcal{L}_A, \mathcal{L}_B) = \{a_1b_1 \, a_2b_2 \cdots a_nb_n \mid n \geq 0, a_1a_2 \cdots a_n \in \mathcal{L}_A, b_1b_2 \cdots b_n \in \mathcal{L}_B\}.$$

The problems that we formalize in this paper come down to the recovery of $\mathcal{L}$ from $\mathcal{L}_A$ and $\mathcal{L}_B$, and the state complexity of the conversion of M_A to DM_A and M_B to DM_B for Aho-Corasick machines.

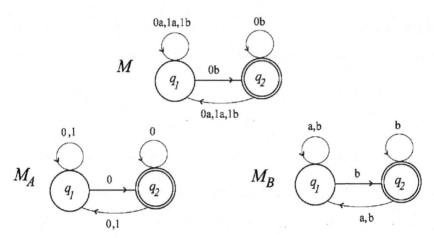

Fig. 1. M_A and M_B from M: $\Sigma = A \times B$ with $A = \{0, 1\}$, $B = \{a, b\}$

Lemma 1. *Suppose* $w = a_1b_1\,a_2b_2\,\cdots\,a_nb_n \in \mathcal{L}$, *where* $\mathcal{L} = \mathcal{L}(M)$ *for a DFA* M *over the alphabet* $A \times B$, *as in Definition 1. Then* $a_1a_2\cdots a_n \in \mathcal{L}_A$ *and* $b_1b_2\cdots b_n \in \mathcal{L}_B$. *In other words*

$$\mathcal{L} \subseteq Alt(\mathcal{L}_A, \mathcal{L}_B). \tag{2}$$

Proof. Suppose $a_1b_1\,a_2b_2\cdots a_nb_n \in \mathcal{L}$. Then there are states $q_{i_1}, q_{i_2}, \ldots, q_{i_{n+1}}$ in Q with $q_1 = q_{i_1}$ and $q_{i_{n+1}} \in F$ with $\delta(q_{i_j}, a_jb_j) = q_{i_{j+1}}$ for $j = 1, 2, \ldots, n$. By the definition of δ_A, $q_{i_{j+1}} \in \delta_A(q_{i_j}, a_j)$ for $j = 1, 2, \ldots, n$. Furthermore $q_{i_{n+1}}$ is also a final state of M_A. Thus $a_1a_2\cdots a_n \in \mathcal{L}_A$. Similarly $b_1b_2\cdots b_n \in \mathcal{L}_B$. Therefore every $a_1b_1\,a_2b_2\cdots a_nb_n \in \mathcal{L}$ belongs to $Alt(\mathcal{L}_A, \mathcal{L}_B)$ and (2) follows.   □

Remark: Equality in (2) does not necessarily hold. For example when $\Sigma = \{0, 1\} \times \{a, b\}$ and $\mathcal{L}$ over Σ is the language denoted by the $(0a + 0b + 1a + 1b)^*(0b + 1a)$, $\mathcal{L}_A$ and $\mathcal{L}_B$ are the languages denoted by the regular expressions $(0 + 1)^*(0 + 1)$ and $(a + b)^*(a + b)$, respectively. Thus $a_1 = 0$ and $b_1 = a$ are in $\mathcal{L}_A$ and $\mathcal{L}_B$, respectively. Therefore $a_1b_1 = 0a \in Alt(\mathcal{L}_A, \mathcal{L}_B)$, but $0a \notin \mathcal{L}$.

Definition 3. *Suppose* $\mathcal{L} = \mathcal{L}(M)$ *where* M *is a DFA over* $\Sigma = A \times B$. $\mathcal{L}$ *satisfies the* alternation property *if for every* $n \geq 0$, $a_i, x_i \in A$, $b_i, y_i \in B$ *for* $i = 1, 2, \ldots, n$,

$$a_1y_1\,a_2y_2\cdots a_ny_n,\ x_1b_1\,x_2b_2\cdots x_nb_n \in \mathcal{L} \text{ implies } a_1b_1\,a_2b_2\cdots a_nb_n \in \mathcal{L}. \tag{3}$$

This property suffices to prove equality in (2).

Proposition 1. *Suppose* $\mathcal{L} = \mathcal{L}(M)$ *over the alphabet* $\Sigma = A \times B$, $\mathcal{L}_A$ *and* $\mathcal{L}_B$ *defined as in Definition 1. If* $\mathcal{L}$ *has the alternation property, then*

$$\mathcal{L} = Alt(\mathcal{L}_A, \mathcal{L}_B) .$$

Proof. By Lemma 1, we have $\mathcal{L} \subseteq Alt(\mathcal{L}_A, \mathcal{L}_B)$. To show $Alt(\mathcal{L}_A, \mathcal{L}_B) \subseteq \mathcal{L}$, assume $a_1 b_1\, a_2 b_2 \cdots a_n b_n \in Alt(\mathcal{L}_A, \mathcal{L}_B)$ for some $n \geq 0$. By definition of $Alt(\mathcal{L}_A, \mathcal{L}_B)$, $a_1 a_2 \cdots a_n \in \mathcal{L}_A$ and $b_1 b_2 \cdots b_n \in \mathcal{L}_B$. First we show that $a_1 a_2 \cdots a_n \in \mathcal{L}_A$ implies that there exist $y_1, y_2, \ldots, y_n \in B$ with $a_1 y_1\, a_2 y_2 \cdots a_n y_n \in \mathcal{L}$. Consider a sequence of states $q_{i_1}, q_{i_2}, \ldots, q_{i_{n+1}}$ in Q with $q_1 = q_{i_1}$ and $q_{i_{n+1}} \in F$ with

$$q_{i_{j+1}} \in \delta_A(q_{i_j}, a_j)$$

for $j = 1, 2, \ldots, n$. By definition of δ_A,

$$q_{i_{j+1}} = \delta(q_{i_j}, a_j \beta_{k_j})$$

for some $\beta_{k_j} \in B$ and we can take $y_j = \beta_{k_j}$ for $j = 1, 2, \ldots, n$. Similarly, $b_1 b_2 \cdots b_n \in \mathcal{L}_B$ implies that there exist $x_1, x_2, \ldots, x_n \in A$ with $x_1 b_1 x_2 b_2 \cdots x_n b_n \in \mathcal{L}$. Since $\mathcal{L}$ satisfies the alternation property, we have $a_1 b_1\, a_2 b_2 \cdots a_n b_n \in \mathcal{L}$. Thus $Alt(\mathcal{L}_A, \mathcal{L}_B) \subseteq \mathcal{L}$. □

Lemma 2. *The language $\mathcal{L} = \mathcal{L}(M)$ accepted by a Aho-Corasick machine M with a single keyword satisfies the alternation property.*

Proof. $\mathcal{L}$ is of the form $\Sigma^* p$ where $\Sigma = A \times B$ and p is the keyword. With the notation of Definition 3,

$$a_1 y_1\, a_2 y_2 \cdots a_n y_n,\ x_1 b_1\, x_2 b_2 \cdots x_n b_n \in \mathcal{L}$$

implies that for some k,

$$a_1 y_1\, a_2 y_2 \cdots a_n y_n = a_1 y_1\, a_2 y_2 \cdots a_k y_k\, p\ ,$$
$$x_1 b_1\, x_2 b_2 \cdots x_n b_n = x_1 b_1\, x_2 b_2 \cdots x_k b_k\, p\ .$$

Therefore $a_1 b_1\, a_2 b_2 \cdots a_n b_n = a_1 b_1\, a_2 b_2 \cdots a_k b_k\, p \in \mathcal{L}$. □

The language $\mathcal{L}$ we are interested in is a finite union of languages of the form $\Sigma^* p$, where the union is over the keywords p. However $\mathcal{L}$ in this generality need not satisfy the alternation property of Proposition 1.

It is possible to have an exponential blow-up in the number of states of a DFA for a language $\mathcal{L}$ and the minimum state DFA for its homomorphic image $h(\mathcal{L})$, even if the homomorphism just identifies a pair of letters of the alphabet, e.g. a homomorphism such as

$$h : \{a, b, c\} \rightarrow \{a, b\}^*, \text{ where } h(a) = a,\ h(b) = b,\ h(c) = b. \tag{4}$$

Example: Let $\Sigma = \{a, b, c\}$. Given an integer $k > 0$, consider the DFA M on $k + 2$ states shown in Figure 2. M accepts the language $\mathcal{L}$ denoted by $(a + b)^* c(a + b)^{k-1}$. The homomorphic image of $\mathcal{L}$ under the homomorphism (4) is given by $(a + b)^* b(a + b)^{k-1}$. It is well-known that the minimum state DFA for this latter language requires $\Omega(2^k)$ states.

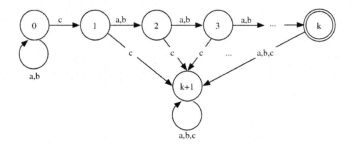

Fig. 2. DFA for a language whose homomorphic image requires $\Omega(2^k)$ DFA states

2.1   NFA to DFA Conversion in Bit-Splitting

We can show that for any Aho-Corasick pattern matching machine, the projection automata M_A and M_B in our construction do not blow up in size when converted to the equivalent DFA DM_A and DM_B.

Recall that the Aho-Corasick algorithm [1] constructs a special state machine which is essentially a trie with back/cross edges, that can be constructed and stored in linear time and space with respect to the total complexity of all the keywords. The preprocessing for the construction is in two stages. The first stage builds up a tree of all keyword strings. The tree has a branching factor equal to the number of symbols in the language, and is thus a *trie*. The root represents the state where no strings have been even partially matched. To match a string, we start at the root node and traverse down the edges according to the input characters observed. The second half of the preprocessing is inserting failure edges. When a string match is not found, it is possible for the suffix of one keyword to match a prefix of another. To handle this case, transitions are inserted which shortcut from a partial match of one string to a partial match of another. In the Aho-Corasick automaton, there is a one-to-one correspondence between accepting states and strings, where each accepting state indicates the match to a unique keyword.

Proposition 2. *Suppose M is a Aho-Corasick automaton on n states over the alphabet $\Sigma = A \times B$ and M_A, M_B are the two NFA obtained from M using bit-splitting. Then the equivalent DFA DM_A and DM_B each have at most n states.*

Proof. M is built on a trie for a set of keywords $P = \{p_1, p_2, \ldots, p_m\}$ with a number of back and cross edges defined by the longest proper suffix that is also a prefix of some keyword, as described above and in detail in [1].

It suffices to show that the trie part of M_A (and M_B) has no more than n states, as the back and cross edges for DM_A and DM_B are constructed by the longest proper suffix condition for the patterns obtained from P after collapsing the alphabets to A and B, and this process does not change the number of states.

Note that we can obtain M_A from M in stages, where in each stage a pair of letters of the current alphabet are identified and the alphabet is reduced in size by one. For example starting with $A \times B = \{0, 1\} \times \{a, b, c\} = \{0a, 0b, 0c, 1a, 1b, 1c\}$, we can identify $1c$ and $1b$, and then $1b$ with $1a$ obtaining the intermediate alphabet $\{0a, 0b, 0c, 1a\}$. Then we can identify $0c$ and $0b$, and then $0b$ with $0a$ obtaining $\{0a, 1a\}$, which is a copy of A. Thus it suffices to show that when only two letters are identified, the resulting machine has a deterministic counterpart with no more than n states.

Suppose we are given a trie T of an Aho-Corasick machine M on some alphabet Σ (which need not be a product of two alphabets), and we identify two letters $b, c \in \Sigma$. In T, we first replace each occurrence of c by b. The resulting structure is a nondeterministic trie, in the sense that a node can have more than one child labeled by the letter b. As the second step, we identify nodes of the trie top down, level by level, and at each level, from left to right. At the root of the trie, we identify the children of the root indexed by the letter b. At other nodes, we may also need to identify children of a node labeled by the same letter for letters other than b, because identifications at the previous level may produce more than one child in an identified node that is labeled by a letter other than b. In addition, if any one of the identified nodes is a final state of the original machine, then the node obtained by the identification is made into a final state of the resulting machine. Since a sequence of identifications can only decrease the number of nodes of the trie, the result follows. $\square$

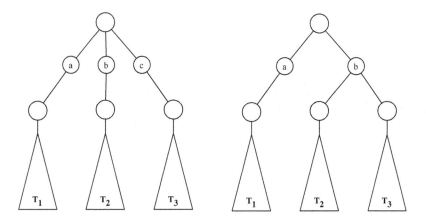

Fig. 3. Identification of b and c: at the root of the trie

Note that the identifications can produce multiple back edges or cross edges if we keep these edges in addition to the trie structure when we execute the two steps in the proof above. The final step in creating the Aho-Corasick machine requires the elimination of multiple edges of this type which may have been created by the identification nodes. In other words, we need not recompute the back and cross edges anew for each the new set of keywords obtained by identifying a pair of letters. Figure 3 and Figure 4 show the operation of identification on root and non-root nodes of the trie.

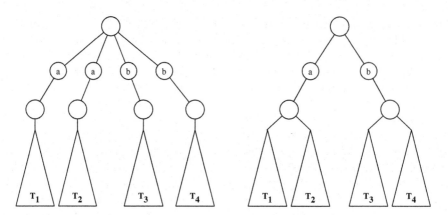

Fig. 4. Identification of b and c: at an arbitrary node of the trie

Example: The trie in Figure 5 is built on the patterns $P = \{abbc, abcc, bab, bba, ca, cba, cc\}$ over $\Sigma = \{a, b, c\}$. Identification of c and b results in the trie in Figure 6 built on the set of patterns $\{abbb, bab, bba, ba, bb\}$ over $\Sigma = \{a, b\}$.

2.2   Recovering $\mathcal{L}$

If there is a single pattern p, then the language $\mathcal{L}_M$ is the form $\Sigma^* p$. Since this language has the alternation property of Definition 3, $\mathcal{L}$ can be recovered completely from the knowledge of $\mathcal{L}_A$ and $\mathcal{L}_B$. Thus by Proposition 1 the input $a_1 b_1\, a_2 b_2 \cdots a_n b_n \in \mathcal{L}$ iff $a_1 a_2 \cdots a_n \in \mathcal{L}_A$ and $b_1 b_2 \cdots b_n \in \mathcal{L}_B$. But this works because both M_A and M_B have a single final state, i.e. the unique final state of M that corresponds to the keyword p. When there is more than one keyword, $\mathcal{L}$ no longer satisfies the alternation property, and therefore equality of the languages in Proposition 1 does not hold. However we can recover $\mathcal{L}$ from M_A and M_B by considering a type of diagonal acceptance as follows

Proposition 3. *Suppose $\mathcal{L} = \mathcal{L}(M)$ over the alphabet $\Sigma = A \times B$ for some Aho-Corasick machine M. Define $M_A(f)$ and $M_B(f)$ as in Definition 1, except a fixed $f \in F$ is made the final state. For $a_1 a_2 \cdots a_n \in \mathcal{L}_A$ and $b_1 b_2 \cdots b_n \in \mathcal{L}_B$, $a_1 b_1\, a_2 b_2 \cdots a_n b_n \in \mathcal{L}$ iff $a_1 a_2 \cdots a_n \in \mathcal{L}(M_A(f))$ and $b_1 b_2 \cdots b_n \in \mathcal{L}(M_B(f))$ for some $f \in F$.*

Proof. An Aho-Corasick machine M accepts languages of the form (1). The condition of the proposition forces M_A and M_B to accept by the same final state. Thus for each final state, the language accepted is of the form $\Sigma^* p_i$, and therefore satisfies the alternation property and Lemma 2 is applicable.   □

Remark: Note that we are not able to recover $\mathcal{L}$ from an arbitrary description of the languages $\mathcal{L}_A$ and $\mathcal{L}_B$ for more than one pattern. However for the packet

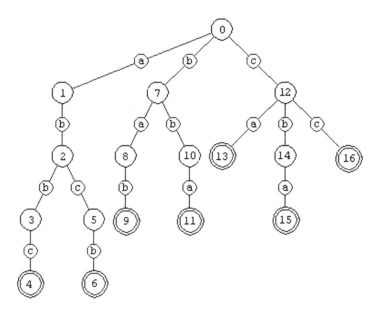

Fig. 5. Trie portion of the Aho-Corasick machine for the keywords $\{abbc, abcc, bab,$ $bba, ca, cba, cc\}$ over $\Sigma = \{a, b, c\}$

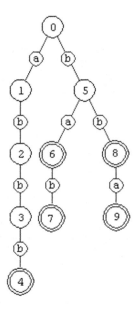

Fig. 6. After identifying c and b, the resulting trie of the Aho-Corasick machine for the keywords $\{abbb, bab, bba, ba, bb\}$ over $\Sigma = \{a, b\}$

scanning application, this presents no problems. We make sure that the M_A and M_B accept on the same final state. Otherwise the input is rejected.

Remark: If we use the deterministic versions of M_A and M_B obtained by the algorithm described in the proof of Proposition 2 and keep the names of the identified final as an equivalence class, then we can still recover $\mathcal{L}$ by acceptance by the "same" final state, meaning that there is a common final state in the two equivalence classes of names after identifications in the resulting DFA.

Remark: The results given above for the Cartesian product of two alphabets readily generalize to $\Sigma = A_1 \times A_2 \times \cdots \times A_m$. We omit the details of the general case. In particular, $\Sigma = \{0, 1\}^8$, results in the 8 binary machines $M_0, M_1, \ldots, M_7$ of the bit-split Aho-Corasick.

3   Conclusions

We proved that bit-splitting Aho-Corasick machines is functionally correct, and provided strict space bounds for this approach. The formal description of how and why bit-splitting works opens the door to new potential applications for other classes of languages in similar problem domains. Future work could address a formal framework for bit-splitting to search for patterns embedded with single character wildcards.

References

[1] Aho, A.V., Corasick, M.J.: Efficient String Matching: An Aid to Bibliographic Search. Comm. of the ACM 18(6), 333–340 (1975)
[2] Baker, Z.K., Prasanna, V.K.: High-throughput Linked-Pattern Matching for Intrusion Detection Systems. In: Proc. of the First Annual ACM Sym. on Arch. for Networking and Comm. Systems (2005)
[3] Eckmann, S.T., Vigna, G., Kemmerer, R.A.: STATL: An Attack Language for State-Based Intrusion Detection. J. of Computer Security 10(1/2), 71–104 (2002)
[4] Newsome, J., Karp, B., Song, D.X.: Polygraph: Automatically Generating Signatures for Polymorphic Worms. In: IEEE Sym. on Security and Privacy, pp. 226–241 (2005)
[5] Roesch, M.: Snort - lightweight intrusion detection for networks. In: Proc. of LISA 1999: 13th Systems Adm. Conf., November 1999, pp. 229–238 (1999)
[6] Tan, L., Sherwood, T.: A High Throughput String Matching Architecture for Intrusion Detection and Prevention. In: ISCA 2005: Proc. of the 32nd Annual Int. Sym. on Computer Architecture, pp. 112–122 (2005)
[7] Tuck, N., Sherwood, T., Calder, B., Varghese, G.: Deterministic Memory-Efficient String Matching Algorithms for Intrusion Detection. In: The 23rd Conf. of the IEEE Comm. Society (Infocomm) (2004)

Pattern Matching in DCA Coded Text[*]

Jan Lahoda[1,2], Bořivoj Melichar[1], and Jan Žďárek[1]

[1] Department of Computer Science and Engineering,
Faculty of Electrical Engineering, Czech Technical University in Prague,
Karlovo náměstí 13, 121 35 Praha 2, Czech Republic
{melichar,zdarekj}@fel.cvut.cz
[2] Sun Microsystems Czech, V Parku 2308/8, 148 00 Praha 4, Czech Republic
Jan.Lahoda@sun.com

Abstract. A new algorithm searching all occurrences of a regular expression pattern in a text is presented. It uses only the text that has been compressed by the text compression using antidictionaries without its decompression. The proposed algorithm runs in $\mathcal{O}(2^m \cdot ||\mathrm{AD}||^2 + n_c + r)$ worst case time, where m is the length of the pattern, AD is the antidictionary, n_C is the length of the coded text and r is the number of found matches.

1 Introduction

We present a new algorithm for searching strings from a set of strings described by a regular expression in a text coded by the Data Compression with Antidictionaries (DCA) compression method (text compression using antidictionaries [1]). The proposed algorithm and its variants run in linear time with respect to the length of the compressed text, not counting the preprocessing costs.

The paper is organized as follows: After resumption of several basic notions at the beginning of Section 2, we continue with a short overview of the DCA compression method itself in Section 2.1 and the KMP based searching in the DCA compressed text in Section 2.3. Section 3 discusses proposed basic (3.1), and enhanced algorithms (using almost antiwords in 3.2 and incremental construction in 3.3). We conclude in Section 5. The experimental evaluation of our algorithms is described in the appendix.

2 Basic Notions and Previous Work

Let A be a finite alphabet and its elements be called symbols. The set of all strings over A is denoted by A^* and A^ℓ is the set of all strings of length ℓ. The empty string is denoted by ε. A power set of set S is denoted by $\mathcal{P}(S)$. Language L is any subset of A^*, $L \subseteq A^*$. Let $P \in A^m$ and $T \in A^n$ be a pattern and a text, respectively, $m \leq n$. An exact occurrence of P in T is an index i, such that $P[1, \ldots, m] = T[i - m + 1, \ldots, i]$, $i \leq n$. Dictionary (antidictionary) AD is a set of words over A, $\mathrm{AD} = \{w_1, w_2, \ldots, w_{|\mathrm{AD}|}\}$, $|\mathrm{AD}|$ denotes the number of

---

[*] This research has been partially supported by the Czech Science Foundation as project No. 201/06/1039 and by the MSMT research program MSM6840770014.

O.H. Ibarra and B. Ravikumar (Eds.): CIAA 2008, LNCS 5148, pp. 151–160, 2008.

strings in AD. By $\|AD\|$ we denote the sum of lengths of all words in AD. A finite automaton (FA) is a quintuple (Q, A, δ, I, F). Q is a finite set of states, A is a finite input alphabet, $F \subseteq Q$ is a set of final states. If FA is nondeterministic (NFA), then δ is a mapping $Q \times (A \cup \{\varepsilon\}) \mapsto \mathcal{P}(Q)$ and $I \subseteq Q$ is a set of initial states. A deterministic FA (DFA) is (Q, A, δ, q_0, F), where δ is a (partial) function $Q \times A \mapsto Q$; $q_0 \in Q$ is the only initial state. A finite transducer (FT) is $(Q, A, \Gamma, \delta, q_0, F)$, where δ is a mapping $Q \times (A \cup \{\varepsilon\}) \mapsto Q \times (\Gamma \cup \{\varepsilon\})$. A regular expression (RE) over finite alphabet A is defined as follows: $\emptyset$, ε, and a are REs, $\forall a \in A$. Let x, y be REs, then $x + y$, $x \cdot y$, x^*, and (x) are REs, priority of operators is: $+$ (the lowest), $\cdot$, * (the highest). Priority of evaluation of a RE can be modified using the parentheses. The length of the regular expression is defined as the count of all symbols in the regular expression except for parentheses and concatenation operator $(\cdot)$ [2].

2.1 DCA Compression Method

The DCA compression method has been proposed by Crochemore *et al.* [1] in 1999. The antidictionary is a *dictionary of antiwords* – words that do not appear in the text to be coded. Let $T \in \{0, 1\}^*$ be the text to be coded. The text is being read from left to right. When a symbol (a bit) is read from the input text and if the suffix of the text read so far is the longest proper prefix of an antiword, nothing is put to the output. Otherwise, the current symbol is output. The text can be decoded since the missing symbol can be inferred from the antiwords.

The coding process is based on finite transducer $E(AD) = (Q_E, \{0, 1\}, \{0, 1\}, \delta_E, q_{E0}, \emptyset)$. The encoding algorithm is shown in Algorithm 1. An example of the encoding finite transducer is given in Figure 1 a).

The decoding process is also based on finite transducer $B(AD) = (Q_B, \{0, 1\}, \{0, 1\}, \delta_B, q_{B0}, \emptyset)$. The decoding transducer is created from the encoding transducer by swapping input and output labels on all transitions. Note that an additional information about the text length is required to decode the original text properly. The decoding algorithm is shown in Algorithm 2. An example of the decoding finite transducer is given in Figure 1 b).

For the construction of the encoding transducer itself, please refer to [1].

Algorithm 1. Text compression using the DCA compression method

---

Input: Encoding transducer $E(AD) = (Q_E, \{0, 1\}, \{0, 1\}, \delta_E, q_{E0}, \emptyset)$.

    $q = q_{E0}$
    while not the end of the input **do**
        let a be the next input symbol
        $(q', u) = \delta_E(q, a)$
        if $u \neq \varepsilon$ **then**
            print a to the output
        end if
        $q = q'$
    end while

Algorithm 2. Text decompression using the DCA compression method

Input: Decoding transducer $B(AD) = (Q_B, \{0,1\}, \{0,1\}, \delta_B, q_{B0}, \emptyset)$, the length of the
original text n.

$q = q_{B0}$
$i = 0$
while not the end of the input **do**
    let a be the next input symbol
    $(q', u) = \delta_B(q, a)$
    print u to the output, $q = q'$, $i = i + 1$
    while $i \leq n$ and $\delta_B(q, \varepsilon)$ is defined **do**
        $(q', u) = \delta_B(q, \varepsilon)$
        print u to the output, $q = q'$, $i = i + 1$
    end while
end while

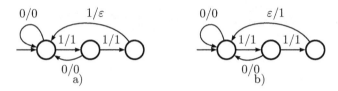

Fig. 1. a) Encoding and b) decoding transducer for AD $= \{110\}$

2.2   Regular Expression Pattern Matching

Regular expressions are commonly used for a specification of a full text search.
The search can be implemented by means of finite automata. Generally, both
nondeterministic (using NFA simulation [3]) and deterministic finite automata
can be used for pattern matching. In this paper, however, we will focus only on
a pattern matching using deterministic finite automata.

The pattern matching using finite automata is a two phase process. In the
first (preprocessing) phase, the searching deterministic finite automaton is constructed for the given pattern (e.g. regular expression). In the second phase,
the input text is processed by the automaton, and each time it enters a final
state, an occurrence of the pattern is reported. This algorithm is outlined in
Algorithm 3.

For regular expression of length m, the corresponding nondeterministic finite
automaton has $m + 1$ states. The corresponding deterministic finite automaton
has therefore $\mathcal{O}(2^m)$ states at most.

Please note that although the exponential growth of the number of states
occurs for certain regular expressions (e.g. $a(a + b)^{m-1}$), the number of states of
the deterministic finite automaton is much smaller in many practical situations,
e.g. $\mathcal{O}(m)$ for exact pattern matching [3].

Algorithm 3. Pattern matching using deterministic finite automaton

Input: Deterministic finite automaton $M = (Q, A, \delta, q_0, F)$.

  $q = q_0$
  $i = 1$
  while not the end of the input **do**
    if $q \in F$ **then**
      mark occurrence of the pattern at index i
    end if
    let a be the next input symbol
    $q = \delta(q, a)$
    $i = i + 1$
  end while
  if $q \in F$ **then**
    mark occurrence of the pattern at index i
  end if

2.3 KMP-Based Pattern Matching in DCA Coded Text

Shibata *et al.* [4] presented a KMP based approach for pattern matching in the DCA compressed text. As a part of this method, the decoding transducer with ε-transitions is converted to a generalized transducer $G(\mathrm{AD}) = (Q_G, \{0,1\}, \{0,1\}, \delta_G, q_{G0}, \emptyset)$ without ε-transitions. The main concept of the conversion is to concatenate sequences of transitions, consisting of a non-ε-transition and at least one ε-transition, into a single transition, see Figure 2.

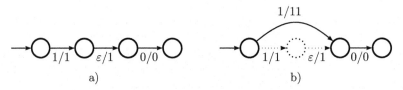

Fig. 2. Generalized decoding transducer construction: a) original decoding transducer, b) generalized decoding transducer

    The original decoding transducer may contain infinite sequences of ε-transitions, which are represented by loops of ε-transitions in the decoding transducer, as shown in Figure 3. Note that the infinite ε-transitions sequence can occur only when the very last character of the coded text is being processed. As the uncoded text is of finite length, the sequence of ε-transitions will not be infinite in fact, it is called semi-infinite [4].

    The infinite ε-transitions sequence handling is as follows. A special state $\perp \in Q_G$ is defined, and transitions sequences leading into a loop of ε-transitions in the original transducer are redirected into this state. The text decoded by this infinite transitions sequence is always in form of uv^* (where $u, v \in \{0,1\}^*$, u is

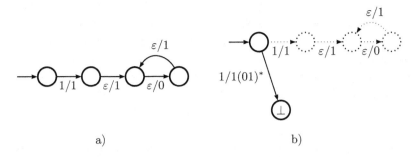

a)   b)

Fig. 3. Infinite ε-transitions sequence

the prefix decoded before entering the infinite loop, v is the text decoded by the infinite loop), as shown in Figure 3.

3   Main Result

We propose the algorithm for pattern matching in DCA coded text in this section. Two extensions to the algorithm are also proposed. The first extension allows to search text coded by the "almost antiwords" extension to the DCA algorithm (Crochemore and Navarro [5]). The second extension allows to dissolve the preprocessing cost into the searching phase, which may lead into faster searches. This assumption has been verified successfully by our experiments, see Section 4.

The proposed algorithm is based on the algorithm by Shibata *et al.* [4] and our method described in [6] and [7].

3.1   Basic Algorithm

The pattern matching in the DCA coded text is based on finite automata. Automaton M_C, $M_C = (Q_C, \{0, 1\}, \delta_C, q_{C0}, \emptyset)$, for pattern matching in DCA coded text is constructed from the decoding transducer and deterministic pattern matching automaton M, $M = (Q, \{0, 1\}, \delta, q_0, F)$, for the given pattern P. Automaton M_C is constructed by "replacing" states from the pattern matching automaton M with copies of the generalized decoding transducer $G(AD)$, $G(AD) = (Q_G, \{0, 1\}, \{0, 1\}, \delta_G, q_{B0}, \emptyset)$. The states of automaton M_C are therefore pairs $[q, q_G], q \in Q, q_G \in Q_G$. The transitions of automaton M_C are then defined as: $\delta_C([q, q_G], a) = [\delta^*(q, \text{output}_G(q_G, a)), \delta_G(q_G, a)]$.

While reading one symbol of the coded text, more than one transition in the original pattern matching automaton M may be performed. Consequently, performing one transition in the automaton M_C may lead into more than one found match. Ordinary final states are not enough to describe this behavior, so we are proposing two auxiliary functions: N and I. Function N maps each transition of M_C to all matches found by this transition, $N : Q_C \times \{0, 1\} \to \mathcal{P}(\mathbb{N})$. Function I maps each transition to the number of symbols that would be decoded by the equivalent transition in the original decoding transducer, $I : Q_C \times \{0, 1\} \to \mathbb{N}$. These two functions allow to report exact match occurrences on exact positions.

The construction of the automaton for pattern matching in DCA coded text and of functions N and I is described in Algorithm 4. An example is given in the appendix.

Algorithm 4. Construction of automaton for pattern matching in DCA coded text

---

Input: Pattern matching automaton $M = (Q, \{0, 1\}, \delta, q_0, F)$, decoding transducer $G(\text{AD}) = (Q_G, \{0, 1\}, \{0, 1\}, \delta_G, q_{B0}, \emptyset)$.
Output: Automaton $M_C = (Q_C, \{0, 1\}, \delta_C, q_{C0}, \emptyset)$ for pattern matching in DCA coded text, auxiliary functions N, I.
$Q_C = Q \times Q_G$
$q_{C0} = (q_0, q_{G0})$
for all $q_C \in Q_C$ $(q_C = (q, q_G))$ and $a \in \{0, 1\}$ **do**
  $(q'_G, u) = \delta_G(q_G, a)$ (where u is the output text)
  if $q'_G \neq \perp$ **then**
    $\delta_C(q_C, a) = [\delta^*(q, u), q'_G]$
    $N(q_C, a) = \{i; \delta^*(q, u[1 : i + 1]) \in F\}$
    $I(q_C, a) = |u|$
  else
    $\delta_C(q_C, a) = \perp$
  end if
end for

Theorem 1. *For pattern P of length m, and the antidictionary* AD *of length* $\|\text{AD}\|$, *worst case time complexity of Algorithm 4 is $\mathcal{O}(2^m \cdot \|\text{AD}\|^2)$, and it uses $\mathcal{O}(2^m \cdot \|\text{AD}\|^2)$ memory in the worst case.*

Proof. The main loop of the algorithm is performed $|Q| \cdot |Q_G|$ times. The maximal number of states of Q is 2^m where m is the length of the pattern (regular expression). The maximal number of states of Q_G is the size of the antidictionary, i.e. $\|\text{AD}\|$.

In each pass through the main loop, it either enters the semi-infinite loop, in which case one pass consumes $\mathcal{O}(1)$ time; or it uses a finite string u, in which case the pass uses $\mathcal{O}(|u|)$ time. As the maximal length of u is $\|\text{AD}\|$, the maximal time to be spent in one pass through the main loop is $\mathcal{O}(\|\text{AD}\|)$.

The total worst case time of the algorithm is therefore $\mathcal{O}(2^m \cdot \|\text{AD}\|^2)$. □

The algorithm for pattern matching in the DCA coded text using the automaton M_C is described in Algorithm 5.

For the following theorem, let us assume the semi-infinite string at the end of the text is shorter than the coded text.

Algorithm 5. Pattern matching in DCA coded text

Input: Automaton $M_C = (Q_C, \{0,1\}, \delta_C, q_{C0}, \emptyset)$ for pattern matching in DCA coded text, auxiliary functions N, I, the length of original text $|T|$.

Output: List of all occurrences of the given pattern in the given text.

$q = q_{C0}$
$i = 1$
while not the end of the input **do**
    a = next symbol from the input
    if $\delta_C(q, a) = \bot$ **then**
        process the remaining text using transducer $B(\text{AD})$ and pattern matching automaton M
    else
        for all $n \in N(q, a)$, $n + i \leq |T|$ **do**
            report found match at index $i + n$ in the original (uncoded) text
        end for
        $i = i + I(q, a)$
        $q = \delta_C(q, a)$
    end if
end while

Theorem 2. *For DCA coded text T_C of length n_C Algorithm 5 runs in $\mathcal{O}(n_C + r)$ worst case time, where r is the number of found matches of the given pattern in the original text.*

Proof. The main loop of the algorithm is performed n_C times. The reporting of matches by the inner for-cycle is performed at most r times for the whole input text. The semi-infinite string handling is (according to the assumptions) $\mathcal{O}(n_C)$. The rest of the inner loop runs in $\mathcal{O}(1)$. The total time complexity of this algorithm is therefore $\mathcal{O}(n_C + r)$.   □

3.2 Almost Antiwords

Algorithm 5 can be extended to handle the extended scheme of compression using almost antiwords [5]. Certain factors of the input text would improve the compression ratio significantly if they would be considered the antiwords. The almost antiwords extension to the DCA compression method uses these factors as antiwords. Exceptions are encoded into a separate list.

Theorem 3. *Algorithm 6 runs in $\mathcal{O}(n_C + r)$ worst case time for DCA coded text T_C of length n_C, r denotes the number of found matches of the given pattern in the original text.*

Proof. As in Crochemore and Navarro [5], let us assume the exceptions are rare and the semi-infinite string at the end of the text is shorter than the coded text. Then the proof is similar to the proof of Theorem 2, except for the exceptions handling. In line with the assumption, the number of exceptions in the coded text is small, hence the impact on the overall time complexity is negligible.   □

Algorithm 6. Pattern matching in text coded by DCA with almost antiwords

Input: Automaton $M_C = (Q_C, \{0, 1\}, \delta_C, q_{C0}, \emptyset)$ for pattern matching in DCA coded text, auxiliary functions N, I, and the sorted list of exceptions.
Output: List of all occurrences of the given pattern in the given text.

$q = q_{C0}$
$i = 1$
while not the end of the input **do**
   $a =$ next symbol from the input
   if $\delta_C(q, a) = \perp$ **then**
      process the remaining text using transducer $B(\text{AD})$ and pattern matching automaton M
   else
      $i' = i + I(q, a)$
      if there is an exception in between i and i' **then**
         use original decoding automaton and pattern matching automaton
      else
         for all $n \in N(q, a)$, $n + i \le |T|$ **do**
            report found match at index $i + n$ in the original (uncoded) text
         end for
         $i = i'$
         $q = \delta_C(q, a)$
      end if
   end if
end while

3.3   An Incremental Algorithm

In the previous algorithms, the automaton M_C is completely constructed during the preprocessing phase, although parts of the M_C automaton may not be used by the pattern matching algorithm. As a possible solution, we propose to construct the automaton M_C "on the fly" during the pattern matching phase.

The incremental algorithm is embeds the preprocessing phase (described in Algorithm 4) into the searching phase (described in Algorithm 6) constructing on-the-fly only the needed parts of the automaton.

This algorithm will construct the whole automaton M_C in the worst case. The worst-case time complexity characteristics are the same as in the case of the previous algorithms 5 and 6. Depending on the pattern and coded text, parts of the automaton M_C may not be created, leading into improved performance. The time complexity of this algorithm may be as low as $\Omega(n_C + r)$.

An important decision is how to address states in set Q_C using its components (states from Q and Q_G). In Algorithm 4, addressing the state is $\mathcal{O}(1)$, as it is a simple addressing in a two-dimensional array. During the incremental construction, creating the two-dimensional array has to be avoided. Instead, we propose to use a hash table with a compound key. First, each state from Q is assigned a unique integer number, in sequence. We do the same for states in Q_G. For state $q \in Q$ and $q_G \in Q_G$ and their unique number i and i_G (respectively), the key for the hash table is determined as $i \cdot |Q_G| + i_G$. Given the key itself is a reasonable hash function, addressing values in this hash table is $\mathcal{O}(1)$ on average.

Algorithm 7. An incremental pattern matching in text coded by DCA with almost antiwords

---

Input: Pattern matching automaton $M = (Q, \{0, 1\}, \delta, q_0, F)$, decoding transducer $G(AD) = (Q_G, \{0, 1\}, \{0, 1\}, \delta_G, q_{G0}, \emptyset)$.

Output: List of all occurrences of the given pattern in the given text.

   create $q_{C0} = (q_0, q_{G0})$
   $q = q_{C0}$
   $i = 1$
   while not the end of the input **do**
      a = next symbol from the input
      if $\delta_C(q, a)$ not defined **then**
         $(q'_G, u) = \delta_G(q_G, a)$ (where u is the output text)
         if $q'_G \neq \perp$ **then**
            $\delta_C(q_C, a) = [\delta^*(q, u), q'_G]$
            $N(q_C, a) = \{i; \delta^*(q, u[0 : i]) \in F\}$
            $I(q_C, a) = |u|$
         else
            $\delta_C(q_C, a) = \perp$
         end if
      end if
      if $\delta_C(q, a) = \perp$ **then**
         process the remaining text using transducer $B(AD)$ and pattern matching automaton M
      else
         $i' = i + I(q, a)$
         if there is an exception in between i and i' **then**
            use original decoding automaton and pattern matching automaton
         else
            for all $n \in N(q, a)$, $n + i \leq |T|$ **do**
               report found match at index $i + n$ in the original (uncoded) text
            end for
            $i = i'$
            $q = \delta_C(q, a)$
         end if
      end if
   end while

---

4   Experimental Results

We have implemented three algorithms: the basic algorithm described in Section 3.1, the incremental algorithm described in Section 3.3, without almost antiwords extension, and the "decompress and search" algorithm[1]. We have then

---

[1] The decoded symbols are passed from the decoder directly into the pattern matching automaton.

compared the performance of these three algorithms on the Canterbury corpus using different lengths of regular expressions.

We have performed our measurements on a PC with Intel Core 2 Duo downscaled to 1 GHz and 2 GB of main memory. Unsuprisingly, the preprocessing costs of the basic algorithm were prohibiting. The incremental algorithm, however, greatly outperformed the decompress and search algorithm. The average running time of the incremental algorithm over the entire corpus was between 50 % and 52 % of the running time of the "decompress and search" algorithm, depending on the length of the regular expression.

5   Conclusion

We introduced the first algorithm for searching strings from a set of strings described by regular expression in a text coded by the DCA compression method.

Besides a basic variant of this algorithm, there were proposed two enhancements in this paper. The algorithm of incremental pattern matching improves performance of our algorithm in practice and our implementation outperforms the decompress-and-search algorithm significantly.

Asymptotical time complexity of our algorithm and its variants is linear with respect to the length of the compressed text, not counting the preprocessing costs.

References

1. Crochemore, M., Mignosi, F., Restivo, A., Salemi, S.: Text compression using antidictionaries. In: Wiedermann, J., Van Emde Boas, P., Nielsen, M. (eds.) ICALP 1999. LNCS, vol. 1644, pp. 261–270. Springer, Heidelberg (1999)
2. Crochemore, M., Hancart, C.: Automata for matching patterns. In: Rozenberg, G., Salomaa, A. (eds.) Handbook of Formal Languages, pp. 399–462. Springer, Berlin (1997)
3. Holub, J.: Simulation of Nondeterministic Finite Automata in Pattern Matching. PhD thesis, Faculty of Electrical Engineering, Czech Technical University, Prague, Czech Republic (2000)
4. Shibata, Y., Takeda, M., Shinohara, A., Arikawa, S.: Pattern matching in text compressed by using antidictionaries. In: Crochemore, M., Paterson, M. (eds.) CPM 1999. LNCS, vol. 1645, pp. 37–49. Springer, Heidelberg (1999)
5. Crochemore, M., Navarro, G.: Improved antidictionary based compression. In: SCCC, pp. 7–13 (2002)
6. Lahoda, J., Melichar, B.: Pattern matching in Huffman coded text. In: Proceedings of the 6th IS 2003, Ljubljana, Slovenia, pp. 274–279. Institut "Jožef Stefan" (2003)
7. Lahoda, J., Melichar, B.: Pattern matching in text coded by finite translation automaton. In: Proceedings of the 7th IS 2004, Ljubljana, Slovenia, pp. 212–214. Institut "Jožef Stefan" (2004)

Five Determinisation Algorithms

Rob van Glabbeek[1,2] and Bas Ploeger[3,*]

[1] National ICT Australia, Locked Bag 6016, Sydney, NSW1466, Australia
[2] School of Computer Science and Engineering, The University of New South Wales,
Sydney, NSW 2052, Australia
[3] Department of Mathematics and Computer Science, Eindhoven University of Technology,
P.O. Box 513, 5600 MB Eindhoven, The Netherlands

Abstract. Determinisation of nondeterministic finite automata is a well-studied problem that plays an important role in compiler theory and system verification. In the latter field, one often encounters automata consisting of millions or even billions of states. On such input, the memory usage of analysis tools becomes the major bottleneck. In this paper we present several determinisation algorithms, all variants of the well-known subset construction, that aim to reduce memory usage and produce smaller output automata. One of them produces automata that are already minimal. We apply our algorithms to determinise automata that describe the possible sequences appearing after a fixed-length run of cellular automaton 110, and obtain a significant improvement in both memory and time efficiency.

1 Introduction

Finite state automata (or finite state machines) are an established and well-studied model of computation. From a theoretical point of view, they are an interesting object of study because they are expressive yet conceptually easy to understand and intuitive. They find applications in compilers, natural language processing, system verification and testing, but also in fields outside of (theoretical) computer science like switching circuits and chip design. Over the years, many flavours and variants of finite state machines have been defined and studied for a large variety of purposes.

One of the most classic and elementary type of finite state machine is the *nondeterministic finite automaton* (NFA). Typical applications of finite state automata involve checking whether some sequence of symbols meets some syntactic criterion, such as displaying a prescribed pattern or being correct input for a given program, a problem that can often be recast as checking whether that sequence is accepted by a given NFA.

A more restrictive type of automaton is the *deterministic finite automaton* (DFA). DFAs are as expressive as NFAs, in the sense that for every NFA there exists a DFA that is *language equivalent* (*i.e.* accepts the same input sequences). Contrary to NFAs, for any DFA there is a trivial linear time, constant space, online algorithm to check whether an input sequence is accepted or not. Consequently, lexical-analyser generators like LEX work on DFAs, and so do many implementations of GREP. For this reason, in many applications it pays to convert NFAs into DFAs, even though the worst-case time and space complexities of this conversion are exponential in the size of the input NFA.

---

* This author is partially supported by the Netherlands Organisation for Scientific Research (NWO) under VoLTS grant number 612.065.410.

O.H. Ibarra and B. Ravikumar (Eds.): CIAA 2008, LNCS 5148, pp. 161–170, 2008.

Once a language equivalent DFA of an NFA has been found, it is usually minimised to obtain the smallest such DFA. This minimal DFA is unique and the problem of finding it for a given NFA is called the *canonisation problem.*

Another application of NFAs is in the realm of *process theory* and *system verification* where they are used to model the behaviour of distributed systems. Typically, both a specification and an implementation of a system are represented as NFAs, and the question arises whether the execution sequences of one NFA are a subset of those of another. This is the *trace inclusion problem.* Although PSPACE-hard in general, this problem is decidable in PTIME once the NFAs are converted into equivalent DFAs.

As we see, in both the canonisation problem and the trace inclusion problem, determinisation plays an essential role. The standard determinisation algorithm is called *subset construction* (see *e.g.* [11]). Although the determinisation problem is EXPTIME-hard, this algorithm is renowned for its good performance in practice. For minimisation of DFAs a lot of algorithms have been proposed, of which Watson presents a taxonomy and performance analyses [16]. The algorithm with the best time complexity is by Hopcroft [10]: $\mathcal{O}(n \log n)$ where n is the number of states in the input DFA.

Another algorithm for canonisation is by Brzozowski [2]. It generates the minimal DFA directly from an input NFA by repeating the process of "reversing" and determinising the automaton twice. Tabakov and Vardi compare both approaches to canonisation experimentally by running them on randomly generated automata [15].

On some NFAs, the exponential blow-up by subset construction is unavoidable. However, we have encountered NFAs for which subset construction consumes a lot of memory and generates a DFA that is much larger than the minimal DFA. Therefore, our main goal is to find algorithms that are more memory efficient and produce smaller DFAs than subset construction.

In this paper we present five determinisation algorithms based on subset construction. For all of them we prove correctness. One algorithm generates the minimal DFA directly and hence is a *canonisation algorithm.* However, it calculates language inclusion as a subroutine; as deciding language inclusion is PSPACE-complete, it is unattractive to use in an implementation. The other four produce a DFA that is not necessarily minimal but is usually smaller than the DFA produced by subset construction.

We have implemented subset construction and these four new algorithms. We have benchmarked these implementations by running them on NFAs that describe patterns on the lines of a cellular automaton's evolution. We compare the implementations on the time and memory needed for the complete canonisation process (*i.e.* including minimisation) and the size of the DFA after determinisation.

2   Preliminaries

Finite automata. A *nondeterministic finite automaton* (NFA) $\mathcal{N}$ is a tuple $(S_{\mathcal{N}}, \Sigma_{\mathcal{N}}, \delta_{\mathcal{N}}, i_{\mathcal{N}}, F_{\mathcal{N}})$ where $S_{\mathcal{N}}$ is a finite set of states, $\Sigma_{\mathcal{N}}$ is a finite input alphabet, $\delta_{\mathcal{N}} \subseteq S_{\mathcal{N}} \times \Sigma_{\mathcal{N}} \times S_{\mathcal{N}}$ is a transition relation, $i_{\mathcal{N}} \in S_{\mathcal{N}}$ is the initial state and $F_{\mathcal{N}} \subseteq S_{\mathcal{N}}$ is a set of final (or accepting) states. A *deterministic finite automaton* (DFA) is an NFA $\mathcal{D}$ such that for all $p \in S_{\mathcal{D}}$ and $a \in \Sigma_{\mathcal{D}}$ there is precisely one $q \in S_{\mathcal{D}}$ such that $(p, a, q) \in \delta_{\mathcal{D}}$.

In graphical representations of DFAs we also allow states that have *at most* one outgoing a-transition for each alphabet symbol a. Formally speaking, these abbreviate the

DFA obtained by adding a non-accepting *sink* state as the target of all missing transitions. Note that adding such a state preserves language equivalence (defined below).

For any alphabet Σ, Σ^* denotes the set of all finite strings over Σ and $\varepsilon \in \Sigma^*$ denotes the empty string. Any subset of Σ^* is called a *language over* Σ. For any states $p, q \in S_\mathcal{N}$ of an NFA $\mathcal{N}$ and string $\sigma \in \Sigma_\mathcal{N}^*$ with $\sigma = \sigma_1 \cdots \sigma_n$ and $\sigma_1, \ldots, \sigma_n \in \Sigma_\mathcal{N}$ for some $n \geq 0$, we write $p \xrightarrow{\sigma}_\mathcal{N} q$ to denote the fact that:

$$\exists p_0, \ldots, p_n \in S_\mathcal{N} \cdot p_0 = p \wedge p_n = q \wedge (p_0, \sigma_1, p_1), \ldots, (p_{n-1}, \sigma_n, p_n) \in \delta_\mathcal{N}.$$

Language semantics. The *language of a state* $p \in S_\mathcal{N}$ of an NFA $\mathcal{N}$ is defined as: $\mathcal{L}_\mathcal{N}(p) = \{\sigma \in \Sigma_\mathcal{N}^* \mid \exists q \in F_\mathcal{N} \cdot p \xrightarrow{\sigma}_\mathcal{N} q\}$. The *language of an NFA* $\mathcal{N}$ is defined as: $\mathcal{L}(\mathcal{N}) = \mathcal{L}_\mathcal{N}(i_\mathcal{N})$. For any NFAs $\mathcal{N}$ and $\mathcal{M}$ and states $p \in S_\mathcal{N}$ and $q \in S_\mathcal{M}$, p is *language included* in q, denoted $p \sqsubseteq_L q$, iff $\mathcal{L}_\mathcal{N}(p) \subseteq \mathcal{L}_\mathcal{M}(q)$. Moreover, p and q are *language equivalent*, denoted $p \equiv_L q$, iff $p \sqsubseteq_L q \wedge q \sqsubseteq_L p$. An NFA $\mathcal{N}$ is *language included* in an NFA $\mathcal{M}$ iff $i_\mathcal{N} \sqsubseteq_L i_\mathcal{M}$ and $\mathcal{N}$ and $\mathcal{M}$ are *language equivalent* iff $i_\mathcal{N} \equiv_L i_\mathcal{M}$.

Simulation semantics. Given NFAs $\mathcal{N}$ and $\mathcal{M}$, a relation $R \subseteq S_\mathcal{N} \times S_\mathcal{M}$ is a *simulation* iff for any $p \in S_\mathcal{N}$ and $q \in S_\mathcal{M}$, $p \, R \, q$ implies:

- $p \in F_\mathcal{N} \Rightarrow q \in F_\mathcal{M}$ and
- $\forall a \in \Sigma_\mathcal{N} . \forall p' \in S_\mathcal{N} . p \xrightarrow{a}_\mathcal{N} p' \Rightarrow \exists q' \in S_\mathcal{M} . q \xrightarrow{a}_\mathcal{M} q' \wedge p' \, R \, q'$.

Given NFAs $\mathcal{N}$ and $\mathcal{M}$, for any $p \in S_\mathcal{N}$ and $q \in S_\mathcal{M}$:

- p is *simulated by* q, denoted $p \subsetneq q$, iff there exists a simulation R such that $p \, R \, q$;
- p and q are *simulation equivalent*, denoted $p \rightleftarrows q$, iff $p \subsetneq q \wedge q \subsetneq p$;

Clearly $p \subsetneq q$ implies $p \sqsubseteq_L q$.

Subset construction. The subset construction (or powerset construction) is the standard way of determinising a given NFA. For reasons that will become apparent in the next sections, we slightly generalise the normal algorithm by augmenting it with a function f on sets of states, which is applied to every generated set. The algorithm is Algorithm 1 and shall be referred to as SUBSET(f). It takes an NFA $\mathcal{N}$ and generates a DFA $\mathcal{D}$. Of course, it should be the case that $\mathcal{N} \equiv_L \mathcal{D}$, which depends strongly on the function f. For normal subset construction, SUBSET($\mathcal{I}$), where $\mathcal{I}$ is the identity function, it is known that the language of $\mathcal{N}$ is indeed preserved. In the sequel, whenever we use the term "subset construction" we mean the normal algorithm, *i.e.* SUBSET($\mathcal{I}$).

It is known that in the worst case, determinisation yields a DFA that is exponentially larger than the input NFA. An example of an NFA that gives rise to such an exponential blow-up is the NFA that accepts the language specified by the regular expression $\Sigma^* x \Sigma^n$ for some alphabet Σ, $x \in \Sigma$ and $n \geq 0$. Figure 1(a) shows the NFA for $\Sigma = \{a, b\}$ and $x = a$. This NFA has $n + 2$ states, whereas the corresponding DFA has 2^{n+1} states and is already minimal.

An interesting thing to note is that if the initial state were accepting (Figure 1(b)), the minimal DFA would consist of only one state with an a, b-loop: the accepted language has become Σ^*. However, subset construction still produces the exponentially larger DFA first, which should then be reduced to obtain the single-state, minimal DFA.

Algorithm 1. The SUBSET(f) determinisation algorithm

Pre: $\mathcal{N} = (S_\mathcal{N}, \Sigma_\mathcal{N}, \delta_\mathcal{N}, i_\mathcal{N}, F_\mathcal{N})$ is an NFA
Post: $\mathcal{D} = (S_\mathcal{D}, \Sigma_\mathcal{D}, \delta_\mathcal{D}, i_\mathcal{D}, F_\mathcal{D})$ is a DFA
1: $\Sigma_\mathcal{D} := \Sigma_\mathcal{N}; \delta_\mathcal{D} := \emptyset; i_\mathcal{D} := f(\{i_\mathcal{N}\}); F_\mathcal{D} := \emptyset;$
2: $S_\mathcal{D} := \{i_\mathcal{D}\}; \text{todo} := \{i_\mathcal{D}\}; \text{done} := \emptyset;$
3: **while** todo $\neq \emptyset$ **do**
4:     pick a $P \in$ todo;
5:     **for all** $a \in \Sigma_\mathcal{N}$ **do**
6:         $P' := f(\{p' \in S_\mathcal{N} \mid \exists p \in P . p \xrightarrow{a}_\mathcal{N} p'\});$
7:         $S_\mathcal{D} := S_\mathcal{D} \cup \{P'\};$
8:         $\delta_\mathcal{D} := \delta_\mathcal{D} \cup \{(P, a, P')\};$
9:         $\text{todo} := \text{todo} \cup (\{P'\} \setminus \text{done});$
10:    **end for**
11:    **if** $\exists p \in P . p \in F_\mathcal{N}$ **then**
12:        $F_\mathcal{D} := F_\mathcal{D} \cup \{P\};$
13:    **end if**
14:    $\text{todo} := \text{todo} \setminus \{P\};$
15:    $\text{done} := \text{done} \cup \{P\};$
16: **end while**

3   Determinisation Using Transition Sets

In this section we show that subset construction can just as well be done on sets of
transitions as on sets of states. We observe that the contribution of an NFA state p to the
behaviour of a DFA state P consists entirely of p's outgoing transitions. We no longer
think of a DFA state as being a set of NFA states, but rather a set of NFA *transitions*.

Definition 1. Given an NFA $\mathcal{N}$, a *transition tuple* is a pair (T, b) where $T \in \mathcal{P}(\Sigma_\mathcal{N} \times S_\mathcal{N})$ is a set of transitions and $b \in \mathbb{B}$ is a boolean.

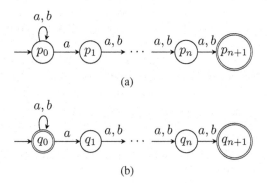

(a)

(b)

Fig. 1. Two NFAs of size $\mathcal{O}(n)$ for which subset construction produces a DFA of size $\mathcal{O}(2^n)$.
Here initial states are marked by unlabelled incoming arrows, and final states by double circles.
In case (a) this DFA is already minimal; in case (b) the minimal DFA has size 1.

Algorithm 2. The TRANSSET(f) determinisation algorithm

Pre: $\mathcal{N} = (S_{\mathcal{N}}, \Sigma_{\mathcal{N}}, \delta_{\mathcal{N}}, i_{\mathcal{N}}, F_{\mathcal{N}})$ is an NFA
Post: $\mathcal{D} = (S_{\mathcal{D}}, \Sigma_{\mathcal{D}}, \delta_{\mathcal{D}}, i_{\mathcal{D}}, F_{\mathcal{D}})$ is a DFA
1: $\Sigma_{\mathcal{D}} := \Sigma_{\mathcal{N}}; \delta_{\mathcal{D}} := \emptyset; i_{\mathcal{D}} := f(\text{tuple}(i_{\mathcal{N}})); F_{\mathcal{D}} := \emptyset;$
2: $S_{\mathcal{D}} := \{i_{\mathcal{D}}\}; \text{todo} := \{i_{\mathcal{D}}\}; \text{done} := \emptyset;$
3: **while** todo $\neq \emptyset$ **do**
4:     pick a $P \in$ todo;
5:     **for all** $a \in \Sigma$ **do**
6:         $P' := f(\bigcup_{(a,p)\in\text{set}(P)} \text{trans}(p), \exists(a,p) \in \text{set}(P) . p \in F_{\mathcal{N}});$
7:         $S_{\mathcal{D}} := S_{\mathcal{D}} \cup \{P'\};$
8:         $\delta_{\mathcal{D}} := \delta_{\mathcal{D}} \cup \{(P, a, P')\};$
9:         $\text{todo} := \text{todo} \cup (\{P'\} \setminus \text{done});$
10:     **end for**
11:     **if** fin(P) **then**
12:         $F_{\mathcal{D}} := F_{\mathcal{D}} \cup \{P\};$
13:     **end if**
14:     $\text{todo} := \text{todo} \setminus \{P\};$
15:     $\text{done} := \text{done} \cup \{P\};$
16: **end while**

For every transition tuple (T, b) we define the projection functions set and fin as: set$(T, b) = T$ and fin$(T, b) = b$. For every state $p \in S_{\mathcal{N}}$ of NFA $\mathcal{N}$, trans(p) is the set of outgoing transitions of p and tuple(p) is the transition tuple belonging to p:

$$\text{trans}(p) = \{(a, q) \in \Sigma_{\mathcal{N}} \times S_{\mathcal{N}} \mid p \xrightarrow{a}_{\mathcal{N}} q\}$$
$$\text{tuple}(p) = (\text{trans}(p), p \in F_{\mathcal{N}}).$$

The DFA state $P \subseteq S_{\mathcal{N}}$ now corresponds to the transition tuple (T, b) where $T = \bigcup_{p\in P} \text{trans}(p)$ and $b \equiv \exists p \in P . p \in F_{\mathcal{N}}$. We need the boolean b to indicate whether the DFA state is final as this can no longer be determined from the elements of the set. Only the labels and target states of the transitions are stored because the source states are irrelevant and would only make the sets unnecessarily large.

Given NFA $\mathcal{N}$, the *language of a transition* $(a, p) \in \Sigma_{\mathcal{N}} \times S_{\mathcal{N}}$ is defined as: $\mathcal{L}_{\mathcal{N}}(a, p) = \{a\sigma \in \Sigma_{\mathcal{N}}^* \mid \sigma \in \mathcal{L}_{\mathcal{N}}(p)\}$. The *language of a set of transitions* T is defined as $\mathcal{L}_{\mathcal{N}}(T) = \bigcup_{t\in T} \mathcal{L}_{\mathcal{N}}(t)$ and the *language of a transition tuple* (T, b) is defined as:

$$\mathcal{L}_{\mathcal{N}}(T, b) = \mathcal{L}_{\mathcal{N}}(T) \cup \begin{cases} \{\varepsilon\} \text{ if } & b \\ \emptyset \quad \text{ if } \neg b. \end{cases}$$

Language inclusion and equivalence for transitions and transition tuples can now be defined in the usual way by means of set inclusion and equality.

The determinisation algorithm that uses transition tuples is Algorithm 2. We shall refer to it as TRANSSET(f) where f is a function on transition tuples. Again, language preservation depends on the specific function f being used. For $f = \mathcal{I}$ this is indeed the case, which we prove in [7], the full version of this paper. Using TRANSSET($\mathcal{I}$) for determinisation can give a smaller DFA than SUBSET($\mathcal{I}$) as is shown by the example in Figure 2. Here, TRANSSET($\mathcal{I}$) happens to produce the minimal DFA directly. This is

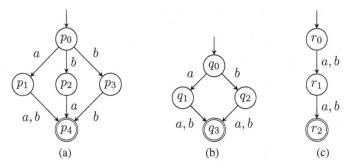

Fig. 2. NFA (a) for which the DFA produced by SUBSET($\mathcal{I}$) (b) is larger than the (minimal) DFA produced by TRANSSET($\mathcal{I}$) (c)

generally not the case: on the NFA of Figure 1(b), TRANSSET($\mathcal{I}$) generates a DFA of size 2^{n+1}, while the minimal DFA has size 1.

4   Determinisation Using Closures

We introduce a *closure* operation that can be used in the SUBSET algorithm instead of the identity function $\mathcal{I}$. It aims to add NFA states to a given DFA state (*i.e.* a set of NFA states) without affecting its language. This results in an algorithm that generates smaller DFAs. In particular, we show that if the criterion to add a state is chosen suitably, SUBSET with closure is an algorithm that produces the minimal DFA directly.

Definition 2. For any set of states $P \subseteq S_\mathcal{N}$ of an NFA $\mathcal{N}$ and relation $\sqsubseteq \, \subseteq S_\mathcal{N} \times \mathcal{P}(S_\mathcal{N})$, the *closure* of P under $\sqsubseteq$, $\mathsf{close}_\sqsubseteq(P)$, is defined as:

$$\mathsf{close}_\sqsubseteq(P) = \{p \in S_\mathcal{N} \mid p \sqsubseteq P\}.$$

The language preorder $\sqsubseteq_L$ can be lifted to operate on states and sets of states in the following way. Define the *language of a set of states* P of an NFA $\mathcal{N}$ as: $\mathcal{L}_\mathcal{N}(P) = \bigcup_{p \in P} \mathcal{L}_\mathcal{N}(p)$. Language equivalence and inclusion can now be defined on any combination of states and sets of states, in terms of set equivalence and inclusion. For instance, for a state $p \in S_\mathcal{N}$ and a set of states $P \subseteq S_\mathcal{N}$, $p \sqsubseteq_L P$ holds if $\mathcal{L}_\mathcal{N}(p) \subseteq \mathcal{L}_\mathcal{N}(P)$.

Applying this, the algorithm SUBSET($\mathsf{close}_{\sqsubseteq_L}$) generates the minimal DFA that is language equivalent to the input NFA. This statement is proven in [7].

5   Simulation Preorder

Although it ensures that the output DFA of SUBSET($\mathsf{close}_{\sqsubseteq_L}$) is minimal, language inclusion is an unattractive preorder to use. Deciding language inclusion is PSPACE-complete [13] which implies that known algorithms have an exponential time complexity. Moreover, most algorithms involve a determinisation step which would render our optimisation useless.

The simulation preorder $\subsetneq$ [12] is finer than language inclusion on NFAs, meaning it relates fewer NFAs. However, considering its PTIME complexity (see *e.g.* [1,9]), it is

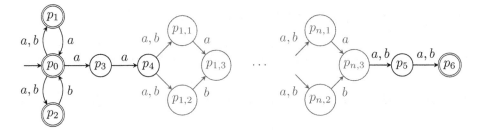

Fig. 3. NFA of size $\mathcal{O}(n)$ for which SUBSET(close$_{\subseteq}$) generates a DFA of size $\mathcal{O}(2^n)$ for any $n \geq 1$. The minimal DFA has 1 state.

an attractive way to "approximate" language inclusion (see also [4]). Hence, as a more practical alternative to SUBSET(close$_{\subseteq_L}$) we define the algorithm SUBSET(close$_{\subseteq}$). The required lifting of $\subseteq$ to states and sets of states is as follows. For any state $p \in S_{\mathcal{N}}$ and set of states $P \subseteq S_{\mathcal{N}}$ of an NFA $\mathcal{N}$, we have $p \subseteq P$ iff:

- $p \in F_{\mathcal{N}} \Rightarrow \exists q \in P . q \in F_{\mathcal{N}}$ and
- there exists a simulation $R \subseteq S_{\mathcal{N}} \times S_{\mathcal{N}}$ such that:

$$\forall a \in \Sigma_{\mathcal{N}} . \forall p' \in S_{\mathcal{N}} . p \xrightarrow{a}_{\mathcal{N}} p' \Rightarrow \exists q, q' \in S_{\mathcal{N}} . q \in P \wedge q \xrightarrow{a}_{\mathcal{N}} q' \wedge p' R q'.$$

The correctness of SUBSET(close$_{\subseteq}$) is established in [7]. The example in Figure 3 shows not only that the resulting DFA is no longer minimal, but moreover that it can be exponentially larger than the minimal DFA. This NFA contains a pattern that repeats itself n times for any $n \geq 1$. It is based on the NFA of Figure 1(b) interwoven with a pattern that prevents SUBSET(close$_{\subseteq}$) from merging states that will later turn out to be equivalent. The NFA accepts the language given by the regular expression $(a \mid b)^*$.

6 Determinisation Using Compressions

Algorithm SUBSET(close$_{\subseteq}$) adds all simulated states to a generated set of states. Another option would be to remove all redundant states from such a set. More specifically, we remove every state that is simulated by another state in the set. For this operation to be well-defined, it is essential that no two different states in the set are simulation equivalent. This can be achieved by minimising the input NFA using simulation equivalence prior to determinisation. In turn, this amounts to computing the simulation preorder that was already necessary in the first place.

Definition 3. Given a set P such that $\neg \exists p, q \in P . p \neq q \wedge p \rightleftarrows q$. Then compress$_{\subseteq}(P)$ denotes the *compression* of P under $\subseteq$ and is defined as:

$$\text{compress}_{\subseteq}(P) = \{p \in P \mid \forall q \in P . p \neq q \Rightarrow p \not\subseteq q\}.$$

The function compress$_{\subseteq}$ can be used not only for sets of states but also for transition tuples. For that, we first define $\subseteq$ on the transitions of an NFA $\mathcal{N}$ as follows. For any $(a, p), (b, q) \in \Sigma_{\mathcal{N}} \times S_{\mathcal{N}}$, we have $(a, p) \subseteq (b, q)$ iff $a = b$ and $p \subseteq q$. By Definition 3 compress$_\subseteq$ is now properly defined on sets of transitions and it can be extended to transition tuples in a straightforward manner: compress$_\subseteq$ (T, b) = (compress$_\subseteq$ (T),b).

This way, we obtain two more determinisation algorithms: SUBSET(compress$_\subseteq$) and TRANSSET(compress$_\subseteq$). Their correctness proofs can be found in [7].

7   Lattice of Algorithms

Figure 4 orders the algorithms described in the previous sections in a lattice: we draw an arrow from algorithm A to algorithm B iff for every input NFA, A produces a DFA that is at most as large as the one produced by B. The algorithms SUBSET(close$_\subseteq$) and TRANSSET(compress$_\subseteq$) are in the same class of the lattice, because they always yield isomorphic DFAs. The relations of Figure 4 are substantiated in [7]; Figures 1(b), 2 and 3 provide counterexamples against further inclusions.

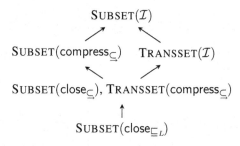

Fig. 4. The lattice of algorithms presented in the previous sections

8   Implementation and Benchmarks

We have implemented the algorithms SUBSET($\mathcal{I}$), TRANSSET($\mathcal{I}$), SUBSET(close$_\subseteq$), SUBSET(compress$_\subseteq$) and TRANSSET(compress$_\subseteq$) in the C++ programming language. A set of states or transitions is stored as a tree with the elements in the leaves. All subtrees are shared among the sets to improve memory efficiency. A hash table provides fast and efficient lookup of existing subtrees.

The benchmarks are performed on a 32-bits architecture computer having two Intel Xeon 3.06 GHz CPUs and 4 GB of RAM. It runs Fedora Core 8 Linux, kernel 2.6.23. The code is compiled using the GNU C++ compiler (version 4.1.2).

Every benchmark starts off by minimising the NFA using simulation equivalence. For this we have implemented our partitioning algorithm [6] which is based on [5] and also computes the simulation preorder on the states of the resulting NFA. Every determinisation algorithm is applied to this minimised NFA, after which the resulting DFA is minimised by the tool ltsmin of the μCRL toolset [3,8] (version 2.18.1).

For the benchmarks we consider a one-dimensional cellular automaton (CA) (see *e.g.* [18]), which is represented by a function $\rho : \Sigma^w \rightarrow \Sigma$ called the *rule* where Σ is an alphabet and w is the *width* of the automaton. Given an infinite sequence $\sigma \in \Sigma^\infty$, a *step* of a CA is an application of ρ to every w-length subsequence of σ, which produces a new sequence. The possible finite sequences appearing as a continuous subsequence

Table 1. Benchmark results for canonising NFAs of steps 4 and 5 of CA 110. Legend: **D** = Determinisation, **M** = Minimisation, **T** = Time (sec), **S** = Space (peak memory use, MB), $|S_\mathcal{D}|$ = Size of DFA after determinisation.

	STEP 4					STEP 5				
	DT	**MT**	**DS**	**MS**	$|S_\mathcal{D}|$	**DT**	**MT**	**DS**	**MS**	$|S_\mathcal{D}|$
Subset($\mathcal{I}$)	0.6	0.4	5.4	2.0	58 370	212.5	76.7	688.2	267.2	7 663 165
Transset($\mathcal{I}$)	1.0	0.4	9.0	2.0	58 094	257.3	79.1	1 146.9	263.0	7 541 248
Subset(close$_\subseteq$)	1.6	< 0.1	2.1	0.2	4 720	2 739.7	1.61	123.2	6.3	176 008
Subset(compress$_\subseteq$)	< 0.1	< 0.1	0.6	0.2	4 745	4.3	1.4	16.7	6.4	179 146
Transset(compress$_\subseteq$)	< 0.1	< 0.1	0.7	0.2	4 720	4.1	1.6	22.9	6.3	176 008

of the infinite sequence obtained after n steps of a given CA (starting from a random input sequence) constitute a language that can be described by a DFA [17]. It is known that for some CA rules, the size of these DFAs increases exponentially in n (*cf.* [14]).

For $\Sigma = \{0, 1\}$ and $w = 3$, the CA with number 110 has the following rule:

$$\rho = \{\ 000 \mapsto 0,\ 001 \mapsto 1,\ 010 \mapsto 1,\ 011 \mapsto 1,$$
$$100 \mapsto 0,\ 101 \mapsto 1,\ 110 \mapsto 1,\ 111 \mapsto 0\ \}.$$

It is known to be computationally universal and to exhibit the exponential blow-up phenomenon described above. We have generated the minimal DFAs for steps 1 through 5 of this CA using the various algorithms presented here. The most interesting results are those for steps 4 and 5, which are shown in Table 1. The input NFA has 228 states for step 4 and 1 421 for step 5; the minimal DFAs have sizes 1 357 and 18 824 respectively. The algorithms that use compress$_\subseteq$ clearly outperform the others, in both memory and time efficiency. Every algorithm that uses a function other than $\mathcal{I}$, generates a DFA that is an order of magnitude smaller than that of its $\mathcal{I}$-counterpart.

9   Conclusions

We have presented a schematic generalisation of the well-known subset construction algorithm that allows for a function to be applied to every generated set of states. We have given a similar scheme for a variant of subset construction that operates on sets of transitions rather than states. Next, we instantiated these schemes with several set-expanding or -reducing functions to obtain various determinisation algorithms. One of these algorithms even produces the minimal DFA directly, but its use of the PSPACE-hard language preorder renders it impractical. As our aim is to reduce the average-case workload in practice, we instead use the PTIME-decidable simulation preorder in the other algorithms. We have classified all presented algorithms in a lattice, based on the sizes of the DFAs they produce. This is a natural criterion, as the worst-case complexities are the same for all algorithms. To assess their performance, we have implemented and benchmarked them. The case study comprised NFAs describing patterns in the elementary cellular automaton with rule number 110. On these examples, the algorithms that use a function to reduce the computed sets, convincingly outperformed the others.

Based on our algorithm schemes, many more algorithms can be constructed by substituting various functions, depending on the specific needs and applications. Moreover, the functions we defined here could be equipped with any suitable preorder or partial order, *e.g.* from the linear time – branching time spectrum. We also remark that our optimisations to subset construction are particularly beneficial in cases where normal subset construction leaves a large gap between the generated DFA and the minimal one.

Acknowledgements. We would like to thank Jan Friso Groote, Tim Willemse and Sebastian Maneth for valuable ideas, discussions and/or comments.

References

1. Bloom, B., Paige, R.: Transformational design and implementation of a new efficient solution to the ready simulation problem. Science of Computer Programming 24(3), 189–220 (1995)
2. Brzozowski, J.A.: Canonical regular expressions and minimal state graphs for definite events. In: Proceedings of the Symposium on Mathematical Theory of Automata. MRI Symposia Series, vol. 12, pp. 529–561. Polytechnic Press, Polytechnic Institute of Brooklyn (1963)
3. CWI: μCRL Toolset Home Page, http://www.cwi.nl/~mcrl/
4. Dill, D.L., Hu, A.J., Wong-Toi, H.: Checking for language inclusion using simulation preorders. In: Larsen, K.G., Skou, A. (eds.) CAV 1991. LNCS, vol. 575, pp. 255–265. Springer, Heidelberg (1992)
5. Gentilini, R., Piazza, C., Policriti, A.: From bisimulation to simulation: Coarsest partition problems. Journal of Automated Reasoning 31(1), 73–103 (2003)
6. van Glabbeek, R.J., Ploeger, B.: Correcting a space-efficient simulation algorithm. In: Proc. 20th Int. Conf. on Computer Aided Verification. LNCS. Springer, Heidelberg (to appear, 2008)
7. van Glabbeek, R.J., Ploeger, B.: Five Determinisation Algorithms. CS-Report 08-14, Eindhoven University of Technology (2008)
8. Groote, J.F., Reniers, M.A.: Algebraic process verification. In: Bergstra, J.A., Ponse, A., Smolka, S.A. (eds.) Handbook of Process Algebra, pp. 1151–1208. Elsevier, Amsterdam (2001)
9. Henzinger, M.R., Henzinger, T.A., Kopke, P.W.: Computing simulations on finite and infinite graphs. In: 36th Annual Symposium on Foundations of Computer Science (FOCS 1995), pp. 453–462. IEEE Computer Society Press, Los Alamitos (1995)
10. Hopcroft, J.E.: An $n \log n$ algorithm for minimizing states in a finite automaton. In: Kohavi, Z. (ed.) Theory of Machines and Computations, pp. 189–196. Academic Press, London (1971)
11. Hopcroft, J.E., Ullman, J.D.: Introduction to Automata Theory, Languages, and Computation. Addison-Wesley, Reading (1979)
12. Park, D.M.R.: Concurrency and automata on infinite sequences. In: Deussen, P. (ed.) Proceedings 5th GI-Conference on Theoretical Computer Science. LNCS, vol. 104, pp. 167–183. Springer, Heidelberg (1981)
13. Stockmeyer, L.J., Meyer, A.R.: Word problems requiring exponential time. In: Proc. 5th Annual ACM Symposium on Theory of Computing (STOC 1973), pp. 1–9. ACM, New York (1973)
14. Sutner, K.: The size of power automata. Theor. Comput. Sci. 295(1-3), 371–386 (2003)
15. Tabakov, D., Vardi, M.Y.: Experimental evaluation of classical automata constructions. In: Sutcliffe, G., Voronkov, A. (eds.) LPAR 2005. LNCS (LNAI), vol. 3835, pp. 396–411. Springer, Heidelberg (2005)
16. Watson, B.W.: Taxonomies and Toolkits of Regular Language Algorithms. PhD thesis, Technische Universiteit Eindhoven (1995)
17. Wolfram, S.: Computation theory of cellular automata. Communications in Mathematical Physics 96(1), 15–57 (1984)
18. Wolfram, S.: A New Kind of Science. Wolfram Media, Inc. (2002)

Persistent Computations of Turing Machines

Harald Hempel[1] and Madlen Kimmritz[2],[*]

[1] Institut für Informatik
Friedrich-Schiller-Universität Jena
07743 Jena, Germany
`hempel@informatik.uni-jena.de`
[2] Mathematisches Seminar
Christian-Albrechts-Universität zu Kiel
24098 Kiel, Germany
`mkimmritz@yahoo.de`

Abstract. In this paper we formally define the notion of persistent Turing machines to model interactive computations. We compare the power of persistent computations with their classical counterparts.

1 Introduction

In many real world applications of algorithms it is often not the case, that computations start with an input and empty memory to produce some output. In human guided search [KL02] human knowledge and computer power interact to achieve better results than humans or computers alone could provide. In a 3-brain approach [A85] two computer programs provide alternative intermediate results with the human having the final say which one to use in the still ongoing computation. These two approaches serve merely as successful examples [KL02, LM03, LM03a, AS03] to illustrate that human-machine-interaction is used in practice. Classical (Turing machine) based models of computation can hardly describe these. A promising approach to do so is the notion of persistent Turing machines [GW98, Ko98]. A persistent Turing machine, or persistent computation (of a Turing machine), receives a sequence of inputs and produces a sequence of outputs while the computation on a single input may depend on all computations on previous inputs. In this paper we give a sound formal definition of the notion of persistent computations that until now was missing in the literature and so will lay the ground for methodically studying the power of persistent computations. We will also show how persistent computations relate to classical Turing machine computations. Since a persistent computation is based on an underlying Turing machine and a sequence of inputs (or an input function) we will look at various restrictions of input functions as well as Turing machines and compare the resulting types of persistent computations with their classical counterparts.

It has been shown that any function can be computed by a persistent computation [Ko98]. We will show that when restricting to computable input functions

---

[*] Work done in part while working at Friedrich-Schiller-Universität Jena.

O.H. Ibarra and B. Ravikumar (Eds.): CIAA 2008, LNCS 5148, pp. 171–180, 2008.

a persistent computation can only produce computable output functions. The power of persistent computations however is illustrated by the fact that a single input function is sufficient to compute all total recursive functions and primitive recursive input funtions suffice to compute all recursive functions (see Theorems 3.1 and 3.2). It also turns out that persistent computations give rise to new classes of functions that have no obvious classical counterparts (see Theorems 3.6 and 3.7).

The paper is organized as follows. In Section 2 we will formally introduce and define the notion of persistent computations and what it means to compute a function with a persistent computation. Section 3 contains some of our results and their proofs. We mention in passing that the authors have also obtained results concerning the notions of persistent-decidability as well as persistent-enumerability [HK].

2   Basic Concepts and Definitions

In this section we will develop our model of persistent computations.

Let $\Sigma = \{0, 1\}$ be our alphabet. We assume the reader to be familiar with the basic concepts and notations of recursion theory [Ro67]. Depending on the context we will view functions as to map from $\mathbb{N}$ to $\mathbb{N}$, from $\mathbb{N}$ to Σ^* or as to map from Σ^* to Σ^*. Due to the tight connection (there is a polynomial-time computable and invertible bijection) between $\mathbb{N}$ and Σ^* this will not weaken our results but simplify their presentation. Note that we will solely consider functions of that type. Let id be a bijective function and maps from $\mathbb{N}$ to Σ^* such that $id(0) = \varepsilon$, $id(1) = 0$, $id(2) = 1$, $id(3) = 00$ and so on. So, id^{-1} exists and, in particular, id and id^{-1} are primitive recursive. Let nd be the everywhere undefined function, i.e. $nd(n)$ is undefined for all $n \in \mathbb{N}$, which is partial recursive as well. For a function f let D_f and R_f denote the domain of definition and the range of f, respectively. The sets of partial and total recursive functions will be denoted by $\mathbb{P}$ and $\mathbb{R}$, respectively. We will denote $\mathbb{P}r$ as the set of all primitive recursive functions. For any set of functions $\mathcal{F}$, let $\mathcal{F}_{\text{total}}$ and $\mathcal{F}_{\text{bij}}$ denote the sets of all total and bijective functions from $\mathcal{F}$, respectively.

2.1   The Model

In the formal Turing machine model each computation of a Turing machine starts with an input tape containing the input and worktapes that are empty. To model interactive and persistent behavior, as it is to be found in many todays real world scenarios, as already mentioned in the introduction, we introduce the notion of persistent computations of Turing machines. Even though this model has been studied in the literature before [GW98, Ko98] a clear definition has been missing until now.

Before we give formal definitions we recall the intuitive description. In contrast to classical Turing machine computations their persistent counterparts do not start out from an empty worktape. More precisely, the contents of the worktape at the start of the computation on an input x is identical to the content of the worktape at the end of the computation on the input preceeding x. So in fact, we view our machines as to receive sequences of inputs where the starting configuration for each input depends on the end configuration of the machine on previous inputs. That is what gave the model the name "persistent" computations. We now turn to formally define our model.

Definition 2.1. *Let M be a Turing machine with one input tape, one worktape and one output tape, input alphabet Σ and worktape alphabet Γ. Without loss of generality assume $\Sigma \subseteq \Gamma$. Let $f : \mathbb{N} \to \Sigma^*$ be a total function.*

1. *The functions $work_M : \Sigma^* \times \Gamma^* \to \Gamma^*$ and $out_M : \Sigma^* \times \Gamma^* \to \Gamma^*$ are defined as follows:*
   For all $x \in \Sigma^*$ and all $y \in \Gamma^*$, $work_M(x, y)$ and $out_M(x, y)$ are the contents of the worktape and output tape, respectively, of M in the end configuration if the computation of M on input x and initial worktape content y halts. Otherwise $work_M(x, y)$ and $out_M(x, y)$ are undefined.

   The computation $comp_M(x, y)$ of M on input x with initial worktape content y is the sequence of configurations that M on input x with initial worktape content y passes through, if that computation reaches a halting state. Otherwise $comp_M(x, y)$ is undefined.
2. *The mapping $hist_{M,f} : \mathbb{N} \to \Gamma^*$ is recursively defined as:*

$$hist_{M,f}(0) = \varepsilon \text{ and for all } i \in \mathbb{N}^+$$

$$hist_{M,f}(i + 1) = \begin{cases} work_M(f(i), hist_{M,f}(i)), & \text{if } hist_{M,f}(i) \neq n.d., \\ n.d., & \text{if } hist_{M,f}(i) = n.d.. \end{cases}$$

3. *The output function $g_{M,f} : \mathbb{N} \to \Gamma^*$ is, for all $i \in \mathbb{N}$, defined via*

$$g_{M,f}(i) = out_{M,f}(f(i), hist_{M,f}(i)).$$

Thus a persistent computation receives a sequence of inputs, modelled as the function f in the above definition, and produces a sequence of outputs, named $g_{M,f}$ above. Persistence, the survival of information from previous computations, is modelled by the function $hist_{M,f}$. In other words, a persistent computation is a sequence of computations of a classical Turing machine M on inputs $f(0)$, $f(1)$, ... where the contents of the worktape from the previous computation is the initial content of the worktape for the current computation.

The function f in the above definition will be called input function and we denote the set of all total functions mapping from $\mathbb{N}$ to Σ^* by $\mathbb{In}$.

Such persistent computations can produce an infinite or finite sequence of output values depending on whether all "local" computations of M halt or not (see also Figure 1).

In analogy to classical (Turing machine) computations we define the concept of a *persistent computation* via the notion of a configuration in the obvious way.

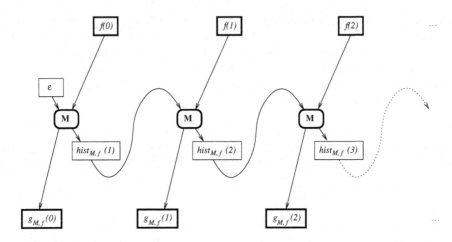

Fig. 1. Schematic illustration of a persistent computation of a Turing machine M on input sequence $f(0)$, $f(1)$, $f(2)$, ... if all values of $hist_{M,f}$ are defined

Definition 2.2. *Let M be a Turing machine with one input tape, one worktape and one output tape, input alphabet Σ and worktape alphabet Γ. Without loss of generality assume $\Sigma \subseteq \Gamma$. Let $f \in \mathbb{In}$. The persistent computation of M on input f, i.e., on the input sequence $f(0)$, $f(1)$, $f(2)$, ... is denoted by $M(f)$ and defined as*

$$M(f) =_{df} (comp_M(f(i), hist_{M,f}(i)))_{i \in \mathbb{N}},$$

if $comp_M(f(i), hist_{M,f}(i))$ is defined for all $i \in \mathbb{N}$. If $comp_M(f(i), hist_{M,f}(i))$ is not defined for all $i \in \mathbb{N}$ we define

$$M(f) =_{df} (comp_M(f(0), hist_{M,f}(0)), \ldots, comp_M(f(i_0), hist_{M,f}(i_0)))$$

where i_0 is the smallest $i \in \mathbb{N}$ such that $comp_M(f(i), hist_{M,f}(i))$ is undefined.

Note that all definitions of this section can easily be modified to deal with Turing machines having more than one worktape. Also, the general concept of persistence can be generalized to other models of computation, such as RAM-programs, MARKOV-algorithms and others, where all inner program variables persist between the end of a computation and the start of a new computation.

2.2   Persistent Computations of Functions

Note that the mapping from $f(i)$ to $g_{M,f}(i)$ in Definition 2.2 is in general not a function, since we might have $f(i) = f(j)$ and yet $g_{M,f}(i) \neq g_{M,f}(j)$ for some $i \neq j$. This observation leads to the following definition.

Definition 2.3 ([Ko98]). *Let M be a Turing machine and $f \in \mathbb{In}$.*

1. *The persistent computation $M(f)$ is called consistent if and only if for all $i, j \in \mathbb{N}$ the following condition holds for all $i, j \in \mathbb{N}$:*

$$f(i) = f(j) \rightarrow g_{M,f}(i) = g_{M,f}(j).$$

2. A function $h : \Sigma^* \to \Sigma^*$ is said to be persistent computable (p-computable) if and only if there exists a Turing machine M and a function $f \in \mathbb{In}$ such that
   (a) $M(f)$ is consistent,
   (b) $D_h \subseteq R_f$ and
   (c) for all $i \in \mathbb{N}$, $g_{f,M}(i) = h(f(i))$.
   In that case we say that M on input f p-computes the function h.
3. A function $h : \mathbb{N} \to \mathbb{N}$ is said to be p-computable if and only if the mapping $\widehat{h} : \Sigma^* \to \Sigma^*$ being defined via $\widehat{h}(n) = id^{-1}(\widehat{h}(id(n)))$ for all $n \in \mathbb{N}$ is p-computable.
4. The set of all p-computable functions $h : \mathbb{N} \to \mathbb{N}$ is denoted by $\mathrm{p}\mathbb{F}$.

Note that the requirement $D_h \subseteq R_f$ (instead of $D_h = R_f$) in Part 2b of Definition 2.3 gives more flexibility when it comes to p-computing partial functions. In particular there are two ways to realize $h(x) = n.d.$ for some x during a p-computation $M(f)$ of h, either x never shows up as an input, $x \notin R_f$, or even though $x \in R_f$, some prior runs of M do not terminate during the p-computation.

An interesting result concerning the persistent computation of functions was first observed in [Ko98].

Theorem 2.4 (Kosub). *[Ko98] Every function $h : \mathbb{N} \to \mathbb{N}$ is p-computable.*

The idea of the proof is to construct a (piecewise constant) input function f, such that the length of a constant part of the input function encodes the function value of the function h to be computed, on the input that will be provided by f when it changes its value the next time. The underlying Turing machine simply counts, how often the input value does not change and outputs that number when the input value changes. Note that since there are no restrictions on the input functions for persistent computations the encoding of otherwise uncomputable functions into the input leads to the above statement.

So in order to be fair, the power of p-computability should be studied when all input functions are required to be computable. In the process we will not only study restrictions to the input functions but also restrictions to the underlying machine model.

Definition 2.5. *Let $\Phi \subseteq \mathbb{In}$, and $\mathfrak{M}$ be a collection of programs or machines.*

1. *The set of p-Φ-computable functions is defined as*

$$\mathrm{p}\mathbb{F}(\Phi) =_{df} \{h \in \mathbb{F} \,|\, (\exists \mathrm{TM}\ M)(\exists f \in \Phi)[M \text{ on input } f \text{ p-computes } h]\}.$$

2. *The set of p-$(\Phi, \mathfrak{M})$-computable functions is defined as*

$$\mathrm{p}\mathbb{F}(\Phi, \mathfrak{M}) =_{df} \{h \in \mathbb{F} \,|\, (\exists \mathrm{TM}\ M \in \mathfrak{M})(\exists f \in \Phi)[M \text{ on input } f \text{ p-computes } h]\}.$$

Note that the Turing machine used in the above proof sketch of Theorem 2.4 does not do much more then counting. So any set Ψ of machines which are flexible enough to count will be able to p-$(\mathbb{In}, \Psi)$-compute all functions. Hence, the focus in the upcoming section will be on restricting the set of input functions.

3   The Power of Persistent Computations

As already mentioned above the true power of persistent computations can only be judged if the set of input functions is restricted to computable functions. It turns out that with this restriction, persistent computations can only compute recursive functions and, even stronger, primitive recursive input functions suffice to p-compute all recursive functions.

Theorem 3.1. $\mathbb{P} = p\mathbb{F}(\mathbb{R}) = p\mathbb{F}(\mathbb{Pr})$.

Proof. Since we clearly have $p\mathbb{F}(\mathbb{Pr}) \subseteq p\mathbb{F}(\mathbb{R})$ it suffices to prove $p\mathbb{F}(\mathbb{R}) \subseteq \mathbb{P}$ and $\mathbb{P} \subseteq p\mathbb{F}(\mathbb{Pr})$.

We first show $p\mathbb{F}(\mathbb{R}) \subseteq \mathbb{P}$. Let $h \in p\mathbb{F}(\mathbb{R})$. Hence, there exist a Turing machine M and an input function $f \in \mathbb{R}$ such that $M(f)$ p-computes h. In particular, for every $n \in D_h$ there is an $i \in \mathbb{N}$ such that $id(n) = f(i)$ and $h(n) = id^{-1}(g_{M,f}(i))$. It is not hard to see that $g_{M,f}$ is a recursive function, since f itself is total and recursive and in order to compute $g_{M,f}(i)$ for some $i \in \mathbb{N}$ we simply have to run the machine M $i+1$ times on the inputs $f(0), f(1),\ldots, f(i)$ (in that order) while preserving the content of the worktapes between consecutive runs of M. More formally, the following recursive scheme clearly holds:

$$
\begin{aligned}
hist_{M,f}(0) &= \epsilon \\
g_{M,f}(0) &= out_M(f(0), hist_{M,f}(0)) \\
hist_{M,f}(i+1) &= work_M(f(i), hist_{M,f}(i)) \text{ for all } i \geq 0 \\
g_{M,f}(i+1) &= out_M(f(i), hist_{M,f}(i)), \text{ for all } i \geq 0.
\end{aligned}
$$

Since out_M, $work_M$, and f are recursive functions and $hist_{M,f}$ and $g_{M,f}$ are defined via a simultaneous recursion, based on out_M, $work_M$, and f, we conclude that also $hist_{M,f}$ and $g_{M,f}$ are recursive. Furthermore, for all $n \in \mathbb{N}$ we have $h(n) = id^{-1}(g_{M,f}(\min\{i \in \mathbb{N} : f(i) = id(n)\}))$. Since id, id^{-1}, f and $g_{M,f}$ are recursive functions and the class of recursive functions is closed with respect to the μ-operator it follows that h is recursive.

The inclusion $\mathbb{P} \subseteq p\mathbb{F}(\mathbb{Pr})$ can be shown as follows. Let $h \in \mathbb{P}$. It is well known that for all $g_1 \in \mathbb{P}$ there exists a function $g_2 \in \mathbb{Pr}$ with $D_{g_1} = R_{g_2}$. So let $f \in \mathbb{Pr}$ be a function such that $D_h = R_f$. Let M be the Turing machine that computes the function h such that in each halting configuration the worktape is empty. Then, M on input f clearly p-computes h and thus $h \in p\mathbb{F}(\mathbb{Pr})$.   □

Further restricting the input functions to total and surjective recursive functions ($\mathbb{R}_{\text{surj}}$) or to the single function id (recall that $id : \mathbb{N} \to \Sigma^*$ is bijective), we obtain the following results.

Theorem 3.2. *1.* $p\mathbb{F}(\mathbb{R}_{\text{surj}}) = \mathbb{R} \cup \{f \in \mathbb{P}\,|\,|D_f| < \infty\}$.
   2. $p\mathbb{F}(\{id\}) = \mathbb{R} \cup \{f \in \mathbb{P}\,|\,(\exists n \in \mathbb{N})[D_f = \{0, 1, 2,\ldots, n\}]\}$.
   3. $p\mathbb{F}_{\text{total}}(\{id\}) = \mathbb{R}$.

The proof is omitted due to space restrictions. Note that the classes $\mathbb{R}$, $\mathbb{R} \cup \{f \in \mathbb{P}\,|\,(\exists n \in \mathbb{N})[D_f = \{0, 1, 2,\ldots, n\}]\}$, $\mathbb{R} \cup \{f \in \mathbb{P}\,|\,|D_f| < \infty\}$, and $\mathbb{P}$ form a chain of strict inclusions and thus we have an inclusion structure as shown in Figure 2.

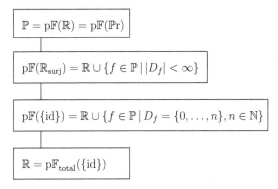

Fig. 2. Classes between $\mathbb{R}$ and $\mathbb{P}$

We will now turn to characterize the function class $\mathbb{P}\mathrm{r}$ in terms of persistent computations. Since we have $\mathrm{p}\mathbb{F}_{total}(\{id\}) = \mathbb{R}$, a restriction of the set of input functions alone will not be sufficient to reduce the power of persistent computations to characterize $\mathbb{P}\mathrm{r}$. We additionally will have to restrict the underlying Turing machine model. Let $\mathcal{TM}_{\mathbb{P}\mathrm{r}}$ denote the set of all Turing machines that compute functions that are primitive recursive and that have a primitive recursive *work* funtions.

Theorem 3.3. $\mathbb{P}\mathrm{r} = \mathrm{p}\mathbb{F}(\{id\}, \mathcal{TM}_{\mathbb{P}\mathrm{r}})$.

Proof. The inclusion $\mathbb{P}\mathrm{r} \subseteq \mathrm{p}\mathbb{F}(\{id\}, \mathcal{TM}_{\mathbb{P}\mathrm{r}})$ is obvious. So it is sufficient to prove $\mathrm{p}\mathbb{F}(\{id\}, \mathcal{TM}_{\mathbb{P}\mathrm{r}}) \subseteq \mathbb{P}\mathrm{r}$.

Let $h \in \mathrm{p}\mathbb{F}(\{id\}, \mathcal{TM}_{\mathbb{P}\mathrm{r}})$ be a function and let M be a Turing machine from $\mathcal{TM}_{\mathbb{P}\mathrm{r}}$ such that M on input id p-computes h. Applying an argument similar to the one in the proof of $\mathrm{p}\mathbb{F}(\mathbb{R}) \subseteq \mathbb{P}$ (see Theorem 3.1) while obeying that all involved functions are primitive recursive and $\mathbb{P}\mathrm{r}$ is closed under simultaneous recursion as well as the bounded μ-operator it is not hard to see that h is primitive recursive. $\qquad\square$

Next we will show that we can even allow more input functions than just id and still get a characterization of $\mathbb{P}\mathrm{r}$. Let $\mathbb{P}\mathrm{r}_{-1}$ denote the set of all functions $f \in \mathbb{P}\mathrm{r}$ such that the inverse f^{-1} is a function and also in $\mathbb{P}\mathrm{r}$, i.e. $\mathbb{P}\mathrm{r}_{-1} = \{f \in \mathbb{P}\mathrm{r} \,|\, f^{-1} \in \mathbb{P}\mathrm{r}\}$.

Theorem 3.4. $\mathbb{P}\mathrm{r} = \mathrm{p}\mathbb{F}(\mathbb{P}\mathrm{r}_{-1}, \mathcal{TM}_{\mathbb{P}\mathrm{r}})$.

Proof. Since clearly $id, id^{-1} \in \mathbb{P}\mathrm{r}$ we have $\mathrm{p}\mathbb{F}(\{id\}, \mathcal{TM}_{\mathbb{P}\mathrm{r}}) \subseteq \mathrm{p}\mathbb{F}(\mathbb{P}\mathrm{r}_{-1}, \mathcal{TM}_{\mathbb{P}\mathrm{r}})$ and thus $\mathbb{P}\mathrm{r} \subseteq \mathrm{p}\mathbb{F}(\mathbb{P}\mathrm{r}_{-1}, \mathcal{TM}_{\mathbb{P}\mathrm{r}})$ by Theorem 3.3. So it remains to show that $\mathrm{p}\mathbb{F}(\mathbb{P}\mathrm{r}_{-1}, \mathcal{TM}_{\mathbb{P}\mathrm{r}}) \subseteq \mathbb{P}\mathrm{r}$.

So let $h \in \mathrm{p}\mathbb{F}(\mathbb{P}\mathrm{r}_{-1}, \mathcal{TM}_{\mathbb{P}\mathrm{r}})$. Hence, there exist a function $f \in \mathbb{P}\mathrm{r}_{-1}$ and a Turing machine $M \in \mathcal{TM}_{\mathbb{P}\mathrm{r}}$ such that M on input f p-computes h. Without loss of generality let $work_M$ be primitive recursive. Similar to the argument in the proof sketch of Theorem 3.3 one can show that $g_{M,f}$ is primitive recursive since it can be described via simultaneous recursion and the functions out_M, $work_M$, and f. Since for all $n \in \mathbb{N}$, $h(n) = g_{M,f}(\min\{i \in \mathbb{N} : i = f^{-1}(n)\})$, using the fact that f^{-1} is primitive recursive and $\mathbb{P}\mathrm{r}$ is closed with respect to the application of the bounded μ-operator we obtain $h \in \mathbb{P}\mathrm{r}$.   □

One might be tempted to conjecture that even $\mathrm{pF}(\mathbb{P}\mathrm{r}, \mathcal{TM}_{\mathbb{P}\mathrm{r}}) = \mathbb{P}\mathrm{r}$ holds. This is not the case, as we will show in the following. Recall that $\mathbb{P}\mathrm{r}_{\mathrm{bij}}$ denotes the set of all functions in $\mathbb{P}\mathrm{r}$ that are bijective. Clearly, $\mathbb{P}\mathrm{r}_{-1} \subseteq \mathbb{P}\mathrm{r}_{\mathrm{bij}}$. We will now argue that $\mathbb{P}\mathrm{r}_{-1} \subset \mathbb{P}\mathrm{r}_{\mathrm{bij}}$.

Lemma 1. $\mathbb{P}\mathrm{r}_{\mathrm{bij}}$ *is not closed with respect to inversion.*

Proof. By a result of Robinson ([Ro50]) we know that

$$\mathbb{R} = \Gamma_{\mathrm{ADD,SUB,INV}}(\{succ,\ x \mathrel{\dot-} \lfloor \sqrt{x} \rfloor^2\})$$

where $succ$ denotes the successor function and for all sets of functions A, the term $\Gamma_{\mathrm{ADD,SUB,INV}}(A)$ denotes the closure of A with respect to addition (ADD), subtraction (SUB) and a limited form of inversion (INV) where inversion can only be applied to bijective functions.

Recall that $\{succ,\ x \mathrel{\dot-} \lfloor \sqrt{x} \rfloor^2\} \subseteq \mathbb{P}\mathrm{r}$, $\mathbb{P}\mathrm{r}$ is closed with respect to ADD and SUB, and $\mathbb{R} \setminus \mathbb{P}\mathrm{r} \neq \emptyset$. Let $h \in \mathbb{R} \setminus \mathbb{P}\mathrm{r}$. The function h can be described by a finite sequence of successive applications of ADD, SUB, and INV on either $succ$ or $x \mathrel{\dot-} \lfloor \sqrt{x} \rfloor^2$. Since during the process of these successive applications of ADD, SUB, and INV, the functions we start from are in $\mathbb{P}\mathrm{r}$ and the function we end with is element of $\mathbb{R} \setminus \mathbb{P}\mathrm{r}$, there exist (intermediate) functions $f \in \mathbb{P}\mathrm{r}$ and $g \in \mathbb{R} \setminus \mathbb{P}\mathrm{r}$ such that:

1. $f \in \Gamma_{\mathrm{ADD,SUB,INV}}(\{succ,\ x \mathrel{\dot-} \lfloor \sqrt{x} \rfloor^2\})$,
2. $f \in \mathbb{P}\mathrm{r}_{\mathrm{bij}}$,
3. $g \in \Gamma_{\mathrm{ADD,SUB,INV}}(\{succ,\ x \mathrel{\dot-} \lfloor \sqrt{x} \rfloor^2\})$,
4. $g = f^{-1}$.

Since $\mathbb{P}\mathrm{r}_{\mathrm{bij}} \subseteq \mathbb{P}\mathrm{r}$ and $g \in \Gamma_{\mathrm{INV}}(\mathbb{P}\mathrm{r}_{\mathrm{bij}})$ we obtain $\Gamma_{\mathrm{INV}}(\mathbb{P}\mathrm{r}_{\mathrm{bij}}) \neq \mathbb{P}\mathrm{r}_{\mathrm{bij}}$ and hence $\mathbb{P}\mathrm{r}_{\mathrm{bij}}$ is not closed under inversion.   □

Since $\mathbb{P}\mathrm{r}_{-1}$ is clearly closed under inversion we have the following corollary.

Corollary 3.5. $\mathbb{P}\mathrm{r}_{-1} \subset \mathbb{P}\mathrm{r}_{\mathrm{bij}}$.

Moreover we can show, that the class $\mathrm{pF}(\mathbb{P}\mathrm{r}_{\mathrm{bij}}, \mathcal{TM}_{\mathbb{P}\mathrm{r}})$ is located between $\mathbb{P}\mathrm{r}$ and $\mathbb{R}$.

Theorem 3.6. $\mathbb{P}\mathrm{r} \subset \mathrm{pF}(\mathbb{P}\mathrm{r}_{\mathrm{bij}}, \mathcal{TM}_{\mathbb{P}\mathrm{r}}) \subset \mathbb{R}$.

Proof. We will first show $\mathbb{P}\mathrm{r} \subset \mathrm{pF}(\mathbb{P}\mathrm{r}_{\mathrm{bij}}, \mathcal{TM}_{\mathbb{P}\mathrm{r}})$.

Since $\mathbb{P}\mathrm{r} = \mathrm{pF}(\mathbb{P}\mathrm{r}_{-1}, \mathcal{TM}_{\mathbb{P}\mathrm{r}})$ due to Theorem 3.4 and $\mathbb{P}\mathrm{r}_{-1} \subseteq \mathbb{P}\mathrm{r}_{\mathrm{bij}}$ we have $\mathbb{P}\mathrm{r} \subseteq \mathrm{pF}(\mathbb{P}\mathrm{r}_{\mathrm{bij}}, \mathcal{TM}_{\mathbb{P}\mathrm{r}})$. It remains to show that there exists a function $h \in \mathrm{pF}(\mathbb{P}\mathrm{r}_{\mathrm{bij}}, \mathcal{TM}_{\mathbb{P}\mathrm{r}})$ that is not primitive recursive.

Let f be a function in $\mathbb{Pr}_{\text{bij}} \setminus \mathbb{Pr}_{-1}$ and M be a Turing machine from $\mathcal{TM}_{\mathbb{Pr}}$ such that $g_{M,f'} = id$ for any input function f'. Clearly $M(f)$ is a consistent p-computation since f is bijective. Let h denote the function computed by the p-computation $M(f)$. Hence $h \in \text{pF}(\mathbb{Pr}_{\text{bij}}, \mathcal{TM}_{\mathbb{Pr}})$. However, we have $h(f(i)) = g_{M,f}(i) = i$ for all $i \in \mathbb{N}$ and thus $h = f^{-1}$. It follows that h is not primitive recursive.

We now proof $\text{pF}(\mathbb{Pr}_{\text{bij}}, \mathcal{TM}_{\mathbb{Pr}}) \subset \mathbb{R}$. The inclusion $\text{pF}(\mathbb{Pr}_{\text{bij}}, \mathcal{TM}_{\mathbb{Pr}}) \subseteq \mathbb{R}$ can be seen as follows. On the one hand it follows immediately from Theorem 3.1 that $\text{pF}(\mathbb{Pr}_{\text{bij}}, \mathcal{TM}_{\mathbb{Pr}}) \subseteq \mathbb{P}$ and on the other hand a p-computation $M(f)$ for a Turing machine M from $\mathcal{TM}_{\mathbb{Pr}}$ and a function $f \in \mathbb{Pr}_{\text{bij}}$ always yields a total function.

To show the strictness of that inclusion we use the Ackermann function p (also known as Peter function) [Ro67]. It is known that $p \in \mathbb{R} \setminus \mathbb{Pr}$. Let the function q be defined as $q(n) = p(n,n)$ for all $n \in \mathbb{N}$. Assume that q is an element of $\text{pF}(\mathbb{Pr}_{\text{bij}}, \mathcal{TM}_{\mathbb{Pr}})$. Hence there exist a function $f \in \mathbb{Pr}_{\text{bij}}$ and a Turing machine $M \in \mathcal{TM}_{\mathbb{Pr}}$ such that $M(f)$ is a p-computation of q. Without loss of generality let $work_M$ be primitive recursive. It follows that $g_{M,f}$ is primitive recursive as well since it can be described via a simultaneous recursion based on out_M and $work_M$ (see the proof of Theorem 3.1). Since $(q \circ f)(n) = q(f(n)) = g_{M,f}(n)$ for all $n \in \mathbb{N}$ we have $q \circ f \in \mathbb{Pr}$. It is a well-known fact that the Peter function grows faster then any primitive recursive function, i.e.,

$$(\forall h \in \mathbb{Pr})(\exists m \in \mathbb{N})(\forall n \in \mathbb{N})[h(n) < p(m,n)].$$

Hence, there exists an $m \in \mathbb{N}$ such that for all $n \in \mathbb{N}$, $q(f(n)) < p(m,n)$. Since f is surjective there exists $n_0 \in \mathbb{N}$ such that $f(n_0) = m$. It follows that

$$q(f(n_0)) = q(m) < p(m,m)$$

which contradicts the definition $q(n) = p(n,n)$ for all $n \in \mathbb{N}$. Hence our assumption $q \in \text{pF}(\mathbb{Pr}_{\text{bij}}, \mathcal{TM}_{\mathbb{Pr}})$ was false. □

Next we will classify the set $\text{pF}(\mathbb{Pr}, \mathcal{TM}_{\mathbb{Pr}})$ which turns out to be not equal to $\mathbb{Pr}$ as the above Theorem 3.6 implies. On the one hand $\text{pF}(\mathbb{Pr}, \mathcal{TM}_{\mathbb{Pr}})$ is a strict superset of $\text{pF}(\mathbb{Pr}_{\text{bij}}, \mathcal{TM}_{\mathbb{Pr}})$ since input functions from $\mathbb{Pr}$ are more flexible than input functions from $\mathbb{Pr}_{\text{bij}}$. On the other hand $\text{pF}(\mathbb{Pr}, \mathcal{TM}_{\mathbb{Pr}})$ remains a subset of $\mathbb{P}$ as the following proposition shows.

Theorem 3.7. $\text{pF}(\mathbb{Pr}_{\text{bij}}, \mathcal{TM}_{\mathbb{Pr}}) \subset \text{pF}(\mathbb{Pr}, \mathcal{TM}_{\mathbb{Pr}}) \subset \mathbb{P} \setminus \{nd\}$.

Proof. The first inclusion, $\text{pF}(\mathbb{Pr}_{\text{bij}}, \mathcal{TM}_{\mathbb{Pr}}) \subset \text{pF}(\mathbb{Pr}, \mathcal{TM}_{\mathbb{Pr}})$ is easy to see. Note that $\mathbb{Pr}_{\text{bij}} \subset \mathbb{Pr}$ and hence $\text{pF}(\mathbb{Pr}_{\text{bij}}, \mathcal{TM}_{\mathbb{Pr}}) \subseteq \text{pF}(\mathbb{Pr}, \mathcal{TM}_{\mathbb{Pr}})$, yet the function $h : \mathbb{N} \to \mathbb{N}$ that, for all $n \in \mathbb{N}$, is defined as

$$h(n) = \begin{cases} n, & \text{if } n \equiv 0 \mod 2, \\ \text{n.d.}, & \text{if } n \equiv 1 \mod 2, \end{cases}$$

is an element of $\text{pF}(\mathbb{Pr}, \mathcal{TM}_{\mathbb{Pr}}) \setminus \text{pF}(\mathbb{Pr}_{\text{bij}}, \mathcal{TM}_{\mathbb{Pr}})$.

To show the other inclusion, $p\mathbb{F}(\mathbb{P}r, \mathcal{TM}_{\mathbb{P}r}) \subset \mathbb{P} \setminus \{nd\}$, first observe that the function nd is not in $p\mathbb{F}(\mathbb{P}r, \mathcal{TM}_{\mathbb{P}r})$ since $g_{M,f}(0)$ is defined for any $M \in \mathcal{TM}_{\mathbb{P}r}$ and any input function f. Second, recall that we have $p\mathbb{F}(\mathbb{P}r) = \mathbb{P}$ by Theorem 3.1 and thus $p\mathbb{F}(\mathbb{P}r, \mathcal{TM}_{\mathbb{P}r}) \subseteq \mathbb{P} \setminus \{nd\}$. And third, note that the strictness of that inclusion follows from the proof of Theorem 3.6. In particular, in that proof a function q was defined and it was shown that q is in $\mathbb{R} \setminus p\mathbb{F}(\mathbb{P}r_{\mathrm{bij}}, \mathcal{TM}_{\mathbb{P}r})$. Using the same argument one can also show that $q \in \mathbb{P} \setminus p\mathbb{F}(\mathbb{P}r, \mathcal{TM}_{\mathbb{P}r})$.   □

Acknowledgments. The authors would like to thank the anonymous referees for their very helpful comments.

References

[A85]   Althöfer, I.: Das Dreihirn—Entscheidungsteilung im Schach. Computerschach & Spiele, 20–22 (December 1985)

[AS03]   Althöfer, I., Snatzke, R.G.: Playing Games with Multiple Choice Systems. In: Schaeffer, J., Müller, M., Björnsson, Y. (eds.) CG 2002. LNCS, vol. 2883, pp. 142–153. Springer, Heidelberg (2003)

[BF04]   Brand, M., Frisken, S., Lesh, N., Marks, J., Nikovski, D., Perry, R., Yedidia, J.: Theory and Applied Computing: Observations and Anecdotes. In: Fiala, J., Koubek, V., Kratochvíl, J. (eds.) MFCS 2004. LNCS, vol. 3153, pp. 106–118. Springer, Heidelberg (2004)

[GW98]   Goldin, D., Wegner, P.: Persistence as a form of interaction, Technical Report CS-98-07, Brown University, Department of Computer Science (1998)

[HK]   Hempel, H., Kimmritz, M.: Aspects of Persistent Computations (unpublished)

[Ko98]   Kosub, S.: Persistent Computations, Technical Report No. 217, Julius-Maximilians-Universität Würzburg, Institut für Informatik (1998)

[KL02]   Klau, G., Lesh, N., Marks, J., Mitzenmacher, M.: Human-guided tabu search. In: Proceedings of the Eighteenth National Conference on Artificial Intelligence, Fourteenth Conference on Innovative Applications of Artificial Intelligence 2002, pp. 41–47. AAAI Press, Menlo Park (2002)

[LM03]   Lesh, N., Mitzenmacher, M., Whitesides, S.: A complete and effective move set for simplified protein folding. In: Proceedings of the Seventh Annual International Conference on Research in Computational Molecular Biology, pp. 188–195 (2003)

[LM03a]   Lesh, N., Marks, J., McMahon, A., Mitzenmacher, M.: New exhaustive, heuristic, and interactive approaches to 2D rectangular strip packing, TR2003-05. Mitsubishi Electric Research Laboratories, Cambridge (May 2003)

[Ro50]   Robinson, R.: General recursive functions. Proceedings of the American Mathematical Society 1, JO 3-718 (1950)

[Ro67]   Rogers, H.: The Theory of Recursive Functions and Effective Computability, 2nd edn. (1987). MIT Press, Cambridge (1967)

[Sch92]   Schöning, U.: Theoretische Informatik kurz gefasst, Mannheim; Leipzig; Wien; Zürich: BI-Wissenschaftsverlag (1992)

On Complexity of Two Dimensional Languages Generated by Transducers

Egor Dolzhenko and Nataša Jonoska

University of South Florida,
4202 E. Fowler Ave Tampa, Fl 33620, USA
edolzhen@mail.usf.edu, jonoska@math.usf.edu

Abstract. We consider two-dimensional languages, called here *2d transducer languages*, generated by iterative applications of transducers (finite state automata with output). To each transducer a two-dimensional language consisting of blocks of symbols is associated: the bottom row of a block is an input string accepted by the transducer and, by iterative application of the transducer, each row of the block is an output of the transducer on the preceding row. We observe that this class of languages is a proper subclass of recognizable picture languages containing the class of all factorial local 2d languages. By taking the average growth rate of the number of blocks in the language as a measure of its complexity, also known as the entropy of the language, we show that every entropy value of a one-dimensional regular language can be obtained as an entropy value of a 2d transducer language.

Keywords: Transducers, Finite State Automata with Output, Entropy, Picture Languages, Local Languages.

1 Introduction and Background

Two-dimensional languages, representing sets of rectangular blocks of symbols are a natural extension of one-dimensional languages, sets of words, or strings of symbols. Although there are fairly well developed classifications and theories to study one-dimensional languages, in particular regular languages, the case of two dimensional languages remains elusive. Two-dimensional recognizable languages, so called class REC, are morphic images of two-dimensional local languages, and were originally defined by A. Restivo and D. Giammarresi [5,6]. They showed that the emptiness problem for these languages is undecidable which implies that many other questions that are easily solved in one-dimensional case become undecidable in two-dimensional case. Recent work by several authors attempts to better understand the class REC through various approaches such as: design of variants of finite state automata that recognize these languages [1,2,12,13], characterization of determinism of two-dimensional recognizable languages [3], or study of the factor languages of two-dimensional shift spaces [9,10].

On the other side there is a natural representation of prolongable local two-dimensional languages with Wang tiles which have been studied extensively for

O.H. Ibarra and B. Ravikumar (Eds.): CIAA 2008, LNCS 5148, pp. 181–190, 2008.

couple of decades. Recently, a physical representation of Wang tiles with DNA molecules has been demonstrated [21,22]. This provides another motivation for studying two-dimensional languages. It is well known that by iteration of generalized sequential machines (finite state machines mapping symbols into strings) all computable functions can be simulated (see for ex. [19,20]). The full computational power depends on the possibility for iterations of a finite state machine. As there is a natural simulation of the process of iteration of transducers and recursive (computable) functions with Wang tiles [8], this idea has been developed further in [4] where a successful experimental simulation of a programmable transducer (finite state machine mapping symbols into symbols) with DNA Wang tiles having iteration capabilities is reported. This experimental development provides means for generating patterns and variety of two-dimensional arrays at the nano level.

Motivated by this recent experimental development, in this note we concentrate on the class of two-dimensional languages generated by iteration of transducers. It is not difficult to see that such languages belong to the REC class (see Proposition 1), however, they do not necessarily belong to the class of local two-dimensional languages (Example 2). Therefore, this is another sub-class of REC languages whose analysis may provide a way to understand some properties of the the whole class of REC. In Section 4 we make some observations about the average growth rate of the number of blocks in a picture language relative their size as a measure of complexity. This measure is known in symbolic dynamics as the entropy of the language and it is well understood in the case of one dimensional regular languages. It is known that in one-dimensional case, the set of entropies of the regular languages coincides with the set of logarithms of Perron numbers (see [18]). However, there is no general theory that describes a way to obtain the entropy of a two-dimensional local, or even less a language belonging to the larger class of recognizable languages. It is known that even languages with so called strong transitivity, i.e., mixing properties, have zero entropy [15,16]. In this note we observe that the value given by a log of a Perron number can be obtained as an entropy value of a transducer generated two-dimensional language. This also shows that the two-dimensional arrays that can be obtained by self-assembly of DNA tiles simulating iterations of transducers have rich complexity.

2   Notation and Definitions

We use A to indicate an alphabet, a finite set of symbols. The cardinality of A is denoted with $\#A$. A finite sequence of symbols is called a word, or a one-dimensional block. The set of all words over alphabet A is denoted with A^*. We also consider A^* as a free monoid with the operation of concatenation of words. The length of a word $w = a_1 \cdot \ldots \cdot a_k$ is k and is denoted with $|w|$. The empty word is denoted with ϵ. The set of all words of length k is denoted with A^k, and set of all words of length less or equal to k is denoted with $A^{\leq k}$.

A *one-dimensional language* is a subset of A^*. For a language L, we extend the notation to $L_k = A^k \cap L$ and $L_{\leq k} = A^{\leq k} \cap L$. A word u such that $w = x_1 u x_2$ for some words $x_1, x_2 \in A^*$ is called a *factor of w*. The set of all factors of w is denoted with $F(w)$, and the set of all factors of length k of w is denoted with $F_k(w)$. We extend this notation such that the set of factors of all words in a language L denoted by $F(L)$ and the set of factors of all words in L of length k is denoted by $F_k(L)$.

Definition 1. *A* nondeterministic transducer *(also known as alphabetic transducer) is a five-tuple*

$$\tau = (A, Q, \delta, q_0, T),$$

where A is a finite alphabet, Q is a finite set of states, q_0 is an initial state ($q_0 \in Q$), T is a set of final (terminal) states ($T \subseteq Q$), $\delta \subseteq Q \times A \times A \times Q$ is the set of transitions. A transducer is called deterministic *if its set of transitions defines a function (which is also denoted with δ) $\delta : Q \times A \to A \times Q$.*

To a transducer we associate a directed labeled graph in a standard way: the set of vertices is the set of states Q and the directed edges are transitions in δ, such that an edge $e = (q, a, a', q')$ starts at q and terminates at q'. To each edge we associate labels $\mathcal{I} : \delta \to A$ and $\mathcal{O} : \delta \to A$ being the *input* and the *output* labels, i.e., for $e = (q, a, a', q')$ we have $\mathcal{I}(e) = a$ and $\mathcal{O}(e) = a'$. The input and the output labels are extended to paths in the transducer.

We say that a word w is *accepted* by a transducer $\tau = (A, Q, \delta, q_0, T)$ if there is a path $p = e_1 \cdots e_k$ which starts at q_0, terminates with a state in T and $\mathcal{I}(p) = \mathcal{I}(e_1) \cdots \mathcal{I}(e_k) = w$. The path p in this case is called an *accepting path for w*. The language which consists of all words that are accepted by τ is called the *input language* of τ and is denoted $\mathcal{I}(\tau)$. A word v is said to be an *output* of τ if there is $w \in \mathcal{I}(\tau)$ and an accepting path p for w such that $\mathcal{O}(p) = v$. In this case we also write $v \in \mathcal{O}(w)$. The language which consist of all outputs of τ is the *output language for τ* denoted with $\mathcal{O}(\tau)$.

Definition 2. *If $S = \{1, \ldots, n\} \times \{1, \ldots, m\}$, then a map $B : S \mapsto A$ is a block of size $n \times m$ or an $n \times m$-block. We say that n is the* number of columns *in B and m is the* number of rows *in B. The empty block is of size $m \times n$ where at least one of m, n equals 0 and is denoted by ϵ.*

The blocks are represented as arrays of symbols: the first row of the block is the bottom row, and every successive row is placed on top of the previous row.

Definition 3. *If B is a block of size $n \times m$, and n', m', x, and y are nonnegative integers, such that $1 \leq x + n' \leq n$ and $1 \leq y + m' \leq m$, then a sub-block of B of size $n' \times m'$ at position (x, y), denoted $B|_{(x,y)}^{n',m'}$ is the $n' \times m'$-block such that $B|_{(x,y)}^{n',m'}(i, j) = B(x+i-1, y+j-1)$ for $1 \leq i \leq n'$ and $1 \leq j \leq m'$. We say that a block B' is a sub-block of B if there are x, y, n', m' such that $B' = B|_{(x,y)}^{n',m'}$.*

The set A^{**} denotes the set of all blocks over alphabet A. A subset L of A^{**} is called a *picture language*. The set of all $k \times k$-blocks is denoted with $A^{k \times k}$. A subset of $A^{k \times k}$ is denoted with $Q_{k,k}$. The set of all $k \times \ell$ sub-blocks of a block B is denoted by $F_{k,\ell}(B)$. The set of all sub-blocks of B is denoted with $F(B)$. We extend this notation naturally to $F(L)$ for all sub-blocks of blocks in L and $F_{k,\ell}(L)$ for the set of all sub-blocks of size $k \times \ell$ of blocks in L.

Now we concentrate on picture languages generated by transducers. If τ is a transducer (deterministic or nondeterministic), we define inductively: $\tau^0(w) = \{w\}$ if $w \in \mathcal{I}(\tau)$ and $\tau^r(w) = \{u \mid$ there is $v \in \tau^{r-1}(w) \cap \mathcal{I}(\tau),\, u \in \mathcal{O}(v)\}$.

Definition 4. *An $n \times m$-block B is generated by transducer τ if $B|_{(1,1)}^{n,1} \in \mathcal{I}(\tau)$ and $B|_{(1,i+1)}^{n,1} \in \tau(B|_{(1,i)}^{n,1})$ for all $1 \leq i \leq m-1$.*

Note that the empty block ϵ is generated by a transducer τ if the initial state is also a terminal state. A $n \times 1$-block is generated by a transducer τ if it belongs to $\mathcal{I}(\tau)$. Every transducer with non-empty input language generates blocks of size $n \times i$ for $i = 1, 2$.

Definition 5. *A picture language which consists of all blocks that are generated by a deterministic (nondeterministic) transducer τ is called a picture language generated by transducer τ and is denoted with L_τ. A picture language L is said to be* transducer generated *if there is a transducer τ such that $L = L_\tau$.*

The class of transducer generated picture languages is denoted with TG.

3   Local Picture Languages and TG

We recall the definition for local languages in one dimensional case. For a language $L \subseteq A^*$ we say that L is a *local language of order k* if there is $P \subseteq A^k$ such that for all $w \in A^{\geq k}$, we have $w \in L$ if and only if $F_k(w) \subseteq P$. The set P is called the *set of allowed words*. This definition naturally extends to two dimensions.

Definition 6. *For a picture language $L \subseteq A^{**}$ we say that L is a* local picture language of order k *if there is a set $Q_{k,k}$ such that for all $n \times m$-blocks B $(n, m \geq k)$ we have $B \in L$ if and only if $F_{k,k}(B) \subseteq Q_{k,k}$. The set $Q_{k,k}$ is called the* set of the allowed blocks.

We note that in the definition of local languages given in [5,6] each block in the language is surrounded by a special symbol indicating the boundary of the block. This requirement may be important in determining certain properties of picture languages, such as the "ambiguity" defined in [3,2]. The boundary may also prevent certain sizes of blocks to appear. For example the boundaries allow a construction of a local language which consists of square block sizes only [3]. However, by Definition 6, local picture languages contain every sub-block of a block in the language. Therefore Definition 6 is a definition of "factorial local picture languages" compared to the definition in [5].

Let $Q_{k,k} \subset A^{k \times k}$ and K be the local picture language defined by $Q_{k,k}$. Consider $\varphi : Q_{k,k} \to A$. Let $\mathcal{A}$ denote the set of all $m \times n$-blocks from K with

$m, n \geq k$. A *projection map* defined by φ is a map $\Phi : \mathcal{A} \to A^{**}$ such that $\Phi(B)(i,j) = \varphi(B|_{(i,j)}^{k,k})$ for an $m \times n$-block B and $1 \leq i \leq n - k$, $1 \leq j \leq m - k$. We say that a picture language L is in class REC if and only if there is a local picture language K and a projection map Φ such that $L = \Phi(K)$. As in the case of local languages, the definition for recognizable languages is somewhat different than the one in [5], i.e., here we consider "factorial recognizable languages".

Proposition 1. *Transducer generated languages are in REC.*

Proof. (sketch) Given Wang prototiles $\mathcal{T}$, a *Wang language* defined by $\mathcal{T}$ is a set or all rectangles obtained by tilings with Wang tiles from $\mathcal{T}$. It is well known that (with the appropriate coding) the class of Wang languages is identical to the class of local picture languages (see for ex. [15,16]). To every transducer τ one can associate a set of Wang prototiles $W(\mathcal{T}_\tau)$ [8]. A representation of a transducer transition with a Wang tile is depicted in Fig. 1. To prove the proposition, it is sufficient to observe that for every transducer τ there is a natural projection map from $W(\mathcal{T}_\tau)$ to the language L_τ which maps each prototile $[q, a, a', q']$ to a' (the top color). This map (with a small modification to take care of the border colors) generates all of the blocks from L_τ.

As noted with the following example there are picture languages in REC that are not in TG.

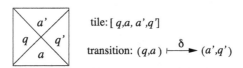

Fig. 1. A computational tile for a transducer

Example 1. Consider the picture language over alphabet $\{a, b\}$ which consists of all blocks containing at most one appearance of b (all other symbols are a). This picture language is in REC [14]. If there were a transducer that generates this language, this transducer would have a transition with an input symbol a and output b, and a transition with input symbol b and output a. But then, there are n, s such that $a^s b a^{n-s-1} \in \tau(a^n)$, i.e., on an input a^n the transducer may output a word containing a symbol b. Hence blocks with more than three rows that are generated by the transducer can have more than one appearance of b.

Although the class of transducer generated languages TG is a subset of REC, it turns out that there is a TG language which is not a local picture language. In fact even for a deterministic transducer τ with input language $\mathcal{I}(\tau)$ being local, the picture language generated by τ, L_τ, may not be.

Example 2. Consider the transducer over alphabet $\{a, b\}$ as depicted in Fig. 2. This transducer is deterministic and all of its states are terminal except the "junk state" indicated by a shaded circle. The initial state is indicated with an arrow. The output symbols for all transitions starting at the same state are the same, so the output symbols are indicated inside the circles denoting the states. The input language of the transducer τ is local of order 3 (the allowed words of length 3 are all but "bbb").

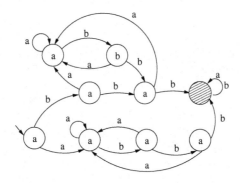

Fig. 2. A deterministic transducer τ such that $\mathcal{I}(\tau)$ is a local language, but L_τ is not

Suppose that L_τ is a local picture language and, there is a set $Q_{k,k}$ of allowed blocks of size $k \times k$ such that every $k \times k$ sub-block of a block in L_τ is in $Q_{k,k}$. Let B, B' be $n \times m$-blocks where $m, n > k$ and C be $(n+1) \times m$-block defined as follows:

$$B = \begin{matrix} a\,a\ \ a\ \ldots a\,a\,a \\ \cdots \\ a\,a\ \ a\ \ldots a\,a\,a \\ a\,b\ \ a\ \ldots a\,a\,b \end{matrix} \qquad B' = \begin{matrix} a\,a\ \ a\ \ldots a\,a\,a \\ \cdots \\ a\,a\ \ a\ \ldots a\,a\,b \\ b\,a\ \ a\ \ldots a\,b\,a \end{matrix} \qquad C = \begin{matrix} a\,a\ \ a\ \ldots a\,a\,a \\ \cdots \\ a\,a\ \ a\ \ldots a\,a\,b \\ a\,b\ \ a\ \ldots a\,b\,a \end{matrix}$$

One can think of C as obtained from B by adding the last column of B' as a last column of C. In this case, $B = C|_{(1,1)}^{n,m}$ and $B' = C|_{(2,1)}^{n,m}$, i.e., $B, B' \in F(C)$. Quick check of the transducer shows that blocks B and B' are in L_τ. Moreover, $F_{k,k}(C) = F_{k,k}(\{B, B'\}) \subseteq Q_{k,k}$. If L_τ is local, then it must be that $C \in L_\tau$, but direct check shows that it, in fact, is not (note that the only way to output symbol b is when the input word starts with b, and this is not the case with the first row of C).

Recall that by enlarging the alphabet accordingly (similarly as going to the higher block system in [18]) one can encode every local language in an "equivalent" local language defined through a 2×2 size blocks. In the following we assume that every local language is determined by a set of blocks $Q_{2,2}$. The relationship between local picture languages as defined by Definition 6 and the transducer generated languages is obtained by the following proposition. We state the following observation without a proof.

Proposition 2. *For every local picture language L there is a transducer τ such that $L_\tau = L$.*

4 Entropy of L_τ

One measure of complexity of a given language is the average growth rate of the number of blocks that appear in the language relative their size. In one dimensional case, this measure is also called the entropy of the language and is derived from the notion of topological entropy of (compact) symbolic dynamical systems (see [7]). The Perron-Frobenious theory provides a straight-forward way of computing the entropy for a one-dimensional regular language. It is the logarithm of the maximal eigen value (also known as Perron numbers) of the adjacency matrix of the minimal deterministic automaton of the language [18]. However, obtaining a general method for computing the entropy of a two-dimensional recognizable language shows to be very difficult, and consequently, there is no general knowledge about what numbers can be realized as the entropy values in two-dimensions. In the following we show that logarithm of every Perron number can be obtained as an entropy value for a transducer generated picture language. In other words, all entropy values realized by one-dimensional regular languages can also be realized by transducer generated picture languages.

Recall that for $L \subseteq A^*$ the *entropy of* L is $h(L) = \limsup\limits_{n \to \infty} \frac{1}{n} \log(\#F_n(L))$.
This definition extends to an equivalent definition in two-dimensions.

Definition 7. *For $L \subseteq A^{**}$ the entropy of the picture language L is*

$$h(L) = \limsup_{n \to \infty} \frac{1}{n^2} \log(\#F_{n,n}(L)).$$

Note. Since the entropy formula "counts" the sub-blocks of a certain size, the value of the entropy of L_τ and $\mathcal{I}(\tau)$ does not change if we consider these languages to be factorial, hence we can assume that all transducers in this sections have all their states initial and terminal. In this case, $F(L_\tau) = L_\tau$, and $F(L) = L$.

Note that the entropy of L is always bounded by $\log \#A$. The entropy of L_τ is zero for any deterministic transducer τ, since for each n it contains at most $\#A^n$ blocks of size $n \times n$ (each word w can generate at most one block of height n). However, if L_τ is a two dimensional language generated by a nondeterministic transducer, its entropy may no longer be zero. For example, the transducer $\tau = (A, \{q\}, \delta, \{q\}, q)$ with $\delta = \{(q, a, b, q) | a, b \in A\}$, which consists of one state with transitions having all possible labels generates $L_\tau = A^{**}$ and for each n, $\#F_{n,n}(L_\tau) = \#(A^{n \times n}) = \#A^{n^2}$. Thus $h(L_\tau) = h(A^{**}) = \log \#A$.

For a given transducer τ and w in $\mathcal{I}(\tau)$ define $\deg(w) = \#\tau(w)$, i.e., $\deg(w)$ is the number of distinct words that τ can output on input w. We extend this notation to finite sets of words by setting $\deg(S) = \max_{w \in S} \{\deg(w)\}$.

Observe that the number of distinct blocks of height n with the bottom row w contained in L_τ is bounded above by

$$\prod_{i=0}^{n-1} \deg(\tau^i(w)).$$

Suppose $\deg(w) \leq n^k$ for all w in $\mathcal{I}(\tau)$ with $|w| = n$. Then we observe that

$$h(L_\tau) = \limsup_{n \to \infty} \frac{1}{n^2} \log(F_{n,n}(L_\tau))$$

$$\leq \limsup_{n \to \infty} \frac{1}{n^2} \log \left(\sum_{\substack{|w|=n \\ w \in \mathcal{I}(\tau)}} \left(\prod_{i=0}^{n-1} (\deg(\tau^i(w))) \right) \right)$$

$$\leq \limsup_{n \to \infty} \frac{1}{n^2} \log \left(\#A^n \cdot n^{nk} \right) = \limsup_{n \to \infty} \left[\frac{1}{n} \log \#A + \frac{k}{n} \log n \right] = 0.$$

Thus if there is some positive integer k, such that for any w in $\mathcal{I}(\tau)$, $\#\tau(w) \leq |w|^k$, the entropy of L_τ is zero. This proves:

Proposition 3. *Let τ be a transducer. If there is a polynomial p such that $\#\tau(w) \leq p(|w|)$ for every $w \in \mathcal{I}(w)$, then the entropy of L_τ is 0.*

Proposition 4. *For any regular language L there is a nondeterministic transducer τ such that $\mathcal{I}(\tau) = L$ and $h(L_\tau) = h(L)$.*

Proof. Let M be a finite state automaton accepting language L. Denote the set of transitions of M by φ, and construct a transducer τ from M as follows. The set of states remains the same and the set of transitions in τ is $\{(q_1, a, b, q_2) \mid (q_1, a, q_2) \in \varphi$ and $b \in A\}$. Observe that $\mathcal{I}(\tau) = L$.

Now consider L_τ. Note that for an $n \times n$-block $B \in L_\tau$, every row of B must be in $\mathcal{I}(\tau)$, except maybe the last, n^{th} row which may not belong to $\mathcal{I}(\tau)$. Let $B_{p,k}$ denote the set of all $n \times p$-blocks $B \in L_\tau$ with $B|_{(1,p)}^{n,1}$ (the pth row of block B) in $\mathcal{I}(\tau)$. Thus we conclude that $\#F_{n,n}(L_\tau) \leq \#B_{n,n-1}\#A^n \leq \#B_{n,n}\#A^n$. Hence

$$h(L_\tau) = \limsup_{n \to \infty} \frac{1}{n^2} \log \#F_{n,n}(L_\tau)$$

$$\leq \limsup_{n \to \infty} \frac{1}{n^2} \log(\#B_{n,n} \cdot \#A^n)$$

$$= \limsup_{n \to \infty} \frac{1}{n^2} \log \#B_{n,n}$$

Since $\#B_{n,n} \leq \#F_{n,n}(L_\tau)$, we have that

$$h(L_\tau) = \limsup_{n \to \infty} \frac{1}{n^2} \log \#B_{n,n}$$

Since the transducer can output every word of length n on any given input of length n, the number of $n \times n$-blocks in L_τ having each of its rows in $\mathcal{I}(\tau)$ is exactly $[\#F_n(\mathcal{I}(\tau))]^n$, i.e., $\#B_{n,n} = [\#F_n(\mathcal{I}(\tau))]^n$. Thus

$$h(L_\tau) = \limsup_{n \to \infty} \frac{1}{n} \log \#F_n(\mathcal{I}(\tau)) = h(L)$$

Corollary 1. *Let L be a regular language. Then the entropy of L is an upper bound for the entropy of L_τ for any nondeterministic transducer τ with $\mathcal{I}(\tau) = L$.*

Proof. Let L be a regular language and let $\tau = (A, Q, \delta, q_0, F)$ be such that $\mathcal{I}(\tau) = L$. Then consider $\tau' = (A, Q, \delta', q_0, F)$, with $\delta' = \{(q, a, b, p) \mid (q, a, s, p) \in \delta$ and $b \in A\}$. Hence $\delta \subseteq \delta'$ and $h(L_\tau) \leq h(L_{\tau'})$. By the proof of the Proposition 4, $h(L_{\tau'}) = h(\mathcal{I}(\tau)) = h(L)$.

5   Concluding Remarks

In this paper we introduced a new class of two-dimensional languages which is a sub-class of REC and contains all factorial local picture languages. This class comes naturally as a class generated by iterative applications of transducers, and if entropy is taken as a measure of complexity, this class shows to have rich pattern generation capabilities. Characterization of patterns that can be generated by iteration of transducers may be of interest in applications, in particular, in algorithmic self-assembly of two-dimensional arrays with DNA tiles. Also, it may be of interest to investigate some decidability questions for these languages as well: for example, given a language in TG, is there an $m \times n$-block in the language for every m, n? The relationship of the class TG with the class of unambiguous (or non-deterministic) picture languages as well as transitivity and mixing properties of these languages remain to be investigated as well.

Acknowledgement. This work has been supported in part by the NSF grants CCF #0523928 and CCF #0726396.

References

1. Anselmo, M., Giammarresi, D., Madonia, M.: Tiling automaton: a computational model for recognizable two-dimensional languages. In: Holub, J., Žd'árek, J. (eds.) CIAA 2007. LNCS, vol. 4783, pp. 290–302. Springer, Heidelberg (2007)
2. Anselmo, M., Giammarresi, D., Madonia, M.: From determinism to non-determinism in recognizable two-dimensional languages. In: Harju, T., Karhumäki, J., Lepisto, A. (eds.) DLT 2007. LNCS, vol. 4588, pp. 36–47. Springer, Heidelberg (2007)
3. Anselmo, M., Giammarresi, D., Madonia, M., Restivo, A.: Unambiguous recognizable two-dimensional languages. RAIRO - Inf. Theor. Appl. 40, 277–293 (2006)
4. Chakraborty, B., Jonoska, N., Seeman, N.C.: Programmable tranducer by DNA self-assembly (submitted)
5. Giammarresi, D., Restivo, A.: Recognizable picture languages. In: Nivat, M., Saoudi, A., Wang, P.S.P. (eds.) Proc. 1st Internat. Colloq. on Parallel Image Processing; also in Internat. J. Pattern Recognition Artif. Intell. 6, 231–256 (1992)
6. Giammarresi, D., Restivo, A.: Two-dimensional languages. In: Handbook of Formal Languages, vol. 3, pp. 215–267. Springer, Berlin (1997)
7. Gottschalk, W.H., Hedlund, G.A.: Topological Dynamics. AMS Colloquium Pubs. 36 (1955)
8. Jonoska, N., Liao, S., Seeman, N.C.: Transducers with programmable input by DNA self-assembly. In: Jonoska, N., Păun, G., Rozenberg, G. (eds.) Aspects of Molecular Computing. LNCS, vol. 2950, pp. 219–240. Springer, Heidelberg (2003)

9. Jonoska, N., Pirnot, J.B.: Transitivity in two-dimensional local languages defined by dot systems. International Journal of Foundations of Computer Science 17, 435–464 (2006)
10. Jonoska, N., Pirnot, J.B.: Finite state automata representing two-dimensional subshifts. In: Holub, J., Žd'árek, J. (eds.) CIAA 2007. LNCS, vol. 4783, pp. 277–289. Springer, Heidelberg (2007)
11. Kari, J.: A small aperiodic set of Wang tiles. Discrete Math. 160(1-3), 259–264 (1996)
12. Kari, J., Moore, C.: Rectangles and squares recognized by two-dimensional automata, http://www.santafe.edu/~moore/pubs/picture.html
13. Kari, J., Moore, C.: New results on alternating and non-deterministic two-dimensional finite automata. In: Ferreira, A., Reichel, H. (eds.) STACS 2001. LNCS, vol. 2010, pp. 396–406. Springer, Heidelberg (2001)
14. Kari, J.: private communication
15. Kitchens, B., Schmidt, K.: Automorphisms of compact groups. Ergod. Th. & Dynam. Sys. 9, 691–735 (1989)
16. Kitchens, B., Schmidt, K.: Markov subgroups of $(\mathbb{Z}/2\mathbb{Z})^{\mathbb{Z}^2}$. In: Walters, P. (ed.) Symbolic Dynamics and its Applications; Contemporary Mathematics 135, 265–283 (1992)
17. Latteux, M., Simplot, D., Terlutte, A.: Iterated Length-Preserving Rational Transductions. In: Brim, L., Gruska, J., Zlatuška, J. (eds.) MFCS 1998. LNCS, vol. 1450, pp. 286–295. Springer, Heidelberg (1998)
18. Lind, D., Marcus, B.: An Introduction to Symbolic Dynamics and Coding. Cambridge University Press, Cambridge (1995)
19. Manca, V., Martin-Vide, C., Păun, G.: New computing paradigms suggested by DNA computing: computing by carving. BioSystems 52, 47–54 (1999)
20. Păun, G.: On the iteration of gsm mappings. Rev. Roum. Math. Pures Appl. 23(4), 921–937 (1978)
21. Winfree, E., Liu, F., Wenzler, L.A., Seeman, N.C.: Design and self-assembly of two-dimensional DNA crystals. Nature 394, 539–544 (1998)
22. Winfree, E.: Algorithmic self-assembly of DNA: theoretical motivations and 2D assembly experiments. Journal of Biomolecular Structure and Dynamics 11 (S2), 263–270 (2000)

Games for Temporal Logics on Trees

Z. Ésik[1,*] and Sz. Iván[2]

[1] GRLMC, Rovira i Virgili University, Tarragona, Spain
[2] Dept. of Computer Science, University of Szeged, Hungary

Abstract. We associate a temporal logic XTL($\mathcal{L}$) with each class $\mathcal{L}$ of (regular) tree languages and provide both an algebraic and a game-theoretic characterization of the expressive power of the logic XTL($\mathcal{L}$).

1 Introduction

The characterization of the expressive power of first-order logic on trees (with both the successor relations and the partial order relation derived from the successor relations) has been a long standing open problem, cf. [12,14,19].[1] With a few exceptions, there is no decidable characterization known for temporal logics on (finite and/or infinite) trees. Most notably, the decidable characterization of the logic CTL [5] is open.

In this paper we consider only finite trees. In [6], a logic FTL($\mathcal{L}$) was associated with each class $\mathcal{L}$ of regular tree languages. Under the assumption that the next modalities are expressible (and an additional technical condition), we obtained a characterization of the languages definable in FTL($\mathcal{L}$) using pseudovarieties of finite tree automata and cascade products. We argued that by selecting particular (finite) language classes $\mathcal{L}$, most of the familiar temporal logics can be covered. In [8], we removed the extra condition on the next modalities by making use of a modified version of the cascade product, called the Moore-product. The logics FTL($\mathcal{L}$) contain "built in" atomic formulas describing the root of a tree. This has the disadvantage that several natural classes of tree languages do not possess a characterization in terms of the logics FTL($\mathcal{L}$).

In this paper, we introduce a generalization of the logics FTL($\mathcal{L}$). We associate yet another logic, called XTL($\mathcal{L}$), with each class $\mathcal{L}$ of tree languages. In the first part of the paper we show that, when $\mathcal{L}$ ranges over subclasses of regular tree languages (and satisfies a technical condition), then the classes of languages definable in XTL($\mathcal{L}$) are in a one-to-one correspondence with those pseudovarieties of finite tree automata which are closed under a variant of the Moore-product.

In the second part of the paper we provide a game-theoretic characterization of the logics XTL($\mathcal{L}$). With each class $\mathcal{L}$ of tree languages, we associate an

---

* Partially supported by MEC grant. no. MTM2007-63422.
[1] The case when one has only the successor relations has been studied in [3] where a decidable characterization has been found.

O.H. Ibarra and B. Ravikumar (Eds.): CIAA 2008, LNCS 5148, pp. 191–200, 2008.

Ehrenfeucht-Fraïssé-type game, called the XTL($\mathcal{L}$)-game, between "Spoiler" and "Duplicator". We obtain that two trees s, t can be separated by an XTL($\mathcal{L}$)-formula of "depth n" iff Spoiler has a winning strategy in the n-round XTL($\mathcal{L}$)-game on (s, t). We also discuss a modification of the game that characterizes the logics FTL($\mathcal{L}$).

The paper is ended by a few examples derived from the main theorems providing game-theoretic characterizations of some familiar logics, including a version of CTL for finite trees, and some of its fragments. All proofs are omitted.

2 Preliminaries

A *rank type* is a nonempty finite set of nonnegative integers containing 0. A *ranked alphabet* Σ (of rank type R) is a union $\bigcup\limits_{n \in R} \Sigma_n$ of pairwise disjoint, finite nonempty sets of symbols. Elements of Σ_0 are also called *constant symbols*. We assume that each ranked alphabet Σ comes with a fixed lexicographic ordering denoted $<_\Sigma$, or just $<$ when Σ is understood.

For the whole paper we now fix an arbitrary rank type R.

Given a ranked alphabet Σ, the set T_Σ of Σ-*trees* is the least set such that whenever $\sigma \in \Sigma_k$, $k \in R$ is a symbol and $t_1, \ldots, t_k$ are Σ-trees, then $\sigma(t_1, \ldots, t_k)$ is also a Σ-tree. When σ is a constant symbol, we often write σ for the tree $\sigma()$. A *(Σ-)tree language L* is any subset of T_Σ.

We can also view a Σ-tree as a map from a tree domain to Σ. In this setting, the *domain* dom(t) of a tree t is defined inductively as follows. When $t = \sigma \in \Sigma_0$, dom(t) $= \{\epsilon\}$, the singleton set whose unique element is the empty word. Suppose that $t = \sigma(t_1, \ldots, t_n)$, where $n > 0$. Then dom(t) $= \{\epsilon\} \cup \bigcup\limits_{i=1}^{n} \{i \cdot v : v \in \text{dom}(t_i)\}$. Elements of dom($t$) are also called *nodes* of t. Then, a Σ-tree $t = \sigma(t_1, \ldots, t_n)$ can be viewed as a mapping $t : \text{dom}(t) \to \Sigma$ defined inductively as follows: $t(\epsilon) = \sigma$, and for any node $i \cdot v \in \text{dom}(t)$, $t(i \cdot v) = t_i(v)$. We define Root(t) $= t(\epsilon)$. When $t(v) \in \Sigma_n$, we also say that v is a node of *rank n*. When t is a Σ-tree and s is a Δ-tree such that dom(t) $=$ dom(s), s is called a Δ-*relabeling* of t.

When t is a Σ-tree and $v \in \text{dom}(t)$ is a node of t, the *subtree* of t rooted at v is defined as the tree $t|_v$ with dom($t|_v$) $= \{w : v \cdot w \in \text{dom}(t)\}$ and $t|_v(w) = t(v \cdot w)$. We extend the above notions to tuples of trees as follows: when $\underline{t} = (t_1, \ldots, t_n)$ is an n-tuple of trees, let dom($\underline{t}$) $= \bigcup\limits_{i=1}^{n} \{i \cdot v : v \in \text{dom}(t_i)\}$ and $\underline{t}(i \cdot v) = t_i(v)$.

Suppose Σ and Δ are ranked alphabets and h is a rank-preserving mapping $\Sigma \to \Delta$. Then h determines a *literal tree homomorphism* $T_\Sigma \to T_\Delta$, also denoted h, defined as follows: for any tree $t \in T_\Sigma$, let dom($h(t)$) $=$ dom(t), and for any node $v \in \text{dom}(t)$, let $h(t)(v) = h(t(v))$.

When Σ is a ranked alphabet, let $\Sigma(\bullet)$ denote its enrichment by a new constant symbol $\bullet$. A Σ-*context* is a tree $\zeta \in T_{\Sigma(\bullet)}$ in which $\bullet$ occurs exactly once. When ζ is a Σ-context and t is a Σ-tree, $\zeta(t)$ denotes the Σ-tree resulting from ζ by substituting t in place of the "hole" $\bullet$. When $L \subseteq T_\Sigma$ is a tree language and ζ is a Σ-context, the *quotient of L with respect to* ζ is the tree language $\zeta^{-1}(L) = \{t : \zeta(t) \in L\}$.

Suppose Σ is a ranked alphabet. A Σ-*algebra* $\mathbb{A} = (A, \Sigma)$ consists of a nonempty *set A of states* and for each symbol $\sigma \in \Sigma_n$ an associated *elementary operation* $\sigma^{\mathbb{A}} : A^n \to A$. *Subalgebras, homomorphisms, quotients* etc. are defined as usual, cf. [11]. A Σ-*tree automaton* is a Σ-algebra which contains no proper subalgebra. A tree automaton $\mathbb{A} = (A, \Sigma)$ is called *finite* if A is finite.

In any Σ-algebra $\mathbb{A}$, any tree $t \in T_\Sigma$ *evaluates* to a state $t^{\mathbb{A}} \in A$ defined as usual. The *connected part* of a Σ-algebra $\mathbb{A}$ is the tree automaton which is the subalgebra of $\mathbb{A}$ determined by the states $t^{\mathbb{A}}$, where t ranges over T_Σ.

Suppose that $\mathbb{A}$ is a Σ-tree automaton. When also a set $A' \subseteq A$ is given, $\mathbb{A}$ *recognizes* the tree language $L_{\mathbb{A},A'} = \{t : t^{\mathbb{A}} \in A'\}$ with the set A' of *final states*. A tree language L is *recognizable by the tree automaton* $\mathbb{A}$ if $L = L_{\mathbb{A},A'}$ for some set $A' \subseteq A$ of final states. A tree language is called *regular* if it is recognizable by some finite tree automaton.

We say that the tree automaton $\mathbb{B} = (B, \Delta)$ is a *renaming* of the tree automaton $\mathbb{A} = (A, \Sigma)$ if $B \subseteq A$ and each elementary operation of $\mathbb{B}$ is a restriction of an elementary operation of $\mathbb{A}$.

When $\mathbb{A} = (A, \Sigma)$ and $\mathbb{B} = (B, \Sigma)$ are tree automata, their *direct product* $\mathbb{A} \times \mathbb{B}$ is the connected part of the Σ-algebra $\mathbb{C} = (A \times B, \Sigma)$, where for each $\sigma \in \Sigma_n$ and states $a_1, \ldots, a_n \in A$, $b_1, \ldots, b_n \in B$,

$$\sigma^{\mathbb{C}}((a_1, b_1), \ldots, (a_n, b_n)) = (\sigma^{\mathbb{A}}(a_1, \ldots, a_n), \sigma^{\mathbb{B}}(b_1, \ldots, b_n)).$$

We call a nonempty class **V** of finite tree automata a *pseudovariety of finite tree automata* if it is closed under renamings, direct products and quotients.

A closely related notion is that of literal varieties of tree languages: a nonempty class $\mathcal{V}$ of regular tree languages is a *literal variety of tree languages* if it is closed under the Boolean operations, quotients and inverse literal homomorphisms.

There exists an *Eilenberg correspondence* between the lattice of pseudovarieties of finite tree automata and the lattice of literal varieties of tree languages: the mapping

$$\mathbf{K} \mapsto \mathcal{V}_{\mathbf{K}} = \{L : L \text{ is recognizable by some member of } \mathbf{K}\},$$

restricted to pseudovarieties, establishes an order isomorphism between the two lattices. For more information on (literal) varieties of tree languages the reader is referred to [15,16,17,6].

3   The Logic XTL($\mathcal{L}$)

In this section we introduce an extension of the logics FTL($\mathcal{L}$) defined in [6] and further investigated in [8,9].

Let $\mathcal{L}$ be a class of tree languages and Σ a ranked alphabet. The set of XTL($\mathcal{L}$)-*formulas* over Σ is the least set satisfying the following conditions:

1. The symbol $\downarrow$, and for any ranked alphabet Δ, rank-preserving mapping $\pi : \Sigma \to \Delta$ and Δ-tree language $L \in \mathcal{L}$, (L, π) is an (atomic) $\mathrm{XTL}(\mathcal{L})$-formula (of depth 0).
2. When φ is an $\mathrm{XTL}(\mathcal{L})$-formula (of depth d), then $(\neg\varphi)$ is also an $\mathrm{XTL}(\mathcal{L})$-formula (of depth d).
3. When φ and ψ are $\mathrm{XTL}(\mathcal{L})$-formulas (of maximal depth d), then $(\varphi \vee \psi)$ is also an $\mathrm{XTL}(\mathcal{L})$-formula (of depth d).
4. When Δ is a ranked alphabet, $L \in \mathcal{L}$ is a Δ-tree language and for each $\delta \in \Delta$, φ_δ is an $\mathrm{XTL}(\mathcal{L})$-formula (of maximal depth d), then $L(\delta \mapsto \varphi_\delta)_{\delta \in \Delta}$ is an $\mathrm{XTL}(\mathcal{L})$-formula (of depth $d+1$).

We now turn to the definition of the semantics. We need to define what it means that a Σ-tree T *satisfies* an $\mathrm{XTL}(\mathcal{L})$-formula φ over Σ, in notation $t \models \varphi$. Since boolean connectives and the falsity symbol $\downarrow$ are handled as usual, we only concentrate on two types of formulas.

1. If $\varphi = (L, \pi)$ for some rank-preserving mapping $\pi : \Sigma \to \Delta$ and Δ-tree language L, then $t \models \varphi$ iff $\pi(t)$ is contained in L;
2. If $\varphi = L(\delta \mapsto \varphi_\delta)_{\delta \in \Delta}$ then $t \models \varphi$ iff the *characteristic tree* $\hat{t}$ of t determined by the family $(\varphi_\delta)_{\delta \in \Delta}$ is contained in L.
   Here $\hat{t}$ is a Δ-relabeling of t, defined as follows: for every node $v \in \mathrm{dom}(t)$ with $t(v) \in \Sigma_n$, $\hat{t}(v) = \delta$, where δ is either the first symbol in Δ_n with $t|_v \models \varphi_\delta$; or there is no such symbol and δ is the last element of Δ_n.

An $\mathrm{XTL}(\mathcal{L})$-formula over the ranked alphabet Σ *defines* the tree language $L_\varphi = \{t \in T_\Sigma : t \models \varphi\}$. **$\mathrm{XTL}(\mathcal{L})$** denotes the class of tree languages definable by some $\mathrm{XTL}(\mathcal{L})$-formula.

The logic $\mathrm{FTL}(\mathcal{L})$ [6] differs from the logic $\mathrm{XTL}(\mathcal{L})$ in that the atomic formulas over Σ are $\downarrow$ and the the formulas p_σ, where $\sigma \in \Sigma$, defining the language of all Σ-trees whose root is labeled σ. We let **$\mathrm{FTL}(\mathcal{L})$** denote the class of tree languages definable by the formulas of the logic $\mathrm{FTL}(\mathcal{L})$. Let Bool denote the ranked alphabet which contains exactly two symbols, $\uparrow_n$ and $\downarrow_n$ for each $n \in R$. As a shorthand, let $\mathrm{UP} = \{\uparrow_n : n \in R\}$ and $\mathrm{DOWN} = \{\downarrow_n : n \in R\}$.

Example 1. Let $R = \{0, 2\}$, $\Sigma_2 = \{f\}$, $\Sigma_0 = \{a, b\}$. Consider the rank preserving mapping $\pi : \Sigma \to \mathrm{Bool}$ given by $\pi(f) = \downarrow_2$, $\pi(a) = \uparrow_0$ and $\pi(b) = \downarrow_0$. Let L_{even} be the set of all trees in T_{Bool} with an even number of nodes labeled in UP. Then the formula $\psi = \neg(L_{\mathrm{even}}, \pi)$ defines the set of all Σ-trees having an odd number of leaves labeled a. Let $\varphi_{\uparrow_2}$ be the formula ψ defined above, and let $\varphi_\delta = \downarrow$ for all $\delta \in \mathrm{Bool}$, $\delta \neq \uparrow_2$. Then the formula $L_{\mathrm{even}}(\delta \mapsto \varphi_\delta)_{\delta \in \mathrm{Bool}}$ defines the set of all Σ-trees with an even number of non-leaf subtrees having an odd number of leaves labeled a.

Example 2. In this example let $R = \{0, 1\}$. When Σ is a ranked alphabet (of rank type R), then any Σ-tree determines a word over Σ_1 which is the sequence of node labels from the root to the leaf of the tree not including the leaf label. By extension, each tree language over Σ determines a word language over Σ_1. Let L'_{even} be the set of all trees in T_{Bool} with an even number of nodes labeled $\uparrow_1$, and let $\mathcal{L} = \{L'_{\text{even}}\}$. Then a tree language $K \subseteq T_{\Sigma}$ is definable in XTL($\mathcal{L}$) iff the word language determined by K is a (regular) group language whose syntactic group is a p-group for $p = 2$, see [18]. There is no language class $\mathcal{L}'$ such that FTL($\mathcal{L}'$) would define the same language class.

The operators **FTL** and **XTL** are related by Proposition 1 below. Let us define the Bool-tree language $L_{\uparrow} = \{t \in T_{\text{Bool}} : \text{Root}(t) \in \text{UP}\}$.

Proposition 1. *For any class $\mathcal{L}$ of tree languages, **FTL**$(\mathcal{L}) = $ **XTL**$(\mathcal{L} \cup \{L_{\uparrow}\})$.*

The logics XTL($\mathcal{L}$) behave in the same way as the logics FTL($\mathcal{L}$), cf. [6].

Theorem 1. *1. The operator **XTL** is a closure operator: for any classes $\mathcal{L}, \mathcal{L}'$ of tree languages, it holds that $\mathcal{L} \subseteq $ **XTL**$(\mathcal{L})$, **XTL**(**XTL**$(\mathcal{L})) \subseteq $ **XTL**$(\mathcal{L})$, moreover, if $\mathcal{L} \subseteq \mathcal{L}'$, then **XTL**$(\mathcal{L}) \subseteq $ **XTL**$(\mathcal{L}')$.*
*2. When $\mathcal{L}$ is a class of regular tree languages, then so is **XTL**$(\mathcal{L})$.*
*3. For any class $\mathcal{L}$ of tree languages, **XTL**$(\mathcal{L})$ is closed under the Boolean operations and inverse literal homomorphisms, and is closed under quotients iff each quotient of any language in $\mathcal{L}$ is in **XTL**$(\mathcal{L})$.*

4   Definability and Membership

In this section we recall from [8] the notion of the strict Moore-product of tree automata and that of strict Moore pseudovarieties, and relate the operator **XTL** to strict Moore pseudovarieties.

Suppose $\mathbb{A} = (A, \Sigma)$ and $\mathbb{B} = (B, \Delta)$ are tree automata and $\alpha : A \times R \rightarrow \Delta$ is a rank-preserving mapping, i.e. for any $n \in R$ and $a \in A$, $\alpha(a, n)$ is contained in Δ_n. Then the *strict Moore-product of $\mathbb{A}$ and $\mathbb{B}$ determined by α* is the tree automaton $\mathbb{A} \times_{\alpha} \mathbb{B}$ which is the connected part of the algebra $\mathbb{C} = (A \times B, \Sigma)$, where for each $\sigma \in \Sigma_n$ and $a_1, \ldots, a_n \in A$, $b_1, \ldots, b_n \in B$,

$$\sigma^{\mathbb{C}}((a_1, b_1), \ldots, (a_n, b_n)) = (\sigma^{\mathbb{A}}(a_1, \ldots, a_n), \delta^{\mathbb{B}}(b_1, \ldots, b_n))$$

with $\delta = \alpha(\sigma^{\mathbb{A}}(a_1, \ldots, a_n), n)$.

A pseudovariety **V** of finite tree automata is called a *strict Moore pseudovariety* if it is also closed under the strict Moore-product. It is clear that for any class **K** of finite tree automata there exists a least strict Moore pseudovariety $\langle \mathbf{K} \rangle_s$ containing **K**.

Proposition 2. *Suppose $\mathbb{A} = (A, \Sigma)$ is a tree automaton and $\mathcal{L}$ is a class of tree languages such that each tree language recognizable by $\mathbb{A}$ is in **XTL**$(\mathcal{L})$. Then any tree language recognizable by a renaming or quotient of $\mathbb{A}$ is also in **XTL**$(\mathcal{L})$.*

Proposition 3. *Suppose $\mathbb{A} = (A, \Sigma)$ and $\mathbb{B} = (B, \Sigma)$ are finite tree automata and $\mathcal{L}$ is a class of tree languages such that each tree language recognizable by either $\mathbb{A}$ or $\mathbb{B}$ is in **XTL**$(\mathcal{L})$. Then each tree language recognizable by the direct product $\mathbb{A} \times \mathbb{B}$ is also in **XTL**$(\mathcal{L})$.*

Proposition 4. *Suppose* $\mathbb{A} = (A, \Sigma)$ *and* $\mathbb{B} = (B, \Delta)$ *are finite tree automata,* $\mathbb{A} \times_\alpha \mathbb{B}$ *is a strict Moore-product and* $\mathcal{L}$ *is a class of tree languages such that each tree language recognizable by either* $\mathbb{A}$ *or* $\mathbb{B}$ *is in* **XTL**$(\mathcal{L})$. *Then each tree language recognizable by* $\mathbb{A} \times_\alpha \mathbb{B}$ *is also in* **XTL**$(\mathcal{L})$.

Using Propositions 2, 3 and 4 we get:

Theorem 2. *For any class* **K** *of finite tree automata,* $\mathcal{V}_{\langle \mathbf{K} \rangle_s} = \mathbf{XTL}(\mathcal{V}_\mathbf{K})$.

Corollary 1. *The mapping* $\mathbf{K} \mapsto \mathcal{V}_\mathbf{K}$ *establishes an order isomorphism between the lattice of strict Moore pseudovarieties of finite tree automata and the lattice of literal varieties of tree languages* $\mathcal{V}$ *satisfying* **XTL**$(\mathcal{V}) = \mathcal{V}$.

5   Ehrenfeucht-Fraïssé-Type Games

In this section we give a game-theoretic characterization of the logics XTL$(\mathcal{L})$.

Let $\mathcal{L}$ be a class of tree languages, $n \geq 0$ an integer, and let s, t be Σ-trees for some ranked alphabet Σ. The *n-round* XTL$(\mathcal{L})$-*game on the pair* (s, t) *of trees* is played between two competing players, Spoiler and Duplicator according to the following rules:

1. If for some tree language $L \in \mathcal{L}$ over some ranked alphabet Δ and a rank-preserving mapping $\pi : \Sigma \to \Delta$, exactly one of the trees $\pi(s)$ and $\pi(t)$ is contained in L, Spoiler wins. Otherwise, Step 2 follows.
2. If $n = 0$, Duplicator wins. Otherwise, Step 3 follows.
3. Spoiler chooses a tree language $L \in \mathcal{L}$, over some ranked alphabet Δ, and Δ-relabelings $\widehat{s}$ and $\widehat{t}$ of s and t, respectively, such that exactly one of $\widehat{s}$ and $\widehat{t}$ is contained in L. If he cannot do so, Duplicator wins; otherwise, Step 4 follows.
4. Duplicator chooses two nodes of the pair (s, t), x and y, of the same rank, such that $(\widehat{s}, \widehat{t})(x) \neq (\widehat{s}, \widehat{t})(y)$. If he cannot do so, Spoiler wins. Otherwise, an $(n-1)$-round XTL$(\mathcal{L})$-game is played on the pair $((s, t)|_x, (s, t)|_y)$. The player winning the subgame also wins the whole game.

Clearly, for any class $\mathcal{L}$ of tree languages, integer $n \geq 0$ and pair (s, t) of Σ-trees, one of the players has a winning strategy in the n-round XTL$(\mathcal{L})$-game played on (s, t). Let $s \sim_\mathcal{L}^n t$ denote that Duplicator has a winning strategy in the the n-round XTL$(\mathcal{L})$-game on the pair (s, t). Also, when s and t are Σ-trees for some ranked alphabet Σ, $\mathcal{L}$ is a class of tree languages and $n \geq 0$ is an integer, let $s \equiv_\mathcal{L}^n t$ denote that s and t satisfy the same set of XTL$(\mathcal{L})$-formulas (over Σ) having depth at most n.

Theorem 3. *For any class* $\mathcal{L}$ *of tree languages and integer* $n \geq 0$, *the relations* $\sim_\mathcal{L}^n$ *and* $\equiv_\mathcal{L}^n$ *coincide.*

Corollary 2. *For any finite class* $\mathcal{L}$ *of tree languages and any tree language* L, $L \in \mathbf{XTL}(\mathcal{L})$ *iff there exists an integer* $n \geq 0$ *such that for all* $s \in L$ *and* $t \notin L$, *Spoiler has a winning strategy in the* n-round XTL$(\mathcal{L})$-game on (s, t).

6   Modified Games

We have argued that the logics $FTL(\mathcal{L})$ may be seen as special cases of the logics $XTL(\mathcal{L})$. We may thus modify the game introduced in the previous section to obtain a game-theoretic characterization of the logics $FTL(\mathcal{L})$. In this section, we introduce for each $n \geq 0$ and class $\mathcal{L}$ of tree languages the *n-round* $FTL(\mathcal{L})$-*game* characterizing the expressive power of $FTL(\mathcal{L})$. Second, we introduce a *modified n-round* $XTL(\mathcal{L})$-*game*, applicable to certain classes $\mathcal{L}$ of tree languages. This game resembles the original Ehrenfeucht-Fraïssé game more than the n-round $XTL(\mathcal{L})$-game of the previous section. A combination of the two modifications is also introduced. By selecting special language classes $\mathcal{L}$, in the last section we derive games for some familiar temporal logics on finite trees related to CTL, cf. [1,20].

Let $\mathcal{L}$ be a class of tree languages, $n \geq 0$, and let s, t be Σ-trees. The *n-round* $FTL(\mathcal{L})$-*game on the pair* (s, t) is played between Spoiler and Duplicator according to the same rules as the n-round $XTL(\mathcal{L})$-game, except for the first step which gets replaced by:

1'. If $\text{Root}(s) \neq \text{Root}(t)$, Spoiler wins. Otherwise, Step 2 follows.

(We may also modify step 4 by dropping the requirement that x and y have the same rank.) The following characterization theorem holds:

Theorem 4. *For any class $\mathcal{L}$ of tree languages, integer $n \geq 0$ and trees $s, t \in T_\Sigma$, Duplicator has a winning strategy in the n-round $FTL(\mathcal{L})$-game if and only if s and t satisfy the same set of $FTL(\mathcal{L})$-formulas of depth at most n. Consequently, if $\mathcal{L}$ is finite, then for any tree language L, $L \in \mathbf{FTL}(\mathcal{L})$ iff there exists an $n \geq 0$ such that Spoiler has a winning strategy in the n-round $FTL(\mathcal{L})$-game on any pair (s, t) of trees with $s \in L$ and $t \notin L$.*

Now we turn to the modified n-round $XTL(\mathcal{L})$-game. We define the following partial order $\preceq_\Sigma$ on Σ-trees: when $s, t \in T_\Sigma$, let $s \preceq_\Sigma t$ if and only if $\text{dom}(s) = \text{dom}(t)$ and for any node $v \in \text{dom}(s)$, either $s(v) = t(v)$ or $t(v)$ is the last element of the corresponding Σ_n with respect to $<_\Sigma$. If in addition $s \neq t$ holds, then we write $s \prec_\Sigma t$.

Let $\mathcal{L}$ be a class of tree languages, let $n \geq 0$, and let s, t be Σ-trees. The *modified n-round* $XTL(\mathcal{L})$-*game on the pair* (s, t) is played between Spoiler and Duplicator according to the following rules:

1-2. These steps are the same as in the n-round $XTL(\mathcal{L})$-game.
3. Spoiler chooses one of the two trees, say s, some Δ-tree language $L \in \mathcal{L}$ and a relabeling $\widehat{s}$ of s such that $\widehat{s} \in L$ and for any $s' \in T_\Delta$, if $\widehat{s} \prec_\Delta s'$ then $s' \notin L$. (That is, $\widehat{s}$ is a *maximal* relabeling of s in L). If he cannot do so, Duplicator wins, otherwise Step 4 follows.
4. Duplicator chooses a maximal relabeling $\widehat{t}$ of t in the language L. If he cannot do so (i.e., t has no relabeling in L), then Spoiler wins, otherwise Step 5 follows.
5. Spoiler chooses a node y of t such that $\delta = \widehat{t}(y)$ is *not* the last element of the respective Δ_n. If he cannot do so, Duplicator wins, otherwise Step 6 follows.

6. Duplicator chooses a node x of s with $\widehat{s}(x) = \delta$. If he cannot do so, Spoiler wins. Otherwise, a modified $(n-1)$-round XTL($\mathcal{L}$)-game is played on the pair $(s|_x, t|_y)$. The player winning the subgame also wins the whole game.

We say that a tree language $L \subseteq T_\Sigma$ is *downwards closed* if whenever $s \preceq_\Sigma t$ are Σ-trees with $t \in L$, then also $s \in L$. The following characterization holds:

Theorem 5. *Suppose $\mathcal{L}$ is a class of downwards closed tree languages. Then for any $n \geq 0$ and trees $s, t \in T_\Sigma$, Duplicator has a winning strategy on (s, t) in the modified n-round XTL($\mathcal{L}$)-game if and only if s and t satisfy the same set of XTL($\mathcal{L}$)-formulas of depth at most n. Consequently, if $\mathcal{L}$ is finite, then for any tree language L, $L \in$ **XTL**($\mathcal{L}$) iff there exists some $n \geq 0$ such that Spoiler has a winning strategy in the modified n-round XTL($\mathcal{L}$)-game on any pair (s, t) of trees with $s \in L$ and $t \notin L$.*

It is possible to combine the FTL($\mathcal{L}$)-game and the modified XTL($\mathcal{L}$)-game. We call the resulting game the *modified n-round FTL($\mathcal{L}$)-game*. A characterization theorem similar to the previous ones again holds:

Theorem 6. *Suppose $\mathcal{L}$ is a class of downwards closed tree languages. Then for any $n \geq 0$ and trees $s, t \in T_\Sigma$, Duplicator has a winning strategy on (s, t) in the modified n-round FTL($\mathcal{L}$)-game if and only if s and t satisfy the same set of FTL($\mathcal{L}$)-formulas of depth at most n. Consequently, if $\mathcal{L}$ is finite, then for any tree language L, $L \in$ **FTL**($\mathcal{L}$) iff there exists some $n \geq 0$ such that Spoiler has a winning strategy in the modified n-round FTL($\mathcal{L}$)-game on any pair (s, t) of trees with $s \in L$ and $t \notin L$.*

7   Examples

Example 3. Let L_{EF^+} and L_{EF^*} denote the Bool-tree languages of those trees having a *non-root* node labeled in UP, and *any* node labeled in UP, respectively. Then the logics FTL($\{L_{\mathrm{EF}^+}\}$) and FTL($\{L_{\mathrm{EF}^*}\}$) are related to the fragments of CTL[2] determined by the strict and non-strict existential future modalities. The modified n-round FTL(EF$^+$)-game and FTL(EF*)-game have the same rules as the corresponding games described in [20]. (Observe that L_{EF^+} and L_{EF^*} are downwards closed.) It is shown in the papers [4,9,20] (using in part different arguments), that it is decidable for a regular tree language whether it is definable in these logics. For fragments of CTL involving the next modality and the strict or non-strict existential future modality, we refer to [4,7].

Example 4. Recall from Example 1 the definition of L_{even}. This language is *not* downwards closed. Let $\mathcal{L} = \{L_{\mathrm{even}}\}$. The n-round FTL($\mathcal{L}$)-game characterizes the modular temporal logic FTL($\mathcal{L}$). The rules of this game on the pair (s, t) of trees are formulated as follows:

1. If Root(s) $\neq$ Root(t), Spoiler wins. Otherwise Step 2 follows.
2. If $n = 0$, Duplicator wins. Otherwise Step 3 follows.

---

[2] CTL was originally introduced in [5] as a logic on Kripke structures, or infinite (unranked) trees. Regarding the definition of CTL on finite trees as used here, cf. [6].

3. Spoiler and marks an even number of nodes of one tree, and an odd number of nodes of the other tree. After that, Step 4 follows.
4. Duplicator chooses a marked node x and an unmarked node y, either in the same tree or in different trees, and an $(n-1)$-round game is played on the subtrees rooted in x and y. If he cannot do so, Spoiler wins. The player winning the subgame also wins the game.

The question whether $\mathbf{FTL}(\mathcal{L})$ is decidable when the rank type R contains an integer greater than 1 is open. For the classical case $R = \{0, 1\}$, see [2,18].

Example 5. Consider the following n-round game on the pair of trees (s, t):

1. If $\mathrm{Root}(s) \neq \mathrm{Root}(t)$, Spoiler wins. Otherwise Step 2 follows.
2. If $n = 0$, Duplicator wins. Otherwise Step 3 follows.
3. Spoiler chooses either to make an EX-move, in which case Step 4 follows, or an EU-move, in which case Step 5 follows.
4. (EX-move.) Spoiler chooses one of the trees, say s, and a node x of s of depth one. If he cannot do so, Duplicator wins. Otherwise, Duplicator chooses a node y of t of depth one (if he cannot, he immediately loses), and an $(n-1)$-round game is played on the trees $(s|_x, t|_y)$. The player winning the subgame also wins the whole game.
5. (EU-move.) Spoiler chooses one of the trees, say s, and a node x of s. After that, Duplicator chooses a node y of t. Then, Spoiler again can make a decision to continue the game either with the pair of trees $(s|_x, t|_y)$, or with $(s|_{x'}, t|_{y'})$, where x' is a strict ancestor of x and y' is a strict ancestor of y.
6. In the first case, an $(n-1)$-round game is played on $(s|_x, t|_y)$ and the winner of the subgame wins the game.
7. In the second case, Spoiler chooses a strict ancestor y' of y, after which Duplicator chooses a strict ancestor x' of x. (If someone cannot choose such a node, the other player wins.) Then, an $(n-1)$-round game is played on $(s|_{x'}, t|_{y'})$. The winner of the subgame also wins the whole game.

This game (resulting from Theorem 6) characterizes the temporal logic CTL: a tree language L is definable in CTL if and only if there exists an integer $n \geq 0$ such that Spoiler wins the n-round game on any pair (s, t) of trees with $s \in L$ and $t \notin L$.

When $R = \{0, 1\}$, our game is similar to the one described in [10] for words. (See also [13] for a similar game for Mazurkiewicz traces). It is also closely related to the game developed for full CTL (over Kripke structures) in [1].

References

1. Adler, M., Immerman, N.: An $n!$ lower bound on formula size. ACM Transactions on Computational Logic 4, 296–314 (2003)
2. Baziramwabo, A., McKenzie, P., Thérien, D.: Modular Temporal Logic. In: 14th Symposium on Logic in Computer Science, pp. 344–351. IEEE Computer Society, Los Alamitos (1999)

3. Benedikt, M., Segoufin, L.: Regular tree languages definable in FO. In: Diekert, V., Durand, B. (eds.) STACS 2005. LNCS, vol. 3404, pp. 327–339. Springer, Heidelberg (2005)

4. Bojańczyk, M., Walukiewicz, I.: Characterizing EF and EX tree logics. Theoretical Computer Science 358(2-3), 255–272 (2006)

5. Emerson, E.A., Clarke, E.M.: Using Branching Time Temporal Logic to Synthesize Synchronization Skeletons. Science of Computer Programming 2(3), 241–266 (1982)

6. Ésik, Z.: Characterizing CTL-like logics on finite trees. Theoretical Computer Science 356(1-2), 136–152 (2006)

7. Ésik, Z.: An algebraic characterization of temporal logics on finite trees, Parts 1,2,3. In: 1st International Conference on Algebraic Informatics, Thessaloniki, pp. 53–77, 79–99, 101–111. Aristotle University of Thessaloniki (2005)

8. Ésik, Z., Iván, S.: Products of tree automata with an application to temporal logic. Fundamenta Informaticae 82(1-2), 61–78 (2008)

9. Ésik, Z., Iván, S.: Some varieties of finite tree automata related to restricted temporal logics. Fundamenta Informaticae 82(1-2), 79–103 (2008)

10. Etessami, K., Wilke, T.: An until hierarchy for temporal logic. In: 11th Annual IEEE Symposium on Logic in Computer Science, New Brunswick, New Jersey, pp. 108–117. IEEE Computer Society Press, Los Alamitos (1996)

11. Grätzer, G.: Universal Algebra, 2nd edn. Springer, Heidelberg (1979)

12. Heuter, U.: First-order properties of trees, star-free expressions, and aperiodicity. In: Cori, R., Wirsing, M. (eds.) STACS 1988. LNCS, vol. 294, pp. 136–148. Springer, Heidelberg (1988)

13. Henriksen, J.G.: An Expressive Extension of TLC. International Journal of Foundations of Computer Science 13(3), 341–360 (2002)

14. Potthoff, A.: Modulo-counting quantifiers over finite trees. Theoretical Computer Science 126(1), 97–112 (1994)

15. Steinby, M.: Syntactic algebras and varieties of recognizable sets. In: Les arbres en algèbre et en programmation (4éme Colloq., 1979), Lille, pp. 226–240. Univ. Lille I (1979)

16. Steinby, M.: General varieties of tree languages. Theoretical Computer Science 205(1-2), 1–43 (1998)

17. Salehi, S., Steinby, M.: Tree algebras and varieties of tree languages. Theoretical Computer Science 377(1-3), 1–24 (2007)

18. Straubing, H.: Finite Automata, Formal Logic, and Circuit Complexity. Birkhäuser, Basel (1994)

19. Thomas, W.: Logical aspects in the study of tree languages. In: Ninth colloquium on trees in algebra and programming, Bordeaux, pp. 31–49. Cambridge University Press, Cambridge (1984)

20. Wu, Z.: A note on the characterization of TL(EF). Information Processing Letters 102, 48–54 (2007)

A Run-Time Efficient Implementation of Compressed Pattern Matching Automata

Tetsuya Matsumoto, Kazuhito Hagio, and Masayuki Takeda

Department of Informatics, Kyushu University, Fukuoka 819-0395, Japan
{tetsuya.matsumoto,kazuhito.hagio,takeda}@i.kyushu-u.ac.jp

Abstract. We present a run-time efficient implementation of automata for compressed pattern matching (CPM), where a text is given as a truncation-free collage system $\langle \mathcal{D}, \mathcal{S} \rangle$ such that variable sequence $\mathcal{S}$ is encoded by any prefix code. We experimentally show that a combination of recursive-pairing compression and byte-oriented Huffman coding allows both a high compression ratio and a high speed CPM.

1 Introduction

Let $\mathbf{c}$ be a given compression function that maps strings A to their compressed representations $\mathbf{c}(A)$. Given a pattern string P and a compressed text string $\mathbf{c}(T)$, the *compressed pattern matching* (CPM) problem is to find all occurrences of P in T without decompressing T. The problem was first defined in the work of Amir and Benson [1], and many studies have been made over different compression formats. A CPM algorithm is said to be *optimal* if it runs in $O(|P| + |\mathbf{c}(T)| + occ)$ time, where occ denotes the number of pattern occurrences [1]. The time/space complexity of the CPM problem can be regarded as a new criterion of compression schemes in addition to the traditional ones: the compression ratio and the time/space complexity of compression/decompression.

Kida et al. [4] introduced a useful CPM-oriented abstraction of compression formats, named *collage systems*, where a text is represented as a pair of a dictionary $\mathcal{D}$ and a sequence $\mathcal{S}$ of variables defined in $\mathcal{D}$. Algorithms designed for collage systems can be implemented for many different compression formats. By generalizing the work of Amir et al. [2] for the LZW compression, they defined in [4] the *CPM automaton* (CPMA in short) which runs over $\mathcal{S}$, based on the Knuth-Morris-Pratt (KMP) automaton, and showed that it can be built from P and $\mathcal{D}$ in $O(|\mathcal{D}| + |P|^2)$ time and space so that it runs over $\mathcal{S}$ in $O(|\mathcal{S}| + occ)$ time for a subclass of collage systems, called truncation-free, which covers a wide-range of existing compression schemes, where $|\mathcal{D}|$ and $h(D)$, respectively, denote the number and the maximum dependence of variables defined in $\mathcal{D}$, and $|\mathcal{S}|$ is the number of variables in $\mathcal{S}$. Since $|\mathbf{c}(T)| = |\mathcal{D}| + |\mathcal{S}|$, the algorithm is optimal under a reasonable assumption that $|P|^2 = O(|\mathcal{D}| + |\mathcal{S}|)$.

From a practical viewpoint, we have two goals. One is to perform the CPM task in less time compared with a decompression followed by an ordinary search (Goal 1), and the other is to perform it in less time compared with an ordinary search over uncompressed text (Goal 2) [7]. An optimal CPM algorithm

O.H. Ibarra and B. Ravikumar (Eds.): CIAA 2008, LNCS 5148, pp. 201–211, 2008.
© Springer-Verlag Berlin Heidelberg 2008

theoretically achieves the two goals if $|\mathbf{c}(T)| = o(|T|)$, but we often observe $|\mathbf{c}(T)| = \Theta(|T|)$ in practice. Hence reducing the constant factors hidden behind the O-notation of time complexity of CPM algorithms play a crucial role in achieving the two goals, especially for Goal 2. There are two conditions for practical speed-up. One is a run-time efficient implementation of the state-transition function $Jump$ of CPMA. Although the algorithm of [4] implements $Jump$ using only $O(|\mathcal{D}| + |P|^2)$ space so that it responds in constant time, the constant is not very small. A naive two-dimensional array implementation using $O(|\mathcal{D}||P|)$ space is preferable if $\mathcal{D}$ is relatively small. The other is a quick decoding of $\mathcal{D}$ and $\mathcal{S}$ that are usually represented as bit-strings using some encoding techniques.

The byte-pair encoding (BPE) [3] satisfies these two conditions, which is a variant of the recursive-pairing [6] such that the dictionary size $|\mathcal{D}|$ is limited to at most 256 and each variable of $\mathcal{S}$ is encoded as a byte. The limitation on $|\mathcal{D}|$ allows us to use the naive two-dimensional array implementation of $Jump$, and the use of byte code avoids slow bitwise operations in decoding. In fact, Shibata et al. [12] reported that CPMA over BPE compressed text runs faster than KMP automaton over original text, and the speed-up ratio is almost the same as the compression ratio. However, the compression ratio of BPE is very poor due to the limitation on $|\mathcal{D}|$. In this paper, we extend BPE to get a higher compression ratio by easing the limitation and using the byte-oriented Huffman coding.

Main contributions. We present a run-time efficient implementation of CPMA for *any* truncation-free collage system $\langle \mathcal{D}, \mathcal{S} \rangle$ such that $\mathcal{S}$ is encoded using any prefix code: We first build CPMA directly from P and $\mathcal{D}$ in $O(|\mathcal{D}||P|)$ time and space, and then convert it into the *decoder-embedded CPMA* (DECPMA in short). We note that the bound $O(|\mathcal{D}||P|)$ improves the bound $O(|\mathcal{D}||P| + |P|^2)$ achieved by a straightforward application of [4]. We experimentally show that a combination of the recursive-pairing compression and the byte-oriented Huffman coding shows a good compression ratio compared to existing Goal 2-oriented compressors. We note that the dictionary size $|\mathcal{D}|$ can be tuned by a parameter n such that the corresponding 256-ary Huffman tree has n internal nodes and $|\mathcal{D}| = 255n+1$ leaves, and BPE is a special case of the compression scheme where $n = 1$. Although the memory requirement grows linearly proportional to n, the compression ratio and the search speed basically get better as n grows (and therefore DECPMA with $n > 1$ runs faster than CPMA over BPE compressed text [12]). Moreover we show that in the case of short patterns, DECPMA with a large n (say $n \geq 10$) runs faster than the algorithm of Rautio et al. [11], which is recognized as one of the fastest Goal 2-oriented CPM methods.

Related work. There are two lines of research work in CPM studies addressing Goal 2. One is to put a restriction on compression scheme so that every pattern occurrence can be identified simply as a substring of encoded text that is identical to encoded pattern. The advantage is that any favored pattern matching algorithm can be used to search encoded text for encoded pattern. The works of Manber [7] and Rautio et al. [11] are along this line. The drawback is that the restriction considerably sacrifices the compression ratio (e.g. 60–70% for typical

English texts). The work of Moura et al. [9] uses a word-based Huffman encoding with a byte-oriented code, and shows a high compression ratio. However it is limited to word-based search. The other line is to develop CPM algorithms for coping with compression scheme in which some occurrences of encoded pattern can be false matches, and/or pattern possibly occurs in several different forms within encoded text. The work of Miyazaki et al. [8], the works of Shibata et al. [12,13] for BPE, and the present paper are along this line. While all of the works [7,11,8,12,13] mentioned here achieve Goal 2, the compression ratios are poor: BPE is the best among them.

2 Preliminaries

Let Σ be a finite alphabet. An element of Σ^* is called *string*. Strings x, y, and z are said to be a *prefix*, *factor*, and *suffix* of the string $s = xyz$, respectively. The length of a string s is denoted by $|s|$. The ith symbol of a string s is denoted by $s[i]$ for $1 \le i \le |s|$, and the factor of s that begins at position i and ends at position j is denoted by $s[i..j]$ for $1 \le i \le j \le |s|$. Denote by $^{[i]}s$ (resp. $s^{[i]}$) the string obtained from s by removing the length i prefix (resp. suffix) for $0 \le i \le |s|$. The concatenation of i copies of the same string s is denoted by s^i. For strings x, y, and z, let $Occ_x(y) = \{|v| \mid \exists u, \exists v : y = uxv\}$ and $Occ_x^\star(y, z) = \{d \mid d \in Occ_x(yz) \wedge |x| + d > |z| > d\}$.

A *collage system* is a pair $\langle \mathcal{D}, \mathcal{S} \rangle$ defined as follows. $\mathcal{D}$ is a sequence of assignments $X_1 = expr_1;\ X_2 = expr_2;\ \cdots\ ; X_n = expr_n$, where X_k is a variable and $expr_k$ is any of the form:

a	for $a \in \Sigma \cup \{\varepsilon\}$,	(*primitive assignment*)
$X_i X_j$	for $i, j < k$,	(*concatenation*)
$^{[j]}X_i$	for $i < k$ and a positive integer j,	(*j length prefix truncation*)
$X_i^{[j]}$	for $i < k$ and a positive integer j,	(*j length suffix truncation*)
$(X_i)^j$	for $i < k$ and a positive integer j,	(*j times repetition*)

for each $k = 1, \ldots, n$, and $\mathcal{S}$ is a sequence $X_{i_1} \cdots X_{i_\ell}$ of variables defined in $\mathcal{D}$. The *size* of $\mathcal{D}$ is the number n of assignments and denoted by $|\mathcal{D}|$. The *height* of $\mathcal{D}$ is the maximum dependence of variables defined in $\mathcal{D}$ and denoted by $h(\mathcal{D})$. The *length* of $\mathcal{S}$ is the number ℓ of variables of $\mathcal{S}$ and denoted by $|\mathcal{S}|$. The variables X_k represent the strings $\overline{X_k}$ obtained by evaluating their expressions. A collage system $\langle \mathcal{D}, \mathcal{S} \rangle$ represents the string obtained by concatenating the strings $\overline{X_{i_1}}, \ldots, \overline{X_{i_\ell}}$ represented by variables $X_{i_1}, \ldots, X_{i_\ell}$ of $\mathcal{S}$.

A collage system is said to be *truncation-free* if $\mathcal{D}$ contains no truncation operation, and *regular* if $\mathcal{D}$ contains neither repetition nor truncation operation. For example, the collage systems for the run-length encoding is truncation-free, and those for the recursive-pairing [6], SEQUITUR [10], BPE [3], and the grammar-transform based compression [5] are regular. In the Lempel-Ziv family, the collage systems for LZ78/LZW are regular, while those for LZ77/LZSS are not truncation-free.

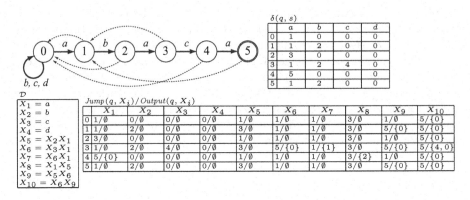

Fig. 1. KMP automaton for $P = abaca$ is shown on the upper-left, where the state-transition function δ is represented by the goto and the failure functions (depicted by the solid and the broken arrows, respectively), and the deterministic version of δ is displayed on the upper-right. The functions $Jump$ and $Output$ built from the KMP automaton for the dictionary $\mathcal{D}$ shown on the lower-left, are shown on the lower-right.

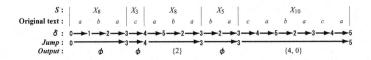

Fig. 2. Move of CPMA of Fig. 1 over $\mathcal{S} = X_8 X_3 X_8 X_5 X_{10}$ is demonstrated

Let $\delta : Q \times \Sigma \to Q$ be the state-transition function of the KMP automaton for a pattern P, where $Q = \{0, \ldots, |P|\}$ is the state set with an initial state 0 and a unique final state $|P|$. We extend δ to $Q \times \Sigma^*$ in a natural way. CPMA is a Mealy-type finite-state machine, consisting of two functions $Jump$ and $Output$ defined as follows: For any state q in Q and any variable X defined in $\mathcal{D}$, let

$$Jump(q, X) = \delta(q, \overline{X}),$$

$$Output(q, X) = \left\{ |\overline{X}| - |w| \,\middle|\, \begin{array}{l} w \text{ is a non-empty prefix of } \overline{X} \\ \text{such that } \delta(q, w) \text{ is the final state.} \end{array} \right\}.$$

An example of CPMA and its move are displayed in Fig. 1 and 2, respectively.

Theorem 1 (Kida et al. [4]). *CPMA can be built in $O(|\mathcal{D}|h(\mathcal{D}) + |P|^2)$ time using $O(|\mathcal{D}| + |P|^2)$ space, so that the values of Jump and Output, respectively, are returned in constant time and in $O(h(\mathcal{D}) + \ell)$ time, where ℓ is the answer size. The factor $h(\mathcal{D})$ disappears if $\mathcal{D}$ is truncation-free.*

Code Φ

variable	codeword	variable	codeword
X_1	B	X_6	AC
X_2	C	X_7	AAA
X_3	D	X_8	AD
X_4	AAD	X_9	AAB
X_5	AB	X_{10}	AAC

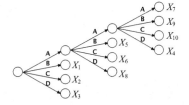

Fig. 3. A prefix code Φ that maps the variables $X_1, \ldots, X_{10}$ to strings over $\Gamma = \{A, B, C, D\}$ is shown on the left, and its code tree is displayed on the right

3   Decoder-Embedded CPMA

3.1   Truncation-Free Collage Systems with $\mathcal{S}$ Encoded by Prefix Code

We encode the variables of $\mathcal{S}$ by a prefix code Φ that maps the variables defined in $\mathcal{D}$ to strings over an alphabet Γ. We illustrate our method using an example with $\Sigma = \{a, b, c, d\}$ and $\Gamma = \{A, B, C, D\}$.

Fig. 3 shows a prefix code Φ that maps variables $X_1, \ldots, X_{10}$ to strings over $\Gamma = \{A, B, C, D\}$ and its code tree. Using this code, the variable sequence $\mathcal{S} = X_8 X_3 X_8 X_5 X_{10}$ of Fig. 2 is encoded as $AD\ D\ AD\ AB\ AAC$. Input to our CPM problem is thus a string over Γ representing $\mathcal{S}$.

The *code tree* $\mathcal{T}_\Phi$ of a prefix code Φ that maps the variables defined in $\mathcal{D}$ to strings over a coding alphabet Γ is a trie representing the set of codewords of Φ such that (1) the leaves are one-to-one associated with variables defined in $\mathcal{D}$, and (2) the path from the root to the leaf associated with X_i spells out the codeword $\Phi(X_i)$. In the sequel we assume code trees are *full*, that is, every internal node has exactly $|\Gamma|$ children. Then any code tree with n internal nodes has exactly $(|\Gamma| - 1)n + 1$ leaves, and hence $|\mathcal{D}| = (|\Gamma| - 1)n + 1$.

We shall mention encoded sizes of $\mathcal{D}$ and Φ. A code tree $\mathcal{T}_\Phi$ with n internal nodes can be represented by the bit-string obtained during a preorder traversal over it such that every internal node is represented by '0' and every leaf is represented by '1' followed by a $\lceil \log_2 |\mathcal{D}| \rceil$-bit integer indicating the corresponding variable, and thus stored in $|\mathcal{D}|(\lceil \log_2 |\mathcal{D}| \rceil + 1) + n$ bits. A dictionary $\mathcal{D}$ can be represented as a list of the right-hand-sides of assignments of $\mathcal{D}$. Suppose that c distinct symbols occurs in the original text, the first c assignments are primitive and the rest are concatenation or repetition. The primitive assignments are stored in $(c + 1) \log_2 |\Sigma|$ bits. Each concatenation assignment $X_k \to X_i X_j$ takes $2\lceil \log_2 k \rceil$ bits and each repetition assignment $X_k \to (X_i)^j$ takes $\lceil \log_2 k \rceil + \ell$ bits, where ℓ is the maximum value of $\lceil \log_2 j \rceil$.

3.2   Embedding Decoder into CPMA

Given a pattern P, a dictionary $\mathcal{D}$, a prefix code Φ, and an encoded variable sequence $\Phi(\mathcal{S})$, one naive solution to the CPM problem would be to build CPMA

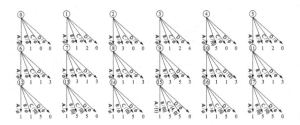

Fig. 4. DECPMA is displayed, where the numbers in circles represent the states, and the numbers not in circles imply the states with the same numbers. The path consisting of the edges $(3, 9)$, $(9, 15)$, and $(15, 5)$ which are labeled $A/\emptyset$, $A/\emptyset$, and $C/\{4, 0\}$, respectively, implies that $Jump(3, X_{10}) = 5$ and $Output(3, X_{10}) = \{4, 0\}$. The number of states of DECPMA is 18, which is 3 times larger than the original CPMA of Fig. 1 as the number of internal nodes of the code tree of Fig. 3 is 3.

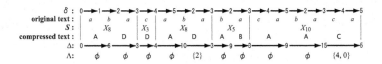

Fig. 5. Move of DECPMA of Fig. 4 over $ADDADABAAC$ is demonstrated

from P and $\mathcal{D}$, decode $\mathcal{S}$ from $\Phi(\mathcal{S})$ by using the code tree $\mathcal{T}_\Phi$ as a decoder and make the CPMA run over the decoded variables on the fly. However, it is slow as shown in Section 5.

Our solution is to embed the decoder into the CPMA. That is, we replace every transition by X_i from state s to state t of CPMA with a consecutive transitions from s to t that spells out the codeword $\Phi(X_i)$. The *decoder-embedded CPMA* (DECPMA for short) is thus a Mealy-type finite-state machine with state-transition function Δ and output function Λ. In the running example, the transition $Jump(3, X_{10}) = 5$ of CPMA is replaced with the transitions $\Delta(3, A) = 9$, $\Delta(9, A) = 15$, and $\Delta(15, C) = 5$, where 9 and 15 are newly introduced states. All but last transitions have no outputs, that is, $\Lambda(3, A) = \Lambda(9, A) = \emptyset$, and $\Lambda(15, C) = Output(3, X_{10})$. The DECPMA for the running example and its move over input $ADDADABAAC$ are shown in Fig. 4 and Fig. 5, respectively.

Let I be the set of internal nodes of the code tree $\mathcal{T}_\Phi$. Let $\tilde{Q} = Q \times I$, which is the set of states of DECPMA. The state transition function Δ and the output function Λ of DECPMA are defined on $\tilde{Q} \times \Gamma$. Let $((j, t), \gamma)$ be any element in $\tilde{Q} \times \Gamma$. Let t' be the child of t such that the edge (t, t') is labeled $\gamma \in \Gamma$ in $\mathcal{T}_\Phi$. The functions Δ and Λ are defined as follows.

- If t' is a leaf of $\mathcal{T}_\Phi$ associated with variable X_i, then $\Delta((j, t), \gamma) = Jump(j, X_i)$ and $\Lambda((j, t), \gamma) = Output(j, X_i)$.
- If t' is an internal node of $\mathcal{T}_\Phi$, then $\Delta((j, t), \gamma) = (j, t')$ and $\Lambda((j, t), \gamma) = \emptyset$.

A two-dimensional table J storing the values of $Jump$ is of size $|Q| \times |\mathcal{D}| = (|P|+1)((|\Gamma|-1)n+1)$ and a two-dimensional table storing Δ is of size $|\tilde{Q}| \times |\Gamma| =$

$(|P| + 1)n|\Gamma|$. The fraction is $\frac{|\Gamma|n}{(|\Gamma|-1)n+1} \leq \frac{|\Gamma|}{|\Gamma|-1}$. Thus, the size of the table storing Δ is almost the same as the table J when $|\Gamma| = 256$.

4 Efficient Implementation of DECPMA

In this section, we present an algorithm that builds DECPMA from a pattern P and a truncation-free collage system $\langle \mathcal{D}, \mathcal{S} \rangle$ and a code Φ. The algorithm first builds CPMA consisting of *Jump* and *Output*, and then convert it into DECPMA according to Φ. If we have built a table J of size $(|P| + 1) \times |\mathcal{D}|$ storing *Jump*, we can construct a table of size $|\tilde{Q}| \times |\Gamma|$ storing Δ in $O(|\tilde{Q}||\Gamma|)$ time and space in a straightforward manner. Similarly, if we have built a data structure storing *Output*, then we can construct a data structure for Λ in $O(|\tilde{Q}||\Gamma|)$ time and space. The conversion thus takes $O(|\mathcal{D}||P|)$ time and space as $|\tilde{Q}||\Gamma| = \Theta(|\mathcal{D}||P|)$.

Theorem 2. *DECPMA can be built in $O(|\mathcal{D}||P|)$ time and space, so that the values of the functions Δ and Λ, respectively, are returned in constant time and in time linear in the answer size, if $\mathcal{D}$ is truncation-free.*

The above theorem follows from Lemmas 1, 2, and 3 (presented below), the proofs of which are based on the Periodicity Lemma, and omitted here due to the page limit.

Direct construction of two-dimensional array storing *Jump*. Consider building a two-dimensional array J that stores the values of *Jump*, namely, $J[q, X] = Jump(q, X)$ for any $q \in Q = \{0, \ldots, |P|\}$ and any variable X defined in $\mathcal{D}$. A straightforward application of the algorithm of [4] requires $O(|\mathcal{D}||P| + |P|^2)$ time and space, where the $O(|P|^2)$ factor is needed for solving a subproblem named "factor concatenation problem" [4]. Since we use the two-dimensional array J, we can avoid this problem and take a more direct way.

Lemma 1. *A two-dimensional array J which stores the function Jump can be built in $O(|\mathcal{D}||P|)$ time and space, if $\mathcal{D}$ is truncation-free.*

We remark that throughout the construction of J, the extra space needed is a one-dimensional array of size $|\mathcal{D}|$ storing $|\overline{X}|$ for all variables X defined in $\mathcal{D}$.

Construction of *Output*. Consider building a data structure which takes $q \in Q$ and variable X in $\mathcal{D}$ as input and returns the set $Output(q, X)$ in linear time w.r.t. its size. A straightforward application of the algorithm of [4] again requires $O(|\mathcal{D}||P| + |P|^2)$ time and space. We reduce this to $O(|\mathcal{D}||P|)$: We have $Output(q, X) = Occ_P^{\star}(P[1..q], \overline{X}) \cup Occ_P(\overline{X})$, where the union is disjoint, and we can prove the following lemmas.

Lemma 2. *A two-dimensional table which stores the sets $Occ_P^{\star}(P[1..q], \overline{X})$ can be built in $O(|\mathcal{D}||P|)$ time and space, if $\mathcal{D}$ is truncation-free.*

Lemma 3. *A data structure can be built in $O(|\mathcal{D}||P|)$ time and space which enumerates $Occ_P(\overline{X})$ in time linear in its size, if $\mathcal{D}$ is truncation-free.*

5   Experimental Results

We experimentally evaluated the performance of the following three implementations of CPMA: (1) the compact implementation [4] (compact-CPMA), (2) the naive two-dimensional array implementation (CPMA), and (3) the two-dimensional array implementation of DECPMA proposed in this paper (DECPMA). The programs were written in C-language, and all the experiments were carried out on a PC with a 2.66 GHz Intel Core 2 Duo processor and 8.0 GB RAM running Linux (kernel 2.6.18). The text files we used are as follows. **Medline:** a clinically-oriented subset of Medline (60.3 MB); **Genbank:** the file consisting only of accession numbers and nucleotide sequences taken from a data set in Genbank (17.1 MB); **DBLP:** XML records of DBLP (52.4 MB). We transformed these texts into collage systems by using the recursive-pairing [6] with restriction $|\mathcal{D}| \leq 255n+1$ for $n = 1, \ldots, 30$. We then encoded the obtained collage systems with the byte-oriented Huffman coding. The patterns searched for are substrings of the original texts.

Table 1. Compression ratios (%) are compared

	standard compressors			Goal 2-oriented compressors					
	compress	gzip	bzip2	SE	BPE	RBH			
						$n = 2$	$n = 10$	$n = 20$	$n = 30$
medline	42.35	33.29	24.13	66.51	56.41	52.33	43.88	39.01	36.21
genbank	26.81	21.98	22.71	51.54	31.37	29.34	28.74	28.36	28.18
dblp	22.97	17.23	11.17	70.39	37.85	31.52	25.39	22.59	21.17

Table 1 compares the compression ratios of the recursive-pairing with byte-oriented Huffman coding (RBH in short) to those of other compressors. Although the performance of RBH is poor compared to the standard compressors gzip and bzip2, it outperforms the Goal 2-oriented compressors SE and BPE, where SE denotes the stopper encoding with 4-bit base symbols [11]. We note that BPE is identical to RBH with $n = 1$. Basically the compression ratio of RBH gets better as n grows [1].

We measured the construction times and the running times of compact-CPMA, CPMA, and DECPMA for $|P| = 2$ to 10. We averaged the values over 10 different patterns with a same length. For a comparison, we also tested KMP automaton for uncompressed text (uncompressed-KMP), and the Boyer-Moore algorithm over SE compressed text (BM-SE) [11], which is recognized as one of the fastest Goal 2-oriented CPM methods. We note that the compressed text data resided in main memory for measurements in order to exclude the disk I/O time.

The graph displayed on the upper-left of Fig. 6 compares the automaton construction times of compact-CPMA, CPMA(naive), CPMA(direct), and DECPMA with n varied from 1 to 30, where CPMA(naive) and CPMA(direct) are, respectively, a straightforward application of [4] which uses $O(|\mathcal{D}||P| + |P|^2)$ time,

---

[1] This is not true for texts T of small size (e.g. 100 KB) for which the encoded size of $\mathcal{D}$ and Φ for a large n is relatively large compared to $|T|$.

and the $O(|\mathcal{D}||P|)$-time direct construction described in the previous section. We showed the results only for $|P| = 10$. We see that CPMA(direct) is indeed faster than CPMA(naive) as expected. The construction times of uncompressed-KMP and Decoder (decoder for $\mathcal{S}$ encoded by the byte-Huffman coding) are also shown, which are very small. We see that compact-CPMA is the fastest among the four in the construction time comparison. We note that the difference between the construction time of DECPMA and that of CPMA(direct) is exactly the time for converting CPMA into DECPMA. Although the construction time of DECPMA is very large compared to other methods, but it is much smaller than the automaton running time for texts of moderate size (e.g. 50–60 MB).

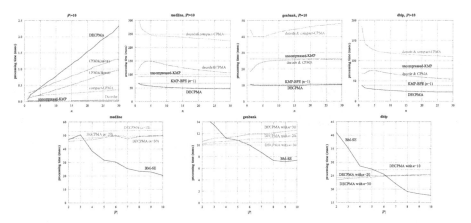

Fig. 6. The graph on the upper-left compares the automaton construction times of three implementations with n varied from 1 to 30 for $|P| = 10$. Construction times of uncompressed-KMP and Decoder are also shown, which are very small. The three graphs on the upper-right show the automaton running times of the five methods for Medline, Genbank and DBLP, respectively. The three graphs on the lower show the total processing time of DECPMA with $n = 10, 20, 30$ for $|P| = 2$ to 10 against Medline, Genbank and DBLP, together with those of BM-SE.

The three graphs displayed on the upper-right of Fig. 6 show the automaton running times for Medline, Genbank and DBLP, respectively. The methods compared are decode&compact-CPMA, decode&CPMA, DECPMA, and uncompressed-KMP, where decode&compact-CPMA (resp. decode&CPMA) is to decode $\mathcal{S}$ and make compact-CPMA (resp. CPMA) run over $\mathcal{S}$ on the fly. The running times of the first three get better as n grows and DECPMA is the fastest. We see no substantial improvement of the compression ratio and the automaton running time when n grows for Genbank. DECPMA with $n = 30$ runs 1.43, 1.04 and 1.70 times faster than DECPMA with $n = 1$ (i.e. KMP algorithm over BPE compressed texts [12]) for Medline, Genbank and DBLP, respectively. The running time of DECPMA is linear in the number of state transitions made, and we remark that the encoded lengths of $\mathcal{S}$ with $n = 1$ for Medline, Genbank and DBLP are, respectively, 1.56, 1.12 and 1.79 times longer than those with $n = 30$.

The three graphs on the lower of Fig. 6 show the total processing time (the construction time plus the running time) of DECPMA with $n = 10, 20, 30$ for $|P| = 2$ to 10 against Medline, Genbank and DBLP. The performance gets worse as $|P|$ grows, mainly due to the increase of construction time. It gets better as n grows for Medline and DBLP, but does not so for Genbank, for which the growth of n makes little improvement on the compression ratio and $|T|$ is relatively small. Compared to BM-SE, we see that DECPMA runs faster in the case of short patterns.

6   Conclusion

We presented a run-time implementation of CPM automata that deals with any truncation-free collage system encoded with any prefix code. We experimentally proved that the combination of recursive-pairing and byte-oriented Huffman coding allows both a good compression ratio and a fast search. There is a trade-off between the memory requirement and the performance of compression and compressed search, and we can tune it with a parameter n. The compressed search of Rautio et al. [11] is faster than ours in long pattern case, but the compression ratio of [11] is much worse than ours.

Recursive-pairing used in our experiments produces regular collage systems, rather than truncation-free. To develop a new compression scheme producing truncation-free collage systems of smaller size is one interesting future work.

References

1. Amir, A., Benson, G.: Efficient two-dimensional compressed matching. In: Proc. Data Compression Conference 1992 (DCC 1992), p. 279 (1992)
2. Amir, A., Benson, G., Farach, M.: Let sleeping files lie: Pattern matching in Z-compressed files. Journal of Computer and System Sciences 52(2), 299–307 (1996)
3. Gage, P.: A new algorithm for data compression. The C Users Journal 12(2) (1994)
4. Kida, T., Matsumoto, T., Shibata, Y., Takeda, M., Shinohara, A., Arikawa, S.: Collage systems: a unifying framework for compressed pattern matching. Theoretical Computer Science 298(1), 253–272 (2003)
5. Kieffer, J.C., Yang, E.-H.: Grammar-based codes: A new class of universal lossless source codes. IEEE Trans. on Information Theory 46(3), 737–754 (2000)
6. Larsson, N.J., Moffat, A.: Offline dictionary-based compression. In: Proc. Data Compression Conference 1999 (DCC 1999), pp. 296–305 (1999)
7. Manber, U.: A text compression scheme that allows fast searching directly in the compressed file. ACM Transactions on Information Systems 15(2), 124–136 (1997)
8. Miyazaki, M., Fukamachi, S., Takeda, M., Shinohara, T.: Speeding up the pattern matching machine for compressed texts. Transactions of Information Processing Society of Japan 39(9), 2638–2648 (1998)
9. Moura, E., Navarro, G., Ziviani, N., Baeza-Yates, R.: Fast and flexible word searching on compressed text. ACM Transactions on Information Systems 18(2), 113–139 (2000)

10. Nevill-Manning, C.G., Witten, I.H., Maulsby, D.L.: Compression by induction of hierarchical grammars. In: Proc. Data Compression Conference 1994 (DCC 1994), pp. 244–253 (1994)
11. Rautio, J., Tanninen, J., Tarhio, J.: String matching with stopper encoding and code splitting. In: Apostolico, A., Takeda, M. (eds.) CPM 2002. LNCS, vol. 2373, pp. 42–52. Springer, Heidelberg (2002)
12. Shibata, Y., Kida, T., Fukamachi, S., Takeda, M., Shinohara, A., Shinohara, T., Arikawa, S.: Speeding up pattern matching by text compression. In: Bongiovanni, G., Petreschi, R., Gambosi, G. (eds.) CIAC 2000. LNCS, vol. 1767, pp. 306–315. Springer, Heidelberg (2000)
13. Shibata, Y., Matsumoto, T., Takeda, M., Shinohara, A., Arikawa, S.: A Boyer-Moore type algorithm for compressed pattern matching. In: Giancarlo, R., Sankoff, D. (eds.) CPM 2000. LNCS, vol. 1848, pp. 181–194. Springer, Heidelberg (2000)

Composed Bisimulation for Tree Automata[*]

Parosh A. Abdulla[1], Ahmed Bouajjani[2], Lukáš Holík[3], Lisa Kaati[1], and Tomáš Vojnar[3]

[1] University of Uppsala, Sweden
{parosh,lisa.kaati}@it.uu.se
[2] LIAFA, University Paris 7, France
abou@liafa.jussieu.fr
[3] FIT, Brno University of Technology, Czech Rep.
{holik,vojnar}@fit.vutbr.cz

Abstract. We address the problem of reducing the size of (nondeterministic, bottom-up) tree automata using suitable, language-preserving equivalences on the states of the automata. In particular, we propose the so-called *composed bisimulation* as a new language preserving equivalence. Composed bisimulation is defined in terms of two different relations, namely upward and downward bisimulation. Moreover, we provide simple and efficient algorithms for computing composed bisimulation based on a reduction to the problem of computing bisimulations on transition systems. The proposal of composed bisimulation is motivated by an attempt to obtain an equivalence that can provide better reductions than what currently known bisimulation-based approaches can offer, but which is not significantly more difficult to compute (and hence stays below the computational requirements of simulation-based reductions). The experimental results we present in the paper show that our composed bisimulation meets such requirements, and hence provides users of tree automata with a finer way to resolve the trade-off between the available degree of reduction and its cost.

1 Introduction

Tree automata are widely used in many areas of computer science such as XML manipulation, natural language processing, or formal verification. For instance, in formal verification, tree automata are—among other uses—at the heart of the so-called regular tree model checking framework developed for a fully automated verification of infinite-state or parameterised systems such as parameterised networks of processes with a tree-like topology or programs with dynamic linked data-structures [9,5,7,8]. In the regular tree model checking framework, tree automata are, in particular, used to finitely represent and manipulate infinite sets of reachable configurations.

In many applications of tree automata, such as in the above mentioned regular tree model checking framework, it is highly desirable to deal with automata which are as

---

[*] This work was supported by the French projects ANR-06-SETI-001 AVERISS and RNTL AVERILES, the Czech Grant Agency (projects 102/07/0322, 102/05/H050), the Barrande project 17356TD, and the Czech Ministry of Education by the project MSM 0021630528 *Security-Oriented Research in Information Technology*.

O.H. Ibarra and B. Ravikumar (Eds.): CIAA 2008, LNCS 5148, pp. 212–222, 2008.
© Springer-Verlag Berlin Heidelberg 2008

small as possible, in order to save memory as well as time. In theory, one can always determinise and minimise any given (bottom-up) tree automaton. However, the determinisation step may lead to an exponential blow-up in the size of the automaton. Therefore, even if the minimal deterministic tree automaton can be small, it might not be feasible to compute it in practice because of the expensive determinisation step.

To avoid determinisation, a tree automaton can be reduced by identifying and collapsing states that are equal wrt a suitable equivalence relation that preserves the language of the automaton. One such an equivalence is *downward bisimulation* (also called backward bisimulation) considered in [11]. The downward bisimulation equivalence can be computed efficiently in time $O(\hat{r}^2 m \log n)$ where $\hat{r}$ is the maximal rank of the input symbols, m the size of the transition table, and n the number of states. Unfortunately, the reduction obtained by using the downward bisimulation equivalence might be limited.

To get a better reduction, some *simulation equivalence* (as, e.g., the *downward simulation* equivalence or the *composed simulation* [2]) can be used. Simulation is weaker than bisimulation and hence it can really offer a better reduction. On the other hand, it is considerably harder to compute—in particular, the time complexity of computing it is in $O(mn)$. Hence, despite the recent advances in efficient heuristics for computing simulation relations on tree automata [2], the choice between bisimulation and simulation is a trade-off between the time consumption of the reduction and the achieved degree of reduction.

In this paper, we propose a new *composed bisimulation* relation, which is a composition of *downward bisimulation* and its dual *upward bisimulation* (also proposed in the paper). The proposal is motivated by an attempt to obtain a relation which is still easy to compute and, on the other hand, can give a better reduction than downward bisimulation, and hence give users of tree automata a finer choice in the above mentioned trade-off.

As another part of our contribution, we then discuss how composed bisimulation can be computed in an efficient way. Inspired by the approach of [2], we show how the computation of upward and downward bisimulation (from which composed bisimulation is subsequently built) can be reduced to computing bisimulations on *transition systems* derived from the automata at hand. This transformation allows us to re-use the results proposed for an efficient computation of bisimulation relations on transition systems (or, equivalently, Kripke structures or finite word automata).

We have implemented a prototype tool in which we have performed thorough experiments with a use of the proposed composed bisimulation framework for reducing tree automata. Our experimental results show that composed bisimulation indeed reduces the size of tree automata much more than downward bisimulation and more than downward simulation, but, as expected, less than composed simulation. Computationally, composed bisimulation is, of course, more difficult to compute than downward bisimulation, but it is still much easier to compute than all relations based on simulation.

Related work. Several algorithms for reducing the size of non-deterministic tree automata while preserving their language have been proposed in the literature. The first attempt was done in [3] where an algorithm inspired by the partition refinement algorithm by Paige and Tarjan [13] was presented. In [11], two different types of bisimulation—backward and forward bisimulation—were presented. The concept of backward bisimulation corresponds to downward bisimulation used in this paper. Forward bisimulation is even cheaper to compute than backward bisimulation and turns out to be especially suited for reducing deterministic tree automata. The experimental results presented in this paper show that, by running backward bisimulation followed by forward bisimulation, one can get a better reduction than using any of the methods alone.

Efficient algorithms for computing simulation equivalences over tree automata have then been discussed in [2]. Our method for computing bisimulations is inspired by the approach of [2], which we here extend to cope with bisimulation relations.

Outline. The rest of the paper is organised as follows. In the next section, we give some preliminaries on tree automata and transition systems. In Section 3, as a basis for composed bisimulation, we present upward and downward bisimulation. In Section 4 we describe the way in which the relations can be computed. Subsequently, in Section 5, composed bisimulation is described. In Section 6, we present our experimental results obtained from a prototype implemented in Java. Finally, in Section 7, we give some concluding remarks and directions for future work.

2   Preliminaries

In this section, we introduce some preliminaries on trees, tree automata, and transition systems (TS).

For an equivalence relation $\equiv$ defined on a set Q, we call each equivalence class of $\equiv$ a *block*, and use $Q/\equiv$ to denote the set of blocks in $\equiv$.

Trees. A *ranked alphabet* Σ is a set of symbols together with a function $Rank : \Sigma \to \mathbb{N}$. For $f \in \Sigma$, the value $Rank(f)$ is called the *rank* of f. For any $n \geq 0$, we denote by Σ_n the set of all symbols of rank n from Σ. Let ε denote the empty sequence. A *tree* t over an alphabet Σ is a partial mapping $t : \mathbb{N}^* \to \Sigma$ that satisfies the following conditions:

- $dom(t)$ is a finite, prefix-closed subset of $\mathbb{N}^*$, and
- for each $p \in dom(t)$, if $Rank(t(p)) = n \geq 0$, then $\{i \mid pi \in dom(t)\} = \{1,\ldots,n\}$.

Each sequence $p \in dom(t)$ is called a *node* of t. For a node p, we define the ith *child* of p to be the node pi, and we define the ith *subtree* of p to be the tree t' such that $t'(p') = t(pip')$ for all $p' \in \mathbb{N}^*$. A *leaf* of t is a node p which does not have any children, i.e., there is no $i \in \mathbb{N}$ with $pi \in dom(t)$. We denote by $T(\Sigma)$ the set of all trees over the alphabet Σ.

Tree Automata. A (finite, non-deterministic, bottom-up) *tree automaton* (TA) is a 4-tuple $A = (Q,\Sigma,\Delta,F)$ where Q is a finite set of states, $F \subseteq Q$ is a set of final states, Σ is a ranked alphabet, and Δ is a set of transition rules. Each transition rule is a triple of the form $((q_1,\ldots,q_n),f,q)$ where $q_1,\ldots,q_n,q \in Q$, $f \in \Sigma$, and $Rank(f) = n$. We use $(q_1,\ldots,q_n) \xrightarrow{f} q$ to denote that $((q_1,\ldots,q_n),f,q) \in \Delta$. In the special case where $n = 0$, we speak about the so-called *leaf rules*, which we sometimes abbreviate as $\xrightarrow{f} q$. We use $Lhs(A)$ to denote the set of *left-hand sides* of rules, i.e., the set of tuples of the form $(q_1, \ldots, q_n)$ where $(q_1, \ldots, q_n) \xrightarrow{f} q$ for some f and q. Finally, we denote by $Rank(A)$ the smallest $n \in \mathbb{N}$ such that $n \geq m$ for each $m \in \mathbb{N}$ where $(q_1, \ldots, q_m) \in Lhs(A)$ for some $q_i \in Q, 1 \leq i \leq m$.

A *run* of A over a tree $t \in T(\Sigma)$ is a mapping $\pi : dom(t) \rightarrow Q$ such that for each node $p \in dom(t)$ where $q = \pi(p)$, we have that if $q_i = \pi(pi)$ for $1 \leq i \leq n$, then Δ has a rule $(q_1, \ldots, q_n) \xrightarrow{t(p)} q$. We write $t \xRightarrow{\pi} q$ to denote that π is a run of A over t such that $\pi(\varepsilon) = q$. We use $t \Longrightarrow q$ to denote that $t \xRightarrow{\pi} q$ for some run π. The *language* of a state q is defined by $L(q) = \{t \mid t \Longrightarrow q\}$, while the *language* of A is defined by $L(A) = \bigcup_{q \in F} L(q)$.

An *environment* is a tuple of the form $((q_1, \ldots, q_{i-1}, \Box, q_{i+1}, \ldots, q_n), f, q)$ obtained by removing a state q_i, $1 \leq i \leq n$, from the ith position of the left hand side of a rule $((q_1, \ldots, q_{i-1}, q_i, q_{i+1}, \ldots, q_n), f, q)$, and by replacing it by a special symbol $\Box \notin Q$ (called a *hole* below). Like for transition rules, we write $(q_1, \ldots, \Box, \ldots, q_n) \xrightarrow{f} q$ provided $((q_1, \ldots, q_{i-1}, q_i, q_{i+1}, \ldots, q_n), f, q) \in \Delta$ for some $q_i \in Q$. Sometimes, we also write the environment as $(q_1, \ldots, \Box_i, \ldots, q_n) \xrightarrow{f} q$ to emphasise that the hole is at position i. We denote the set of all environments of A by $Env(A)$.

Transition Systems. A (finite) *transition system (TS)* is a pair $T = (S, \rightarrow)$ where S is a finite set of states, and $\rightarrow \subseteq S \times S$ is a transition relation. Given a TS $T = (S, \rightarrow)$, and two states $q, r \in S$, we denote by $q \longrightarrow r$ the fact that $(q, r) \in \rightarrow$.

3   Downward and Upward Bisimulation

In this section, we present two different equivalence relations for tree automata: *downward bisimulation* and *upward bisimulation*

Downward Bisimulation. For a tree automaton $A = (Q, \Sigma, \Delta, F)$, a *downward bisimulation R* is an equivalence relation on Q such that if $(q, r) \in R$, then there are $q_1, \ldots, q_n$ such that $(q_1, \ldots, q_n) \xrightarrow{f} q$ if and only if there are $r_1, \ldots, r_n$ such that $(r_1, \ldots, r_n) \xrightarrow{f} r$ and $(q_i, r_i) \in R$ for each $i : 1 \leq i \leq n$.

For a given tree automaton, there is a unique maximal downward bisimulation (referred to as backward bisimulation in [11]) that we hereby denote as $\simeq$.

Upward Bisimulation. Given a tree automaton $A = (Q, \Sigma, \Delta, F)$ and a downward bisimulation $\simeq$, an *upward bisimulation R* wrt $\simeq$ is an equivalence relation on Q such that if $(q, r) \in R$, then

(i) there are $q_1, \ldots, q_n, q'$ such that $(q_1, \ldots, q_n) \xrightarrow{f} q'$ with $q_i = q$ if and only if there are $r_1, \ldots, r_n, r'$ such that $(r_1, \ldots, r_n) \xrightarrow{f} r'$ where $r_i = r$, $(q', r') \in R$, and $q_j \simeq r_j$ for each $j : 1 \leq j \neq i \leq n$; and

(ii) $q \in F$ iff $r \in F$.

Theorem 1. *For any downward bisimulation $\simeq$, there is a unique maximal upward bisimulation R wrt $\simeq$. Furthermore, R is an equivalence relation.*

In the sequel, we will use $\overset{\bullet}{\simeq}$ to denote the (unique) maximal upward bisimulation wrt $\simeq$.

4   Computing Downward and Upward Bisimulation

In this section, we describe how the bisimulation relations described in the previous section are computed.

4.1   Computing Downward Bisimulation

In [2], an approach for computing downward simulation on tree automata via their translation to certain specialised transition systems is proposed. Downward simulation is then computed on the generated TS using standard simulation algorithms such as [10,14]. Since downward bisimulation is a bisimulation counterpart of downward simulation, the TS generated for computing downward simulation can also be exploited for computing the downward bisimulation equivalence using standard algorithms for computing bisimulation such as [13]. This method gives us an algorithm which is easy to implement and runs in time $O(\hat{r}^3 \, m \log n)$ where m is the number of transitions, n is the number of states, and $\hat{r}$ is the maximal rank of the alphabet. We give the details in [1].

An alternative approach for computing downward bisimulation is to use the specialised algorithm proposed in [11]. This algorithm works in time $O(\hat{r}^2 \, m \log n)$.

4.2   Computing Upward Bisimulation

Consider a TS (Q, Δ). Let I be a partitioning of Q, called the *initial partitioning*. A *bisimulation* consistent with I is an equivalence relation $R \subseteq I$ on Q such that if $(q, r) \in R$, then $q \xrightarrow{a} q'$ for some q' if and only if $r \xrightarrow{a} r'$ for some r' such that $(q', r') \in R$. We use $\cong_I$ to denote the largest bisimulation which is consistent with I.

We translate the upward bisimulation problem on tree automata into the bisimulation problem on TS. Consider a tree automaton $A = (Q, \Sigma, \Delta, F)$ and the downward bisimulation $\overset{\bullet}{\simeq}$ induced by a relation $\simeq$. We derive a TS $A^{\bullet} = (Q^{\bullet}, \Delta^{\bullet})$ and an initial partitioning I on the set $Q^{\bullet}$ as follows:

- The set $Q^{\bullet}$ contains a state $q^{\bullet}$ for each state $q \in Q$, and an state $e^{\bullet}$ for each environment e.
- The set $\Delta^{\bullet}$ is the smallest set such that if $(q_1, \ldots, q_n) \xrightarrow{f} q$, where $1 \leq i \leq n$, then the set $\Delta^{\bullet}$ contains both $q_i^{\bullet} \longrightarrow e_i^{\bullet}$ and $e_i^{\bullet} \longrightarrow q^{\bullet}$, where e_i is of the form $(q_1, \ldots, \Box_i, \ldots, q_n) \xrightarrow{f} q$.

Furthermore, we define the initial partitioning I to be the smallest relation containing the following elements:

- $(q_1^{\bullet}, q_2^{\bullet}) \in I$ for all states $q_1, q_2 \in Q$ such that $q_1 \in F \iff q_2 \in F$.

- $(e_1^\bullet, e_2^\bullet) \in I$ if environments e_1 and e_2 are of the forms $(q_1,\ldots,\Box_i,\ldots,q_n) \xrightarrow{f} q$ and $(r_1,\ldots,\Box_i,\ldots,r_n) \xrightarrow{f} r$, respectively, $q_j \simeq r_j$ for each $j : 1 \le j \ne i \le n$, and $q \in F$ iff $r \in F$. In other words, the two environments share the same label, and, moreover, the respective states in the left hand sides are equivalent wrt $\simeq$ at all positions except position i. Furthermore, the states in the right hand sides agree on membership in F.

The following theorem shows the correctness of the translation.

Theorem 2. *For all $q, r \in Q$, we have $q \overset{\bullet}{\simeq} r$ iff $q^\bullet \cong_I r^\bullet$.*

4.3 Complexity of Computing Upward Bisimulation

We analyse the complexity of computing upward bisimulation using the translation scheme presented above. Let $m = |\Delta|$, $n = |Q|$, $\hat{r} = Rank(A)$, and $p = |\Sigma|$.

Given the relation $\simeq$, we can compute the initial partitioning I in time $O(\hat{r}m)$. Furthermore, we observe that $|Q^\bullet| = O(n + \hat{r}m) = O(\hat{r}m)$ and $|\Delta^\bullet| = O(\hat{r}m)$. From the Paige-Tarjan algorithm [13], we know that we can compute $\cong_I$ in time $O(|\Delta^\bullet| \log |Q^\bullet|)$. Therefore, the time complexity of using our method for computing upward bisimulation amounts to $O(\hat{r}m \log(\hat{r}m)) \le O(\hat{r}m \log(\hat{r}n^{\hat{r}}p)) = O(\hat{r}m \log \hat{r} + \hat{r}^2 m \log n + \hat{r}m \log p)$. This means that, for a given Σ, we have time complexity $O(m \log \max(n, p))$.

5 Composed Bisimulation

Consider a tree automaton $A = (Q, \Sigma, \Delta, F)$. We will reduce A with respect to an equivalence relation $\overset{\circ}{\simeq}$, which we call a *composed bisimulation*. Like downward bisimulation, composed bisimulation preserves language equivalence, but it may be much coarser than downward bisimulation (note that upward bisimulation does not preserve the language of tree automata).

For a state $r \in Q$ and a set $B \subseteq Q$ of states, we write $r \simeq B$ to denote that, for all states $q \in B$, it holds that $q \simeq r$. We define $r \overset{\bullet}{\simeq} B$ and $r \overset{\circ}{\simeq} B$ analogously. We define $\overset{\circ}{\simeq}$ to be an equivalence relation such that $\simeq \subseteq \overset{\circ}{\simeq} \subseteq \left(\simeq * \overset{\bullet}{\simeq}\right)$. Here, $*$ denotes the composition of the two relations.

To compute $\overset{\circ}{\simeq}$, the two relations $\overset{\bullet}{\simeq}$ and $\simeq$ are composed, and all states in the relation violating transitivity are removed, while all elements from the $\simeq$ are maintained. In such a manner, we obtain a new relation R. We define $\overset{\circ}{\simeq}$ to be $R \cap R^{-1}$. Notice that depending on how the transitive fragment is computed, there may be several relations satisfying the condition of $\overset{\circ}{\simeq}$.

Language Preservation. Consider a tree automaton $A = (Q, \Sigma, \Delta, F)$ and an equivalence relation $\equiv$ on Q. The *abstract tree automaton* derived from A and $\equiv$ is $A/\equiv = (Q/\equiv, \Sigma, \Delta/\equiv, F/\equiv)$ where:

- $Q/\equiv$ is the set of blocks in $\equiv$. In other words, we collapse all states which belong to the same block into one abstract state.

- $(B_1, \ldots, B_n) \xrightarrow{f} B$ iff $(q_1, \ldots, q_n) \xrightarrow{f} q$ for some $q_1 \in B_1, \ldots, q_n \in B_n, q \in B$. This is, there is a transition in the abstract automaton iff there is a transition between states in the corresponding blocks.
- $F/\equiv$ contains a block B iff $B \cap F \neq \emptyset$. Intuitively, a block is accepting if it contains a state which is accepting.

We will now consider the abstract automaton $A/\overset{\circ}{\simeq}$ where the states of A are collapsed according to $\overset{\circ}{\simeq}$. We will relate the languages of A and $A/\overset{\circ}{\simeq}$.

To do that, we first define the notion of a *context*. Intuitively, a context is a tree with "holes" instead of leaves. Formally, we consider a special symbol $\bigcirc \notin \Sigma$ with rank 0. A *context* over Σ is a tree c over $\Sigma \cup \{\bigcirc\}$ such that for all leaves $p \in c$, we have $c(p) = \bigcirc$. For a context c with leaves $p_1, \ldots, p_n$, and trees $t_1, \ldots, t_n$, we define $c[t_1, \ldots, t_n]$ to be the tree t, where

- $dom(t) = dom(c) \bigcup \{p_1 \cdot p' \mid p' \in dom(t_i)\} \bigcup \cdots \bigcup \{p_n \cdot p' \mid p' \in dom(t_n)\}$,
- for each $p = p_i \cdot p'$, we have $t(p) = t_i(p')$, and
- for each $p \in dom(c) \setminus \{p_1, \ldots, p_n\}$, we have $t(p) = c(p)$.

In other words, $c[t_1, \ldots, t_n]$ is the result of appending the trees $t_1, \ldots, t_k$ to the holes of c. We extend the notion of runs to contexts. Let c be a context with leaves $p_1, \ldots, p_n$. A *run* π of A on c from $(q_1, \ldots, q_n)$ is defined in a similar manner to a run on a tree except that for a leaf p_i, we have $\pi(p_i) = q_i$, $1 \leq i \leq n$. In other words, each leaf labelled with $\bigcirc$ is annotated by one q_i. We use $c[q_1, \ldots, q_n] \xRightarrow{\pi} q$ to denote that π is a run of A on c from $(q_1, \ldots, q_n)$ such that $\pi(\varepsilon) = q$. The notation $c[q_1, \ldots, q_n] \Longrightarrow q$ is explained in a similar manner to runs on trees.

Using the notion of a context, we can relate runs of A with those of the abstract automaton $A/\overset{\circ}{\simeq}$. More precisely, we can show that for blocks $B_1, \ldots, B_n, B \in Q/\overset{\circ}{\simeq}$ and a context c, if $c[B_1, \ldots, B_n] \Longrightarrow B$, then there exist states $r_1, \ldots, r_n, r \in Q$ such that $r_1 \simeq B_1, \ldots, r_n \simeq B_n, r \overset{\bullet}{\simeq} B$, and $c[r_1, \ldots, r_n] \Longrightarrow r$.

In other words, each run in $A/\overset{\circ}{\simeq}$ can be simulated by a run in A which starts from a state that is equivalent with respect to downward bisimulation and ends up in a state that is equivalent with respect to upward bisimulation. This leads to the following lemma.

Lemma 1. *If $t \Longrightarrow B$, then $t \Longrightarrow w$ for some w with $(B, w) \in Q/\overset{\bullet}{\simeq}$. Moreover, if $B \in F/\overset{\circ}{\simeq}$, then also $w \in F$.*

In other words, each tree t which leads to a block B in $A/\overset{\circ}{\simeq}$ will also lead to a state in A which is in the block B with respect to the upward bisimulation relation. Moreover, if t can be accepted at B in $A/\overset{\circ}{\simeq}$ (meaning that B contains a final state of A, i.e., $B \cap F \neq \emptyset$), then it can be accepted at w in A (i.e., $w \in F$) too. This leads to the following theorem.

Theorem 3. $L(A/\overset{\circ}{\simeq}) = L(A)$ *for each tree automaton A.*

6 Experiments

We have implemented our algorithms in a prototype tool written in Java. We have used the tool on a number of automata from the framework of *tree regular model checking*.

Table 1. Reduction of the number of states and rules using downward bisimulation, downward simulation, composed bisimulation, and composed simulation

Original		$\simeq$			$\sim$			$\overset{\circ}{\simeq}$			$\overset{\circ}{\sim}$		
states	rules	states	rules	time	states	rules	time	states	rules	time	states	rules	time
33	876	27	756	0.6	21	418	3.6	16	144	0.8	10	90	5.2
41	1707	28	1698	1.4	24	682	7.8	19	417	3.4	14	148	13.7
41	313	33	285	0.3	33	285	4.2	18	189	0.4	12	158	7.3
50	152	32	88	0.2	32	88	3.7	28	83	0.3	26	78	7.1
109	1248	81	1156	3.1	80	1145	19.8	35	390	4.2	18	231	36.1

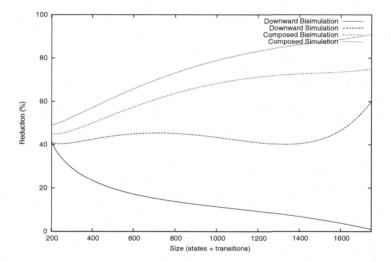

Fig. 1. Reduction of the size of tree automata in percent using downward bisimulation, downward simulation, and composed bisimulation

Tree regular model checking is the name of a family of techniques for analysing infinite-state systems in which configurations of the systems being analysed are represented by trees, sets of the configurations by tree automata, and transitions of the analysed systems by tree transducers.

Most of the algorithms in the framework rely crucially on efficient reduction methods since the size of the generated automata often explodes, making a further computation with the automata infeasible without a reduction. The tree automata that we have considered arose during verification of the *Arbiter* protocol and the *Leader* election protocol [6].

Our experimental evaluation was carried out on an AMD Athlon 64 X2 2.19GHz PC with 2.0 GB RAM. We have compared the size of the considered tree automata after reducing them using composed bisimulation, composed simulation, downward bisimulation, and downward simulation equivalence. It is well known that simulation can give a better reduction but it is harder to compute than bisimulation. Definitions

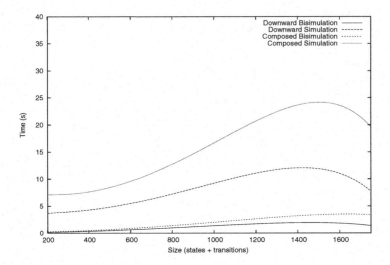

Fig. 2. The time for reducing tree automata using downward bisimulation, downward simulation, composed bisimulation, and composed simulation

and algorithms for computing downward simulation and composed simulation on tree automata can be found in [2].

In Table 1, we show the computation time and the reduction for composed bisimulation $\overset{\circ}{\simeq}$, composed simulation $\overset{\circ}{\sim}$, downward bisimulation $\simeq$, and downward simulation equivalence $\sim$. As can be seen from the results, composed simulation gives the best reduction in all cases, but, on the other hand, it has a much higher computation time than all the other relations. Composed bisimulation gives a better reduction than both downward simulation and downward bisimulation. The time for computing composed simulation is lower than all simulation relations.[1]

Figure 1 shows the amount of reduction in percent for the four different relations. In all the test cases, composed bisimulation gives a much better reduction than downward bisimulation. The computation time is marginally higher, but not comparable with the computation time for downward simulation and composed simulation.

As suggested in [11], running backward bisimulation followed by forward bisimulation gives a better reduction than running backward bisimulation by itself. In all our test cases, backward bisimulation followed by forward bisimulation behaves in a very similar way to composed bisimulation.

Figure 2 shows the computation time when reducing tree automata using the different relations (we point out that no attempt to optimise the implementation of any of the relations was done, and therefore the computation times could probably be lower with an optimised implementation for all of them).

---

[1] From the theoretical point of view, relations $\overset{\circ}{\simeq}$ and $\overset{\circ}{\sim}$ are incomparable as well as relations $\overset{\circ}{\simeq}$ and $\sim$, i.e., for each of the pairs, there exists an automaton for which the relations are incomparable. For any tree automaton, we also have that $\simeq \subseteq \sim \subseteq \overset{\circ}{\sim}$. We investigate these questions in [4].

7   Conclusions and Future Work

We have presented a new equivalence, called *composed bisimulation*, for reducing tree automata while preserving their language. Composed bisimulation is defined in terms of a composition of two relations, namely downward bisimulation proposed earlier in the literature and upward bisimulation proposed in this paper. Our experimental results show that composed bisimulation produces a much better reduction than downward bisimulation and downward simulation (also studied in the literature). Computationally, composed bisimulation is slightly more expensive than downward bisimulation, but significantly faster than downward simulation and composed simulation. These results offer designers of tools based on tree automata a finer choice of the technique to be used for reducing tree automata in terms of the trade-off between reduction capabilities and the cost of the reduction.

There are several interesting directions for future work. First, it is interesting to extend the results to the domain of symbolically encoded tree automata like in the MONA tree automata library [12], allowing one to deal with significantly larger automata. Another interesting direction (considered in the follow-up work [4]) is the possibility of composing not only upward and downward bisimulations, but defining a parametric (bi-)simulation framework allowing one to mix simulations and bisimulations and thus further tune the desired degree of the trade-off between reductions and their costs. Finally, it can be interesting to extend the algorithms presented in this paper to work for other kinds of tree automata such as guided tree automata, weighted tree automata, or unranked tree automata.

References

1. Abdulla, P., Bouajjani, A., Holík, L., Kaati, L., Vojnar, T.: Composed Bisimulation for Tree Automata. Technical Report FIT-TR-2008-04, FIT, Brno Uni. of Technology, Czech Republic (2008)
2. Abdulla, P., Bouajjani, A., Holik, L., Kaati, L., Vojnar, T.: Computing Simulations over Tree Automata: Efficient Techniques for Reducing Tree Automata. In: Proc. of TACAS 2008. LNCS. Springer, Heidelberg (2008)
3. Abdulla, P., Högberg, J., Kaati, L.: Bisimulation Minimization of Tree Automata. In: Ibarra, O.H., Yen, H.-C. (eds.) CIAA 2006. LNCS, vol. 4094, pp. 173–185. Springer, Heidelberg (2006)
4. Abdulla, P., Holík, L., Kaati, L., Vojnar, T.: A Uniform (Bi-)Simulation-Based Framework for Reducing Tree Automata. Technical Report FIT-TR-2008-05, FIT, Brno Uni. of Technology, Czech Republic (2008)
5. Abdulla, P., Jonsson, B., Mahata, P., d'Orso, J.: Regular Tree Model Checking. In: Brinksma, E., Larsen, K.G. (eds.) CAV 2002. LNCS, vol. 2404. Springer, Heidelberg (2002)
6. Abdulla, P., Legay, A., d'Orso, J., Rezine, A.: Tree Regular Model Checking: A Simulation-based Approach. The Journal of Logic and Algebraic Programming 69(1-2), 93–121 (2006)
7. Bouajjani, A., Habermehl, P., Rogalewicz, A., Vojnar, T.: Abstract Regular Tree Model Checking. In: Proc. of INFINITY 2005; ENTCS 149(1) (published, 2006)
8. Bouajjani, A., Habermehl, P., Rogalewicz, A., Vojnar, T.: Abstract Regular Tree Model Checking. ENTCS 149, 37–48 (2006)
9. Bouajjani, A., Touili, T.: Extrapolating Tree Transformations. In: Brinksma, E., Larsen, K.G. (eds.) CAV 2002. LNCS, vol. 2404. Springer, Heidelberg (2002)

10. Henzinger, M., Henzinger, T., Kopke, P.: Computing Simulations on Finite and Infinite Graphs. In: Proc. of FOCS 1995. IEEE, Los Alamitos (1995)
11. Högberg, J., Maletti, A., May, J.: Backward and Forward Bisimulation Minimisation of Tree Automata. In: Holub, J., Žďárek, J. (eds.) CIAA 2007. LNCS, vol. 4783, pp. 109–121. Springer, Heidelberg (2007)
12. Klarlund, N., Møller, A.: MONA Version 1.4 User Manual, BRICS, Department of Computer Science, University of Aarhus, Denmark (2001)
13. Paige, R., Tarjan, R.: Three Partition Refinement Algorithms. SIAM Journal on Computing 16, 973–989 (1987)
14. Ranzato, F., Tapparo, F.: A New Efficient Simulation Equivalence Algorithm. In: Proc. of LICS 2007. IEEE CS, Los Alamitos (2007)

Hyper-Minimization in $O(n^2)$

Andrew Badr

Flowgram Research Division
650 Townsend #315
San Francisco, CA 94103, USA
andrewbadr@gmail.com

Abstract. Two formal languages are *f-equivalent* if their symmetric difference $L_1 \triangle L_2$ is a finite set — that is, if they differ on only finitely many words. The study of f-equivalent languages, and particularly the DFAs that accept them, was recently introduced [1]. First, we restate the fundamental results in this new area of research. Second, our main result is a faster algorithm for the natural minimization problem: given a starting DFA D, find the smallest (by number of states) DFA D' such that $L(D)$ and $L(D')$ are f-equivalent. Finally, we present a technique that combines this *hyper-minimization* with the well-studied notion of a *deterministic finite cover automaton* [2–4], or DFCA, thereby extending the application of DFCAs from finite to infinite regular languages.

1 Introduction, Notation, and Prior Results

We use the standard definition of a DFA as a 5-tuple $(Q, \Sigma, \delta, q_0, A)$ where Q is the state-set, Σ is the alphabet, δ is the extended transition function, q_0 is the starting state, and A is the accepting subset of Q. For more on DFAs, see any standard reference [5,6]. In all algorithm analyses, "n" implicitly refers to the number of states of the DFA in question. Where it is unspecified, L_x is assumed to be a language, D_x a DFA, and q_x a state. Finally, subscripted components such as Q_1, δ_1 etc. should be assumed to be part of a DFA D_1.

The now-classical notions of DFA *equivalence* and *minimization* are well-studied [5,6]. Two DFAs D_1 and D_2 are *equivalent* if the languages they induce ($L(D_1)$ and $L(D_2)$) are equal. We write this as $D_1 \equiv D_2$. In the recently-introduced study of f-*equivalence* [1] [0], this condition is loosened: instead of requiring that the languages be equal, one allows them to differ by finitely many words.

Definition 1 (f-equivalence). *Two languages L_1 and L_2 are said to be f-equivalent if $L_1 \triangle L_2$, their symmetric difference, is a finite set. We write $L_1 \sim L_2$. This relation is extended to DFAs in the obvious way: if $L(D)$ is the language recognized by a DFA D, then we write $D_1 \sim D_2$ whenever $L(D_1) \sim L(D_2)$. Finally, f-equivalence can also be considered on DFA states. States q_1 and q_2*

---

[1] There, f-equivalence is called either "almost equivalence" or "finite difference". We use the new term here because it is shorter, and cannot be misunderstood as excluding total equivalence.

O.H. Ibarra and B. Ravikumar (Eds.): CIAA 2008, LNCS 5148, pp. 223–231, 2008.
© Springer-Verlag Berlin Heidelberg 2008

are f-equivalent ($q_1 \sim q_2$) if their induced languages (sometimes called right-languages) are f-equivalent ($L(q_1) \sim L(q_2)$). States q_1 and q_2 need not be in the same DFA.

Many interesting features of the f-equivalence relation have been discovered. In this section, we restate and explain the most important of these to the reader (since these ideas are still new). One should, however, refer to the original paper for analyses.

Like classical equivalence, *f-equivalence* can be seen as an equivalence relation on either the languages themselves (we write $L_1 \sim L_2$) or the DFAs recognizing them ($D_1 \sim D_2$). DFA f-equivalence (like classical-equivalence) is an equivalence-relation, so it partitions the set of all DFAs into equivalence-classes. Since two classically-equivalent DFAs are also trivially f-equivalent, the classical-equivalence partition is a refinement of the f-equivalence partition.

We begin with two trivial but very useful results:

Proposition 1. *Let q_1 be a state from DFA D_1, and q_2 be a state from D_2. If $q_1 \sim q_2$, then for any input c: $\delta(q_1, c) \sim \delta(q_2, c)$.*

Note the analogous statement about classical equivalence.

Corollary 1. *If $D_1 \sim D_2$, then $(\forall q_1 \in Q_1, \exists q_2 \in Q_2, : q_1 \sim q_2)$.*

Again, this is directly analagous to a statement for classical equivalence: if two DFAs are equivalent, their states occupy the same set of Myhill-Nerode equivalence classes.

Next, we define a partition of every DFA's state set which turns out to be critical to the study of f-equivalence:

Definition 2 (Preamble and Kernel). *For any DFA $D = (Q, \Sigma, \delta, q_0, A)$, Q is partitioned into the preamble and kernel parts: $P(D)$ and $K(D)$. A state q is the preamble $P(D)$ if its left-language is finite — that is, if there are only finitely many strings w such that $\delta(q_0, w) = q$ — and in the kernel otherwise. In short, the states are divided according to whether they are reachable from q_0 by only finitely many or by infinitely many strings.*

Finally, we go through the f-equivalence isomorphism and minimality results. Once again, we emphasize that the interested reader should refer to the original for proofs [1]. The results are presented here primarily as background, and also to give these ideas wider exposure.

Definition 3 (Kernel Isomorphism). *Given DFAs $D_1 = (Q_1, \Sigma, \delta_1, q_{0,1}, A_1)$ and $D_2 = (Q_2, \Sigma, \delta_2, q_{0,2}, A_2)$, we say that D_1 and D_2 have isomorphic kernels (and write $D_1 \cong_K D_2$) when there exists a bijection $f : K(D_1) \to K(D_2)$ such that*

1. $\forall q_1 \in K(D_1) : q \in A_1 \Leftrightarrow f(q) \in A_2$ and
2. $\forall q_1 \in K(D_1), \forall c \in \Sigma : f(\delta_1(q_1, c)) = \delta_2(f(q_1), c)$.

Theorem 1 (Kernel Isomorphism). *If $D_1 \sim D_2$ and both are classically minimized, then $D_1 \cong_K D_2$*

Definition 4 (Hyper-minimality). *A DFA $D_1 = (Q_1, \Sigma, \delta_1, q_{0,1}, A_1)$ is called hyper-minimized if for any DFA $D_2 = (Q_2, \Sigma, \delta_2, q_{0,2}, A_2)$, it holds that $(D_1 \sim D_2) \Rightarrow (|Q_1| <= |Q_2|)$.*

Theorem 2 (Characterizing Hyper-minimality). *A DFA $D=(Q, \Sigma, \delta, q_0, A)$ is hyper-minimal if and only if:*

1. *D is classically minimized, and*
2. *$\forall q_1 \in Q, \forall q_2 \in (Q - \{q\}) : (q_1 \sim q_2) \Rightarrow (q_1 \in K(D) \vee q_2 \in K(D))$.*

Definition 5 (Preamble Isomorphism). *Given DFAs $D_1=(Q_1, \Sigma, \delta_1, q_{0,1}, A_1)$ and $D_2 = (Q_2, \Sigma, \delta_2, q_{0,2}, A_2)$, we say that D_1 and D_2 have isomorphic preambles (and write $D_1 \cong_P D_2$) when there exists a bijection $f : P(D_1) \to P(D_2)$ such that: $\forall q_a \in P(D_1), \forall q_b \in P(D_1), \forall c \in \Sigma : \delta_1(q_a, c) = q_b \to \delta_2(f(q_a), c) = f(q_b)$.*

The definition of preamble isomorphism is weaker than kernel isomorphism because f does not preserve acceptance (membership in A).

Theorem 3 (Preamble Isomorphism). *If $D_1 \sim D_2$ and both are hyper-minimized, then $D_1 \cong_P D_2$*

Notice that Theorem 5 requires that the automata are hyper-minimized while Theorem 1 only requires them to be classically minimized. To conclude this section, we briefly note that these two isomorphism theorems are optimal in the sense that any aspect of the DFA that they do not preserve can indeed vary between f-equivalent and hyper-minimized automata. These are the start state q_0, acceptance in the preamble ($P(D) \cap A$), and transitions leading from the preamble to the kernel.

2   Hyper-Minimization Algorithm

2.1   Algorithm Overview

The problem of hyper-minimization is a fundamental part of the study of f-equivalence, and perhaps the most strongly motivated. Given a starting DFA D, we seek the smallest D' (by number of states) such that $D \sim D'$. Here, we present a new hyper-minimization algorithm, which is the fastest yet known. The original algorithm ran in $O(n^3)$-time; this one runs in $O(n^2)$. Furthermore, this algorithm is more direct, involving no iterative partition refinement, and uses the perhaps surprising technique of constructing the cross-product of a DFA with itself.

We begin with a top-down sketch of hyper-minimization, then explain the components from the bottom up. Both the new and the original hyper-minimization algorithms share the following highest-level structure:

Algorithm 4 (hyper-minimize)
Input: a starting DFA $D = (Q, \Sigma, \delta, q_0, A)$
Output: a hyper-minimized version of D

1. Let $D' = minimize(D)$, where 'minimize' is classical DFA minimization
2. Let $E = f\_equivalence\_classes(D')$ be the partition of Q' into f-equivalence classes, for example via Algorithm 6 (Main Result) below
3. Let $P, K = preamble\_and\_kernel(D')$ be the preamble and kernel subsets of Q', for example via Algorithm 7 below
4. $f\_merge\_states(D', E, P, K)$, for example via Algorithm 8 below. This is the operation of merging states within each f-equivalence class.
5. Return D'

Because the new and original algorithms share this outline, we refer to the original for proof that it is valid [1]. As with classical minimization, the meat of the problem is in finding the state equivalence classes, which is the only step that here differs from the original paper.

We claim that the four steps of Algorithm 4 can be executed in quadratic time. Step 1, famously, can be accomplished in $O(n * log(n))$ time [6] and requires no further explanation. Step 2 is explained in more detail as Algorithm 6. We prove below that it can be accomplished in time $O(n^2)$. For full explanations and analyses of Steps 3 and 4, the reader is referred to the original paper [1], though we do offer an overview below.

Implementations of all the algorithms in this paper are available in the Python programming language at http://ianab.com/hyper/

2.2   Algorithm Details

The above hyper-minimization outline is roughly analagous to one for classical DFA minimization:

1. Remove all unreachable states
2. Partition the states into Myhill-Nerode equivalence-classes
3. Collapse each equivalence class into a representative state

Almost all DFA minimization algorithms fit into this framework [7]. As in hyper-minimization, the meat of the problem is in partitioning the states into equivalence classes, with the other steps being quite straightforward in comparison. (One difference is that the collapsing of classes is more complicated under hyper-minimization, requiring the computation of the kernel and preamble.)

We will now work up towards Step 2 of Algorithm 4, presenting and analyzing the new method by which a partition into f-equivalence classes can be accomplished in time $O(n^2)$. This is our main result. Afterwards, we will discuss Steps 3 and 4 of Algorithm 4.

Our algorithm will use the following version of the standard cross-product DFA construction [6].

Definition 6 (xor_cross_product). *Given DFAs* $D_1 = (Q_1, \Sigma, \delta_1, q_{0,1}, A_1)$ *and* $D_2 = (Q_2, \Sigma, \delta_2, q_{0,2}, A_2)$, *define* $xor\_cross\_product(D_1, D2) = D^{\otimes} = (Q^{\otimes}, \Sigma, \delta^{\otimes}, q_0^{\otimes}, A^{\otimes})$ *as follows:*

1. *Let $Q^\otimes = \{(q_1, q_2) : q_1 \in Q_1 \wedge q_2 \in Q_2\}$*
2. *$\forall q_1 \in Q_1, \forall q_2 \in Q_2, \forall c \in \Sigma$: Let $\delta^\otimes((q_1, q_2), c) = (\delta_1(q_1, c), \delta_2(q_2, c))$*
3. *Let $q_0^\otimes = (q_{0_1}, q_{0_2})$*
4. *Let $A^\otimes = \{(q_1, q_2) : (q_1 \in A_1) \otimes (q_2 \in A_2)\}$ where $\otimes$ is the xor operation*

Note that the three DFAs share the same alphabet Σ.

Algorithm 5 (right_finite_states)

Input: a DFA $D = (Q, \Sigma, \delta, q_0, A)$, and the set S of all states in Q that induce the *empty* language (that is, $S = \{q \in Q : \forall w \in \Sigma^* : \delta(q, w) \notin A\}$).
Output: the subset $F \subset Q$ of all states that induce a *finite* language
Running-time: $O(n)$

1. Let S' be the complement of S
2. For each state q let $Incoming_q$ and $Outgoing_q$ be new empty sets
3. For each $q \in S'$: for each $c \in \Sigma$:
   (a) Let $q' = \delta(q, c)$
   (b) Add (q, c) to the set $Incoming_{q'}$
   (c) Add (q', c) to the set $Outgoing_q$
4. Let F be a new empty list
5. Let *to_process* be a new list equal to S
6. While *to_process* is nonempty:
   (a) Let $q = pop(to\_process)$
   (b) Add q to F
   (c) For each $(q', c) \in Incoming_q$:
       i. Remove (q, c) from $Outgoing_{q'}$
       ii. If $Outgoing_{q'}$ is now empty, add q' to *to_process*.
7. Return F

Proof (Algorithm 5). We seek to prove first that the algorithm is correct, and second that it runs in linear time with respect to Q.

Correctness. When a state is added to F in the processing loop, we call it "removed" from the DFA. This algorithm removes every state in the "sink-set" S, then (while any such state exists) removes all states such that all the state's outgoing transitions lead to removed states. It remains to prove that a state is removed if and only if it induces a finite language.

First, we prove that if a state is removed, then it induces a finite language. Note that there are no transitions from S to a state in S'. Otherwise, the state in S' would also induce an empty language, so by assumption it would be in S. Next, assign to each removed state q a distance $d(q)$ from S, equal to the length of the longest path from q to a state in S. We obtain the result by induction on d. If $d(q) = 0$, then $q \in S$ and $|L(q)| = 0$ by definition. The size of $L(q)$ for any state q in a DFA is bounded above by $1 + \Sigma_{q' \in Outgoing_q} L(q')$. Therefore, if all removed states with $d <= n$ induce finite languages, it follows that all states with $d = n + 1$ also induce a finite language, completing this direction.

Second, we prove that if a state q induces a finite language, it is removed by the algorithm. Again we use a simple inductive proof. Let $l(q)$ be the length of some longest word w in $L(q)$. If $l(q) = 0$ then q is in S, so it is removed by the algorithm. If $l = n$, then for every state $q' \in Outgoing_q$, $l(q') < l(q)$. Therefore, if every state with $l <= n$ is removed by the algorithm, then every state with $l = n + 1$ is also removed, because all states it transitions to are removed.

Speed. Building the *Incoming* and *Outgoing* sets takes linear time because it takes a constant amount of time for each transition and the number of transitions is linear with the number of states. Removing any state takes constant time (for popping it from *to_process* and adding it to F, plus some amount of work for each incoming transition). Again, there are only $O(n)$ transitions, so the latter part adds up to work linear in the number of states. These steps compose the algorithm.   □

Algorithm 6 (f-equivalence-classes (Main Result))
Input: a minimized DFA $D = (Q, \Sigma, \delta, q_0, A)$
Output: a partition of Q (the state-set of D) into the equivalence-classes determined by the f-equivalence relation (the "f-equivalence classes")
Running-time: $O(n^2)$

1. Let $D^{\otimes} = xor\_cross\_product(D, D)$
2. Let $S = \{(q, q) : q \in Q\}$ be the set of all self-pair states in $D^{\otimes}$.
3. Let $F = right\_finite\_states(D^{\otimes}, S)$ be the set of all states (q, r) such that (q, r) induces a finite language in $D^{\otimes}$. (Algorithm 5)
4. Use the state-pairs in F to construct a partition P of Q:
   (a) Let P be a new Union-Find data structure [8]
   (b) For each state $q \in Q$: make a new set $\{q\}$ in U
   (c) For each (q, r) in F:
       i. Let $P_q = P.find(q)$
       ii. Let $P_r = P.find(r)$
       iii. If $P_r \neq P_q$, then $P.union(P_q, P_r)$
5. Return P

Proof (Algorithm 6)

Correctness. For every word $w \in \Sigma^*$ and state $(q, r) \in Q^{\otimes}$ we have $w \in L((q, r)) \Leftrightarrow \delta^{\otimes}((q, r), w) \in A^{\otimes} \Leftrightarrow (\delta(q, w) \in A) \otimes (\delta(r, w) \in A)$ by definition. In other words, the language $L((q, r))$ of every state in the $D^{\otimes}$ context equals the language $L(q) \triangle L(r)$ in the D context. The first consequence of this is that S is exactly the set of states in $D^{\otimes}$ that induce the empty language, because the given DFA D is minimized (so no two distinct states induce the same language). This proves that the input to $right\_finite\_states$ is correct, and the result F is as desired. Thus, as a second consequence of the above, we see that $L((q, r))$ is finite if and only if $q \sim r$. Therefore, F is the f-equivalence relation on the states in D. Step 4 turns this relation, represented as a set of pairs, into a partition.

Speed. The DFA cross-product construction in Step 1 clearly takes $O(n^2)$ time. Constructing S in Step 2 clearly takes $O(n)$ time. In Step 3, we construct F using *right_finite_states* (Algorithm 5), which was proven to take time linear in the number of states. Since the input DFA has n^2 states, Step 3 takes time $O(n^2)$. In Step 4, we iterate through $O(n^2)$ pairs and do an equivalent number of Find operations. Since there are only n states, at most $n-1$ Union operations are performed. Therefore, by using a Union-Find data-structure that has constant-time Find and linear-time Union [8], this step also takes $O(n^2)$ time.   □

This concludes the main result of the paper. We now continue with Steps 3 and 4 from Algorithm 4. Once again, since these are exactly the same as in the original paper[1], the reader is directed there for additional analysis.

Algorithm 7 (preamble_and_kernel)
Input: a DFA $D = (Q, \Sigma, \delta, q_0, A)$
Output: a pair of sets, the first containing the preamble states of D, and the second containing the kernel states of D
Running-time: $O(n^2)$

1. Let K be an empty set
2. For each $q \in Q$: let R_q be the set of states nontrivially reachable from q
3. For each $q \in Q$: if $q \in R_q$: Let $K = K \cup R_q$
4. Return $(Q - K, K)$

Algorithm 8 (f_merge_states)
Input: a minimized DFA $D = (Q, \Sigma, \delta, q_0, A)$, the partition E of its states into f-equivalence classes, and the partition (P, K) of its states into the preamble and kernel
Output: D is hyper-minimized
Running-time: $O(n)$

1. For each set S in E:
   (a) Let $P_S = S \cap P$
   (b) Let $K_S = S \cap K$
   (c) If K_S is non-empty: Let $R = pop(K_S)$
   (d) Else: Let $R = pop(P_S)$
   (e) For each state q in P_S: merge q into R

The "merge" in the final step above refers to a procedure that is familiar from classical minimization: all transitions to the first state are redirected to the second state, and the first state is deleted from the automaton.

3 Finite-Factoring with the DFCA

In some sense, hyper-minimization pares down a regular language to its core. Outlier words are added or removed to make the DFA as small as possible. However, in some circumstances, one may want to keep track of exactly *which* words were changed in the course of hyper-minimization. Such a list is not difficult to obtain: if D is the original DFA and D' is the hyper-minimized version, the xor_cross_product of D and D' recognizes precisely the finite difference that was changed. (A more complicated algorithm could keep track of which words change during the minimization process.)

The DFCA, or deterministic finite cover automaton, is a fairly well-studied [2–4] variation on the classical DFA. A DFCA can save space in recognizing finite languages, in proportion to their redundancy, essentially by removing the need of the DFA to "count" the length of the string. A DFCA C can be understood as a pair $C = (D, l)$ where D is a DFA and l is a non-negative integer. Now C accepts a word w if $|w| < l$ and D accepts w (where $|w|$ is the length of w). Minimization algorithms have been given [3] that, given a starting DFA D_1 and maximum desired length l, can quickly reduce the DFA to minimal DFCA $C = (D_2, l)$ that agrees with D_1 on all words of length less than l.

An obvious weakness of the DFCA is that its ability to remove the redundant computation necessitated by counting can only be applied to finite languages. By combining hyper-minimization with the DFCA, this weakness can for the first time be overcome.

Definition 7 (Finite-Factored Automaton). *A finite-factored automaton is a pair (D, C) where the first item is a DFA and the second is a DFCA. A finite-factored automaton accepts a word w if and only if exactly one of D and C accepts w.*

Algorithm 9 (finite-factor)
Input: a DFA D
Output: a finite-factored automaton pair (D', C), where D' is a DFA and C a DFCA, such that for all words w, D accepts w if and only if (D', C) accepts w.
Running-time: $O(n^2 * log(n))$

  1. Let $D' = hyper\_minimize(D)$
  2. Let $D_f = xor\_cross\_product(D, D')$
  3. Let $l = max(|w| : w \in L(D_f))$
  4. Minimize the DFCA (D_f, l) [3]
  5. Return $(D', (D_f, l))$

It is clear from a simple example that finite-factoring can greatly reduce the number of states required to recognize a regular language. Consider a language over $\Sigma = \{0, 1, a, b, c, d, e\}$ that accepts a word w if w contains only numbers and is up to nine characters long, or if w contains only letters (of any length). This language L requires eleven states to represent with a minimized DFA, and a DFCA cannot be used directly because L is infinite. However, finite-factoring results in two states for the DFA, and two states for the DFCA, for a total reduction of seven states.

This reduction seems to have been possible because L contains a finite-sized subset of words that are amenable to reduction with a DFCA, and hyper-minimization can be used to isolate this component. Analysis of this technique is left for future research.

4   Conclusion and Open Problems

The question we address in this paper — in short, "What can be said about finitely-different automata?" — is a quite natural one. However, it has (until recently) gone unaddressed in the now half-century-long study of DFAs. In this paper, we reviewed the fundamental results in this new area, then provided a significantly improved algorithm for the central problem of hyper-minimization. We conclude with a few open problems:

1. DFA minimization is famously solvable in time $O(n * logn)$. DFCA mini-mization, too, was quickly reduced from $O(n^4)$ in the original paper [2] to an $O(n * logn)$ algorithm [3]. Can hyper-minimization also be achieved in $O(n * logn)$?
2. There are numerous open problems surrounding finite-factored automata. For example: does the method presented here always result in the smallest total number of states? If not, are some hyper-minimized automata in the same equivalence class better than others?
3. Starting with a minimized DFA, first change the acceptance values of selected preamble states, then minimize the DFA again. It is clear that for some automata, this process can produce a hyper-minimized result. For exactly which automata is this true?

References

1. Badr, A., Geffert, V., Shipman, I.C.: Hyper-minimizing minimized deterministic fi-nite state automata. RAIRO - Theoretical Informatics and Applications (to appear), http://www.rairo-ita.org/articles/ita/abs/first/ita07033/ita07033.html
2. Câmpeanu, C., Santean, N., Yu, S.: Minimal cover-automata for finite languages. In: Workshop on Implementing Automata, pp. 43–56 (1998)
3. Körner, H.: A time and space efficient algorithm for minimizing cover automata for finite languages. International Journal of Foundations of Computer Science 14(2), 1071–1086 (2003)
4. Câmpeanu, C., Paun, A., Smith, J.R.: Incremental construction of minimal deter-ministic finite cover automata. Theor. Comput. Sci. 363(2), 135–148 (2006)
5. Sipser, M.: Introduction to the Theory of Computation. International Thomson Publishing (1996)
6. Hopcroft, J.E., Motwani, R., Ullman, J.D.: Introduction to Automata Theory, Lan-guages and Computability. Addison-Wesley Longman Publishing Co., Inc., Boston (2000)
7. Watson, B.W.: A taxonomy of finite automata minimization algorithms. Technical report (1994)
8. Cormen, T.H., Leiserson, C.E., Rivest, R.L., Stein, C.: Introduction to algorithms. MIT Press, Cambridge (2001)

Deterministic Pushdown Automata
and Unary Languages

Giovanni Pighizzini

Dipartimento di Informatica e Comunicazione, Università degli Studi di Milano
via Comelico 39, I-20135 Milano, Italy
pighizzini@dico.unimi.it

Abstract. The simulation of deterministic pushdown automata defined over a one letter alphabet by finite state automata is investigated from a descriptional complexity point of view. We show that each unary deterministic pushdown automaton of size s can be simulated by a deterministic finite automaton with a number of states which is exponential in s. We prove that this simulation is tight. Furthermore, its cost cannot be reduced even if it is performed by a two-way nondeterministic automaton. We also prove that there are unary languages for which deterministic pushdown automata cannot be exponentially more succinct than finite automata. In order to state this result, we investigate the conversion of deterministic pushdown automata into context-free grammars. We prove that in the unary case the number of variables in the resulting grammar is strictly lower than the number of variables needed in the case of nonunary alphabets.

1 Introduction

Deterministic context-free languages and their corresponding devices, deterministic pushdown automata (dpda's), have been extensively studied in the literature (e.g., [5,10,15,16,17]). They are interesting not only from a theoretical point of view, but even, and perhaps mainly, for their relevance in connection with the implementation of efficient parsers. It is well-known that the class of deterministic context-free languages is a proper subclass of that of context-free languages, characterized by (nondeterministic) pushdown automata (pda's). In the case of languages defined over a one-letter alphabet, called *unary* or *tally* languages, these classes collapse: in fact, as proved in [6], each unary context-free language is regular. This implies that unary pda's and unary dpda's can be simulated by finite automata.

In this paper we study the simulation of unary dpda's by finite automata, from a *descriptional complexity* point of view. As a main result, we get the cost, in terms of the sizes of the descriptions, of the optimal simulation between these kinds of devices.

The problem of the simulation of dpda's by finite automata was already studied in the literature in the case of general alphabets: in [16] it was proved that each dpda of size s accepting a regular language can be simulated by a finite automaton with a number of states bounded by a function which is triple

O.H. Ibarra and B. Ravikumar (Eds.): CIAA 2008, LNCS 5148, pp. 232–241, 2008.

exponential in s. That bound was reduced to a double exponential in [17]. It cannot be further reduced because there is a matching lower bound [13].

We show that in the unary case the situation is different. In fact, we are able to prove that each unary dpda of size s can be simulated by a one-way deterministic automaton (1dfa) with a number of states exponential in s. We prove that this simulation is tight, by showing a family of languages exhibiting an exponential gap between the size of dpda's accepting them, and the number of states of equivalent 1dfa's.

As proved in [12], each n-state unary two-way nondeterministic finite automaton (2nfa) can be simulated by a 1dfa with $2^{O(\sqrt{n \log n})}$ states. This suggests the possibility of a smaller gap between the descriptional complexities of unary dpda's and 2nfa's. However, we show that even in this case the gap can be exponential.

We further deepen the investigation in this subject, in order to discover whether or not *for each* unary regular language there exists an exponential gap between the sizes of deterministic pushdown automata and of finite automata. We give a negative answer to this question, by showing a family of languages for which unary dpda's cannot be exponentially more succinct than finite automata.

In order to prove this last result, we study the problem of converting unary dpda's into equivalent context-free grammars. In general, given a pda with n states and m input symbols, the standard conversion technique produces an equivalent grammar with $n^2 m + 1$ variables. As proved in [7], this number cannot be reduced, even if given pda is deterministic. Here, we show that in the case of a unary alphabet, a reduction to $2mn$ is possible.

We briefly mention that the cost of the simulation of unary (nondeterministic) pda's by finite automata was studied in [14], where the authors proved that each unary pda with n states and m stack symbols, such that each push adds exactly one symbol, can be simulated by a 1dfa with $2^{O(n^4 m^2)}$ states. Our main result reduces this bound to 2^{nm}, when the given pda is deterministic.

Due to space limits, many of the proofs are omitted in this version of the paper.

2   Preliminaries

Given a set S, we denote by $\#S$ its cardinality, and by 2^S the family of all its subsets.

A language L is said to be *unary* if it is defined over a one letter alphabet. In this case, we let $L \subseteq a^*$. In a similar way, an automaton is unary if its input alphabet contains only one letter. It is easy to prove the following:

Theorem 1. *Let L be a unary language. Then L is regular if and only if there exist two integers $\mu \geq 0$, $\lambda \geq 1$ such that for each integer $n \geq \mu$, $a^n \in L$ if and only if $a^{n+\lambda} \in L$.*

If the constant μ in Theorem 1 is 0, then L is said to be *cyclic* or even λ-*cyclic*. Furthermore, in this case, L is said to be *properly λ-cyclic*, when it is not λ'-cyclic for any $\lambda' < \lambda$. It is immediate to see that the minimum 1dfa accepting a properly λ-cyclic language consists of a cycle of λ states.

A pushdown automaton [9] $M = (Q, \Sigma, \Gamma, \delta, q_0, Z_0, F)$ is said to be *deterministic* [5] if and only if for each $q \in Q$, $Z \in \Gamma$ the following hold:

1. if $\delta(q, \epsilon, Z) \neq \emptyset$ then $\delta(q, a, Z) = \emptyset$, for each $a \in \Sigma$, and
2. for each $\sigma \in \Sigma \cup \{\epsilon\}$, $\delta(q, \sigma, Z)$ contains at most one element.

A *configuration* of M is a triple (q, w, γ) where q is the current state, w the unread part of the input, and γ the current content of the pushdown store. The leftmost symbol of γ is the topmost stack symbol. As usual, we denote by $\vdash$ the relation between configurations such that for two configurations α and β, $\alpha \vdash \beta$ if and only if β is reached from α in one move. We also write $\alpha \overset{t}{\vdash} \beta$ if and only if β can be reached from α in $t \geq 0$ moves, and $\alpha \overset{*}{\vdash} \beta$ if and only if $\alpha \overset{t}{\vdash} \beta$ for some $t \geq 0$.

While in the nondeterministic case the acceptance by final states is equivalent to the acceptance by empty stack, for dpda's the second condition is strictly weaker (dpda's accepting with empty stack characterize the class of deterministic context-free languages having the prefix property). Hence, the acceptance condition we will consider in the paper is that by *final states*. In particular, given a pda M, we will denote by $L(M)$ the language accepted by it under such a condition, i.e., $L(M) = \{w \in \Sigma^* \mid \exists q \in F, \gamma \in \Gamma^* : (q_0, w, Z_0) \overset{*}{\vdash} (q, \epsilon, \gamma)\}$.

In order to simplify the exposition and the proofs of our results, in this paper it is useful to consider pda's in a certain normal form [14].

1. At the start of the computation the pushdown store contains only the start symbol Z_0; this symbol is never pushed or popped on the stack;
2. the input is accepted if and only if the automaton reaches a final state, and all the input has been scanned;
3. if the automaton moves the input head, then no operations are performed on the stack;
4. every push adds exactly one symbol on the stack.

The transition function δ of a pda M then can be written as

$$\delta : Q \times (\Sigma \cup \{\epsilon\}) \times \Gamma \to 2^{Q \times (\{\text{read}, \text{pop}\} \cup \{\text{push}(A) \mid A \in \Gamma\})}.$$

In particular, for $q, p \in Q$, $A, B \in \Gamma$, $\sigma \in \Sigma \cup \{\epsilon\}$, $(p, \text{read}) \in \delta(q, \sigma, A)$ means that the pda M, in the state q, with A at the top of the stack, by consuming the input $\sigma \in \Sigma$ or not consuming any input symbol if $\sigma = \epsilon$, can reach the state p without changing the stack contents. $(p, \text{pop}) \in \delta(q, \epsilon, A)$ $((p, \text{push}(B)) \in \delta(q, \epsilon, A)$, resp.), means that M, in the state q, with A at the top of the stack, without reading any input symbol, can reach the state p by popping off the stack the symbol A on the top (by pushing the symbol B on the top of the stack, respectively).

It can be easily observed that each pda can be converted into an equivalent pda satisfying these conditions. Furthermore, if the given pda is deterministic, then the resulting pda is deterministic too. Hence, in the following we will consider dpda's in the above form. According to the discussion in [8], the size of a pda should be defined by considering the total number of symbols needed to write down its description. It can be easily shown that the transformation of a pda of size s into normal form produces an equivalent pda of size $O(s)$. Furthermore, the size of a pda in normal form is linear in the number of rules of its transition function. This permit us of using, as a measure for the size of a dpda in normal form, the product of the number of its states and of the number its stack symbols. In the paper, we will denote the size of a pda M as $size(M)$. The size of a finite automaton is defined to be the number of its states.

A *mode* of a pda M is a pair belonging to $Q \times \Gamma$. In the paper, the mode defined by a state q and a symbol Z will be denoted as $[qZ]$. The *mode of the configuration* $(q, x, Z\alpha)$ is $[qZ]$. Note that in a unary dpda, the mode of a configuration defines the only possible move.

A dpda M is *loop-free* if and only if for each $w \in \Sigma^*$ there are $q \in Q$, $\gamma \in \Gamma^*$, $Z \in \Gamma$ such that $(q_0, w, Z_0) \vdash^* (q, \epsilon, Z\gamma)$ and $\delta(q, \epsilon, Z) = \emptyset$, i.e., for each input string the computation cannot enter in an infinite loop of ϵ-moves. It is known that each dpda can be converted into an equivalent loop-free dpda [5]. In the unary case such a conversion can be done without increasing the size of the given dpda. In fact, we can write a procedure that given a mode $[qA]$ simulates the ϵ-moves of M in order to make a list of the modes reachable from the configuration (q, ϵ, A). If a mode is visited twice, then the computation enters a loop. In this case, the transition function of M can be modified by setting $\delta(p, \epsilon, B) = \emptyset$ for each mode visited in the simulation. Note that the procedure ends before $size(M)$ steps. Hence, in the following, without loss of generality, we will suppose that each unary dpda we consider is loop-free.

3   Simulation of Unary dpda's by Finite Automata

In this section we prove our main result: in fact we show that each unary dpda M can be simulated by a 1dfa whose number of states is exponential in the size of M. We will also show that this simulation is tight.

Let us consider a given unary dpda M. We start by introducing some useful notions and lemmas:

Definition 1. *Given two modes $[qA]$ and $[pB]$, we define $[qA] \leq [pB]$ if and only if there are integers $k, h \geq 0$ and strings $\alpha, \beta \in \Gamma^*$, such that:*

- $(q_0, a^k, Z_0) \vdash^* (q, \epsilon, A\alpha)$, $(q, a^h, A) \vdash^* (p, \epsilon, B\beta)$, *and*
- *if $(q_0, a^{k'}, Z_0) \vdash^* (p, \epsilon, B\beta')$ for some $k' < k$, $\beta' \in \Gamma^*$, then there is an integer k'' with $k' + k'' < k$ and a state $p' \in Q$, such that $(p, a^{k''}, B) \vdash^* (p', \epsilon, \epsilon)$.*

Intuitively, $[qA] \leq [pB]$ means that M from the initial configuration can reach a configuration with mode $[qA]$ by a computation $(q_0, a^k, Z_0) \vdash^* (q, \epsilon, A\alpha)$ and, after that, it can reach a configuration with mode $[pB]$, by a computation which does not use the portion of the stack below A, i.e., the portion containing α. Furthermore, if during the computation $(q_0, a^k, Z_0) \vdash^* (q, \epsilon, A\alpha)$ a configuration with mode $[pB]$ and stack height h is reached, then in some subsequent step of the same computation the stack height must decrease below height h. In other word, for all integers k' and k'' with $k' + k'' = k$, it is not possible that $(q_0, a^{k'}, Z_0) \vdash^* (p, \epsilon, B\beta')$ and $(p, a^{k''}, B) \vdash^* (q, \epsilon, A\alpha')$, for some $\alpha', \beta' \in \Gamma^*$.

Lemma 1. *The relation $\leq$ defines a partial order on the set of the modes.*

A configuration completely describes the status of a pda in a given instant and gives enough information to simulate the remaining steps of a computation. However, in order to study the properties of dpda's computations, it is useful to have a richer description, which also takes into account the states reached in some previous computation steps. To this aim we now introduce the notion of history. Before doing that, we observe that the next move from a configuration of a unary dpda depends only on the current mode. If such a move requires the reading of an input symbol and all the input has been consumed, then the computation stops. Hence, given a unary dpda M, for each integer t there exists at most one configuration that can be reached after t computation steps. Such a configuration will be reached if the input is long enough.

Definition 2. *For each integer $t \geq 0$, the* history h_t *of M at the time t is a sequence of modes $[q_m Z_m][q_{m-1} Z_{m-1}] \ldots [q_1 Z_1]$ such that:*

- *$Z_m Z_{m-1} \ldots Z_1$ is the content of the pushdown store after the execution of t transitions from the initial configuration,*
- *for each integer i, $1 \leq i \leq m$, $[q_i Z_i]$ was the mode of the last configuration having stack height i, in the computation $(q_0, x, Z_0) \vdash^t (q_m, \epsilon, Z_m Z_{m-1} \ldots Z_1)$, for a suitable $x \in a^*$.*

The mode *at the time t, denoted as m_t, is the leftmost symbol in h_t, i.e., the pair representing the state and the stack top of M after t transitions.*

In the following we will denote by H the set of all histories of M, i.e., $H = \{h_t \mid t \geq 0\}$.

Lemma 2. *Let $h_t = [q_m Z_m][q_{m-1} Z_{m-1}] \ldots [q_1 Z_1]$ be the history at the time t. Then:*

1. *For $i = 1, \ldots, m-1$, there is an integer t_i s.t. $h_{t_i} = [q_i Z_i][q_{i-1} Z_{i-1}] \ldots [q_1 Z_1]$, $(q_i, x, Z_i) \vdash^* (q_{i+1}, \epsilon, Z_{i+1} Z_i)$, for some $x \in a^*$, and h_{t_i} is a suffix of each h_j, for each integer j such that $t_i < j \leq m$. Furthermore $0 \leq t_1 < t_2 < \ldots < t_{m-1} < t$.*
2. *If all the modes in h_t are different then $[q_1 Z_1] \leq \ldots \leq [q_m Z_m]$.*
3. *If $h_\mu = h_{\mu+\lambda}$ for some $\mu \geq 0$, $\lambda \geq 1$, then $h_{\mu+i} = h_{\mu+\lambda+i}$, for each $i \geq 0$.*

Lemma 3. *The set H contains infinitely many histories if and only if there exist two integers $\mu \geq 0$, $\lambda \geq 1$, and λ nonempty sequences of modes $\tilde{h}_1, \ldots, \tilde{h}_\lambda$, such that:*

$$h_{\mu+1} = \tilde{h}_1 h_\mu, \quad h_{\mu+2} = \tilde{h}_2 h_\mu, \quad \ldots, \quad h_{\mu+k\lambda+i} = \tilde{h}_i (\tilde{h}_\lambda)^k h_\mu,$$

for all integers $k \geq 0$, $0 \leq i < \lambda$.

Furthermore, if such μ and λ exist then their sum does not exceed $2^{\#Q \cdot \#\Gamma}$, while if H is finite then its cardinality is less than $2^{\#Q \cdot \#\Gamma}$.

Lemma 4. *The sequence $(m_t)_{t \geq 0}$ is ultimately periodic. More precisely, there are integers $\mu \geq 0, \lambda \geq 1$ such that $\mu + \lambda \leq 2^{\#Q \#\Gamma}$ and $m_t = m_{t+\lambda}$, for each $t \geq \mu$.*

Now, we are ready to prove our main result:

Theorem 2. *Let $L \subseteq a^*$ be accepted by a dpda M in normal form with n states and m stack symbols. Then L is accepted by a 1dfa with at most 2^{mn} states.*

Proof. The acceptance or rejection of a word depends only on the states that are reached by consuming it (and possibly performing some ϵ-moves). By Lemma 4 the sequence of the modes that can be reached in computation steps is ultimately periodic. This implies that also the sequence of the reached states, which gives the acceptance or the rejection, is ultimately periodic. Hence, it is possible to build a 1dfa accepting the language. The upper bound on the number of the states derives from Lemma 4.   □

We now prove that the simulation presented in Theorem 2 is optimal. In particular, we show that for each integer s there exists a language which is accepted by a dpda of size $O(s)$ such that any equivalent 1dfa needs 2^s states.

More precisely, for each integer s, we consider the set of the multiples of 2^s, written in unary notation, namely the language $L_s = \{a^{2^s}\}^*$.

Given $s > 0$, we can build a dpda accepting L_s that, from the initial configuration, reaches a configuration with the state q_0 and the pushdown containing only Z_0, every time it consumes an input factor of length 2^s, i.e., $(q_0, a^{2^s}, Z_0) \vdash^* (q_0, \epsilon, Z_0)$. The state q_0 is the only final state and it cannot be reached in the other steps of the computation. The computation from (q_0, a^{2^s}, Z_0) to (q_0, ϵ, Z_0) uses a procedure that, given an integer i, consumes 2^i input symbols. For $i > 0$ the procedure makes two recursive calls, each one of them consuming 2^{i-1} symbols. In the implementation, two stack symbols A_{i-1} and B_{i-1} are used, respectively, to keep track of the first and of the second recursive call of the procedure. For example, for $s = 3$, a configuration with the pushdown store containing $B_0 A_1 B_2 Z_0$ will be reached after consuming $2^2 + 2^0$ input symbols and performing some ϵ-moves. The formal definition is below:

- $Q = \{q_0, q_1, q_2, q_3\}$
- $\Gamma = \{Z_0, A_0, A_1, \ldots, A_{s-1}, B_0, B_1, \ldots, B_{s-1}\}$
- $\delta(q_0, \epsilon, Z_0) = \{(q_1, \mathrm{push}(A_{s-1}))\}$
  $\delta(q_1, a, A_0) = \{(q_3, \mathrm{read})\}$
  $\delta(q_1, a, B_0) = \{(q_3, \mathrm{read})\}$
  $\delta(q_1, \epsilon, A_i) = \delta(q_1, \epsilon, B_i) = \{(q_1, \mathrm{push}(A_{i-1}))\}$, for $i = 1, \ldots, s-1$
  $\delta(q_2, \epsilon, A_i) = \delta(q_2, \epsilon, B_i) = \{(q_1, \mathrm{push}(B_{i-1}))\}$, for $i = 1, \ldots, s-1$
  $\delta(q_3, \epsilon, A_i) = \{(q_2, \mathrm{pop})\}$, for $i = 0, \ldots, s-1$
  $\delta(q_3, \epsilon, B_i) = \{(q_3, \mathrm{pop})\}$, for $i = 0, \ldots, s-1$
  $\delta(q_2, \epsilon, Z_0) = \{(q_1, \mathrm{push}(B_{s-1}))\}$
  $\delta(q_3, \epsilon, Z_0) = \{(q_0, Z_0)\}$
- $F = \{q_0\}$.

By induction we can show that $(q_1, a^{2^i}, A_i) \vdash^* (q_2, \epsilon, \epsilon)$ and $(q_1, a^{2^i}, B_i) \vdash^* (q_3, \epsilon, \epsilon)$, for $i = 1, \ldots, s - 1$, easily concluding that the dpda so described accepts L_s.

Theorem 3. *For each integer $s > 0$, the language L_s is accepted by a dpda of size $8s + 4$ but the minumum 1dfa accepting it contains exactly 2^s states.*

Using Theorem 9 of [11], it is possible to prove that also any 2nfa accepting the language L_s must have at least 2^s states. Hence we get the following:

Corollary 1. *Unary determistic pushdown automata can be exponentially more succinct than two-way nondeterministic finite automata.*

4   Unary dpda's and Context-Free Grammars

In this section we study the conversion of unary dpda's into context-free grammars. Given a pda with n states and m stack symbols, the standard conversion produces a context-free grammar with n^2m+1 variables. In [7] it has been proved that such a number cannot be reduced, even if the given pda is deterministic. As we prove in this section, in the unary case the situation is different. In fact, we show how to get a grammar with $2nm$ variables. This transformation will be useful in the last part of the paper to prove the existence of languages for which dpda's cannot be exponentially more succinct than 1dfa's.

Let $M = (Q, \{a\}, \Gamma, \delta, q_0, Z_0, F)$ be a unary dpda in normal form.

First of all, we observe that for each mode $[qA]$ there exists at most one state p such that $(q, x, A) \vdash^* (p, \epsilon, \epsilon)$ for some $x \in a^*$. We denote such a state by $\mathrm{exit}[qA]$ and we call the sequence of moves from (q, x, A) to (p, ϵ, ϵ), the *segment of computation* from $[qA]$. Note that given two modes $[qA]$ and $[q'A]$, if $(q, x, A) \vdash^* (q', \epsilon, A)$, for some $x \in a^*$, then $\mathrm{exit}[qA] = \mathrm{exit}[q'A]$.

We now define a grammar $G = (V, \{a\}, P, S)$ and we will show that it is equivalent to M. The set of variables is $V = Q \times \Gamma \times \{0, 1\}$. The elements of V will be denoted as $[qA]_b$, where $[qA]$ is a mode and $b \in \{0, 1\}$. The start symbol of the grammar is $S = [q_0Z_0]_1$.

The productions of G are defined in order to derive from each variable $[qA]_0$ the string x consumed in the segment of computation from $[qA]$, and from each variable $[qA]_1$ all the strings x such that M, from a configuration with mode $[qA]$ can reach a final configuration, consuming x, before completing the segment from $[qA]$. They are listed below, by considering the possible moves of M:

- *Push moves:* For $\delta(q, \epsilon, A) = \{(p, \mathrm{push}(B))\}$, there is the production
    (a) $[qA]_1 \rightarrow [pB]_1$
    Furthermore, if $\mathrm{exit}[pB]$ is defined, with $\mathrm{exit}[pB] = q'$, then there are the productions
    (b) $[qA]_0 \rightarrow [pB]_0[q'A]_0$
    (c) $[qA]_1 \rightarrow [pB]_0[q'A]_1$
- *Pop moves:* For $\delta(q, \epsilon, A) = \{(p, \mathrm{pop})\}$, there is the production
    (d) $[qA]_0 \rightarrow \epsilon$

– *Read moves:* For $\delta(q, \sigma, A) = \{(p, \text{read})\}$, with $\sigma \in \{\epsilon, a\}$, and for each
  $b \in \{0, 1\}$, there is the production
   (e) $[qA]_b \rightarrow \sigma[pA]_b$
– *Acceptance:* For each final state $q \in F$, there is the production
   (f) $[qA]_1 \rightarrow \epsilon$

The productions from a variable $[qA]_0$ are similar to those used in the standard conversion from pda's (accepting by empty stack) to context-free grammars.[1] The productions from modes $[qA]_1$ are used to guess that in some place the computation will stop in a final state. For example, for the push move $(p, \text{push}(B)) \in \delta(q, \epsilon, A)$, we can guess that the acceptance will be reached in the segment of computation which starts from the mode $[pB]$ (hence, ending the computation before reaching the same stack level as in the starting mode $[qA]$, see production (a)), or after that segment is completed (production (c)).

In order to show that the grammar G is equivalent to M, it is useful to prove the following lemma:

Lemma 5. *For each mode $[qA]$, $x \in a^*$, it holds that:*

1. $[qA]_0 \overset{*}{\Rightarrow} x$ *if and only if* $(q, x, A) \overset{*}{\vdash} (\text{exit}[qA], \epsilon, \epsilon)$.
2. $[qA]_1 \overset{*}{\Rightarrow} x$ *if and only if* $(q, x, A) \overset{*}{\vdash} (q', \epsilon, \gamma)$, *for some* $q' \in F$, $\gamma \in \Gamma^+$.

As a consequence of Lemma 5, it turns out that, for each $x \in a^*$, $[q_0 Z_0]_1 \overset{*}{\Rightarrow} x$ if and only if x is accepted by M. Hence, we get the following result:

Theorem 4. *For any unary deterministic pushdown automaton M there exists an equivalent context-free grammar with at most $2\text{size}(M)$ variables, such that the right hand side of each production contains at most two symbols.*

Finally, we can observe that from the grammar G above defined, it is easy to get a grammar in Chomsky normal formal, accepting $L(M) - \{\epsilon\}$. This can require one more variable.

5   Languages with Complex dpda's

In Section 3, we proved that dpda's can be exponentially more succinct than finite automata. In this section we show the existence of languages for which this dramatic reduction of the descriptional complexity cannot be achieved. More precisely, we prove that for each integer m there exists a unary 2^m-cyclic language L_m such that the size of each dpda accepting it is exponential in m.

Let us start by introducing the definition of the language L_m. To this aim, we first recall that a *de Bruijn word* [3] of order m on $\{0, 1\}$ is a word w_m of length $2^m + m - 1$ such that each string of length m is a factor of w_m occurring

---

[1] In that case, variables of the form $[qAp]$ are used, where p represents one possible "exit" from the segment from $[qA]$. In the case under consideration, there is at most one possible exit, namely $\text{exit}[qA]$.

in w_m exactly one time. Furthermore, the suffix and the prefix of length $m - 1$ of w_m coincide.

We consider the following language:[2]

$$L_m = \{a^k \mid \text{ the } (k \bmod' 2^m)\text{th letter of } w_m \text{ is } 1\},$$

where $x \bmod' y = \begin{cases} x \bmod y & \text{if } x \bmod y > 0 \\ y & \text{otherwise.} \end{cases}$

For example, $w_3 = 0001011100$ and $L_3 = \{a^0, a^4, a^6, a^7\}\{a^8\}^*$.

By definition and by the above mentioned properties of de Bruijn words, L_m is a properly 2^m-cyclic unary language. Hence, the minimal 1dfa accepting it has exactly 2^m states (actually, by Theorem 9 in [11], this number of states is required even by each 2nfa accepting L_m). We show that even the size of each dpda accepting L_m must be exponential in m. More precisely:

Theorem 5. *There is a constant d, such that for each $m > 0$ the size of any dpda accepting L_m is at least $d\frac{2^m}{m^2}$.*

Proof. Let us consider a dpda M of size s accepting L_m. We will show that from M it is possible to build a grammar with $O(sm)$ variables generating the language which consists only of the word w_m. Hence, the result will follow from a lower bound presented in [4], related to the generation of w_m.

First of all, from M it is possible to get an equivalent dpda M' of size $2s + 1$, such that M' is able to accept or reject each string a^k immediately after reading the kth letter of the input.

We also consider a 1dfa A accepting the language L which consists of all strings x on the alphabet $\{0, 1\}$, such that $x = yw$, where w is the suffix of length m of w_m, and w is not a proper factor of x, i.e., $x = x'w$, and $x = x''ww'$ implies $w' = \epsilon$. Note that A can be implemented with $m + 1$ states. The automaton A will be used in the following to modify the control of M', in order to force it to accept only the string $a^{2^m + m - 1}$.

To this aim, we describe a new dpda M''. Each state of M'' simulates one state of M' and one state of A. The initial state of M'' is the pair of the initial states of M' and A. M'' simulates M' moves step by step. When a transition which reads an input symbol is simulated, then M'' simulates also one move of A on input $\sigma \in \{0, 1\}$, where $\sigma = 1$ if the transition of M' leads to an accepting state, 0 otherwise. In this way, the automaton A will finally receive as input the word w_m. When the simulation reaches the accepting state of A, namely the end of w_m has been reached, M'' stops and accepts. Thus, the only string accepted by M'' is $a^{2^m + m - 1}$.

Using the construction presented in Section 4, we can build a context-free grammar G equivalent to M''. We modify the productions of G that correspond to operations which consume input symbols: each production $[qA]_b \to a[pA]_b$ is replaced by $[qA]_b \to 1[pA]_b$ if p corresponds to a final state of M', and by $[qA]_b \to 0[pA]_b$ otherwise. It is easy to observe that the grammar G' so obtained

---

[2] The same language was considered in [2] for a different problem.

generates the language $\{w_m\}$. Furthermore, the size of G' is bounded by ksm, for some constant k. By a result presented in [4] (based on a lower bound from [1]), the number of variables of G' must be at least $c\frac{2^m}{m}$ for some constant c. Hence, from $ksm \geq c\frac{2^m}{m}$, we finally get that the size of the original dpda M must be at least $d\frac{2^m}{m^2}$ for some constant d. $\qquad\square$

References

1. Althöfer, I.: Tight lower bounds for the length of word chains. Information Processing Letters 34, 275–276 (1990)
2. Berstel, J., Carton, O.: On the complexity of Hopcroft's State Minimization Algorithm. In: Domaratzki, M., Okhotin, A., Salomaa, K., Yu, S. (eds.) CIAA 2004. LNCS, vol. 3317, pp. 35–44. Springer, Heidelberg (2005)
3. de Bruijn, N.: A combinatorial problem. Proc. Kon. Nederl. Akad. Wetensch 49, 758–764 (1946)
4. Domaratzki, M., Pighizzini, G., Shallit, J.: Simulating finite automata with context-free grammars. Information Processing Letters 84, 339–344 (2002)
5. Ginsburg, S., Greibach, S.: Deterministic context-free languages. Information and Control 9, 563–582 (1966)
6. Ginsburg, S., Rice, H.: Two families of languages related to ALGOL. Journal of the ACM 9, 350–371 (1962)
7. Goldstine, J., Price, J., Wotschke, D.: A pushdown automaton or a context-free grammar – Which is more economical? Theoretical Computer Science 18, 33–40 (1982)
8. Harrison, M.A.: Introduction to Formal Language Theory. Addison-Wesley, Reading (1978)
9. Hopcroft, J., Ullman, J.: Introduction to Automata Theory, Languages, and Computation. Addison-Wesley, Reading (1979)
10. Knuth, D.: On the translation of languages from left to right. Information and Control 8, 607–639 (1965)
11. Mereghetti, C., Pighizzini, G.: Two-way automata simulations and unary languages. J. Aut.Lang.Combin. 5, 287–300 (2000)
12. Mereghetti, C., Pighizzini, G.: Optimal simulations between unary automata. SIAM J. Comput. 30, 1976–1992 (2001)
13. Meyer, A., Fischer, M.: Economy of description by automata, grammars, and formal systems. In: Proc.12th Ann. IEEE Symp.on Switching and Automata Theory, pp. 188–191 (1971)
14. Pighizzini, G., Shallit, J., Wang, M.-W.: Unary context-free grammars and pushdown automata, descriptional complexity and auxiliary space lower bounds. Journal of Computer and System Sciences 65, 393–414 (2002)
15. Sénizergues, G.: The equivalence problem for deterministic pushdown automata is decidable. In: Degano, P., Gorrieri, R., Marchetti-Spaccamela, A. (eds.) ICALP 1997. LNCS, vol. 1256, pp. 671–682. Springer, Heidelberg (1997)
16. Stearns, R.: A regularity test for pushdown machines. Information and Control 11, 323–340 (1967)
17. Valiant, L.: Regularity and related problems for deterministic pushdown automata. Journal of the ACM 22, 1–10 (1975)

Finite Eilenberg Machines

Benoît Razet

INRIA Paris-Rocquencourt, Aden
benoit.razet@inria.fr

Abstract. Eilenberg machines define a general computational model. They are well suited to the simulation of problems specified using finite state formalisms such as formal languages and automata theory. This paper introduces a subclass of them called finite Eilenberg machines. We give a formal description of complete and efficient algorithms which permit the simulation of such machines. We show that our finiteness condition ensures a correct behavior of the simulation. Interpretations of this condition are studied for the cases of non-deterministic finite automata (NFA) and transducers, leading to applications to computational linguistics. The given implementation provides a generic simulation procedure for any problem encoded as a composition of finite Eilenberg machines.

Introduction

Samuel Eilenberg introduced in chapter 10 of his book [4], published in 1974, a notion of *Machine* which he claimed to be a *very efficient tool* for studying formal languages of the Chomsky hierarchy. They are sometimes referred to as *X-machines*. Many variants have appeared in the last twenty years [8] in several scientific domains different from formal languages.

Eilenberg machines define a general computational model. Assumed given an abstract data set X (it motivates X-machine terminology), a *machine* is defined as an automaton labelled with binary relations on X. Two generalizations result from this. Firstly, the set X abstracts the traditional tape used by automata on words, transducers *etc.* Secondly, compared to functions, binary relations give a built-in notion of non-determinism. Many translations of other machines into Eilenberg's machines were also given [4]: automata, transducers, real-time transducers, two-way automata, push-down automata and Turing machines.

The remainder of this paper recalls the definitions of Eilenberg machines in Section 1. It also introduces a new subclass of them called *finite Eilenberg machines*. The Section 2 discusses the adaptation to the models of non-deterministic finite automata (NFA) and transducers which motivate their use for computational linguistics. The next two sections provide algorithms simulating finite Eilenberg machines. Since relations are central to Eilenberg machines, Section 3 proposes an encoding of them using streams. The Section 4 gives a formal description of algorithms which permit the simulation of finite Eilenberg machines in the spirit of the *reactive engine* introduced by Huet [5].

O.H. Ibarra and B. Ravikumar (Eds.): CIAA 2008, LNCS 5148, pp. 242–251, 2008.

1   Finite Eilenberg Machines

We consider a monoid with carrier M, $\cdot$ an associative product on M and 1 its unit element. A finite monoid automaton $\mathcal{A}$ over M, also called a M-automaton, is a tuple (Q, δ, I, T) with Q a finite set of elements called *states*, δ a function from Q to finite subsets of $(M \times Q)$ called the *transition function*, I a subset of Q of *initial states* and T a subset of Q of *terminal states*.

A *path* p is a sequence $p = q_0 \xrightarrow{m_1} q_1 \xrightarrow{m_2} \cdots \xrightarrow{m_n} q_n$ with $n \in \mathbb{N}$ and $\forall i \leq n \ q_i \in Q$, $\forall i < n \ m_{i+1} \in M$ and $\forall i < n \ (m_{i+1}, q_{i+1}) \in \delta(q_i)$. The path p is *successful* when $q_0 \in I$ and $q_n \in T$; its *length* is n. The *label* of p written $\bar{p}$ is 1 if $n = 0$ or $m_1 \cdot \ldots \cdot m_n$ otherwise. Finally, the *behavior* of the M-automaton $\mathcal{A}$, written $|\mathcal{A}|$, is defined as the set of all labels of successful paths of $\mathcal{A}$. We introduce the *type of* $\mathcal{A}$, written $\Phi_\mathcal{A}$, as the finite subset of M of elements appearing in the image of δ: $\Phi_\mathcal{A} = \{ \ m \in M \mid \exists q \ q' \in Q, \ (m, q') \in \delta(q) \ \}$.

Let us now precise some notations for relations which are central to the remainder of this paper. A relation ρ from some set $\mathcal{D}$ to a set $\mathcal{D}'$ written $\rho : \mathcal{D} \to \mathcal{D}'$ is a set of pairs from $\wp(\mathcal{D} \times \mathcal{D}')$. The functional notation of its type is justified by the isomorphism between $\wp(\mathcal{D} \times \mathcal{D}')$ and $\mathcal{D} \to \wp(\mathcal{D}')$. The converse of a relation $\rho : \mathcal{D} \to \mathcal{D}'$ is written $\rho^{-1} : \mathcal{D}' \to \mathcal{D}$. Let us use $\rho(d)$ as notation for $\{ \ d' \mid d' \in \mathcal{D}', \ (d, d') \in \rho \}$. The identity relation is written $id_\mathcal{D} = \{(d, d) \mid d \in \mathcal{D}\}$.

Let us recall Eilenberg's definition of machines. Let $\mathcal{D}$ be an arbitrary set called the *data* (it replaces the original notation X). We consider the set $R_\mathcal{D}$ of binary relations from $\mathcal{D}$ to $\mathcal{D}$. We consider here the *relations monoid* $R_\mathcal{D}$ with the *relation composition* $\circ$ as associative product and the *identity* relation id as unit element. A $\mathcal{D}$-*machine* $\mathcal{M}$ is a $R_\mathcal{D}$-automaton (Q, δ, I, T). With respect to the previous definitions the label of a path $p = q_0 \xrightarrow{\phi_1} q_1 \xrightarrow{\phi_2} \cdots \xrightarrow{\phi_n} q_n$ is the composition of relations $\bar{p} = \phi_1 \circ \cdots \circ \phi_n$. The behavior of $\mathcal{M}$ as an automaton, $|\mathcal{M}|$, is the set of relations of all labels of successful paths. The distinction between an automaton and a machine lies in the use of the union operation available on relations. The machine $\mathcal{M}$ defines a particular relation, written $||\mathcal{M}||$, as the relation union extended over all relations in $|\mathcal{M}|$:

$$||\mathcal{M}|| = \bigcup_{\rho \in |\mathcal{M}|} \rho \ .$$

We call the relation $||\mathcal{M}||$ the *characteristic relation* of the machine $\mathcal{M}$. We have given until now what we call the *kernel* of an Eilenberg machine which refers only to the automaton part.

The complete description of an Eilenberg machine requires what we call its *interface*. That is, consider $\mathcal{D}_-$ and $\mathcal{D}_+$ be two sets called respectively the *input* and *output* sets, an input relation $\phi_- : \mathcal{D}_- \to \mathcal{D}$ and an output relation $\phi_+ : \mathcal{D} \to \mathcal{D}_+$. Intuitively, the relation ϕ_- feeds the kernel with inputs and ϕ_+ interprets kernel results as outputs. A machine kernel with its interface defines a relation $\rho : \mathcal{D}_- \to \mathcal{D}_+$ as $\rho = \phi_- \circ ||\mathcal{M}|| \circ \phi_+$. The usefulness of kernel and interfaces will be clear with examples provided in section 2.

Remark 1 (on modularity of Eilenberg machines). Any Eilenberg machine $\mathcal{M}$ of type $\Phi_{\mathcal{M}}$ defines a characteristic relation $\|\mathcal{M}\|$ that may belong to a type $\Phi_{\mathcal{M}'}$ of another Eilenberg machine $\mathcal{M}'$. This gives an idea that Eilenberg machines describe a modular computational model.

We are now going to introduce a new subclass of Eilenberg machines. For this purpose let us first define useful notions specific to machines rather than automata. Let us consider a $\mathcal{D}$-machine $\mathcal{M} = (Q, \delta, I, T)$. We call *cell* a pair $c = (d, q)$ of $\mathcal{D} \times Q$. An *edge* is a triple $((d, q), \phi, (d', q'))$, written $(d, q) \xrightarrow{\phi} (d', q')$ and satisfying the following two conditions $(\phi, q') \in \delta(q)$ and $d' \in \phi(d)$. A *trace* is a sequence of consecutive edges $t = c_0 \xrightarrow{\phi_1} c_1 \cdots \xrightarrow{\phi_n} c_n$. The integer n is the *length* of the trace. The cell c_0 is called its *beginning* and c_n its *end*. For each data d and state q, the cell (d, q) defines a null trace with itself as beginning and end. A cell (d, q) is said to be *terminal* whenever q is terminal. A trace t is said to be *terminal* when its end is terminal. Remark that each trace can be projected as the corresponding path when data are forgotten.

Definition 1

1. *Let $\mathcal{D}_1$ and $\mathcal{D}_2$ be two sets, we say that a relation $\rho : \mathcal{D}_1 \to \mathcal{D}_2$ is **locally finite** iff for all data d in $\mathcal{D}_1$ the set $\rho(d)$ is finite.*
2. *We say that a machine $\mathcal{M}$ is **locally finite** iff every relation ϕ in $\Phi_{\mathcal{M}}$ is locally finite.*
3. *The machine $\mathcal{M}$ is **globally finite** iff its characteristic relation $\|\mathcal{M}\|$ is locally finite.*
4. *The machine $\mathcal{M}$ is **nœtherian** iff there is no infinite trace $c_0 \xrightarrow{\phi_1} c_1 \cdots \xrightarrow{\phi_n} c_n \cdots$.*
5. *The machine $\mathcal{M}$ is called **finite** iff it is locally finite and nœtherian.*

Remark 2. A locally finite machine may or may not be globally finite and conversely a globally finite machine may or may not be locally finite.

Proposition 1. *If the machine $\mathcal{M}$ is finite then it is globally finite.*

Proof. Using König's lemma; the locally finite condition corresponds to the finite branching condition and the nœtherian condition to the non existence of infinite traces. $\square$

Corollary 1. *Let ϕ_- and ϕ_+ be two partial functions. If the machine $\mathcal{M}$ is finite with interface ϕ_- and ϕ_+ then the relation $\phi_- \circ \|\mathcal{M}\| \circ \phi_+$ is locally finite.*

Let us now discuss the nœtherian condition. This definition with both the control and data may be arbitrarily complex. Of course an easy subcase is when there is no cycle in the automaton part of $\mathcal{M}$. Also it is easy to formulate a sufficient condition for a machine to be nœtherian:

Definition 2. *The machine $\mathcal{M}$ is of **nœtherian type** iff the relation $\bigcup_{\rho \in |\Phi_{\mathcal{M}}|} \rho$ is nœtherian.*

Proposition 2. *If the machine $\mathcal{M}$ is of nœtherian type then it satisfies the nœtherian condition.*

2   Examples and Applications

We consider a finite set Σ of *letters* called the *alphabet*. We consider the free monoid Σ^* of *words* over Σ with the word concatenation as monoid product and the *empty word* ϵ as unit element. Formal languages are sets of words. Four basic operations on words are to be considered for defining Eilenberg machines for the next examples. For each letter σ of Σ:

- $L_\sigma = \{ (w, \sigma w) \mid w \in \Sigma^* \}$, $L_\sigma^{-1} = \{ (\sigma w, w) \mid w \in \Sigma^* \}$,
- $R_\sigma = \{ (w, w\sigma) \mid w \in \Sigma^* \}$, $R_\sigma^{-1} = \{ (w\sigma, w) \mid w \in \Sigma^* \}$.

The L and R denotations indicate operations respectively on the *left* or the *right* of a word. The last two relations are respectively the converse relations of the first ones. The *identity relation* on Σ^* is written id_{Σ^*}.

Remark 3. Relations L_σ, R_σ, L_σ^{-1}, R_σ^{-1} and id_{Σ^*} described above are in fact partial functions, thus they are locally finite relations.

Examples from Eilenberg show that his machine model implements many other computational paradigms. They use a notion of *"relabelling"* formally presented by Sakarovitch [11]. We use them in the two following examples.

Example 1 (NFA). We consider here an alphabet Σ and words as elements of Σ^*. An NFA on alphabet Σ is a Σ^*-automaton $\mathcal{A}$ such that $\Phi_{\mathcal{A}} \subseteq \Sigma^*$ (ϵ-transitions are allowed). The set of words $|\mathcal{A}|$, the behavior of $\mathcal{A}$, is a formal language that belongs to the class of rational languages.

Let us define a relabelling procedure translating any NFA into an Eilenberg machine solving its word problem. Let $\mathcal{A} = (Q, \delta, I, T)$ be an NFA. We choose a data set $\mathcal{D} = \Sigma^*$. Since $\Phi_{\mathcal{A}} \subseteq \Sigma^*$, we recall the relabelling morphism α defined on Σ as $\alpha(\sigma) = L_\sigma^{-1}$ and then extended on Σ^*. Thus the machine $\mathcal{M}$ relabelled from $\mathcal{A}$ by α has the following characteristic relation: $||\mathcal{M}|| = \{ (w\,w', w') \mid w \in |\mathcal{A}|, w' \in \Sigma^* \}$. That is, a given input $w \cdot w'$ is truncated by the word w recognized by the automaton $\mathcal{A}$. The encoding is completed with the following interface: $\mathcal{D}_- = \Sigma^*$, the input relation $\phi_- = id_{\Sigma^*}$, $\mathcal{D}_+ = \mathbb{B}$ the Boolean set composed of the two values $\top$ and $\bot$ and the output function $\phi_+ : \Sigma^* \to \mathbb{B}$ defined by $\phi_+(w)$ being $\top$ when $w = \epsilon$ and $\bot$ otherwise. Now we have $(\phi_- \circ ||\mathcal{M}|| \circ \phi_+)^{-1}(\top) = |\mathcal{A}|$. It shows that the relabelling is correct.

Let us now discuss the case when $\mathcal{M}$ is a *finite* Eilenberg machine. $\mathcal{M}$ is locally finite (Remark 3) and it satisfies the nœtherian condition whenever there is no ϵ-cycle in it. By ϵ-cycle we mean cycle labelled with id_{Σ^*}. Also $\mathcal{M}$ is of *nœtherian type* iff there is no ϵ-transition at all in it. It is true because for every edge $(u, q) \xrightarrow{L_w^{-1}} (v, q')$ we have $|w| > 1$ and then $|v| < |u|$, this shows that the length of traces is bounded by the length of their beginning word in their initial cell and thus there may not be infinite traces.

Example 2 (Transducers). Let Σ and Γ be two finite alphabets. The empty word ϵ will denote both empty words for Σ^* and for Γ^*. We consider here the monoid $\Sigma^* \times \Gamma^*$ with its traditional concatenation as associative product and the pair (ϵ, ϵ) as unit element. A rational transducer from Σ^* to Γ^* is a monoid automaton $\mathcal{A}$ over $\Sigma^* \times \Gamma^*$ such that $\Phi_{\mathcal{A}} \subseteq (\Sigma \times \epsilon) \cup (\epsilon \times \Gamma)$. The subset of pairs of words from $|\mathcal{A}|$, the behavior of $\mathcal{A}$, defines a relation which belongs to the subclass of *rational relations*. Three problematics arise naturally:

– *Recognition* Given a couple of words (w, w') of $\Sigma^* \times \Gamma^*$, does (w, w') belong to $|\mathcal{A}|$.
– *Synthesis* Given a word w in Σ^* compute the set $|\mathcal{A}|(w)$ of words from Γ^*.
– *Analysis* Given a word w in Γ^* compute the set $|\mathcal{A}|^{-1}(w)$ of words from Σ^*.

For a given transducer these three problems may be encoded with the same automaton but using different relabellings and interfaces. The relabelling for the *synthesis* problem is defined as a morphism α on $\Phi_{\mathcal{A}}$ such that $\alpha(\sigma, \epsilon) = L_{\sigma}^{-1} \times id_{\Gamma^*}$ and $\alpha(\epsilon, \gamma) = id_{\Sigma^*} \times R_{\gamma}$. This encoding is completed with the following interface: $\mathcal{D}_- = \Sigma^*$, $\mathcal{D}_+ = \Gamma^*$, the input relation $\phi_- = \{ (w, (w, \epsilon)) \mid w \in \Sigma^* \}$ and the output relation $\phi_+ = \{ ((\epsilon, w'), w') \mid w' \in \Gamma^* \}$. Then we obtain $(\phi_- \circ || \mathcal{M} || \circ \phi_+) = |\mathcal{A}|$. $\mathcal{M}$ is locally finite (Remark 3) and satisfies the nœtherian condition whenever there is no cycle labelled with relation of $id_{\Sigma^*} \times R_{\gamma}$. $\mathcal{M}$ is of nœtherian type whenever there is no transition labelled with a relation of $id_{\Sigma^*} \times R_{\gamma}$ at all. As for NFA, this property is true with the same kind of argument concerning the length of the input tape.

Automata, transducers and more generally finite state machines are a popular technology for solving many computational linguistics problems [10]. We believe that the Eilenberg machines model is promising for this purpose. In fact, our restriction of *finite Eilenberg machines* is the formalism underlying the works concerning general morphological and phonetical modelings [5,6] which have been applied to the Sanskrit language. Furthermore this application needs the modularity of such Eilenberg machine as sketched in the Remark 1. In the following we provide algorithms that simulate in a complete fashion any finite Eilenberg machine.

3   Streams Representing Relations

We consider now that the data set $\mathcal{D}$ is representable as an abstract ML datatype. We recall that **unit** is the singleton ML datatype containing the unique value denoted $()$. In our implementation we will use streams which are objects for enumerating on demand. In ML notation stream values are encoded with the following type parametrized with $\mathcal{D}$:

```
type  stream  D  = |  EOS
                   |  Stream of  D  ×  (delay  D )
  and  delay  D  = unit  →  stream  D ;
```

A stream value is either the empty stream *EOS* ("*End of Stream*") for encoding the empty enumeration or else a value *Stream d del* that provides the new element d of the enumeration and a value *del* as a delayed computation of the rest of the enumeration. Since ML computes with the restriction of λ-calculus to weak reduction, a value of type *delay* $\mathcal{D}$ such as *del* is delayed because it is a functional value. This well known technique permits computation on demand. Note that this technique would not apply in a programming language evaluating inside a function body (strong reduction in λ-calculus terminology).

ML being a Turing-complete programming language, not all ML functions terminate and since our streams contain function values we shall restrict their computational power:

Definition 3

1. *The ML function* f: **unit** $\to \alpha$ *is said to be total iff the evaluation of* f () *terminates (yielding a value of type* α).
2. *The ML stream str: stream $\mathcal{D}$ is said to be progressive iff*
   - *either str is EOS*
   - *or else str is of the form Stream d f with f total, and f () is progressive.*

We define the *head* function hd from non-empty streams to data defined as follows: $hd(Stream\ d\ del) = d$. We define also the *tail* function tl from streams to streams as $tl(EOS) = EOS$ and $tl(Stream\ d\ del) = del()$. Let n be an integer, we introduce the function tl^n that iterates the tl function n times:

$$\begin{cases} tl^0(str) & = str \\ tl^{n+1}(str) = tl^n(tl(str)) \end{cases} \tag{1}$$

We introduce the predicate $InStream(d, str)$ that checks whether a data d appears in the stream str:

Definition 4. $InStream(d, str)$ *is true iff there exists an integer n such that* $(tl^n(str))$ *is non-empty and* $hd(tl^n(str)) = d$.

Definition 5. *A progressive stream str is finite iff there exists an integer n such that* $tl^n(str) = EOS$.

The *length* of a finite stream str, written $|str|$, is defined inductively as follows:

$$\begin{cases} |EOS| & = 0 \\ |Stream\ d\ del| = 1 + |del()| \end{cases} \tag{2}$$

All finite streams of positive length end with a value of type *delay* $\mathcal{D}$ that associates to the unit element () the *EOS* stream announcing the end of the enumeration, typically:

   value *delay_eos* () = *EOS;*

We consider now relations of $R_{\mathcal{D}}$ representable as ML functions of the following type:

   type *relation* $\mathcal{D}$ = $\mathcal{D}$ $\to$ *stream* $\mathcal{D}$;

That is, if a relation *rel* of type *relation* $\mathcal{D}$ corresponds to a relation ρ of $R_{\mathcal{D}}$ then:

$$\forall d\ d' \in \mathcal{D},\ d' \in \rho(d) \Leftrightarrow InStream(d', rel\ d).$$

In the following we will use this technique only for representing locally finite relations. That is, relations are encoded using finite streams which are *progressive* by definition 5. From now on, we shall assume that our Eilenberg machines are *effective* in the sense that their data domain $\mathcal{D}$ are implemented as an ML datatype and that every relation used in their labeling is progressive.

4 A Reactive Engine for Finite Eilenberg Machines

We provide an implementation for the simulation of finite Eilenberg machines using higher-order recursive definitions. Algorithms are presented using ML notations which are directly executable in the OCaml programming language [7]. An essential feature of our formal notations is to possibly compose parametrized modules called functors. Algorithms are variants of the *reactive engine* [5]. They are presented completely using only a dozen of elegant definitions.

Let $\mathcal{M} = (Q, \delta, I, T)$ be a $\mathcal{D}$-machine. We specify $\mathcal{M}$ as a module with the following signature:

```
module type Kernel = sig
    type D ;
    type state ;
    value transition : state → list (relation D × state );
    value initial : list state ;
    value terminal : state → bool ;
end ;
```

The type parameter *state* encodes the set Q, the function *transition* encodes the function δ, the value *initial* encodes the initial states I as a list and the function *terminal* encodes the set of terminal states T as its characteristic predicate.

We aim at providing the algorithms implementing the characteristic relation of $\mathcal{M}$. For this purpose we use a functor that is a module parametrized by a *Kernel* machine. We call *Engine* this functor declared as the following:

```
module Engine (M: Kernel) = struct
    open M;
    ... (* body *) ...
end ;
```

Firstly, the body of the functor contains type declarations:

```
type choice = list (relation D × state );
type backtrack =
  | Advance of D × state
  | Choose of D × state × choice × (delay D ) × state
  ;
type resumption = list backtrack ;
```

The type *choice* is an abbreviation for the list of transitions of the machine as used in the machine M. Eilenberg machines are possibly non-deterministic and need thus a backtracking mechanism for their implementation. Values of type *backtrack* allow to save the multiple choices due to the non-deterministic nature of the machine. The enumerating procedure will stack such backtrack values in a resumption of type *resumption*.

Secondly, the engine contains four functions. Three of them are internal and mutually recursive: *react*, *choose* and *continue*. They perform the non-deterministic search enriching the resumption as the computation goes on. The computation is performed in a depth-first search manner stacking the transition choices and streams within backtrack values in the resumption:

```
(* react: D → state → resumption → stream D *)
value rec react d q res =
  let ch = transition q in
  if terminal q then (* Solution found *)
    Stream d (fun () → choose d q ch res)
  else choose d q ch res

(* choose: D → state → choice → resumption → stream D *)
and choose d q ch res =
  match ch with
  | [] → continue res
  | (rel, q') :: rest →
    match (rel d) with
    | EOS → choose d q rest res
    | Stream d' del →
      react d' q' (Choose(d,q,rest,del,q') :: res)

(* continue: resumption → stream D *)
and continue res =
  match res with
  | [] → EOS
  | (Advance(d,q) :: rest) → react d q rest
  | (Choose(d,q,ch,del,q') :: rest) →
    match (del ()) with
    | EOS → choose d q ch rest
    | Stream d' del' →
      react d' q' (Choose(d,q,ch,del',q') :: rest)
;
```

The function *react* checks whether the state is terminal and then provides an element of the stream delaying the rest of the exploration calling to the function *choose*. This function *choose* performs the non-deterministic search over transitions, choosing them in the natural order induced by the **list** data structure. The function *continue* manages the backtracking mechanism and the enumeration of finite streams of relations, it always chooses to backtrack on the last pushed value in the resumption. Remark that these three mutually recursive functions do not use any side effect and are written in a pure functional style completely tail-recursive using the resumption as a continuation mechanism.

The machine $\mathcal{M}$ implemented as a module M has its characteristic relation $||\mathcal{M}||$ simulated by the following function:

```
(* characteristic_relation: relation D *)
value characteristic_relation d =
  let rec init_res l acc =
    match l with
    | [] → acc
    | (q :: rest) → init_res rest (Advance(d,q) :: acc)
  in continue (init_res initial []);
```

The function *characteristic_relation* first initializes the resumption with *Advance* backtrack values for each initial state and then call the function *continue* on it. We summarize the presented algorithms as follows: the machine $\mathcal{M}$ implemented as a module M has its characteristic relation $\|\mathcal{M}\|$ simulated by *Engine(M). characteristic_relation*, the function given by the instantiation of functor *Engine* with module M. We now provide the formalization with all arguments ensuring the correctness of our so-called reactive engine.

The formalization is inspired by the original one for the reactive engine [5]. We formalize the fact that data d and d' are in relation by the characteristic relation of $\mathcal{M}$ using the predicate $Solution(d, d')$ which is true iff there exists an initial state q and a terminal trace t beginning with cell (d, q) and ending with data d'. Now we give the correctness theorem of the reactive engine including its termination, its soundness and its completeness.

Theorem 1. *If the machine $\mathcal{M}$ is finite then characteristic_relation is a finite progressive relation (termination) and for all data d and d'*

$$InStream(d', characteristic\_relation\ d) \Leftrightarrow Solution(d, d').$$

Proof. The proof has been completely formalized and verified mechanically using the Coq proof assistant in the companion paper [9]. It uses the *well-founded multiset ordering* technique as presented by Dershowitz and Manna [3] to prove termination. It also gives us a nœtherian induction principle needed for the proofs of soundness and completeness (the two directions of the equivalence).   □

Theorem 1 is a constructive version of Proposition 1. The reactive engine presented here *computes on demand* the solutions of a machine. This feature is important for combining in a modular fashion finite Eilenberg machines and keeping under control their evaluation.

5   Conclusion

Eilenberg machines provide a powerful and elegant framework for simulating specifications presented as finite automata variants. Eilenberg gave easy encodings into machines of formalisms at various levels of the Chomsky hierarchy. We have introduced a subclass of them called *finite Eilenberg machines* which are still general. They are *a priori* non-deterministic machines and we have shown that they behave as relations that associate to an input a **finite** number of computed outputs. Our machines are not restricted to treatments for the rational level of the Chomsky hierarchy. This particular point makes us believe that finite Eilenberg machines have applications to computational linguistics. In fact they are already efficient for explaining recognition or transduction problems that manipulate two levels of finite state formalisms for the modeling of the Sanskrit language [6]. This multi-level ability is the modularity feature of Eilenberg machines. For this purpose implementations need to be lazy. We anticipate future works in this spirit providing lazy algorithms. Our small but efficient *reactive engine* computes lazily the simulation of any finite Eilenberg machines.

Our methodology using higher-order recursive definitions of functional programming language leads to formal proofs amenable to a complete formalization using higher-order logic. Such a formal development is available in the companion paper [9] using the Coq proof assistant [1]. Remark that this methodology leads to the same programs as shown here, by Coq's extraction mechanism from the formal development.

The enumeration of solutions implemented by the above algorithms uses a relatively naive lexicographic ordering. It is easy to refine these algorithms with more complex strategies, yielding weighted automata and stochastic methods such as *hidden Markov chains*. Such experiments will guide the design of the specification language for Eilenberg machines using regular expressions and compilation techniques such as presented by Allauzen and Mohri [2].

Acknowledgments

Gérard Huet and Jean-Baptiste Tristan helped in the elaboration of this paper; I thank them for their participation.

References

1. The Coq proof assistant. Software and documentation (1995–2008), http://coq.inria.fr/
2. Allauzen, C., Mohri, M.: A unified construction of the Glushkov, Follow, and Antimirov automata. In: Královič, R., Urzyczyn, P. (eds.) MFCS 2006. LNCS, vol. 4162, pp. 110–121. Springer, Heidelberg (2006)
3. Dershowitz, N., Manna, Z.: Proving termination with multiset orderings. Commun. ACM 22(8), 465–476 (1979)
4. Eilenberg, S.: Automata, Languages and Machines, vol. A. Academic Press, London (1974)
5. Huet, G.: A functional toolkit for morphological and phonological processing, application to a Sanskrit tagger. J. Functional programming 15 (2005)
6. Huet, G., Razet, B.: The reactive engine for modular transducers. In: Jouannaud, J.-P., Futatsugi, K., Meseguer, J. (eds.) Algebra, Meaning, and Computation. LNCS, vol. 4060, pp. 355–374. Springer, Heidelberg (2006)
7. Leroy, X., Doligez, D., Garrigue, J., Vouillon, J.: The Objective Caml system. Software and documentation (1996–2008), http://caml.inria.fr/
8. Theory of X-machines, http://www.x-machines.com
9. Razet, B.: Simulating Eilenberg machines with a reactive engine: Formal specification, proof and program extraction. INRIA Research Report (2008), http://hal.inria.fr/inria-00257352/en/
10. Roche, E., Schabes, Y.: Finite-state language processing. MIT press, Cambridge (1997)
11. Sakarovitch, J.: Eléments de théorie des automates. Vuibert, Paris (2003)

The Number of Runs in Sturmian Words

Paweł Baturo[1], Marcin Piątkowski[1], and Wojciech Rytter[1,2,*]

[1] Faculty of Mathematics and Computer Science, Nicolaus Copernicus University
[2] Institute of Informatics, Warsaw University, Warsaw, Poland

Abstract. Denote by $\mathcal{S}$ the class of *standard Sturmian* words. It is a class of highly compressible words extensively studied in combinatorics of words, including the well known Fibonacci words. The suffix automata for these words have a very particular structure. This implies a simple characterization (described in the paper by the Structural Lemma) of the periods of runs (maximal repetitions) in Sturmian words. Using this characterization we derive an explicit formula for the number $\rho(w)$ of runs in words $w \in \mathcal{S}$, with respect to their *recurrences (directive sequences)*. We show that $\frac{\rho(w)}{|w|} \leq \frac{4}{5}$ for each $w \in \mathcal{S}$, and there is an infinite sequence of strictly growing words $w_k \in \mathcal{S}$ such that $\lim_{k \to \infty} \frac{\rho(w_k)}{|w_k|} = \frac{4}{5}$. The complete understanding of the function ρ for a large class $\mathcal{S}$ of complicated words is a step towards better understanding of the structure of runs in words. We also show how to compute the number of runs in a standard Sturmian word in linear time with respect to the size of its compressed representation (recurrences describing the word). This is an example of a very fast computation on texts given implicitly in terms of a special grammar-based compressed representation (usually of logarithmic size with respect to the explicit text).

1 Introduction

The runs (maximal repetitions) in strings are important in combinatorics on words and in practical applications: data compression, computational biology, pattern-matching. A run is a non-extendable (with the same period) periodic segment in a string in which the period repeats at least twice. In 1999 Kolpakov and Kucherov [10] showed that the number $\rho(w)$ of runs in a string w is $O(|w|)$, but the exact multiplicative constant coefficient is unknown, recent bounds are given in [11,5]. In order to better understand the behavior of the function ρ for general words we give **exact** estimations for a class $\mathcal{S}$ of highly compressible words: the standard Sturmian words (standard words, in short). The class $\mathcal{S}$ of standard Sturmian words is of particular interest due to their importance in combinatorics on words, [2,3]. The standard words are a generalization of Fibonacci words and, like Fibonacci words, are described by recurrences.

The recurrence for a standard word is related to so called *directive sequence* – an integer sequence of the form

$$\gamma = (\gamma_0, \gamma_1, ..., \gamma_n), \text{ where } \gamma_0 \geq 0, \gamma_i > 0 \text{ for } 0 < i \leq n.$$

The standard word corresponding to γ, denoted by $S(\gamma) = x_{n+1}$, is defined by recurrences:

$$x_{-1} = b, \ x_0 = a, \ x_1 = x_0^{\gamma_0} x_{-1}, \ x_2 = x_1^{\gamma_1} x_0, \tag{1}$$

* Supported by grant N206 004 32/0806 of the Polish Ministry of Science and Higher Education.

O.H. Ibarra and B. Ravikumar (Eds.): CIAA 2008, LNCS 5148, pp. 252–261, 2008.

$$x_3 = x_2^{\gamma_2} x_1, \ \ldots, \ x_n = x_{n-1}^{\gamma_{n-1}} x_{n-2}, \ x_{n+1} = x_n^{\gamma_n} x_{n-1} \tag{2}$$

For example the recurrence for the 4-th Fibonacci word is

$$fib_{-1} = b, \ fib_0 = a, \ fib_1 = fib_0^1 b, \ fib_2 = fib_1^1 fib_0,$$

$$fib_3 = fib_2^1 fib_1, \ fib_4 = fib_3^1 fib_2.$$

$$fib_4 \ = \ abaababa \ = \ S(\gamma_0, \gamma_1, \gamma_2, \gamma_3) \ \text{where} \ (\gamma_0, \gamma_1, \gamma_2, \gamma_3) = \ (1, 1, 1, 1)$$

We consider here standard words starting with the letter a, hence assume $\gamma_0 > 0$. The case $\gamma_0 = 0$ can be considered similarly. For even $n > 0$ a word x_n has suffix ba, and for odd n it has suffix ab.

The number $N = |x_{n+1}|$ is the (real) size, while n can be thought of as the compressed size.

Example 1. Consider more complicated example (used later to demonstrate counting of runs), let $\gamma = (1, 2, 1, 3, 1)$, we have

$$S(\gamma) \ = \ ababaababababaababababaababababaababaab$$

The corresponding recurrence is

$$x_{-1} = b; \ x_0 = a, \ x_1 = x_0^1 x_{-1}, \ x_2 = x_1^2 x_0, \ x_3 = x_2^1 x_1, \ x_4 = x_3^3 x_2, \ x_5 = x_4^1 x_3.$$

A number i is a period of the word w iff $w[j] = w[i + j]$ for all i with $i + j \leq |w|$. The minimal period of w will be denoted by $period(w)$. We say that a word w is **periodic** iff $period(w) \leq \frac{|w|}{2}$. A word w is said to be *primitive* iff w is not of the form z^k, where z is a finite word and $k \geq 2$ is a natural number.

A **run** in a string w is an interval $\alpha = [i...j]$ such that $w[i...j]$ is a periodic word with the period $p = period(w[i...j])$ and this period is not extendable to the left or to the right of $[i...j]$. In other words, $[i...j]$ is a run iff $j - i + 1 \geq 2p$, $i = 1$ or $w[i - 1] \neq w[i - 1 + p]$ and $j = n$ or $w[j + 1] \neq w[j + 1 - p]$.

A run α can be properly included as an interval in another run β, but in this case $period(\alpha) < period(\beta)$. The value of the run $\alpha = [i...j]$ is $val(\alpha) = w[i...j]$

When it creates no ambiguity we identify sometimes runs with their values, although two different runs could correspond to identical subwords, if we disregard positions of these runs. Hence runs are also called maximal *positioned* repetitions.

Let $\rho(w)$ be the number of runs in a word w. The most interesting and open conjecture about runs is: $\rho(|w|) < |w|$. The first linear bound was given by Kolpakov and Kucherov [10], the best upper bound is by [6,5] and the best lower bound is by [5,7]. The structure of runs and squares is almost completely understood for the class of Fibonacci words, see [9,13,4]. We continue the work of [8], where it was shown how to compute the number of runs for block-complete Sturmian words (not all standard Sturmian words have this property) in time linear with respect to the size of the whole word

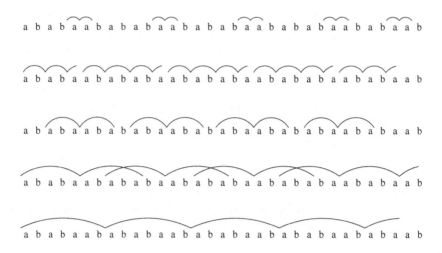

Fig. 1. The structure of runs of $S(1, 2, 1, 3, 1)$. There are 5 runs with period $|a|$, 5 with period $|ab|$. We have 10 *short* runs (period of size at most $|x_1| = |ab|$), 8 medium (with period $|x_1| < p \leq |x_2| = 5$, and 1 large run. Consequently $\rho(1, 2, 1, 3, 1) = 19$.

(while our algorithm is linear with respect to the size of compressed representation). A similar approach as in [8] is used in this paper – a kind of a reduction sequence, however our reductions are different than those in [8] and correspond closely to the structure of the recurrences (directive sequences). Also our aim is different – derivation of a simple formula for $\rho(w)$ and asymptotic behavior of $\rho(w)$.

Our results. We show that $\sup_{w \in S} \frac{\rho(w)}{|w|} = 0.8$ and provide an easily computable formula for the number of runs. We give also a fast algorithm computing $\rho(w)$ in time linear with respect to the length of the directive sequence defining w: this gives an algorithm efficient with respect to the compressed size of the input.

2   Morphic Representations and the Numbers $N_\gamma(k)$

Essentially we use an idea of a *reduction sequence* introduced in [8]. The computation of runs in $S(\gamma_0, \gamma_1, \ldots, \gamma_n)$ is reduced to a computation for $S(\gamma_1, \gamma_2, \ldots, \gamma_n)$. The relation between $S(\gamma_0, \gamma_1, \ldots, \gamma_n)$ and $S(\gamma_1, \gamma_2, \ldots, \gamma_n)$ is described in terms of morphisms transforming one of them to the other.

For $\gamma = (\gamma_0, \gamma_1, \ldots, \gamma_n)$ define the sequence of morphisms:

$$h_i(a) = a^{\gamma_i}b, \quad h_i(b) = a, \quad \text{for } 0 \leq i \leq n$$

Lemma 1. *Assume* $0 \leq i < n$. *We have*

$$S(\gamma_n) = h_n(a), \quad S(\gamma_i, \gamma_{i+1} \ldots, \gamma_n) = h_i\big(S(\gamma_{i+1}, \gamma_{i+2} \ldots, \gamma_n)\big).$$

Let $|w|_r$ denote the number of occurrences of a letter $r \in \{a, b\}$ in the word w. Denote

$$N_\gamma(k) \;=\; |S(\gamma_k, \gamma_{k+1}, \ldots \gamma_n)|_a, \;\; M_\gamma(k) \;=\; |S(\gamma_k, \gamma_{k+1}, \ldots \gamma_n)|_b$$

The numbers $N_\gamma(k)$, $M_\gamma(k)$ satisfy the equation:

$$N_\gamma(k) \;=\; \gamma_k \, N_\gamma(k+1) + N_\gamma(k+2); \;\; M_\gamma(k) \;=\; N_\gamma(k+1) \tag{3}$$

Observation. In case of the directive sequence $(1, 1, \ldots, 1)$ describing the Fibonacci word the numbers $N_\gamma(k)$ are Fibonacci numbers, since the number of letters a in fib_n equals the size of fib_{n-1}.

Example 2. For the word $S(1, 2, 1, 3, 1) \;=\; ababaababababaabababaabababaababaab$ from Figure 1 we have $\gamma \;=\; (1, 2, 1, 3, 1)$ and:

$$S(1) = ab, \; S(3, 1) = aaaba, \; S(1, 3, 1) = (ab)^3 a \, ab,$$

$$N_\gamma(3) = |S(3, 1)|_a = 4, \; N_\gamma(2) = |S(1, 3, 1)|_a = 5$$

Lemma 2. *Let* $A \;=\; N_\gamma(2)$, $B \;=\; N_\gamma(3)$ *and* $w \;=\; S(\gamma_0, \gamma_1, \ldots, \gamma_n)$. *Then*

$$|w| \;=\; ((\gamma_0 + 1) \, \gamma_1 + 1) \, A \;+\; (\gamma_0 + 1) \, B$$

Proof. We have $|w| \;=\; N_\gamma(0) + M_\gamma(0)$ and $M_\gamma(0) = N_\gamma(1)$. Hence $|w| \;=\; N_\gamma(0) + N_\gamma(1)$ and by equation (3):

$$|w| = \gamma_0 N_\gamma(1) + (\gamma_1 + 1) N_\gamma(2) + N_\gamma(3).$$

Now Equation (3) directly implies the thesis.

For our example word $A = 5$, $B = 4$, $\gamma_0 = 1$, $\gamma_1 = 2$. The formula gives the number $(4 + 1) \, 5 + 8 = 33$, which is the correct length of $S(1, 2, 1, 3, 1)$.

3   Counting Runs and Repetition Ratios in Standard Words

We introduce a zero-one function $unary$ testing if the number equals 1,

$$\text{if } x = 1 \text{ then } unary(x) = 1 \text{ else } unary(x) = 0.$$

Similarly define zero-one functions $even(k)$ and $odd(k)$ with the value equal 1 iff k is even (odd respectively).

We use the following notation in this section:

$$A \;=\; N_\gamma(2) \;=\; |S(\gamma_2, \gamma_3 \ldots, \gamma_n)|_a, \; B \;=\; N_\gamma(3) \;=\; |S(\gamma_3, \gamma_4 \ldots, \gamma_n)|_a$$

$$\Delta(\gamma) = n - 1 - (\gamma_1 + \ldots + \gamma_n) - unary(\gamma_n).$$

The following theorem will be proven later.

Theorem 1. [Formula for the number of runs]
Let $n \geq 3$ and $\gamma = (\gamma_0, \ldots, \gamma_n)$. Then the number of runs in $S(\gamma)$ equals

$$
\rho(\gamma) = \begin{cases}
2\,A + 2\,B + \Delta(\gamma) - 1 & \text{if } \gamma_0 = \gamma_1 = 1 \\
(\gamma_1 + 2)\,A + B + \Delta(\gamma) - odd(n) & \text{if } \gamma_0 = 1;\ \gamma_1 > 1 \\
2A + 3B + \Delta(\gamma) - even(n) & \text{if } \gamma_0 > 1;\ \gamma_1 = 1 \\
(2\,\gamma_1 + 1)\,A + 2\,B + \Delta(\gamma) & Otherwise
\end{cases}
$$

Example 3. We now show how to compute $\rho(1, 2, 1, 3, 1)$, using our formula, for the word shown in Figure 1. In this case

$$\gamma = (\gamma_0, \gamma_1\gamma_2, \gamma_3, \gamma_4) = (1, 2, 1, 3, 1) \text{ and } n = 4$$

$$A = N_\gamma(2) = 5,\ B = N_\gamma(3) = 4,\ \Delta = (4 - 1) - 8 = -5,\ odd(4) = 0$$

Theorem 1 implies correctly (see Figure 1):

$$\rho(\gamma) = (\gamma_1 + 2)A + B + \Delta - odd(4) = 4A + B - 5 = 4 \cdot 5 + 4 - 5 = 19.$$

Example 4. As the next example derive the formula for the number of runs in Fibonacci word $fib_n = S(1, 1, \ldots, 1)$ (n ones) for $n \geq 3$. Let F_n be the n-th Fibonacci number. In this case $N_\gamma(k) = F_{n-k-1}$. According to formula from Theorem 1 we have

$$\rho(fib_n) = 2N_\gamma(2) + 2N_\gamma(3) + n - 1 - n - 1 - 1$$

$$= 2\,F_{n-3} + 2\,F_{n-4} - 3 = 2\,F_{n-2} - 3.$$

Theorem 2. $\rho(w) \leq \frac{4}{5}\,|w|$ *for each $w \in S$*

Proof. The easy when $n \leq 2$ can be considered separately, we omit a simple proof for this case. Assume now that $n \geq 3$ and consider 4 cases.

Let $w = S(\gamma_0, \ldots, \gamma_n)$. Observe that $\Delta(\gamma) \leq 0$.

Case 1: $\gamma_0 = \gamma_1 = 1$. We have, due to Lemma 2: $|w| = 3A + 2B$.
According to Theorem 1 we have $\rho(\gamma) \leq 2\,A + 2\,B$. Then

$$\frac{\rho(w)}{|w|} \leq \frac{2A + 2B}{3A + 2B} \leq \frac{4}{5}$$

due to inequalities $A \geq B \geq 1$. This completes the proof in this case.

Case 2: $\gamma_0 = 1;\ \gamma_1 > 1$. We have, due to Lemma 2:

$$|w| = (2\,\gamma_1 + 1)\,A + 2B$$

We have also, due to Theorem 1, that $\rho(w) \leq (\gamma_1 + 2)\,A + B$. Consequently:

$$\frac{\rho(w)}{|w|} \leq \frac{(\gamma_1 + 2)\,A + B}{(2\,\gamma_1 + 1)\,A + 2B} \leq \frac{4}{5}$$

because $\gamma_1 \geq 2$ and $\frac{\gamma_1 + 2}{2\,\gamma_1 + 1} \leq \frac{4}{5}$.

Case 3: $\gamma_0 > 1$; $\gamma_1 = 1$. In this case we have $\rho(w) \leq 2A + 3B$, due to Theorem 1, and , due to Lemma 2,

$$|w| = (\gamma_0 + 2) A + (\gamma_0 + 1) B \geq 4A + 3B$$

Consequently we have

$$\frac{\rho(w)}{|w|} \leq \frac{2A + 3B}{4A + 3B} \leq \frac{3A + 2B}{4A + 3B} \leq \frac{3}{4}$$

Case 4: $\gamma_0 > 1$; $\gamma_1 > 1$. In this case, due to Theorem 1 and Lemma 2, we have

$$\rho(w) \leq (2\,\gamma_1 + 1) A + 2\,B,$$

$$|w| = \big((\gamma_0 + 1)\,\gamma_1 + 1\big) A + (\gamma_0 + 1) B.$$

We have

$$\frac{\rho(w)}{|w|} \leq \frac{(2\,\gamma_1 + 1) A + 2\,B}{\big((\gamma_0 + 1)\,\gamma_1 + 1\big) A + (\gamma_0 + 1) B} \leq \frac{(2\,\gamma_1 + 1) A + 2\,B}{(3\,\gamma_1 + 1) A + 3\,B} \leq \frac{4}{5}$$

because

$$\frac{2\,\gamma_1 + 1}{3\,\gamma_1 + 1} \leq \frac{4}{5}$$

This completes the proof.

Theorem 3

For the class $\mathcal{S}$ of standard words we have
$$\sup\{\, \tfrac{\rho(w)}{|w|} \; : \; w \in \mathcal{S}\,\} = 0.8.$$

Proof. Let

$$w_k = S(1, 2, k, k) = \big((ababa)^k\, ab\big)^k ababa,$$

see the figure 2 for the case $k = 3$. We have $|w_k| = 5k^2 + 2k + 5$. Theorem 1 implies that $|\rho(1, 2, k, k)| = 4k^2 - k + 3$. Consequently

$$\lim_{k \to \infty} \frac{\rho(w_k)}{|w_k|} = \lim_{k \to \infty} \frac{4k^2 - k + 3}{5k^2 + 2k + 5} = 0.8$$

Theorem 4

We can count number of runs in standard word $S(\gamma_0, \ldots, \gamma_n)$ in time $O(n)$.

Proof. We need only to compute in $O(n)$ time the numbers $N_\gamma(k)$ for $k = 1, 2, 3$. We can compute it iterating Equation 2.

```
Algorithm Compute N_γ(k);
x := 1; y := 0;
for i := n downto k do
    (x, y) := (γ_i · x + y, x)
return x;
```

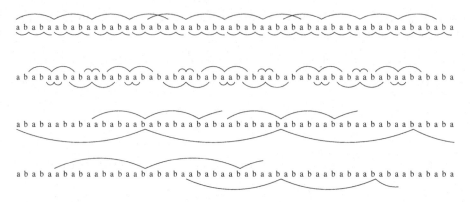

Fig. 2. The structure of runs of $S(1, 2, k, k)$ for $k = 3$, there are $4k^2 - k + 3 = 36$ runs

4   The Proof of Theorem 1

We assume now that x_i are as given by recurrences described in Equations 1,2. The structure of subword graphs for standard Sturmian words is very special [14,13], in particular it implies the following fact.

Lemma 3. [Structural Lemma]
The period of each run of $S(\gamma_0, \gamma_1, \ldots, \gamma_n)$ is of the form $x_i^j x_{i-1}$, where $0 \le j < \gamma_i$.

We say that a run is **short** if the length of its period does not exceed $|x_1|$, **large** if the period exceeds $|x_2|$, and **medium** otherwise. Denote by $\rho_{short}(\gamma)$, $\rho_{med}(\gamma)$, $\rho_{large}(\gamma)$ the number of short, medium and large runs in $S(\gamma)$, respectively. For example we have 10 short, 8 medium and 1 large run in Figure 1.

Lemma 4. [Short Runs] *The number of short runs in $S(\gamma)$ is*

$$\rho_{short}(\gamma) = \begin{cases} N_\gamma(2) + N_\gamma(3) - 1 & \text{if } \gamma_0 = \gamma 1 = 1 \\ 2\,N_\gamma(2) - odd(n) & \text{if } \gamma_0 = 1; \gamma 1 > 1 \\ N_\gamma(1) + N_\gamma(3) - even(n) & \text{if } \gamma_0 > 1; \gamma 1 = 1 \\ N_\gamma(1) + N_\gamma(2) & \text{otherwise} \end{cases}$$

Proof. We estimate separately numbers of runs with periods x_0 and x_1

Claim. Let $\gamma = (\gamma_0, \ldots, \gamma_n)$ be directive sequence. There are:

    (a) $N_\gamma(1)$ runs with period x_0 if $\gamma_0 > 1$,
    (b) $M_\gamma(1)$ runs with period x_0 if $\gamma_0 = 1$,
    (c) $N_\gamma(2)$ runs with period x_1 if $\gamma_1 > 1$,
    (d) $M_\gamma(2)$ runs with period x_1 if $\gamma_1 = 1$.

Point (a). Let us define morphism $h(a) = a^{\gamma_0} b$ and $h(b) = a$. Every run with period x_0 in $S(\gamma)$ is equal to a^{γ_0} or a^{γ_0+1}. Every such run is separated by the letter b and corresponds to the letter a in $h^{-1}(S(\gamma_0, \ldots, \gamma_n)) = S(\gamma_1, \ldots, \gamma_n)$.

Point (b). The proof of this point is similar to (a).

Points (c,d). A run with the period x_1 in $S(\gamma)$ corresponds to a run with the period x_0 in $h^{-1}(S(\gamma))$ and now validity of this case follows from points (a) and (b). This completes the proof of the claim and the lemma.

Lemma 5. [Medium Runs, n $\geq$ 3] *If $n \geq 3$ then*

$$\rho_{med}(\gamma) = N_\gamma(1) - N_\gamma(2) - \gamma_1 + 1$$

Proof. The thesis follows directly from the following stronger claim (the proof is omitted in this version)

Claim. Let $\gamma = (\gamma_0, \ldots, \gamma_n)$. There are:

(a) $N_\gamma(2) - 1$ runs with period $x_1^i x_0$ for each $0 < i < \gamma_1$.
(b) $N_\gamma(3)$ runs with period x_2.

The claim of the lemma follows by summing formulas from the points (a) and (b). We have

$$\left(N_\gamma(2) - 1\right)(\gamma_1 - 1) + N_\gamma(3) =$$
$$\left(\gamma_1 N_\gamma(2) + N_\gamma(3)\right) - N_\gamma(2) - \gamma_1 + 1 = N_\gamma(1) - N_\gamma(2) - \gamma_1 + 1$$

This completes the proof of the lemma.

Lemma 6. [Medium Runs, n=2] *If $n = 2$ then*

$$\rho_{med}(\gamma) = N_\gamma(1) - N_\gamma(2) - \gamma_1 + 1 - unary(\gamma_n)$$

Proof. The proof for the case $\gamma_n > 1$ is similar to the one for Lemma 5. In the case $\gamma_n = 1$ there are no intermediate runs, and we have to subtract $unary(\gamma_n) = 1$ in this case.

We reduce the problem of counting large runs to the one for counting medium runs, using the morphic representation of $S(\gamma)$. Let h be a morphism and let $y = a_1 a_2 \ldots a_t$ be a word of length t.

The morphism partitions $x = h(y)$ into segments $h(a_1)$, $h(a_2), \ldots, h(a_t)$. These segments are called here h-blocks.

We say that a subword w of x is **synchronized** with h in x iff each occurrence of w in x starts at the beginning of some h-block and ends at the end of some h-block. Figure 3 shows examples of synchronized and non-synchronized subwords with the morphism $h_0 : S(2,1,3,1) \to S(1,2,1,3,1)$ related to the morphic structure of $S(1,2,1,3,1)$. Recall that $h_0(a) = a^{\gamma_0} b$, $h_0(b) = a$.

Lemma 7. [Synchronization Lemma]
The large run-periods are synchronized with h_0 in $S(\gamma_0, \ldots, \gamma_n)$

Proof. We omit the proof of the following *syntactical* fact.

Claim

(a) If $i \geq 2$ then $x_i x_{i-1}$ ends with $a^{\gamma_0} b$ or with $(a^{\gamma_0} b)^{\gamma_1+1} a$
(b) a^{γ_1+2} is not a sub-word in $S(\gamma_1, \ldots, \gamma_n)$

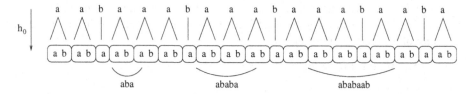

Fig. 3. The medium run-periods $x_1 x_0 = aba$ and $x_2 = ababa$ do not synchronize with h_0 on the string from Figure 1, while the large run-period $x_3 = ababaab$ is synchronized with h_0

In the inverse morphism h_0^{-1} the block $a^{\gamma_0} b$ goes to a and the block a goes to b. If the word starts and ends with $a^{\gamma_0} b$ then it is obviously synchronized with the morphism. The word $x_i x_{i-1}$, for $i \geq 2$, starts with $a^{\gamma_0} b$. The only problem is when it ends with a and this occurrence of a is followed by $a^{\gamma_0 - 1} b$. However, due to the point (a) of the claim, we have an occurrence of the sequence $(a^{\gamma_0} b)^{\gamma_1 + 2}$ in $S(\gamma_1, \ldots, \gamma_n)$. After applying the inverse of h_0 this sequence goes to $a^{\gamma_1 + 2}$ in $S(\gamma_1, \ldots, \gamma_n)$. However this is impossible due to point (b) of the claim. This completes the proof.

The following fact is implied by synchronization lemma.

Lemma 8.   [Recurrence Lemma]

$$\rho_{large}(\gamma_0, \gamma_1, \ldots, \gamma_n) = \rho_{large}(\gamma_1, \gamma_2, \ldots, \gamma_n) + \rho_{med}(\gamma_1, \gamma_2, \ldots, \gamma_n).$$

4.1   Completing the Proof of Theorem 1

The claim of the next lemma follows from Lemma 5 and the recurrence from Lemma 8.

Lemma 9. [Large Runs]

$$\rho_{large} + \rho_{med} = N_\gamma(1) + n - 1 - (\gamma_1 + \ldots + \gamma_n) - unary(\gamma_n)$$

Proof. According to Lemma 5 we have

$$\rho_{large} + \rho_{med} = \big(N_\gamma(1) - N_\gamma(2) - \gamma_1 + 1\big) +$$

$$\big(N_\gamma(2) - N_\gamma(3) - \gamma_2 + 1\big) + \ldots + \big(N_\gamma(n-1) - N_\gamma(n) - \gamma_{n-1} + 1 - unary(\gamma_n)\big)$$

$$= N_\gamma(1) + n - 1 - (\gamma_1 + \ldots + \gamma_n) - unary(\gamma_n),$$

since $N_\gamma(n) = \gamma_n$. This completes the proof.

Now the formula in Theorem 1 results by combining the formulas for ρ_{short} and for the sum $\rho_{large} + \rho_{med}$ using the equalities

$$\rho(\gamma) = \rho_{short}(\gamma) + \rho_{med}(\gamma) + \rho_{large}(\gamma), \text{ and } N_\gamma(1) = \gamma_1 N_\gamma(2) + N\gamma(3).$$

References

1. Baturo, P., Rytter, W.: Occurrence and lexicographic properties of standard Sturmian words. In: LATA 2007 (2007)
2. Berstel, J., Seebold, P.: Sturmian words. In: Lothaire, M. (ed.) Algebraic combinatorics on words. Encyclopedia of Mathematics and its Applications, ch.2, vol. 90, pp. 45–110. Cambridge University Press, Cambridge (2002)
3. Berstel, J., Karhumäki, J.: Combinatorics on words - a tutorial. Bull. EATCS 79, 178–228 (2003)
4. Iliopoulos, C., Moore, D., Smyth, W.F.: Characterization of the Squares in a Fibonacci String. Theor. Comput. Sci. 172(1-2), 281–291 (1997)
5. Crochemore, M., Ilie, L.: Analysis of Maximal Repetitions in Strings. In: Kučera, L., Kučera, A. (eds.) MFCS 2007. LNCS, vol. 4708, pp. 465–476. Springer, Heidelberg (2007)
6. Crochemore, M., Ilie, L., Tinta, I.: Towards a solution to the "runs" conjecture (to be published, CPM 2008)
7. Franek, F., Simpson, R.J., Smyth, W.F.: The maximum number of runs in a string. In: Miller, M., Park, K. (eds.) Proceeding of 14th Australian Workshop on Combinatorial Algorithms, pp. 26–35 (2003)
8. Franek, F., Karaman, A., Smyth, W.F.: Repetitions in Sturmian strings. Theoretical Computer Science 249(2), 289–303 (2000)
9. Kolpakov, R., Kucherov, G.: On Maximal Repetitions in Words. In: Ciobanu, G., Păun, G. (eds.) FCT 1999. LNCS, vol. 1684, pp. 374–385. Springer, Heidelberg (1999)
10. Kolpakov, R., Kucherov, G.: Finding Maximal Repetitions in a Word in Linear Time. In: FOCS 1999, pp. 596–604 (1999)
11. Rytter, W.: The number of runs in a string. Information and Computation 205(9), 1459–1469 (2007)
12. Rytter, W.: Grammar Compression, LZ-Encodings, and String Algorithms with Implicit Input. In: Díaz, J., Karhumäki, J., Lepistö, A., Sannella, D. (eds.) ICALP 2004. LNCS, vol. 3142, pp. 15–27. Springer, Heidelberg (2004)
13. Rytter, W.: The structure of subword graphs and suffix trees of Fibonacci words. Theoretical Computer Science 363(2), 211–223 (2006)
14. Sciortino, M., Zamboni, L.: Suffix Automata and Standard Sturmian Words. In: Harju, T., Karhumäki, J., Lepistö, A. (eds.) DLT 2007. LNCS, vol. 4588, pp. 382–398. Springer, Heidelberg (2007)
15. Smyth, B.: Computing patterns in strings. Addison Wesley, Reading (2003)

3-Way Composition
of Weighted Finite-State Transducers

Cyril Allauzen[1,*] and Mehryar Mohri[1,2]

[1] Courant Institute of Mathematical Sciences,
251 Mercer Street, New York, NY 10012, USA
[2] Google Research,
76 Ninth Avenue, New York, NY 10011, USA

Abstract. Composition of weighted transducers is a fundamental algorithm used in many applications, including for computing complex edit-distances between automata, or string kernels in machine learning, or to combine different components of a speech recognition, speech synthesis, or information extraction system. We present a generalization of the composition of weighted transducers, 3-*way composition*, which is dramatically faster in practice than the standard composition algorithm when combining more than two transducers. The worst-case complexity of our algorithm for composing three transducers T_1, T_2, and T_3 resulting in T, is $O(|T|_Q \min(d(T_1)d(T_3), d(T_2)) + |T|_E)$, where $| \cdot |_Q$ denotes the number of states, $| \cdot |_E$ the number of transitions, and $d(\cdot)$ the maximum out-degree. As in regular composition, the use of perfect hashing requires a pre-processing step with linear-time expected complexity in the size of the input transducers. In many cases, this approach significantly improves on the complexity of standard composition. Our algorithm also leads to a dramatically faster composition in practice. Furthermore, standard composition can be obtained as a special case of our algorithm. We report the results of several experiments demonstrating this improvement. These theoretical and empirical improvements significantly enhance performance in the applications already mentioned.

1 Introduction

Weighted finite-state transducers are widely used in text, speech, and image processing applications and other related areas such as information extraction [8,10,12,11,4]. They are finite automata in which each transition is augmented with an output label and some weight, in addition to the familiar (input) label [14,5,7]. The weights may represent probabilities, log-likelihoods, or they may be some other costs used to rank alternatives. They are, more generally, elements of a semiring [7].

Weighted transducers are used to represent models derived from large data sets using various statistical learning techniques such as pronunciation dictionaries, statistical grammars, string kernels, or complex edit-distance models

---

* This author's current address is: Google Research, 76 Ninth Avenue, New York, NY 10011.

O.H. Ibarra and B. Ravikumar (Eds.): CIAA 2008, LNCS 5148, pp. 262–273, 2008.

[11,6,2,3]. These models can be combined to create complex systems such as a speech recognition or information extraction system using a fundamental transducer algorithm, *composition of weighted transducers* [12,11]. Weighted composition is a generalization of the composition algorithm for unweighted finite-state transducers which consists of matching the output label of the transitions of one transducer with the input label of the transitions of another transducer. The weighted case is however more complex and requires the introduction of an ϵ-filter to avoid the creation of redundant ϵ-paths and preserve the correct path multiplicity [12,11]. The result is a new weighted transducer representing the relational composition of the two transducers.

Composition is widely used in computational biology, text and speech, and machine learning applications. In many of these applications, the transducers used are quite large, they may have as many as several hundred million states or transitions. A critical problem is thus to devise efficient algorithms for combining them. This paper presents a generalization of the composition of weighted transducer, 3-*way composition*, that is dramatically faster than the standard composition algorithm when combining more than two transducers. The complexity of composing three transducer T_1, T_2, and T_3, with the standard composition algorithm is $O(|T_1||T_2||T_3|)$ [12,11]. Using perfect hashing, the worst-case complexity of computing $T = (T_1 \circ T_2) \circ T_3$ using standard composition is

$$O(|T|_Q \min(d(T_3), d(T_1 \circ T_2)) + |T|_E + |T_1 \circ T_2|_Q \min(d(T_1), d(T_2)) + |T_1 \circ T_2|_E), \quad (1)$$

which may be prohibitive in some cases even when the resulting transducer T is not large but the intermediate transducer $T_1 \circ T_2$ is.[1] Instead, the worst-case complexity of our algorithm is

$$O(|T|_Q \min(d(T_1)d(T_3), d(T_2)) + |T|_E). \quad (2)$$

In both cases, the use of perfect hashing requires a pre-processing step with linear-time expected complexity in the size of the input transducers.

Our algorithm also leads to a dramatically faster computation of the result of composition in practice. We report the results of several experiments demonstrating this improvement. These theoretical and empirical improvements significantly enhance performance in a series of applications: string kernel-based algorithms in machine learning, the computation of complex edit-distances between automata, speech recognition and speech synthesis, and information extraction. Furthermore, as we shall see later, standard composition can be obtained as a special case of 3-way composition.

The main technical difficulty in the design of our algorithm is the definition of a *filter* to deal with a path multiplicity problem that arises in the presence of the empty string ϵ in the composition of three transducers. This problem, which we shall describe in detail, leads to a word combinatorial problem [13]. We will present two solutions for this problem: one requiring two ϵ-filters and a generalization of the ϵ-filters used for standard composition [12,11]; and another

---

[1] Moreover both $T_1 \circ T_2$ and $T_2 \circ T_3$ may be very large compared to T, hence both $(T_1 \circ T_2) \circ T_3$ and $T_1 \circ (T_2 \circ T_3)$ may be prohibitive.

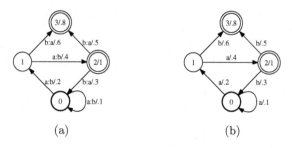

(a)   (b)

Fig. 1. (a) Example of a weighted transducer T. (b) Example of a weighted automaton A. $[\![T]\!](aab, bba) = [\![A]\!](aab) = .1 \times .2 \times .6 \times .8 + .2 \times .4 \times .5 \times .8$. A bold circle indicates an initial state and a double-circle a final state. The final weight $\rho[q]$ of a final state q is indicated after the slash symbol representing q.

direct and symmetric solution where a single filter is needed. Remarkably, this 3-way filter can be encoded as a finite automaton and painlessly integrated in our 3-way composition.

The remainder of the paper is structured as follows. Some preliminary definitions and terminology are introduced in the next section (Section 2). Section 3 describes our 3-way algorithm in the ϵ-free case. The word combinatorial problem of ϵ-path multiplicity and our solutions are presented in detail Section 4. Section 5 reports the results of experiments using the 3-way algorithm and compares them with the standard composition.

2   Preliminaries

This section gives the standard definition and specifies the notation used for weighted transducers.

Finite-state transducers are finite automata in which each transition is augmented with an output label in addition to the familiar input label [1,5]. Output labels are concatenated along a path to form an output sequence and similarly with input labels. *Weighted transducers* are finite-state transducers in which each transition carries some weight in addition to the input and output labels [14,7]. The weights are elements of a semiring, that is a ring that may lack negation [7]. Some familiar semirings are the tropical semiring $(\mathbb{R}_+ \cup \{\infty\}, \min, +, \infty, 0)$ related to classical shortest-paths algorithms, and the probability semiring $(\mathbb{R}, +, \cdot, 0, 1)$. A semiring is *idempotent* if for all $a \in \mathbb{K}$, $a \oplus a = a$. It is *commutative* when $\otimes$ is commutative. We will assume in this paper that the semiring used is commutative, which is a necessary condition for composition to be an efficient algorithm [10]. The following gives a formal definition of weighted transducers.

Definition 1. *A* weighted finite-state transducer T over $(\mathbb{K}, \oplus, \cdot, 0, 1)$ *is an 8-tuple* $T = (\Sigma, \Delta, Q, I, F, E, \lambda, \rho)$ *where* Σ *is the finite input alphabet of the transducer,* Δ *is the finite output alphabet,* Q *is a finite set of states,* $I \subseteq Q$ *the set of*

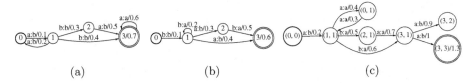

(a)   (b)   (c)

Fig. 2. Example of transducer composition. (a) Weighted transducer T_1 and (b) Weighted transducer T_2 over the probability semiring $(\mathbb{R}, +, \cdot, 0, 1)$. (c) Result of the composition of T_1 and T_2.

initial states, $F \subseteq Q$ the set of final states, $E \subseteq Q \times (\Sigma \cup \{\epsilon\}) \times (\Delta \cup \{\epsilon\}) \times \mathbb{K} \times Q$ a finite set of transitions, $\lambda : I \to \mathbb{K}$ the initial weight function, and $\rho : F \to \mathbb{K}$ the final weight function mapping F to $\mathbb{K}$.

The weight of a path π is obtained by multiplying the weights of its constituent transitions using the multiplication rule of the semiring and is denoted by $w[\pi]$. The weight of a pair of input and output strings (x, y) is obtained by $\oplus$-summing the weights of the paths labeled with (x, y) from an initial state to a final state.

For a path π, we denote by $p[\pi]$ its origin state and by $n[\pi]$ its destination state. We also denote by $P(I, x, y, F)$ the set of paths from the initial states I to the final states F labeled with input string x and output string y. A transducer T is *regulated* if the output weight associated by T to any pair of strings (x, y):

$$T(x, y) = \bigoplus_{\pi \in P(I, x, y, F)} \lambda(p[\pi]) \cdot w[\pi] \cdot \rho[n[\pi]] \tag{3}$$

is well-defined and in $\mathbb{K}$. $T(x, y) = \overline{0}$ when $P(I, x, y, F) = \emptyset$. If for all $q \in Q$ $\bigoplus_{\pi \in P(q, \epsilon, \epsilon, q)} w[\pi] \in \mathbb{K}$, then T is regulated. In particular, when T does not admit any ϵ-cycle, it is regulated. The weighted transducers we will be considering in this paper will be regulated. Figure 1(a) shows an example.

The *composition* of two weighted transducers T_1 and T_2 with matching input and output alphabets Σ, is a weighted transducer denoted by $T_1 \circ T_2$ when the sum:

$$(T_1 \circ T_2)(x, y) = \bigoplus_{z \in \Sigma^*} T_1(x, z) \otimes T_2(z, y) \tag{4}$$

is well-defined and in $\mathbb{K}$ for all $x, y \in \Sigma^*$ [14,7]. *Weighted automata* can be defined as weighted transducers A with identical input and output labels, for any transition. Thus, only pairs of the form (x, x) can have a non-zero weight by A, which is why the weight associated by A to (x, x) is abusively denoted by $A(x)$ and identified with the *weight associated by A to x*. Similarly, in the graph representation of weighted automata, the output (or input) label is omitted.

3 Epsilon-Free Composition

3.1 Standard Composition

Let us start with a brief description of the standard composition algorithm for weighted transducers [12,11]. States in the composition $T_1 \circ T_2$ of two weighted transducers T_1 and T_2 are identified with pairs of a state of T_1 and a state of T_2. Leaving aside transitions with ϵ inputs or outputs, the following rule specifies how to compute a transition of $T_1 \circ T_2$ from appropriate transitions of T_1 and T_2: (q_1, a, b, w_1, q_2) and $(q'_1, b, c, w_2, q'_2) \Longrightarrow ((q_1, q'_1), a, c, w_1 \otimes w_2, (q_2, q'_2))$.

Figure 2 illustrates the algorithm. In the worst case, all transitions of T_1 leaving a state q_1 match all those of T_2 leaving state q'_1, thus the space and time complexity of composition is quadratic: $O(|T_1||T_2|)$. However, using perfect hashing on the input transducer with the highest out-degree leads to a worst-case complexity of $O(|T_1 \circ T_2|_Q \min(d(T_1), d(T_2)) + |T_1 \circ T_2|_E)$. The pre-processing step required for hashing the transitions of the transducer with the highest out-degree has an expected complexity in $O(|T_1|_E)$ if $d(T_1) > d(T_2)$ and $O(|T_2|_E)$ otherwise.

The main problem with the standard composition algorithm is the following. Assume that one wishes to compute $T_1 \circ T_2 \circ T_3$, say for example by proceeding left to right. Thus, first T_1 and T_2 are composed to compute $T_1 \circ T_2$ and then the result is composed with T_3. The worst-case complexity of that computation is:

$$O(|T_1 \circ T_2 \circ T_3|_Q \min(d(T_1 \circ T_2), d(T_3)) + |T_1 \circ T_2 \circ T_3|_E +$$
$$|T_1 \circ T_2|_Q \min(d(T_1), d(T_2)) + |T_1 \circ T_2|_E). \tag{5}$$

But, in many cases, computing $T_1 \circ T_2$ creates a very large number of transitions that may never match any transition of T_3. For example, T_2 may represent a complex edit-distance transducer, allowing all possible insertions, deletions, substitutions and perhaps other operations such as transpositions or more complex edits in T_1 all with different costs. Even when T_1 is a simple non-deterministic finite automaton with ϵ-transitions, which is often the case in the applications already mentioned, $T_1 \circ T_2$ will then have a very large number of paths, most of which will not match those of the non-deterministic automaton T_3. Both $T_1 \circ T_2$ and $T_2 \circ T_3$ would be much larger than T in this example. In other applications in speech recognition, or for the computation of kernels in machine learning, the central transducer T_2 could be far more complex and the set of transitions or paths of $T_1 \circ T_2$ not matching those of T_3 could be even larger.

3.2 3-Way Composition

The key idea behind our algorithm is precisely to avoid creating these unnecessary transitions by directly constructing $T_1 \circ T_2 \circ T_3$, which we refer to as a *3-way composition*. Thus, our algorithm does not include the intermediate step of creating $T_1 \circ T_2$ or $T_2 \circ T_3$. To do so, we can proceed following a *lateral* or *sideways strategy*: for each transition e_1 in T_1 and e_3 in T_3, we search for matching transitions in T_2.

The pseudocode of the algorithm in the ϵ-free case is given below. The algorithm computes T, the result of the composition $T_1 \circ T_2 \circ T_3$. It uses a queue S containing the set of pairs of states yet to be examined. The queue discipline of S can be arbitrarily chosen and does not affect the termination of the algorithm. Using a FIFO or LIFO discipline, the queue operations can be performed in constant time. We can pre-process the transducer T_2 in expected linear time $O(|T_2|_E)$ by using perfect hashing so that the transitions G (line 13) can be found in worst-case linear time $O(|G|)$. Thus, the worst-case running time complexity of the 3-way composition algorithm is in $O(|T|_Q d(T_1) d(T_3) + |T|_E)$, where T is transducer returned by the algorithm.

Alternatively, depending on the size of the three transducers, it may be advantageous to direct the 3-way composition from the center, i.e., ask for each transition e_2 in T_2 if there are matching transitions e_1 in T_1 and e_3 in T_3. We refer to this as the *central strategy* for our 3-way composition algorithm. Pre-processing the transducers T_1 and T_3 and creating hash tables for the transitions leaving each state (the expected complexity of this pre-processing being $O(|T_1|_E + |T_3|_E)$), this strategy leads to a worst-case running time complexity of $O(|T|_Q d(T_2) + |T|_E)$. The lateral and central strategies can be combined by using, at a state (q_1, q_2, q_3), the lateral strategy if $|E[q_1]| \cdot |E[q_3]| \leq |E[q_2]|$ and the central strategy otherwise. The algorithm leads to a natural lazy or on-demand implementation in which the transitions of the resulting transducer T are generated only as needed by other operations on T. The standard composition coincides with the 3-way algorithm when using the central strategy with either T_1 or T_2 equal to the identity transducer.

3-WAY-COMPOSITION(T_1, T_2, T_3)

```
1   Q ← I₁ × I₂ × I₃
2   S ← I₁ × I₂ × I₃
3   while S ≠ ∅ do
4       (q₁, q₂, q₃) ← HEAD(S)
5       DEQUEUE(S)
6       if (q₁, q₂, q₃) ∈ I₁ × I₂ × I₃ then
7           I ← I ∪ {(q₁, q₂, q₃)}
8           λ(q₁, q₂, q₃) ← λ₁(q₁) ⊗ λ₂(q₂) ⊗ λ₃(q₃)
9       if (q₁, q₂, q₃) ∈ F₁ × F₂ × F₃ then
10          F ← F ∪ {(q₁, q₂, q₃)}
11          ρ(q₁, q₂, q₃) ← ρ₁(q₁) ⊗ ρ₂(q₂) ⊗ ρ₃(q₃)
12      for each (e₁, e₃) ∈ E[q₁] × E[q₃] do
13          G ← {e ∈ E[q₂] : i[e] = o[e₁] ∧ o[e] = i[e₃]}
14          for each e₂ ∈ G do
15              if (n[e₁], n[e₂], n[e₃]) ∉ Q then
16                  Q ← Q ∪ {(n[e₁], n[e₂], n[e₃])}
17                  ENQUEUE(S, (n[e₁], n[e₂], n[e₃]))
18              E ← E ∪ {((q₁, q₂, q₃), i[e₁], o[e₃], w[e₁] ⊗ w[e₂] ⊗ w[e₃], (n[e₁], n[e₂], n[e₃]))}
19  return T
```

4   Epsilon Filtering

The algorithm described thus far cannot be readily used in most cases found in practice. In general, a transducer T_1 may have transitions with output label ϵ and T_2 transitions with input ϵ. A straightforward generalization of the ϵ-free case would generate redundant ϵ-paths and, in the case of non-idempotent semirings,

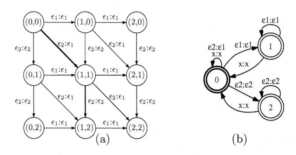

Fig. 3. (a) Redundant ϵ-paths. A straightforward generalization of the ϵ-free case could generate all the paths from $(0,0)$ to $(2,2)$ for example, even when composing just two simple transducers. (b) Filter transducer M allowing a unique ϵ-path.

would lead to an incorrect result, even just for composing two transducers. The weight of two matching ϵ-paths of the original transducers would be counted as many times as the number of redundant ϵ-paths generated in the result, instead of one. Thus, a crucial component of our algorithm consists of coping with this problem.

Figure 3(a) illustrates the problem just mentioned in the simpler case of two transducers. To match ϵ-paths leaving q_1 and those leaving q_2, a generalization of the ϵ-free composition can make the following moves: (1) first move forward on a transition of q_1 with output ϵ, or even a path with output ϵ, and stay at the same state q_2 in T_2, with the hope of later finding a transition whose output label is some label $a \neq \epsilon$ matching a transition of q_2 with the same input label; (2) proceed similarly by following a transition or path leaving q_2 with input label ϵ while staying at the same state q_1 in T_1; or, (3) match a transition of q_1 with output label ϵ with a transition of q_2 with input label ϵ.

Let us rename existing output ϵ-labels of T_1 as ϵ_2, and existing input ϵ-labels of T_2 ϵ_1, and let us augment T_1 with a self-loop labeled with ϵ_1 at all states and similarly, augment T_2 with a self-loop labeled with ϵ_2 at all states, as illustrated by Figures 5(a) and (c). These self-loops correspond to staying at the same state in that machine while consuming an ϵ-label of the other transition. The three moves just described now correspond to the matches (1) $(\epsilon_2 : \epsilon_2)$, (2) $(\epsilon_1 : \epsilon_1)$, and (3) $(\epsilon_2 : \epsilon_1)$. The grid of Figure 3(a) shows all the possible ϵ-paths between composition states. We will denote by $\tilde{T}_1$ and $\tilde{T}_2$ the transducers obtained after application of these changes.

For the result of composition to be correct, between any two of these states, all but one path must be disallowed. There are many possible ways of selecting that path. One natural way is to select the shortest path with the diagonal transitions (ϵ-matching transitions) taken first. Figure 3(a) illustrates in bold-face the path just described from state $(0,0)$ to state $(1,2)$. Remarkably, this filtering mechanism itself can be encoded as a finite-state transducer such as the transducer M of Figure 3(b). We denote by $(p,q) \preceq (r,s)$ to indicate that (r,s) can be reached from (p,q) in the grid.

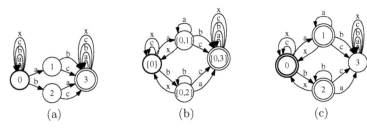

Fig. 4. (a) Finite automaton A representing the set of disallowed sequences. (b) Automaton B, result of the determinization of A. Subsets are indicated at each state. (c) Automaton C obtained from B by complementation, state 3 is not coaccessible.

Proposition 1. *Let M be the transducer of Figure 3(b). M allows a unique path between any two states (p, q) and (r, s), with $(p, q) \preceq (r, s)$.*

Proof. Let a denote $(\epsilon_1{:}\epsilon_1)$, b denote $(\epsilon_2{:}\epsilon_2)$, c denote $(\epsilon_2{:}\epsilon_1)$, and let x stand for any $(x{:}x)$, with $x \in \Sigma$. The following sequences must be disallowed by a shortest-path filter with matching transitions first: ab, ba, ac, bc. This is because, from any state, instead of the moves ab or ba, the matching or diagonal transition c can be taken. Similarly, instead of ac or bc, ca and cb can be taken for an earlier match. Conversely, it is clear from the grid or an immediate recursion that a filter disallowing these sequences accepts a unique path between two connected states of the grid.

Let L be the set of sequences over $\sigma = \{a, b, c, x\}$ that contain one of the disallowed sequence just mentioned as a substring that is $L = \sigma^*(ab + ba + ac + bc)\sigma^*$. Then $\overline{L}$ represents exactly the set of paths allowed by that filter and is thus a regular language. Let A be an automaton representing L (Figure 4(a)). An automaton representing $\overline{L}$ can be constructed from A by determinization and complementation (Figures 4(a)-(c)). The resulting automaton C is equivalent to the transducer M after removal of the state 3, which does not admit a path to a final state.   □

Thus, to compose two transducers T_1 and T_2 with ϵ-transitions, it suffices to compute $\tilde{T}_1 \circ M \circ \tilde{T}_2$, using the rules of composition in the ϵ-free case.

The problem of avoiding the creation of redundant ϵ-paths is more complex in 3-way composition since the ϵ-transitions of all three transducers must be taken into account. We describe two solutions for this problem, one based on two filters, another based on a single filter.

4.1   2-Way ϵ-Filters

One way to deal with this problem is to use the 2-way filter M, by first dealing with matching ϵ-paths in $U = (T_1 \circ T_2)$, and then $U \circ T_3$. However, in 3-way composition, it is possible to remain at the same state of T_1 and the same state of T_2, and move on an ϵ-transition of T_3, which previously was not an option. This corresponds to staying at the same state of U, while moving on a transition of T_3 with input ϵ. To account for this move, we introduce a new symbol ϵ_0 matching

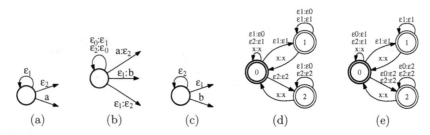

Fig. 5. Marking of transducers and 2-way filters. (a) $\tilde{T}_1$. Self-loop labeled with ϵ_1 added at all states of T_1, regular output ϵs renamed to ϵ_2. (b) $\tilde{T}_2$. Self-loops with labels $(\epsilon_0:\epsilon_1)$ and $(\epsilon_2:\epsilon_0)$ added at all states of T_2. Input ϵs are replaced by ϵ_1, output ϵs by ϵ_2. (c) $\tilde{T}_3$. Self-loop labeled with ϵ_2 added at all states of T_3, regular input ϵs renamed to ϵ_1. (d) Left-to-right filter M_1. (e) Left-to-right filter M_2.

ϵ_1 in T_3. But, we must also ensure the existence of a self-loop with output label ϵ_0 at all states of U. To do so, we augment the filter M with self-loops $(\epsilon_1:\epsilon_0)$ and the transducer T_2 with self-loops $(\epsilon_0:\epsilon_1)$ (see Figure 5(b)). Figure 5(d) shows the resulting filter transducer M_1. From Figures 5(a)-(c), it is clear that $\tilde{T}_1 \circ M_1 \circ \tilde{T}_2$ will have precisely a self-loop labeled with $(\epsilon_1:\epsilon_1)$ at all states.

In the same way, we must allow for moving forward on a transition of T_1 with output ϵ, that is consuming ϵ_2, while remaining at the same states of T_2 and T_3. To do so, we introduce again a new symbol ϵ_0 this time only relevant for matching T_2 with T_3, add self-loops $(\epsilon_2:\epsilon_0)$ to T_2, and augment the filter M by adding a transition labeled with $(\epsilon_0:\epsilon_2)$ (resp. $(\epsilon_0:\epsilon_1)$) wherever there used to be one labeled with $(\epsilon_2:\epsilon_2)$ (resp. $(\epsilon_2:\epsilon_1)$). Figure 5(e) shows the resulting filter transducer M_2.

Thus, the composition $\tilde{T}_1 \circ M_1 \circ \tilde{T}_2 \circ M_2 \circ \tilde{T}_3$ ensures the uniqueness of matching ϵ-paths. In practice, the modifications of the transducers T_1, T_2, and T_3 to generate $\tilde{T}_1$, $\tilde{T}_2$, and $\tilde{T}_3$, as well as the filters M_1 and M_2 can be directly simulated or encoded in the 3-way composition algorithm for greater efficiency. The states in T become quintuples $(q_1, q_2, q_3, f_1, f_2)$ with f_1 and f_2 are states of the filters M_1 and M_2. The introduction of self-loops and marking of ϵs can be simulated (line 12-13) and the filter states f_1 and f_2 taken into account to compute the set G of the transition matches allowed (line 13).

Note that while 3-way composition is symmetric, the analysis of ϵ-paths just presented is left-to-right and the filters M_1 and M_2 are not symmetric. In fact, we could similarly define right-to-left filters M_1' and M_2'. The advantage of the filters presented in this section is however that they can help modify easily an existing implementation of composition into 3-way composition. The filters needed for the 3-way case are also straightforward generalizations of the ϵ-filter used in standard composition.

4.2   3-Way ϵ-Filter

There exists however a direct and symmetric method for dealing with ϵ-paths in 3-way composition. Remarkably, this can be done using a single filter automaton

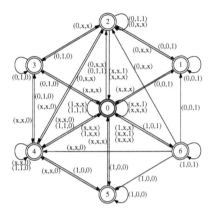

Fig. 6. 3-way matching ϵ-filter W

whose labels are 3-dimensional vectors. Figure 6 shows a filter W that can be used for that purpose. Each transition is labeled with a triplet. The ith element of the triplet corresponding to the move on the ith transducer. 0 indicates staying at the same state or not moving, 1 that a move is made reading an ϵ-transition, and x a move along a matching transition with a non-empty symbol (i.e., non-ϵ output in T_1, non-ϵ input or output in T_2 and non-ϵ input in T_3).

Matching ϵ-paths now correspond to a three-dimensional grid, which leads to a more complex word combinatorics problem. As in the two-dimensional case, $(p, q, r) \preceq (s, t, u)$ indicates that (s, t, u) can be reached from (p, q, r) in the grid. Several filters are possible, here we will again favor the matching of ϵ-transitions (i.e. the diagonals on the grid).

Proposition 2. *The filter automaton W allows a unique path between any two states (p, q, r) and (s, t, u) of a three-dimensional grid, with $(p, q, r) \preceq (s, t, u)$.*

Proof. Due to lack of space, we give a sketch of the proof, which is similar to that of Proposition 1. As in that proof, we can enumerate disallowed sequences of triplets. The triplet $(0, 0, 0)$ is always forbidden since it corresponds to remaining at the same state in all three transducers. Observe that in two consecutive triplets, for $i \in [1, 3]$, 0 in the ith machine of the first triplet cannot be followed by 1 in the second. Indeed, as in the 2-way case, if we stay at a state, then we must remain at that state until a match with a non-empty symbol is made. Also, two 0s in adjacent transducers (T_1 and T_2, or T_2 and T_3), cannot become both xs unless all components become xs. For example, the sequence $(0, 0, 1)(x, x, 1)$ is disallowed since instead $(x, x, 1)(0, 0, 1)$ with an earlier match can be followed. Similarly, the sequence $(0, 0, 1)(x, x, 0)$ is disallowed since instead the single and shorter move $(x, x, 1)$ can be taken. Conversely, it is not hard to see that a filter disallowing these sequences accepts a unique path between two connected states of the grid.

Thus, a filter can be obtained by taking the complement of the automaton accepting the sequences admitting such forbidden substrings. The resulting deterministic and minimal automaton is exactly the filter W shown in Figure 6. □

Table 1. Comparison of 3-way composition with standard composition. The computation times are reported in seconds, the size of T_2 in number of transitions. These experiments were performed on a dual-core AMD Opteron 2.2GHz with 16GB of memory, using the same software library and basic infrastructure.

| | n-gram Kernel | | | | | | Edit distance | |
	≤ 2	≤ 3	≤ 4	≤ 5	≤ 6	≤ 7	standard	+transpositions
Standard	65.3	68.3	71.0	73.5	76.3	78.3	586.1	913.5
3-way	8.0	8.1	8.2	8.2	8.2	8.2	3.8	5.9
Size of T_2	70K	100K	130K	160K	190K	220K	25M	75M

The filter W is used as follows. A triplet state (q_1, q_2, q_3) in 3-way composition is augmented with a state r of the filter automaton W, starting with state 0 of W. The transitions of the filter W at each state r determine the matches or moves allowed for that state (q_1, q_2, q_3, r) of the composed machine.

5   Experiments

This section reports the results of experiments carried out in two different applications: the computation of a complex edit-distance between two automata, as motivated by applications in text and speech processing [9], and the computation of kernels between automata needed in spoken-dialog classification and other machine learning tasks.

In the edit-distance case, the standard transducer T_2 used was one based on all insertions, deletions, and substitutions with different costs [9]. A more realistic transducer T_2 was one augmented with all transpositions, e.g., $ab \rightarrow ba$, with different costs. In the kernel case, n-gram kernels with varying n-gram order were used [3].

Table 1 shows the results of these experiments. The finite automata T_1 and T_3 used were extracted from real text and speech processing tasks. The results show that in all cases, 3-way composition is orders of magnitude faster than standard composition.

6   Conclusion

We presented a general algorithm for the composition of weighted finite-state transducers. In many instances, 3-way composition benefits from a significantly better time and space complexity. Our experiments with both complex edit-distance computations arising in a number of applications in text and speech processing, and with kernel computations, crucial to many machine learning algorithms applied to sequence prediction, show that our algorithm is also substantially faster than standard composition in practice. We expect 3-way composition to further improve efficiency in a variety of other areas and applications in which weighted composition of transducers is used.[2]

References

1. Berstel, J.: Transductions and Context-Free Languages. Teubner (1979)
2. Chen, S., Goodman, J.: An empirical study of smoothing techniques for language modeling. Technical Report, TR-10-98, Harvard University (1998)
3. Cortes, C., Haffner, P., Mohri, M.: Rational Kernels: Theory and Algorithms. Journal of Machine Learning Research 5, 1035–1062 (2004)
4. Culik II, K., Kari, J.: Digital Images and Formal Languages. In: Rozenberg, G., Salomaa, A. (eds.) Handbook of Formal Languages, vol. 3, pp. 599–616. Springer, Heidelberg (1997)
5. Eilenberg, S.: Automata, Languages and Machines. Academic Press, London (1974–1976)
6. Katz, S.M.: Estimation of probabilities from sparse data for the language model component of a speech recogniser. IEEE Transactions on Acoustic, Speech, and Signal Processing 35(3), 400–401 (1987)
7. Kuich, W., Salomaa, A.: Semirings, Automata, Languages. Springer, Heidelberg (1986)
8. Mohri, M.: Finite-State Transducers in Language and Speech Processing. Computational Linguistics 23(2) (1997)
9. Mohri, M.: Edit-Distance of Weighted Automata: General Definitions and Algorithms. Int. J. Found. Comput. Sci. 14(6), 957–982 (2003)
10. Mohri, M.: Statistical Natural Language Processing. In: Lothaire, M. (ed.) Applied Combinatorics on Words. Cambridge University Press, Cambridge (2005)
11. Mohri, M., Pereira, F.C.N., Riley, M.: Weighted Automata in Text and Speech Processing. In: Proceedings of the 12th biennial European Conference on Artificial Intelligence (ECAI 1996). John Wiley and Sons, Chichester (1996)
12. Pereira, F., Riley, M.: Finite State Language Processing. In: Speech Recognition by Composition of Weighted Finite Automata. The MIT Press, Cambridge (1997)
13. Perrin, D.: Words. In: Lothaire, M. (ed.) Combinatorics on words, Cambridge Mathematical Library. Cambridge University Press, Cambridge (1997)
14. Salomaa, A., Soittola, M.: Automata-Theoretic Aspects of Formal Power Series. Springer, Heidelberg (1978)

---

[2] The research of Cyril Allauzen and Mehryar Mohri was partially supported by the New York State Office of Science Technology and Academic Research (NYSTAR). This project was also sponsored in part by the Department of the Army Award Number W81XWH-04-1-0307. The U.S. Army Medical Research Acquisition Activity, 820 Chandler Street, Fort Detrick MD 21702-5014 is the awarding and administering acquisition office. The content of this material does not necessarily reflect the position or the policy of the Government and no official endorsement should be inferred.

Progressive Solutions to FSM Equations

Khaled El-Fakih[1] and Nina Yevtushenko[2,*]

[1] Verimag, University Joseph Fourier (France), American University of Sharjah (UAE)
[2] Tomsk State University (Russia)
elfakih@imag.fr, yevtushenko@elefot.tsu.ru

Abstract. The *equation solving* problem is to derive the behavior of the unknown component X knowing the joint behavior of the other components (or the context) C and the specification of the overall system S. The component X can be derived by solving the Finite State Machine (FSM) equation $C \lozenge X \sim S$, where $\lozenge$ is the parallel composition operator and $\sim$ is the trace equivalence or the trace reduction relation. A solution X to an FSM equation is called *progressive* if for every external input sequence the composition $C \lozenge X$ does not fall into a livelock without an exit. In this paper, we formally define the notion of a progressive solution to a parallel FSM equation and present an algorithm that derives a largest progressive solution (if a progressive solution exists). In addition, we generalize the work to a system of FSM equations. Application examples are provided.

1 Introduction

The equation solving problem can be formulated as solving an equation $C \lozenge X \sim S$, where $\lozenge$ is a composition operator and $\sim$ is a conformance relation. Usually the behavior of X, S, and A, is represented using finite state models such as finite state automata, I/O automata, Labeled Transition Systems (LTSs), and Finite Sate Machines (FSMs) [for references, see, for example, 1, 2]. The conformance relation $\sim$ often is the trace equivalence relation, denoted $\cong$, or the trace containment (or reduction) relation, denoted $\leq$, and the composition operator is either the synchronous $\bullet$ or the parallel $\lozenge$ composition operator. The applications of the equation solving problem were considered in the context of the design of communication protocols and protocol converters, selection of test cases, and the design of controllers for discrete event systems.

If an equation has a solution, then it is known to have a largest solution that includes all other solutions [3]. However, not every solution of a largest solution is of a practical use. Usually, we are interested in so-called *progressive solutions* [3, 4] where for every external input sequence the composition $C \lozenge X$ does not fall into a livelock without an exit. If an automata equation has a progressive solution then the equation is known to have a largest progressive solution [1] that contains all progressive solutions. However, not each solution of a largest progressive solution is

* The second author acknowledges the support of RFBR-NSC grant 06-08-89500.

O.H. Ibarra and B. Ravikumar (Eds.): CIAA 2008, LNCS 5148, pp. 274–282, 2008.

progressive. The problem of deriving and characterizing progressive solutions has been studied for I/O automata, finite automata, and for FSMs over the synchronous composition operator.

In the first part of this paper, we first, define the notion of a progressive solution for the FSM equation $C \Diamond X \cong S$ and for the FSM inequality $C \Diamond X \le S$ [2, 3]. Given, possibly non-deterministic, FSMs context C and specification S, we present an algorithm that provides a largest complete progressive FSM solution to the equation $C \Diamond X \cong S$ (inequality $C \Diamond X \le S$) if the equation (the inequality) has a progressive solution. A largest progressive solution is derived by trimming a proper largest solution. We note that the results [2] obtained for deriving a progressive solution in the area of finite automata cannot be directly applied for deriving a progressive solution over FSMs, since, by definition, a progressive solution to an FSM equation can block output actions allowed by the specification. Moreover, in this paper, we propose a simpler algorithm for deriving a largest progressive solution than that for automata equations [1]. In addition, the results obtained for deriving a progressive solution of an FSM equation over the synchronous composition operator [4] cannot be directly applied for deriving a progressive solution over the parallel composition operator, since the notions of the parallel and synchronous composition operators are different; the parallel composition operator allows to produce an external output not directly after external input but, possibly after a sequence of internal actions.

In some application areas, given a finite set of $k > 1$ contexts C_i and service specifications S_i, one is interested in finding a solution (the unknown component) X that combined with C_i meets the specification S_i, for $i = 1, ..., k$. The problem of finding such a solution X is the problem of solving a *system of equations*. A largest solution to a system of FSM equations can be derived as given in [5]. In the second part of this paper, we deal with a progressive solution to a system of FSM equations. A largest progressive solution to the system of equations is derived by intersecting largest progressive solutions of every equation and then by deriving the largest submachine of this intersection that is progressive for every equation.

2 Preliminaries

Finite State Machine (FSMs). A FSM, or *machine* hereafter, is a quintuple $A = \langle S, I, O, T_A, s_0 \rangle$, where S is a finite nonempty set of states with the initial state s_0, I and O are input and output alphabets, and $T_A \subseteq S \times I \times O \times S$ is a transition relation. In this paper, we consider only *observable* FSMs, i.e. for each triple $(s,i,o) \in S \times I \times O$ there exists at most one state $n \in S$ such that $(s,i,n,o) \in T$. An FSM A is called *complete*, if $\forall s \in S$ and $\forall i \in I$ $\exists o \in O$ and $\exists s' \in S$, such that $(s, i,o, s') \in T_A$. If A is not complete, then it is called *partial*. An FSM A is called *deterministic*, if $\forall s \in S$ and $\forall i \in I$ there exist at most one pair of output o and state s', such that $(s, i,o, s') \in T_A$. An FSM $B = (Q,I,O,T_B,q_0)$ is a sub-machine of A if $Q \subseteq S$ and $T_B \subseteq T_A$. The *largest complete submachine* of FSM A can be obtained by iterative deleting states where the behavior of the FSM is not defined at least for a single input. Each complete sub-machine of A is a submachine of the largest complete sub-machine of A (if it exists). As usual, the transition relation T_A of FSM $A = \langle S, I, O, T_A, s_0 \rangle$ can be extended to sequences over the alphabet I. In this paper, we consider only initially connected FSMs, i.e., each state of an FSM is reachable from the initial state.

Given an FSM A, the set of all I/O sequences generated at state s of A is called the *language* of A *generated at state* s, or simply the set of I/O sequences at s, written $L_s(A)$. The language, generated by the FSM A at the initial state is called the language of the FSM A and is denoted by $L(A)$, for short. The FSM $\langle \{t_0\}, I, O, T, t_0 \rangle$, denoted $MAX(I,O)$, where $T = \{t_0\} \times I \times O \times \{t_0\}$, is called *maximum* over the input alphabet I and the output alphabet O. The maximum machine $MAX(I,O)$ accepts the language $(IO)^*$. An FSM $B = \langle Q, I, O, T_B, q_0 \rangle$ is a *reduction* of FSM $A = \langle S, I, O, T_A, s_0 \rangle$, written $A \leq B$, if $L_B \subseteq L_A$. If $L_B = L_A$ then FSMs A and B are *equivalent*. For complete deterministic FSMs the reduction and the equivalence relations coincide.

The common behavior of two FSMs can be described by the intersection of these machines. The *intersection* $A \cap B$ of FSMs $A = \langle S, I, O, T_A, s_0 \rangle$ and $B = \langle Q, I, O, T_B, q_0 \rangle$ is the largest connected sub-machine of the FSM $\langle S \times Q, I, O, T_{A \cap B}, s_0 q_0 \rangle$. Formally, $T_{A \cap B} = \{(sq, i, o, s'q') \mid (s, i, o, s') \in T_A \wedge (q, i, o, q') \in T_B\}$. The language of $A \cap B$ is the intersection $L(A) \cap L(B)$. The intersection of two observable FSMs is an observable FSM; however, the intersection of complete FSMs can be partial. FSM languages are regular, and thus, the underlying model for an FSM is a finite automaton. When solving a parallel equation an FSM is represented by an automaton by unfolding each transition of the FSM [2 - 4].

Automata and FSMs. A *finite automaton*, is a quintuple $S = \langle S, V, \delta_S, s_0, F_S \rangle$, where S is a finite nonempty set of states with the initial state s_0 and a subset F_S of *final* (or *accepting*) states, V is an alphabet of actions, and $\delta_S \subseteq S \times V \times S$ is a transition relation. An automaton $\langle S', V, \delta'_S, s'_0, F'_S \rangle$ is a *submachine* of the automaton S if $S' \subseteq S$, $\delta'_S \subseteq \delta_S$, and $F'_S \subseteq F_S$. The automaton S is *deterministic*, if $\forall s \in S$ and $\forall v \in V$, $\exists$ at most one state s', such that $(s, v, s') \in \delta_S$. The language $L(S)$ *generated* or *accepted* by S is known to be regular. Given a sequence $\alpha \in V^*$ and an alphabet W, a *W-restriction* of α, written $\alpha_{\downarrow W}$, is obtained by deleting from α all symbols that belong to the set $V \setminus W$. Given a sequence $\alpha \in V^*$ and an alphabet W, a *W-expansion* of α, written $\alpha_{\uparrow W}$, is a set that contains each sequence over alphabet $(V \cup W)$ with the V–projection α.

Well-known results state that regular languages are closed under the union, intersection, complementation, restriction and expansion and the constructions for deriving corresponding automata could be found, for example, in [1, 3, 6]. Let $P = \langle P, V, \delta_P, p_0, F_P \rangle$ be an automaton which accepts the language L. *Restriction* ($\downarrow$): Given a non-empty subset U of V, the automaton $P_{\downarrow U}$ that accepts the language $L_{\downarrow U}$ over U is obtained by replacing each edge (s,a,s') in P by the edge (s,ε,s').[1] *Expansion* ($\uparrow$): Given alphabet U, the automaton $P_{\uparrow U}$ that accepts the language $L_{\uparrow U}$ over $U \cup V$ is obtained by adding $(s,a,s) \ \forall a \in U \setminus V$ for each state s of P.

We note that not each automaton has an FSM language. However, it is known that given an automaton B over alphabet $I \cup O$, $I \cap O = \varnothing$, there exists a largest subset of the language of the automaton B that is the language of an FSM, denoted B^{FSM}, which

---

[1] Apply the closure procedure to obtain an equivalent deterministic automaton without ε-moves [6].

can be constructed by intersecting B with $(IO)^*$ and deleting all non-accepting states from the resulting automaton, which have an incoming transition labeled with an output action o. The language of an FSM C over input I and output O is a subset of the language of an automaton B if and only if C is a reduction of B^{FSM} [3].

Parallel Composition of FSMs. Consider a system of two complete communicating FSMs $A = \langle A, I_1 \cup V, O_1 \cup U, T_A, s_0 \rangle$ and $B = \langle T, I_2 \cup U, O_2 \cup V, T_B, t_0 \rangle$ [1 - 3]. As usual, for the sake of simplicity, we assume that alphabets I_1, V, O_1, U, I_2, O_2 are pair-wise disjoint. The alphabet $Ext_{in} = I_1 \cup I_2$ represents the external inputs of the composition, while the alphabet $Ext_{out} \subseteq O_1 \cup O_2$ represents the external outputs of the composition; $Ext = Ext_{in} \cup Ext_{out}$, $Int = U \cup V$. The two FSMs communicate under a single message in transit, i.e., the next external input is submitted to the system only after it produced an external output to the previous input. The collective behavior of the two communicating FSMs can be described by an FSM. The *parallel composition of FSMs* A and B, denoted $C \lozenge_{Ext} B$ or simply $C \lozenge B$, can be obtained as follows [2, 3]: First, for FSMS A and B, the corresponding automata $Aut(A)$ and $Aut(B)$ are derived. Then, the intersection $(Aut(A)_{\uparrow I_2 \cup O_2} \cap Aut(B)_{\uparrow I_1 \cup O_1})_{\downarrow Ext} \cap Aut(MAX(I,O))$ is converted into an FSM. It is known that the parallel composition of two complete FSMs can be partial, since the communicating FSMs can fall into an infinite dialogue (live-lock) without producing an external output. In this case, the projection of $(Aut(A)_{\uparrow I_2 \cup O_2} \cap Aut(B)_{\uparrow I_1 \cup O_1})_{\downarrow Ext}$ onto I does not coincide with I^*. Formally, the composition falls into live-lock if $Aut(A)_{\uparrow I_2 \cup O_2} \cap Aut(B)_{\uparrow I_1 \cup O_1} \cap Aut(MAX(I,O)_{\uparrow Int}$ has a state where the generated language is empty.

FSM Equations. Let $C = (C, I_1 \cup V, O_1 \cup U, T_C, c_0)$ and $S = (S, Ext_{in}, Ext_{out}, T_S, s_0)$ be two complete FSMs. An expression "$C \lozenge_{Ext} X \cong S$" ("$C \lozenge_{Ext} X \le S$") is called an *FSM equation* (an *FSM inequality*) w.r.t. the unknown X that represents an FSM over the input alphabet $I_2 \cup U$, $I_2 = Ext_{in} \backslash I_1$, and the output alphabet $O_2 \cup V$, $O_2 = Ext_{out} \backslash O_1$. The FSM C is usually called the *context*, and the FSM S is usually called the *specification*. As usual, an FSM equation can have no solution while an FSM inequality is always solvable, as the trivial FSM with the language that contains only the empty sequence always is a solution to an FSM inequality. If an FSM inequality and a solvable FSM equation have a complete solution then they are known to have a largest complete solution [2, 3]. A largest complete solution M to the equation $C \lozenge_{Ext} X \cong S$ can be obtained as the largest complete submachine of the FSM over input alphabet $I_2 \cup U$ and output alphabet $O_2 \cup V$ which corresponds to the automaton $\Lambda(C,S,MAX)$ = $\underline{(Aut(C)_{\uparrow I_2 \cup O_2} \cap Aut(S)_{\uparrow U \cup V})_{\downarrow I_2 \cup O_2 \cup U \cup V}} \cap Aut(MAX(I_2 \cup U, O_2 \cup V))$, if such a complete submachine exists. We note that in this paper, we do not merge equivalent states (for the reasons shown later) of the automaton $\Lambda(C,S,MAX)$ when applying the closure procedure for deriving an equivalent deterministic automaton without ε-moves after the restriction operator. If such a machine M does not exist the equation and the inequality have no complete solutions. If the machine M exists then M is a largest complete solution to the inequality $C \lozenge_{Ext} X \leq S$. Moreover, each reduction of M also is a solution to the inequality. If the composition $C \lozenge_{Ext} M$ is equivalent to S [2] then M is a largest complete solution to the equation. If the composition $C \lozenge_{Ext} M$ is not equivalent to S, then the equation has no complete solution. However, not each complete reduction of M is a solution to the equation.

As an example of a largest complete solution of an FSM equation, consider the specification FSM S_1 with transitions $(1,x,o_3,1)(1,i,o_1,1)$ $(1,x,o_2,1)$ and the context C shown in Fig. 1. The context C is defined over external inputs $I_1 = \{i\}$, external outputs $O_1 = \{o_1, o_2, o_3\}$, internal inputs $V = \{v_1, v_2, v_3\}$ and internal outputs $U = \{u_1, u_2\}$. Specification S_1 is defined over external inputs $Ext_{in} = \{i, x\}$ and external outputs $Ext_{out} = \{o_1, o_2, o_3\}$. A solution to an FSM equation $C \lozenge_{Ext} X \cong S_1$ is defined over the external input alphabet $I_2 = \{x\}$, the internal input alphabet $U = \{u_1, u_2\}$ and the internal output alphabet $V = \{v_1, v_2, v_3\}$. A largest complete solution to the equation is shown in Fig. 2.

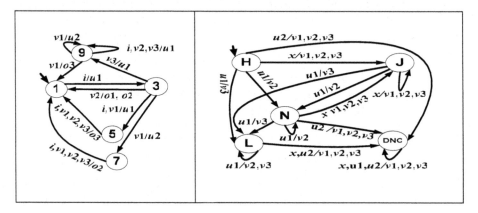

Fig. 1. Context FSM C **Fig. 2.** A largest complete solution to $C \lozenge_{Ext} X \cong S_1$

3 Progressive Solutions to FSM Equations

Consider an FSM equation $C \lozenge X \cong S$, where C and S are FSMs over input alphabets $I_1 \cup V$ and $I_1 \cup I_2$ and over output alphabets $O_1 \cup U$ and $O_1 \cup O_2$ correspondingly, while X is the unknown FSM over input alphabet $I_2 \cup U$ and output alphabet $O_2 \cup V$. A solution $Prog$ to an FSM equation $C \lozenge X \cong S$ (or inequality) is *progressive* if the system $C \lozenge Prog$ cannot fall into a live-lock under any external input sequence, i.e., for each external input action of an input sequence the composition eventually produces an external output. Formally, a solution $Prog$ to an FSM equation $C \lozenge X \cong S$ (or to inequality $C \lozenge X \leq S$) is progressive if $Prog$ is a complete FSM and the intersection $Aut(C)\uparrow_{(I_2 \cup O_2)} \cap Aut(Prog)\uparrow_{(I_1 \cup O_1)} \cap Aut(MAX(I,O))\uparrow_{I \cup V}$ has no states where the empty language is generated. The definition of a progressive solution requires that the above intersection has no cycles over internal actions without an exit from the cycle with an external output. If we consider a deterministic context FSM then each complete deterministic solution to the equation is progressive.

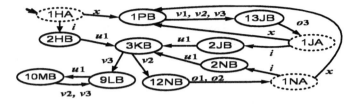

Fig. 3. The intersection $Aut(C)_{\uparrow(I_2\cup O_2)}\cap Aut(Largest)_{\uparrow(I_1\cup O_1)}\cap Aut(MAX(I,O))_{\uparrow U\cup V}$

As an example of a non-progressive solution, consider a largest complete FSM solution *Largest*, shown in Fig. 2. At the initial states 1 of context C (Fig. 1) and H of *Largest*, if the external input i is applied to the context, FSM C produces the internal output u_1. In response to the input u_1, the FSM *Largest* may produce the output v_3, and then the system $C \lozenge Largest$ falls into a livelock. This is due to the fact that states (9,L,B) and (10,M,B) of the intersection shown in Fig. 3 are non-progressive. The O-restriction of the language generated at these states is empty.

In the following, we identify a property of a solution *Sol* to an FSM equation such that a largest progressive reduction of *Sol* can be derived as an appropriate submachine of *Sol*. In particular, the largest complete submachine of an FSM corresponding to the automaton $\Lambda(C,S,MAX)$ (without merging equivalent states) possesses this property.

A solution $P = (P, I_2\cup U, O_2\cup V, T_P, p_0)$ to an FSM inequality $C \lozenge_{Ext} X \leq S$ is called *perfect in the context* C (or simply *perfect*) if for each state (c,p,t_0) of the intersection $Aut(C)_{\uparrow(I_2\cup O_2)}\cap Aut(P)_{\uparrow(I_1\cup O_1)}\cap Aut(MAX(I,O))_{\uparrow U\cup V}$ that has an incoming transition labeled with an action $a \in O_2\cup V$, the $(I_2\cup O_2\cup U\cup V)$-projection of the language accepted at state (c,p,t_0) equals to the set of I/O sequences which take the FSM P from the initial state to state p.

Given a solution F to the inequality, an equivalent perfect solution can be obtained by splitting states of F [4]. However, if we do not merge equivalent states when deriving the automaton $\Lambda(C,S,MAX)$ then the largest complete submachine M of an FSM corresponding to the automaton (if it exists) is perfect w.r.t. the context C. However, if the obtained FSM M is not reduced then the reduced form of M does not generally possess the property.

Theorem 1. Given an FSM equation $C \lozenge X \cong S$ (inequality $C \lozenge X \leq S$), the largest complete submachine M of an FSM corresponding to the automaton $\Lambda(C,S,MAX)$ (without merging equivalent states) is a perfect solution (w.r.t. the context C) to the inequality $C \lozenge_{Ext} X \leq S$.

Theorem 2. Let P be a perfect solution (w.r.t. the context C) to the inequality $C \lozenge X \leq S$. 1. Every complete submachine P_{sub} of P is perfect. 2. A complete intersection of P and some FSM is perfect.

Algorithm 1. Deriving a largest complete progressive solution to an FSM equation (inequality)

Input: Observable FSMs C and S.
Output: A largest progressive solution to $C \lozenge X \cong S$ (if it exists).

Step-1. Derive the largest complete submachine M of the FSM corresponding to the automaton $\Lambda(C,S,MAX)$. If M does not exist or M is not a solution to the equation, then the equation has no complete solution. End Algorithm 1. Otherwise, construct the intersection $Aut(C)_{\uparrow I2 \cup O2} \cap Aut(M)_{\uparrow I1 \cup O1} \cap Aut(MAX(I,O))_{\uparrow Int}$ and Go-to Step-2.

Step-2. If there is no triplet in the intersection where the language generated at the triplet is empty and there is no accepting triplet (c,m,t) where at least one transition under an external input is undefined, then Go-to Step-4. Otherwise; Go-to Step-3.

Step-3. Iteratively delete from the intersection every triplet (c,m,t) where the external restriction of language generated at the triplet is empty and each accepting triplet (c,m,t) where at least one transition under an external input is undefined.

1. If the initial state of the intersection is deleted then there is no progressive solution. End Algorithm 1. Otherwise,
2. For each deleted triplet (c,m,t), delete state m from the FSM M and iteratively delete from M states where at least one input is undefined.
   If the initial state of M is deleted then there is no progressive solution. End Algorithm 1. When a state m is deleted from the FSM M each triplet (c,m,t) is deleted from the intersection. If the initial state of the intersection is deleted then there is no progressive complete solution. End Algorithm 1. Otherwise, Go-to Step-2.

Step-4. If $C \Diamond M \cong S$ then M is a largest progressive solution. End Algorithm 1. If $C \Diamond M \ncong S$ then there is no progressive solution. End Algorithm 1.

Theorem 3. If the equation $C \Diamond X \cong S$ has a progressive solution then Algorithm 1 returns a largest progressive solution.

As an example, consider a largest solution M shown in Fig. 2. In order to derive a largest progressive solution to the equation, at Step-2, derive the intersection in Fig. 3. Let $Aut(F)$ denote the obtained intersection. State $(10,M,B)$ of $Aut(F)$ is non-progressive, i.e., delete this state from $Aut(F)$ and correspondingly delete state M from $Aut(M)$. Furthermore, state $(9,L,B)$ is also non-progressive, i.e., delete this state from the automaton and correspondingly delete state L from $Aut(M)$. The remaining states of the obtained automaton are all progressive. End Algorithm 1. The FSM corresponding to the resulting automaton $Aut(M)$ is a submachine of the FSM in Fig. 2 without state L, and this FSM is a largest complete progressive solution to the equation.

4   A System of FSM Equations

Given an integer $k>1$, complete context FSMs $C_i = (C_i, I_1 \cup V, O_1 \cup U, T_{Ci}, c_{i0})$, specifications $S_i = (S_i, Ext_{in}, Ext_{out}, T_{Si}, s_{i0})$, $k > 1$, and a system of equations $C_i \Diamond_{Ext} X \cong S_i$, $i = 1, ..., k$. An FSM X over the input alphabet $Ext_{in} \backslash I_1 \cup U$ and over the output alphabet $Ext_{out} \backslash O_1 \cup V$ is a solution to the system if it is a solution to each equation, i.e., $C_i \Diamond_{Ext} X \cong S_i$, $i = 1, ..., k$.

If a system of FSM equations has a complete solution then the system has a largest complete solution. A complete solution to the system $C_i \Diamond_{Ext} X \cong S_i$, $i = 1, ..., k$, is called a *largest complete solution* if it includes all complete solutions as reductions. A largest complete solution M to a system of equations $C_i \lozenge_{Ext} X \cong S_i$ can be obtained similar to that in [5]. Given a system of equations $C_i \lozenge_{Ext} X \cong S_i$, $i = 1, ..., k$, a solution B to the system is called *progressive* if it is a progressive solution to every equation of the system. In general, the intersection of two largest progressive solutions to two equations not necessary is a progressive solution to the system of two equations.

Algorithm 2. Deriving a largest progressive solution to a system of FSM equations

   Input: Observable FSMs C_i and S_i, $i = 1, ..., k$.

   Output: A largest progressive solution over the input alphabet $I_2 \cup U$ and output alphabet $O_2 \cup V$ to the system $C_i \lozenge_{Ext} X \cong S_i$, $i = 1, ...,k$ (if a progressive solution exists).

   Step-1: For $i = 1, ..., k$, call Algorithm 1 and obtain a largest progressive solution M_i to the equation $C_i \lozenge_{Ext} X \cong S_i$. If for some $i = 1, ..., k$, there is no progressive solution to the equation $C_i \lozenge_{Ext} X \cong S_i$, then there is no progressive solution to the system of equations, End Algorithm 2. Else; Go-to Step-2.

   Step-2: Derive the largest complete submachine F of the intersection $\cap M_i$. If the intersection has no complete submachine, then there is no progressive solution to the system of equations, End Algorithm 2. Else, Go-to Step-3.1.

   Step-3.1) If F is a progressive solution to each equation, then F is a largest progressive solution to the system of equations. End Algorithm 2. Else, Go-to Step-3.2.

   Step-3.2) For every $j \in 1, ..., k$ such that F is not a progressive solution to an equation $C_j \lozenge_{Ext} X \cong S_j$, assign $M = F$, construct the intersection $Aut(C_j)_{\uparrow I_2 \cup O_2} \cap Aut(M)_{\uparrow I_1 \cup O_1} \cap Aut(MAX(I,O))_{\uparrow Int}$ and call Steps 2 and 3 of Algorithm 1 in order to derive a largest complete submachine F_j of F that is a progressive solution to the equation. If at least for one equation there is no such submachine then the system of equations has no progressive solution; END Algorithm 2. Else, assign $M_j := F_j$ and Go-to Step-2.

Theorem 4. If a system of equations $C_i \lozenge_{Ext} X \cong S_i$, $i = 1, ..., k$, has a progressive solution then Algorithm 2 returns a largest progressive solution.

   As an example, consider the specification S_1 [with $(1,x,o_3,1)(1,i,o_1,1)$ $(1,x,o_2,1)$] and the context C_1 which is that of Fig. 1 where the output label o_3 of the transition $(9,v_1,o_3,1)$ is changed to o_1. Moreover, consider the specification S_2 with a single state 1 and transitions $(1,x,o_3,1)(1,i,o_1,1)$ $(1,x,o_3,1)$. Consider also, the context C_2 shown in Fig. 4 and the system of two equations $C_1 \lozenge_{Ext} X \cong S_1$ and $C_2 \lozenge_{Ext} X \cong S_2$. For each of these equations, at Step-1 of Algorithm 2, apply Algorithm 1 and obtain the largest complete progressive solutions LP_1 and LP_2. The intersection of these solutions is shown in Fig. 5. The corresponding FSM F is not a progressive solution to the equation $C_1 \lozenge_{Ext} X \cong S_1$, since states (9,LS,B), (10,MW,B), and (9,LT,B) of the intersection in Fig. 6 are non-progressive. Correspondingly, in Step-3.2, in order to derive a largest complete submachine of F that is a progressive solution to the equation $C_1 \lozenge_{Ext} X \cong S_1$, derive the intersection in Fig. 6 and apply Steps 2 and 3 of Algorithm 1. States (9,LS,B), (10,MW,B) and (9,LT,B) of the intersection are non-progressive, thus, delete states LS, MW, and LT from $Aut(F)$. The obtained automaton $Aut(F)$ is that of Fig. 5 without deleted states LS, MW, and LT and its corresponding FSM is a complete progressive solution to the system of two equations.

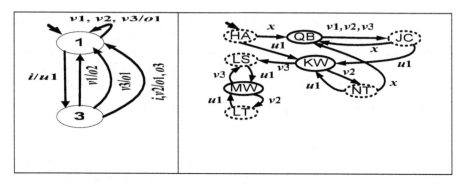

Fig. 4. Context C_2 **Fig. 5.** The intersection $Aut(F)$

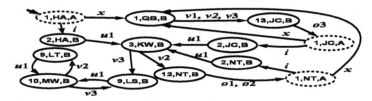

Fig. 6. The intersection $Aut(C_1)\uparrow_{(I2\cup O2)} \cap Aut(F)\uparrow_{(I1\cup O1)} \cap Aut(MAX(I,O))\uparrow_{Int=U\cup V}$

References

1. El-Fakih, K., Yevtushenko, N., Buffalov, S., Bochmann, G.: Progressive Solutions to a Parallel Automata Equation. Theoretical Computer Science 362, 17–32 (2006)
2. Petrenko, A., Yevtushenko, N.: Solving Asynchronous Equations. In: Formal Description Techniques and Protocol Specification, Testing, and Verification, pp. 231–247 (1998)
3. Yevtushenko, N., Villa, T., Brayton, R., Petrenko, A., Sangiovanni-Vincentelli, A.: Solution of Parallel Language Equations for Logic Synthesis. In: ICCAD, pp. 103–110 (2001)
4. Yevtushenko, N., Villa, T., Brayton, R., Petrenko, A., Sangiovanni-Vincentelli, A.: Compositionally Progressive Solutions of Synchronous FSM Equations. Discrete Event Dynamic Systems 18(1), 51–89 (2008)
5. Yevtushenko, N., Zharikova, S., Vetrova, M.: Multi Component Digital Circuit Optimization by Solving FSM Equations. In: Euromicro Symposium on Digital System Design, pp. 62–68. IEEE Computer society, Los Alamitos (2003)
6. Hopcroft, J., Ullman, J.: Introduction to automata theory, Languages, and Computation. Addison-Wesley, Reading (1979)

Combination of Context-Free Grammars and Tree Automata for Unranked and Ranked Trees

Akio Fujiyoshi

Department of Computer and Information Sciences, Ibaraki University
4-12-1 Nakanarusawa, Hitachi, Ibaraki, 316-8511, Japan
fujiyosi@mx.ibaraki.ac.jp

In this paper we will study the use of context-free grammars (CFGs) for the verification of tree structures. Because of the long history of the study of CFGs, parsing techniques for CFGs are well-established. The aim of this paper is to make use of those parsing techniques for the verification of tree structures.

CFGs are known as a formalism for strings. However, a CFG can define a set of unranked trees because every tree can be encoded into a string as follows:

Definition 1. Let Σ be an alphabet. Let '$<$', '$>$' and '$/$' be symbols not included in Σ. Let us denote the set of unranked trees over Σ as T_Σ. The function $tag : T_\Sigma \to (\Sigma \cup \{<, >, /\})^*$ is defined inductively as follows:

- For $t = a \in \Sigma$, $tag(t) = $ `<a></a>`.
- For $t = a(t_1, \ldots, t_n)$, $tag(t) = $ `<a>` $\cdot tag(t_1) \cdot \cdots \cdot tag(t_n) \cdot$ `</a>`.

The *tag-encoding* of a tree $t \in T_\Sigma$ is the string $tag(t)$.

The author's motivation is to obtain a suitable verification method of structural analysis of mathematical formulae for a mathematical OCR system. As shown in Fig. 1, an OCR system offers a tree representation of a mathematical formula from a scanned image. A tree representation is usually formed as a MathML document. We want to check whether or not a result from an OCR system, a MathML document, represents a well-formed mathematical formula.

As a formalism for well-formed mathematical formula, we think of a context-free hedge automaton (CFHA), that is, a hedge automata [1] whose horizontal languages are context-free languages. We could show that the verification of an unranked tree by a CFHA can be reduced to the verification by a CFG.

Definition 2. A *context-free hedge automaton* (CFHA) over Σ is a four-tuple $M = (Q, \Sigma, Q_f, \Delta)$ where Q is a finite set of *states*, Σ is an alphabet, $Q_f \subseteq Q$ is a set of *final states*, and Δ is a finite set of *transition rules* of the form: $a(L) \to q$ where $a \in \Sigma$, $q \in Q$, and $L \subseteq Q^*$ is a context-free language over Q.

Theorem 1. *For any CFHA M over Σ, we can construct a CFG G over $(\Sigma \cup \{<, >, /\})$ such that, for any $t \in T_\Sigma$, t is accepted by A if and only if $tag(t)$ is generated by G.*

O.H. Ibarra and B. Ravikumar (Eds.): CIAA 2008, LNCS 5148, pp. 283–285, 2008.

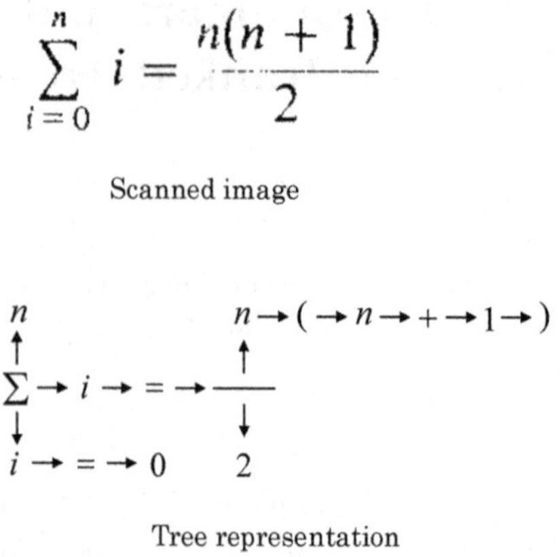

$$\sum_{i=0}^{n} i = \frac{n(n+1)}{2}$$

Scanned image

```
<math xmlns="http://www.w3.org/1998/Math/MathML">
  <munderover>
    <mi>&sum;</mi>
    <mrow><mi>i</mi><mo>=</mo><mn>0</mn></mrow>
    <mi>n</mi>
  </munderover>
  <mi>i</mi>
  <mo>=</mo>
  <mfrac>
    <mrow><mi>n</mi><mo>(</mo><mi>n</mi>
        <mo>+</mo><mn>1</mn><mo>)</mo></mrow>
    <mn>2</mn>
  </mfrac>
</math>
```

Tree representation   MathML document

Fig. 1. A result of structural analysis of a mathematical formula

CFGs are not perfect. Let Σ be the ranked alphabet consisting of the binary symbols a, b and the zeroary symbols c, d, e. Think of the following ranked trees:

$$\{a(b(e,c),d),\ a(a(b(b(e,c),c),d),d),\ a(a(a(b(b(b(e,c),c),c),d),d),d),\ \cdots\ \}.$$

The string language of tag-encodings of the ranked trees is the following non-context-free language:

$$\{(\texttt{<a>})^n(\texttt{<b>})^n\texttt{<e></e>}(\texttt{<c></c></b>})^n(\texttt{<d></d></a>})^n \mid n \geq 1\}.$$

A linear pushdown tree automaton (L-PDTA) [2] can recognize the above-mentioned ranked trees. For another formalism to define well-formed mathematical formula, we will also look at L-PDTAs.

The recognition capability of the following subclasses of L-PDTAs will be compared with regard to tree languages and yield languages:

- All L-PDTAs
- Deterministic L-PDTAs
- Real-time L-PDTAs
- Real-time deterministic L-PDTAs

Let **RtDet, Det, Rt** and **ALL** represent the classes of tree languages recognized by real-time deterministic L-PDTAs, deterministic L-PDTAs, real-time L-PDTAs and any L-PDTAs, respectively.

Theorem 2. $\mathbf{RtDet} \subsetneq \mathbf{Det} \subsetneq \mathbf{Rt} = \mathbf{ALL}$.

Let **yRtDet, yDet, yRt** and **yALL** represent the classes of yield languages corresponding to **RtDet, Det, Rt** and **ALL**, respectively.

Theorem 3. $\mathbf{yRtDet} = \mathbf{yDet} = \mathbf{yRt} = \mathbf{yALL}$.

References

1. Comon, H., Dauchet, M., Gilleron, R., Jacquemard, F., Lugiez, D., Löding, C., Tison, S., Tommasi, M.: Tree automata techniques and applications (release October 12, 2007) (2007), `http://www.grappa.univ-lille3.fr/tata`
2. Fujiyoshi, A., Kawaharada, I.: Deterministic recognition of trees accepted by a linear pushdown tree automaton. In: Farré, J., Litovsky, I., Schmitz, S. (eds.) CIAA 2005. LNCS, vol. 3845, pp. 129–140. Springer, Heidelberg (2006)

Approximate Periods with Levenshtein Distance[*]

Martin Šimůnek and Bořivoj Melichar

Department of Computer Science and Engineering,
Czech Technical University in Prague, Czech Republic
{simunem1,melichar}@fel.cvut.cz

Abstract. We present a new algorithm deciding for strings t and w whether w is an approximate generator of t with Levenshtein distance at most k. The algorithm is based on finite state transducers.

1 Introduction

A generator of a string is one of basic notions of regularities searching. In this paper, we deal with approximate generators with Levenshtein distance. We show a new transducer-based algorithm deciding for strings w and t whether w is a k-approximate generator of t.

A string w is a k-approximate generator of t with respect to a distance measure D if and only if t is composed of disjoint blocks of factors similar to the string w. The last block may be similar to some prefix of w instead of w itself. More formally, t has to be composed of factors $t = w_1 w_2 \ldots w_l u$ and $D(w_i, w) \le k$ for all $i \in \{1, 2 \ldots, l\}$. $D(u, w') \le k$ for some $w' \in \mathrm{Pref}(w)$, $|w'| \le |w|$.

In this paper, the Levenshtein distance is used as a measure of string similarity, even though we offer a more general scheme that can be used for other distance measures.

2 A Transducer Based Algorithm

A basic notion of our algorithm is a distance resolver for sets of strings. Given a set of strings W, a distance measure D, an input string v and a distance bound k, distance resolver $R_{W,D,k}$ is a finite state transducer such that a set of output symbols after reading the last symbol of v is a set of of distance bounds k': $k' \le k$ and $D(v, w') \le k'$ for some $w' \in W$.

In analogy with solution of approximate string matching problems, we define $L(R_{W,D,k})$ to be the language of all input strings w' such that the minimum of the outputs of $R_{W,D,k}$ after reading w' is lower than or equal to k. Then, we

---

[*] This research has been partially supported by the Ministry of Education, Youth, and Sport of the Czech Republic under research program MSM6840770014 and by the Czech Science Foundation as project No. 201/06/1039.

O.H. Ibarra and B. Ravikumar (Eds.): CIAA 2008, LNCS 5148, pp. 286–287, 2008.

check whether tested string w is in the language $L(R_{\{w\},D,k})^{+}L(R_{\text{Pref}(w),D,k})$, where Pref (w) is a set of prefixes of a string w.

We show the modification of a well-known automaton used in pattern matching (see [1]) to meet the requirements of the distance resolver definition.

3 Implementation

As an implementation method for the transducer-based computation, we have chosen simulation using dynamic programming.

Considering Levenshtein distance, a distance bound k and lengths of strings $n = |t|$ and $m = |w|$, our algorithm reads n symbols and for each of them handles $2(m+1)$ groups of states. Thus, time complexity is $\mathcal{O}(nm)$. The space complexity is $\mathcal{O}(m)$.

Sim, Iliopoulos, Park and Smyth ([2]) have shown an algorithm for the optimisation version of the same problem with Levenshtein distance. The time complexity for the algorithm is $\mathcal{O}(nm)$, the space complexity is $\mathcal{O}(n^2)$. The computed distance matrices of Sims algorithm can be reused when checking longer generators. Our solution is intended to become a base for deriving automata based algorithms solving evolutive periods and evolutive tandem repeat problems.

4 Conclusion

In this paper, a new transducer based algorithm is presented. The algorithm decides for given strings w and t whether w is an approximate generator of t.

References

1. Melichar, B., Holub, J., Polcar, T.: Text searching algorithms. Tutorial to the Athens Course (2005). http://www.stringology.org/athens/
2. Sim, J.S., Iliopoulos, C.S., Park, K., Smyth, W.F.: Approximate periods of strings. Theoretical Computer Science 262(1-2), 557–568 (2001)

Author Index

Lecture Notes in Computer Science

Sublibrary 1: Theoretical Computer Science and General Issues

For information about Vols. 1– 4838
please contact your bookseller or Springer

Vol. 4985: M. Ishikawa, K. Doya, H. Miyamoto, T. Ya-makawa (Eds.), Neural Information Processing, Part II. XXX, 1091 pages. 2008.

Vol. 4984: M. Ishikawa, K. Doya, H. Miyamoto, T. Ya-makawa (Eds.), Neural Information Processing, Part I. XXX, 1147 pages. 2008.

Vol. 4981: M. Egerstedt, B. Mishra (Eds.), Hybrid Systems: Computation and Control. XV, 680 pages. 2008.

Vol. 4978: M. Agrawal, D. Du, Z. Duan, A. Li (Eds.), Theory and Applications of Models of Computation. XII, 598 pages. 2008.

Vol. 4975: F. Chen, B. Jüttler (Eds.), Advances in Geometric Modeling and Processing. XV, 606 pages. 2008.

Vol. 4974: M. Giacobini, A. Brabazon, S. Cagnoni, G.A. Di Caro, R. Drechsler, A. Ekárt, A.I. Esparcia-Alcázar, M. Farooq, A. Fink, J. McCormack, M. O'Neill, J. Romero, F. Rothlauf, G. Squillero, A.Ş. Uyar, S. Yang (Eds.), Applications of Evolutionary Computing. XXV, 701 pages. 2008.

Vol. 4973: E. Marchiori, J.H. Moore (Eds.), Evolutionary Computation, Machine Learning and Data Mining in Bioinformatics. X, 213 pages. 2008.

Vol. 4972: J. van Hemert, C. Cotta (Eds.), Evolutionary Computation in Combinatorial Optimization. XII, 289 pages. 2008.

Vol. 4971: M. O'Neill, L. Vanneschi, S. Gustafson, A.I. Esparcia Alcázar, I. De Falco, A. Della Cioppa, E. Tarantino (Eds.), Genetic Programming. XI, 375 pages. 2008.

Vol. 4967: R. Wyrzykowski, J. Dongarra, K. Karczewski, J. Wasniewski (Eds.), Parallel Processing and Applied Mathematics. XXIII, 1414 pages. 2008.

Vol. 4963: C.R. Ramakrishnan, J. Rehof (Eds.), Tools and Algorithms for the Construction and Analysis of Systems. XVI, 518 pages. 2008.

Vol. 4962: R. Amadio (Ed.), Foundations of Software Science and Computational Structures. XV, 505 pages. 2008.

Vol. 4961: J.L. Fiadeiro, P. Inverardi (Eds.), Fundamental Approaches to Software Engineering. XIII, 430 pages. 2008.

Vol. 4960: S. Drossopoulou (Ed.), Programming Languages and Systems. XIII, 399 pages. 2008.

Vol. 4959: L. Hendren (Ed.), Compiler Construction. XII, 307 pages. 2008.

Vol. 4957: E.S. Laber, C. Bornstein, L.T. Nogueira, L. Faria (Eds.), LATIN 2008: Theoretical Informatics. XVII, 794 pages. 2008.

Vol. 4943: R. Woods, K. Compton, C. Bouganis, P.C. Diniz (Eds.), Reconfigurable Computing: Architectures, Tools and Applications. XIV, 344 pages. 2008.

Vol. 4942: E. Frachtenberg, U. Schwiegelshohn (Eds.), Job Scheduling Strategies for Parallel Processing. VII, 189 pages. 2008.

Vol. 4941: M. Miculan, I. Scagnetto, F. Honsell (Eds.), Types for Proofs and Programs. VII, 203 pages. 2008.

Vol. 4935: B. Chapman, W. Zheng, G.R. Gao, M. Sato, E. Ayguadé, D. Wang (Eds.), A Practical Programming Model for the Multi-Core Era. VI, 208 pages. 2008.

Vol. 4934: U. Brinkschulte, T. Ungerer, C. Hochberger, R.G. Spallek (Eds.), Architecture of Computing Systems – ARCS 2008. XI, 287 pages. 2008.

Vol. 4927: C. Kaklamanis, M. Skutella (Eds.), Approximation and Online Algorithms. X, 289 pages. 2008.

Vol. 4926: N. Monmarché, E.-G. Talbi, P. Collet, M. Schoenauer, E. Lutton (Eds.), Artificial Evolution. XIII, 327 pages. 2008.

Vol. 4921: S.-i. Nakano, M.. S. Rahman (Eds.), WAL-COM: Algorithms and Computation. XII, 241 pages. 2008.

Vol. 4919: A. Gelbukh (Ed.), Computational Linguistics and Intelligent Text Processing. XVIII, 666 pages. 2008.

Vol. 4917: P. Stenström, M. Dubois, M. Katevenis, R. Gupta, T. Ungerer (Eds.), High Performance Embedded Architectures and Compilers. XIII, 400 pages. 2008.

Vol. 4915: A. King (Ed.), Logic-Based Program Synthesis and Transformation. X, 219 pages. 2008.

Vol. 4912: G. Barthe, C. Fournet (Eds.), Trustworthy Global Computing. XI, 401 pages. 2008.

Vol. 4910: V. Geffert, J. Karhumäki, A. Bertoni, B. Preneel, P. Návrat, M. Bieliková (Eds.), SOFSEM 2008: Theory and Practice of Computer Science. XV, 792 pages. 2008.

Vol. 4905: F. Logozzo, D.A. Peled, L.D. Zuck (Eds.), Verification, Model Checking, and Abstract Interpretation. X, 325 pages. 2008.

Vol. 4904: S. Rao, M. Chatterjee, P. Jayanti, C.S.R. Murthy, S.K. Saha (Eds.), Distributed Computing and Networking. XVIII, 588 pages. 2007.

Vol. 4878: E. Tovar, P. Tsigas, H. Fouchal (Eds.), Principles of Distributed Systems. XIII, 457 pages. 2007.

Vol. 4875: S.-H. Hong, T. Nishizeki, W. Quan (Eds.), Graph Drawing. XIII, 402 pages. 2008.

Vol. 4873: S. Aluru, M. Parashar, R. Badrinath, V.K. Prasanna (Eds.), High Performance Computing – HiPC 2007. XXIV, 663 pages. 2007.

Vol. 4863: A. Bonato, F.R.K. Chung (Eds.), Algorithms and Models for the Web-Graph. X, 217 pages. 2007.

Vol. 4860: G. Eleftherakis, P. Kefalas, G. Păun, G. Rozenberg, A. Salomaa (Eds.), Membrane Computing. IX, 453 pages. 2007.

Vol. 4855: V. Arvind, S. Prasad (Eds.), FSTTCS 2007: Foundations of Software Technology and Theoretical Computer Science. XIV, 558 pages. 2007.

Vol. 4854: L. Bougé, M. Forsell, J.L. Träff, A. Streit, W. Ziegler, M. Alexander, S. Childs (Eds.), Euro-Par 2007 Workshops: Parallel Processing. XVII, 236 pages. 2008.

Vol. 4851: S. Boztaş, H.-F.(F.) Lu (Eds.), Applied Algebra, Algebraic Algorithms and Error-Correcting Codes. XII, 368 pages. 2007.

Vol. 4848: M.H. Garzon, H. Yan (Eds.), DNA Computing. XI, 292 pages. 2008.

Vol. 4847: M. Xu, Y. Zhan, J. Cao, Y. Liu (Eds.), Advanced Parallel Processing Technologies. XIX, 767 pages. 2007.

Vol. 4846: I. Cervesato (Ed.), Advances in Computer Science – ASIAN 2007. XI, 313 pages. 2007.